CAPITAL RULES

RAWI ABDELAL

Capital Rules

The Construction of Global Finance

HARVARD UNIVERSITY PRESS
Cambridge, Massachusetts, and London, England   2007

Library of Congress Cataloging-in-Publication Data
Abdelal, Rawi, 1971–
    Capital rules : the construction of global finance / Rawi Abdelal.
      p. cm.
    Includes bibliographical references and index.
    ISBN-13: 978-0-674-02369-7 (alk. paper)
    ISBN-10: 0-674-02369-2 (alk. paper)
    1. International finance. 2. Capital movements. I. Title.

HG3881.A23 2007
332'.042—dc22   2006043549

To Alexander and Traci, with love

Contents

Preface

This is a book about the institutional foundations of global financial markets. The project began as my attempt to make sense of the ideas that helped to create and continue to sustain the contemporary era of globalization—first for my students, and then for myself.

In the winter of 2000, during my first year as a professor, my students and I were discussing the devastating financial crisis that had swept across Asia during 1997 and 1998. Unlike its neighbors, the government of Malaysia restricted the outflow of capital in September 1998 as part of its management of an apparently ongoing crisis. The reaction of the international financial community to the Malaysian capital controls was swift and severe. Echoing these sentiments, some of my students labeled the controls "unorthodox" and "heretical." Malaysia had violated the rules of globalization, but some of those rules were unwritten. Although members of the European Union (EU) and Organization for Economic Cooperation and Development (OECD) had legally renounced their right to regulate capital movements, Malaysia, a member of neither organization, had not. Such restrictions on the outflow of capital were generally understood in 1998 to be heretical, but orthodoxy had been determined in significant part by norms of appropriate policy practices and the collective expectations of market participants.

The content of financial orthodoxy had shifted profoundly during the previous century more than once. During the 1940s capital controls were perfectly orthodox tools of macroeconomic management. And forty years before that, prior to the outbreak of World War I in 1914, capital controls had then been heretical. All of which left my class with an enormous, unanswered question: Why were capital controls heretical at the beginning of the twentieth century, orthodox in the middle, and heretical again at the end? It seemed to me an important question then, and I had no compelling answer for my students. In subsequent years the question increasingly seemed to me to be fundamental to our understanding of the history of capitalism.

Although the question had not, to my knowledge, been formulated in quite this way before, the scholarly and popular literatures on financial globalization presented answers that constituted an emerging conventional wisdom. The United States generally was seen to have been instrumental in creating global finance; optimists congratulated liberal American policies, while skeptics lamented the coincidence of interests of Wall Street financial firms and the U.S. Treasury. The rise of the Right in the United States and Europe—U.S. President Ronald Reagan and Britain's Prime Minister Margaret Thatcher, for example—was presumed to have led to the implementation of "neoliberal" policy ideas. The "neo-" modifier suggested a renaissance of the old, classical liberalism of the late nineteenth and early twentieth centuries. The most fervent believers in the efficiency of all markets assumed that scientific knowledge of the proven advantages of capital liberalization underpinned the move to global capital markets. And the end of systemwide fixed exchange rates during the early 1970s was often portrayed as an opportunity for governments to liberalize capital movements without giving up autonomy over their monetary policies. Besides, policymakers and scholars regularly announced, with equal amounts confidence and cliché, that capital controls "do not work," and so, of course, governments had liberalized.

The obviousness and taken-for-grantedness of the conventional wisdom was impressive. I was personally impressed, and some version of that account guided my initial attempts to write an intellectual, legal, and political history of financial globalization. I certainly did not set out to turn the conventional account very nearly on its head. Whereas I had sought to synthesize, instead I found over the course of my research that the prevailing understandings of the origins and institutional foundations of global finance were deeply problematic. A few of the big pieces of the story were just plain wrong.

I set out to recover this recent history from the archival record and interviews with the policymakers and members of the private financial community who had personally debated and created the most fundamental changes in the international financial architecture of the last quarter century. I assumed that I would find ample evidence of American leadership, Wall Street's enthusiasm, the U.S. Treasury's guidance, Rightist politicians, and "neoliberal" economists and policymakers. I found nothing of the sort.

Instead, I discovered European leadership in writing the liberal rules of global finance, Wall Street's caution and skepticism, the U.S. Treasury's ambivalence, disillusioned but reenergized Leftist politicians, and organization-building bureaucrats. The story that emerged from documents and personal interviews differed so profoundly from my initial premises that I struggled to make sense of what I interpreted as paradox and contradiction. I was reassured by the hope that my book had, in the words of Herman Melville, a "mighty theme," along with an intriguing question and a provocative answer. Understanding the answer would take a long time, however.

Finally, a fundamental distinction became clear to me. Under way was a contest between two competing visions for globalization. The American approach, shared by the private financial community and the Treasury, was of an ad hoc globalization of finance, emerging organically through the accumulation of unilateral policymaking and bilateral negotiation. Ad hoc globalization was to be governed primarily by U.S. firms and policymakers. The European—and especially the French—vision was, like the American, essentially liberal, but even a liberal financial architecture would be managed by international organizations, each with powerful tools, a broad mandate, and the appropriate jurisdiction over member governments' policies. The Europeans sought to delegate to the European Commission, the Executive Board of the International Monetary Fund (IMF), and the OECD Secretariat and committees. U.S. policymakers and investors preferred to manage global finance on their own or delegate to American firms, Moody's and Standard & Poor's. This contest over the character of globalization—ad hoc or managed—continues today. And it helps to explain these paradoxes in the making of a liberal regime to govern global finance.

CAPITAL RULES

CHAPTER 1

Orthodoxy and Heresy

Il faut bien connaître les préjugés de son siècle, afin de ne les choquer pas trop, ni trop les suivre. (It is necessary to understand the prejudices of one's time, in order not to offend, nor to follow, them too much.)

—Charles-Louis de Secondat, Baron de Montesquieu

The rise of global financial markets in the last decades of the twentieth century was premised on one fundamental idea: that capital ought to flow across country borders with minimal restriction and regulation. Freedom for capital movements became the new orthodoxy. Any disputes were generally prejudged against governments and in favor of markets, the bearers of discipline. The International Monetary Fund (IMF) began informally to promote capital liberalization. The rules of the European Union (EU) and the Organization for Economic Cooperation and Development (OECD) obliged members, the world's richest thirty or so countries, to allow virtually all cross-border flows of capital. By the end of the 1980s, global finance was built upon and maintained by formal institutional foundations.

It was not always thus. Transactions routinely executed by bankers, managers, and investors during the 1990s—trading foreign stocks and bonds, borrowing in foreign currencies, for example—had been illegal in many countries only decades, and sometimes just a year or two, earlier. Circumventing such restrictions was possible, of course, but usually difficult and expensive. The rules of the international financial system written during the 1940s and 1950s had been restrictive by design and doctrine. At that time members of the international financial community collectively shared a set of beliefs about the destabilizing consequences of short-term, speculative

1

capital flows, or "hot money," and the need for government autonomy from international financial markets.[1] To regulate and control capital was then the prevailing orthodoxy.

Subsequently, as the rules were liberalized, managers and investors enjoyed an era of extraordinary freedom. All sorts of transactions flourished. Perhaps most emblematic was foreign exchange trading, necessary for many cross-border capital flows and essentially nonexistent in 1945. By 1973 the average daily turnover in foreign currency markets was $15 billion, then a nearly inconceivable sum. By 1998 $1.5 trillion changed hands each day in the markets. In 2004 the daily turnover was $1.9 trillion.[2]

The current era of global finance and attendant norms of openness to international capital are not without precedent, however. The heyday of the classical gold standard, circa 1870–1914, was similarly defined by liberal principle and practice. Policymakers understood that to restrict freedom of capital violated the rules, albeit unwritten, of the gold standard. Restrictions being neither normal nor legitimate, capital was as free to flow from one country to another as it has ever been. Economist and statesman John Maynard Keynes once evoked the ease and seeming naturalness of the age by describing a London investor who might, by telephone, "adventure his wealth" around the world, buying shares of firms or bonds of municipalities all while "sipping his morning tea in bed."[3]

This thumbnail sketch of the history of capital controls suggests a number of important questions.[4] How and why did the world shift from an orthodoxy of free capital movements in 1914 to an orthodoxy of capital controls in 1944 and then back again by 1994? How are such standards of appropriate behavior codified and transmitted internationally? In this book I offer answers to these questions that diverge significantly from the scholarly literature on and conventional wisdom about the current era of globalization.

Conventional accounts of the rise of a new era of global finance and a liberal regime to govern it are so widely credited that they constitute truisms and starting assumptions for many scholars and policymakers. While I acknowledge substantial differences of emphasis, a synthesis would go something like this: The U.S. Treasury and Wall Street conceived and promoted a liberal regime for international finance because it served the interests of the United States. Ideological support for the movement away from regulation was provided by the rise of the Right and "neoliberalism." The accumulation of scientific findings that capital liberalization promotes growth, in some versions of the "Washington Consensus," bolstered proponents' claims that a world of mobile capital would yield great benefits. Policymakers recognized that in an age of rapid technological change and well-articulated financial markets, capital controls "do not work." And governments were free to experiment with capital liberalization after the end of systemwide fixed exchange rates in 1971.

Each element of this familiar story, albeit plausible, is also in some way problematic, and collectively they comprise a wholly inadequate account. The alternative I propose in this book, an account informed by heretofore unavailable primary documents and scores of interviews with the policymakers who enacted many of these changes, suggests that both scholarly and popular understandings of the origins and politics of financial globalization should be significantly revised.

The most important misconception of the conventional account concerns the role of the United States. Undoubtedly, the United States played an important role in the creation of a world of mobile capital, through its agents in international financial markets (the public one, the Treasury, and the private one, Wall Street). Unilateral liberalization, bilateral pressure, crisis management, and massive flows of capital in both directions have put the country at the center of global finance. But neither the U.S. Treasury nor Wall Street has preferred or promoted multilateral, liberal rules for global finance. The U.S. approach to globalization has been neither organized nor rule-based, but rather ad hoc.

European policymakers conceived and promoted the liberal rules that compose the international financial architecture. The most liberal rules in international finance are those of the EU, and the United States was irrelevant to their construction. Nearly as liberal and almost as free of U.S. influence, the OECD's rules codifying the norm of capital mobility for developed countries mark another instance of European leadership and deliberate design. Europeans also conceived and embraced a proposal to codify in the IMF's charter a commitment to capital liberalization. The U.S. Treasury was indifferent to such an amendment and Wall Street entirely hostile. While a number of Europeans—particularly the British, Germans, and Dutch—supported liberal rules for capital movements, three French policymakers in the EU, OECD, and IMF played crucial roles. The decisive confluence of worldviews was in Europe—in Brussels, London, Frankfurt, Amsterdam, and, most important, Paris. Europe did not merely acquiesce; Europe made financial globalization. Without an EU open to the world's financial markets—Europe's "open regionalism"—this era of global finance could not have emerged.[5]

The paradoxes do not end with the displacement of the United States by Europe in the story of the making of global finance. The disillusionment of the European Left, rather than the increasing power of the Right, led to the liberalization of capital movements in Europe, as well as to the codification of capital freedom in the rules of its common market. The Left was disillusioned, most profoundly in France, by the recognition that in an age of interdependence capital controls constrained only the middle classes. Socialists came to believe that capital controls did not work to prevent the rich and well-connected from spiriting their funds out of the country, but that they worked all too well to lock up the bank accounts of their working- and middle-class constituents and voters. These processes took place in the absence of clear or systematic evidence that capital liberalization leads to improved economic performance. And capital became most free, and the rules most liberal, in Europe, where governments had fixed the exchange rates of their currencies intermittently since the 1970s and did so permanently in 1999 when the euro came into existence.

My account of the emergence of the rules of global finance, counterintuitive in so many of its particulars, is based on these paradoxes. Refuting conventional wisdom is a daunting task under any circumstances, but when the evidence so convincingly demands it, the creation of an alternate explanation becomes a serious and necessary challenge. I resolve the paradoxes in this book by focusing on processes of social learning after financial crises, explaining the politics of international organizations, and demonstrating the consequences of codifying the boundaries of legitimate government policies. Most essential is to supplement the insights of the economists and political scientists who have written about the globalization of finance with the analytical tools of sociology and the perspective of history.

The End of the First Globalization, 1914–1944

The classical gold standard ushered in an era of unprecedented liberalism in the world economy. Although governments sometimes made exceptions and central banks often subtly manipulated the system, broadly speaking exchange rates were fixed, trade was free, and capital flowed smoothly from country to country. Even people moved across national borders with little interference. Firms and banks became multinational with relative ease.

Governments were insulated from societal demands to reduce interest rates to stimulate domestic economic activity, or to raise them to cool off an over-heating economy. Monetary policy was instead geared toward maintaining the value of the currency in terms of gold.

At the time these arrangements seemed natural. Keynes wrote eloquently of the sense of privilege a cosmopolitan enjoyed while traveling freely, and bearing gold and currency, across borders. Such a person, he observed,

> would consider himself greatly aggrieved and much surprised at the least interference. But, most important of all, he regarded this state of affairs as normal, certain, and permanent, except in the direction of further improvement, and any deviation from it as aberrant, scandalous, and avoidable.[6]

Consensus on the essential rightness of the system was also extraordinarily widespread. Few respectable policy makers, and fewer still serious economists, would have dared suggest that the gold standard and its informal, unwritten rules of fixed exchange rates and free capital flows were inappropriate or undesirable. Although the political Left in Europe would later acquire a reputation for economic irresponsibility, the consensus was shared across the political spectrum. The gold standard, the "money issue," was sacrosanct. The politics of the Right (associated with the orthodox economist David Ricardo) and the Left (symbolized by the Communist Karl Marx) had converged. "Where Ricardo and Marx were as one," Karl Polanyi wrote, "the nineteenth century knew not doubt."[7]

The practice of capital freedom broke down before the principle. The outbreak of World War I in 1914 led the combatant governments to suspend the convertibility of their currencies into gold and, often, other currencies. Fixed exchange rates, international commerce, and cross-border investment collapsed—though only temporarily, most thought. In the early 1920s European governments sought in vain to reestablish on the same principle the prewar system in political circumstances that were much changed. Europe's continental empires had disintegrated into successor states whose governments often carefully guarded their economic autonomy. The working classes, long disenfranchised, empowered the Left and politicized macroeconomic policymaking for the first time. Factories had been destroyed, public finances ruined, and currencies debauched throughout the continent. Germany, severely punished by the economic and political terms of the Treaty of Versailles (1919), struggled to make a success of the fragile Weimar Republic. And the United States withdrew into isolation. Conditions could hardly have been less conducive to the reconstruction of the liberal prewar order.

The onset of the Great Depression in 1929 unraveled all the international links by which the world economy had once flourished. The decisive blow to the principle of capital freedom was the financial crisis of 1931–1933, which began in Austria in the spring of 1931 and spread throughout Europe. As the crisis threatened their banking systems and exchange-rate commitments, governments throughout Europe again took recourse to their wartime capital controls. More important, the crisis, coming as it did at the end of a decade of unstable international currency markets and huge, rapid flows of capital from one country to another, undermined policymakers' trust in unregulated financial markets. If the financial crisis represented the discipline of the market, governments concluded that their financial punishments far exceeded their modest fiscal and monetary transgressions.[8]

When U.S. and European policymakers began to debate the rules by which the international economy ought to be reconstructed, they agreed with their forebears that exchange rates should be fixed and trade free. Regarding capital, however, they would embrace a new principle.

Embedding Liberalism, 1944–1961

The postwar consensus on regulating capital was opposite the nineteenth century's validation of capital mobility. The newly formulated principle was to preserve the existence of markets by taming their social consequences, thereby preempting societal demands to destroy them altogether. Policymakers were keenly aware that such demands had undermined international cooperation in trade and money during the 1920s and 1930s. John Gerard Ruggie describes this reconciliation of markets with the values of social community and domestic welfare as the "embedded liberalism compromise." Markets were to be "embedded" in social and political relations, rather than exist beyond them. Capital controls were understood to be essential to the success of embedded liberalism.[9] Policymakers sought to encourage long-term "productive" capital and regulate tightly short-term "speculative" capital. Short-term capital movements not only constrained the autonomy of governments, but also tended to be "disequilibrating," in the policy idiom of the time. Economists and policymakers also worried about "self-aggravating" flows of capital that could, even in a country without problematic fundamentals, incite and exacerbate a financial crisis. Having emerged informally, this new consensus was at first, like its predecessor, unwritten.

Policymakers then wrote the consensus into the institutional architecture of the international monetary system. The rules were codified in three international organizations: the IMF, the European Community (EC), and the OECD. In each organization the debate about capital's freedom focused on the undesirability of "hot money" flows. The right of IMF, EC, and OECD members to regulate movements of capital, and especially short-term capital, across their borders was protected by the IMF's Articles of Agreement (1945), the EC's Treaty of Rome (1957), and the OECD's liberally named Code of Liberalization of Capital Movements (1961).

Accompanying this legal right was the collective expectation that capital controls would be normal and legitimate for the foreseeable future.[10] As Keynes, one of the authors of the IMF's Articles, explained with typical elegance to the House of Lords: "Not merely as a feature of the transition, but as a permanent arrangement, the plan accords to every member government the explicit right to control all capital movements. What used to be a heresy is now endorsed as orthodox."[11]

Ad Hoc Globalization, 1961–1986

During the 1960s managers, investors, and speculators creatively began to find their way around the myriad regulations designed to constrain their practices. Although some of this creativity expressed itself illegally through outright evasion, much of it took advantage of the invention of the Eurocurrency markets. Eurocurrency markets, ambiguously named, consisted of transactions based in currencies other than that of the host country. The quintessential Eurocurrency transaction was in London, where the market flourished most; Eurocurrencies were primarily Eurodollars. (So, for example, a German firm might issue dollar-denominated bonds in London.)

The Eurocurrency markets burgeoned also because the U.K. government permitted them in London. Although the United Kingdom had at that time an extensive capital controls regime, the Eurocurrency markets were allowed to operate almost completely without regulation.

The U.S. government also tolerated that managers of multinational American firms were, by conducting transactions in the Eurocurrency markets, violating the spirit of U.S. capital controls. The United States instituted in

1963 the interest-equalization tax to eliminate the incentive to take advantage of higher returns abroad. Along with voluntary controls on capital outflows, U.S. policy was designed in principle to avoid some of the transactions that occurred with increasing regularity through the 1960s.[12]

The pace of financial internationalization increased over the course of the 1960s. The Eurocurrency markets represented the ad hoc evolution of international capital markets. The rules of the system remained nonliberal, and no sovereign state, or any international organization, stepped forward to govern global finance. These early indications of the direction of globalization emerged from the market participants with the tacit approval of the United States and the United Kingdom. Both governments came to embrace the globalization of finance not by reconsidering the multilateral rules, but by unilaterally liberalizing implicitly and explicitly.[13]

The markets that resulted soon wrought havoc on the entire multilateral system of fixed exchange rates. The increasing ability of financial market participants to move from one country (and currency) to another was fundamentally incompatible with an international monetary system designed around fixed exchange rates and autonomy for central bankers to manage domestic interest rates. Although a concatenation of events ultimately undermined the system of fixed exchange rates in August 1971, when the United States suspended the convertibility of dollars into gold, many fingers were pointed at the widely denounced "currency speculators."

As the United States and the United Kingdom unilaterally liberalized capital flows during the middle and late 1970s, financial internationalization grew further. Even sovereign governments, for the first time since the 1930s, began systematically to tap international financial markets—and particularly the vast U.S. investing public.

Sovereign bond markets also evolved without a change in the formal rules of the system. Yet market participants quickly came to accept, even to acclaim, the authority of the credit-rating agencies, particularly Standard & Poor's (S&P) and Moody's, as judges of the creditworthiness of governments. The influence of S&P and Moody's derived in part from the information content of their ratings, but also from the widespread incorporation of credit ratings into national financial regulations. The United States in particular effectively delegated regulatory responsibilities to the agencies by using their ratings as benchmarks for the public's exposure to credit risk. S&P's and Moody's sovereign ratings thus carry the force of law in the United States and, today, in many countries around the world. The agencies' sovereign ratings, moreover, indirectly affect every other bond rating in the world because of the "sovereign ceiling": the agencies almost never rate a domestic firm's foreign-currency debt higher than that of its government.[14]

The rating agencies' interpretive frameworks—their sense of and attempt to mirror the prevailing orthodoxy of the markets—have significant consequences, but their authority to govern international financial markets is not codified in any treaty or international agreement. By the middle of the 1980s the rating agencies began to interpret capital controls as unorthodox and governments that employed them as riskier borrowers. S&P managers at the time wrote of the critical importance of a "country's degree of political and economic integration with other 'Western' nations."[15] S&P analysts observed that although developing countries have "extensive capital controls," developed countries are more deeply integrated into international financial markets.[16] Over time, and subtly, the emerging orthodoxy represented and reinforced by the rating agencies increasingly rejected capital controls and embraced liberalization.

The dominance of S&P and Moody's epitomized this ad hoc globalization, an internationalized finance without multilateral rules.[17] U.S. policymakers tended to welcome the growing influence of these distinctly American firms, empowered by U.S. laws, propagating and diffusing credit practices well suited to U.S. economic institutions and familiar to U.S. investors. But the United States had no intention of formalizing the role of these firms at the center of the international financial system, and no other countries formally agreed to their predominance.

Rewriting the Rules, 1986–

Even as the legal rules of the system remained nonliberal for decades, a new era of global capital was in the making. By the middle of the 1980s, four states—the United States, the United Kingdom, Germany, and Japan—had liberalized capital flows across their borders. U.S., British, German, and Japanese banks and firms began to operate in financial markets that were no longer national, but also not yet global.

The unwritten rules of the international monetary system continued to evolve. Policymakers and bankers within these four states began to anticipate an informal trend toward the liberalization of capital by other governments. International financial markets were growing beyond national laws and domestic social norms; the compromise of embedded liberalism was unraveling.[18] Capital controls, once orthodoxy, were, according to a growing number of policymakers, becoming heretical again.[19] The internationalization of finance proceeded, but unevenly. Most governments continued to restrict capital flows, and those that had liberalized were free to reverse course.

Liberal Rules for European and Developed Countries

Two of the formal institutions of the international monetary system were remade at the end of the 1980s. The only partially liberal rules of the EC and OECD, which had slowed the progress toward global financial markets, were revised to embrace a liberal financial system fully. By that time the EC's and OECD's rules obliged members to liberalize almost all foreign direct investment, but short-term, portfolio capital movements were still excluded. Hot money remained officially untrustworthy.

Then a 1988 directive issued by the ministerial Council, Europe's main decision-making body, obliged EC members to remove all restrictions on the movement of capital among member states, as well as between members and nonmembers.[20] France, Germany, and the European Commission were, as always, essential to this major new initiative in European integration. The French government had blocked every attempt to liberalize capital within Europe for more than twenty years. Without a reversal of the French position the directive would have been impossible.

Not only were French Socialists disillusioned with the perverse distributional consequences of capital controls that no longer constrained the rich, but they also came to recognize that monetary union promised greater influence for France in a European economy dominated by the German mark and central bank. In the place of a Bundesbank governed by a dozen German central bankers the French envisioned a European central bank governed by a dozen European policymakers, of whom only one would be German and at least one would be French. The former French finance minister Jacques Delors, in concert with a number of other French policymakers, "decided that it would be better to live in an EMU zone than in a Deutsche mark zone."[21]

The Germans, for their part, had long sought to make capital liberalization central to the European project. Europe's drive toward capital freedom constituted a quid pro quo: French acceptance of capital freedom for the German promise of monetary union. The Germans also insisted on the *erga omnes* principle for European capital liberalization: all capital flows, no matter the source or direction, would have to be liberalized.[22] The *erga omnes* principle, according to Bundesbank President Karl Otto Pöhl, "was absolutely a prerequisite for monetary union. Germany never would have agreed to a single currency area with the possibility of capital controls on third countries."[23] For German policymakers the principle of *erga omnes* was connected to their commitment to the absolute depoliticization of money, which in turn was based on their interpretation of the practice of capital controls during the 1930s and 1940s.[24] Full convertibility removes the temptation, and the possibility, for authorities to serve "other political aims" by influencing the monetary system.[25]

This bargain between France and Germany was conceived and brokered in Brussels, the home of the European Commission. Two French policymakers—Delors, then president of the Commission, and his chief of staff Pascal Lamy—played decisive roles in the codification of the norm of capital mobility in Europe. Not only did Delors and Lamy propose the plan for capital liberalization and monetary union, but the French government would never have agreed to the bargain without the knowledge that Delors himself, a prominent French Socialist, had weighed the trade-offs. Brussels thus became the source of the most liberal set of multilateral rules of international finance ever written. The financial integration of Europe entailed, as a matter of European law, Europe's embrace of the internationalization of finance.

In 1989 the OECD's Code of Liberalization of Capital Movements, which had previously excluded short-term capital flows, was amended to oblige members to liberalize virtually all capital movements. As had been true for the EC in 1988, the amendment became possible only when the French government dropped its opposition to such a sweeping legal obligation to liberalize. Another French policymaker and Socialist, Henri Chavranski, was essential to the emergent consensus. Chavranski chaired during the critical years between 1982 and 1994 the OECD's Committee on Capital Movements and Invisible Transactions (CMIT), which oversaw amendments to and members' compliance with the Code of Liberalization. The United States, as an OECD member, was involved in these negotiations, but the impetus again had come from European policymakers, particularly French, German, Dutch, and British.

For EC and OECD states such as Germany and the United Kingdom these new rules merely codified an obligation to continue to be liberal, a sort of ratification of choices their leaders had already made. But it took several years of entreaties and demands from Brussels and Paris to coax other states such as Italy and Greece to catch up to their peers.

The new rules exerted their most profound effect in negotiations with prospective members. The privileges of membership being contingent on meeting the liberal standards articulated in the rules, the six countries that joined the OECD between 1994 and 2000 and the ten that joined Europe (renamed the European Union by the 1991 Maastricht Treaty) in 2004 liberalized capital flows quickly and comprehensively. In 2005 the liberal rules of the EU and OECD governed some 70 to 80 percent of the world's capital flows, which were concentrated among these organizations' overlapping memberships of, respectively, twenty-five and thirty countries. Global finance had become an affair primarily of rich countries.[26]

Liberal Rules for All?

The last nonliberal rule was potentially the most consequential for patterns of openness and closure in international finance. The IMF's Articles of Agreement apply to nearly every sovereign state in the world, 184 in all. The Articles endow the IMF with a legal mandate to promote trade, but not capital liberalization, and although the Fund has jurisdiction over the current account restrictions imposed by its members, it has no jurisdiction over their capital controls.[27] By the early 1990s the Fund had begun informally to promote capital liberalization, though it did not have the policy tools to oblige member governments to liberalize.[28]

In the middle of the 1990s IMF management proposed and actively promoted an amendment to the articles conceived to transform the IMF's formal role in global capital markets. Ultimately the proposal would fail. Two fundamental and distinct changes were envisioned. First, the IMF was to be endowed with a new purpose: to promote the liberalization of capital flows. Listing capital account liberalization among its official purposes would have enabled the Fund, for the first time in its history, to include capital liberalization in the conditions attached to its loans. Second, the IMF was to assume jurisdiction over the international financial regulations of its members, which were, as a general rule, to be prohibited from imposing restrictions on capital movements without Fund approval.

IMF management, following the lead of Managing Director Michel

Camdessus, another French policymaker, conceived and promoted the proposal. European executive directors of the Fund were the amendment's most enthusiastic proponents. Camdessus and other policymakers within the Fund were most responsible for the organization's embrace of capital liberalization as a practice and the amendment as a legal rule. With no incentive to take responsibility for the failed initiative, Camdessus, along with others involved, continues to insist that the idea to amend the Articles "came from within the Fund."[29]

This finding contrasts sharply with the view widely held among scholars and policymakers that the U.S. Treasury and Wall Street financial firms, the "Wall Street-Treasury Complex," proposed and embraced the capital account amendment.[30] There is, remarkably, almost no evidence to support this conventional wisdom. Instead, I show that Treasury policymakers were at best indifferent to the capital liberalization amendment, and some senior officials even opposed its progress. Wall Street was unambiguously against the amendment. The only decisive American influence on the process came when the U.S. Congress eventually, and single-handedly, defeated the proposal.

The proposal to amend the IMF's Articles generated enormous controversy both within and without the organization, in part because the stakes were so high. Still, many supporters of the amendment believed this fundamental revision of the rules of the system to be imminent during the summer of 1997. The financial crisis that swept across Asia and beyond that very summer dealt the proposal, albeit indirectly, a fatal blow. Although IMF management never officially abandoned the proposal, by the spring of 1999 it was clear that the Articles would not be amended. IMF members, at least those not also members of the EU or OECD, remained free to regulate international capital movements as they wished.

Resolving the Paradoxes of Globalization

Why did Leftist French policymakers, and not the U.S. Treasury and Wall Street financial firms, seek to codify the norm of capital mobility in the world's most influential international organizations? "There is a paradox," observes Lamy, "of the French role in globalization. There is an obvious difference between the traditional French view on the freedom of capital movements and the fact that French policymakers played crucial roles in promoting the liberalization of capital in the EC, OECD, and IMF."[31] Although it has not yet been satisfactorily answered by scholars, this question is less paradoxical than it at first appears.

Managed Globalization

These French policymakers, as well as many other Europeans, have since the late 1980s sought to foster "managed globalization"—a *mondialisation maîtrisée*.[32] Writing the rules of global finance has necessarily entailed strengthening the organizations of which the rules are a part. According to the doctrine of managed globalization, the organizations—the EU, OECD, and IMF—that oversee the rules ought to consist of bureaucracies that are autonomous from the demands of member governments.[33]

Although these international organizations had been at the center of the world economy when it was reconstructed during the 1940s and 1950s, the process of ad hoc globalization had enhanced the influence of multinational firms and banks, as well as the U.S. Treasury. The international financial regime came to be governed less by multilateral legal rules and more by the informal practices and coordination among private financial firms and central banks. The increasing relevance of the Bank for International Settlements (BIS), which represented a more incremental, central-bank centered evolution of the regime, mirrored the diminishing influence of the IMF as the manager of intergovernmental rules.[34]

The European policymakers who held leadership positions in Europe, the OECD, and the IMF—Delors, Chavranski, and Camdessus among them—sought to make their organizations more relevant to the process of globalization by codifying their jurisdiction over their members' capital controls. Through these international organizations and their rules, French and European policymakers might thereby gain more influence over global finance. Observes Lamy, "One resolution of this paradox is the French approach to the problem of liberalization: If you liberalize, you must organize."[35] The liberal rules of the international financial regime were constructed not to limit the interventions of individual governments but to build the capacity of international organizations. Those organizations could then supersede the authority of the capital markets' most powerful states, Germany and the United States.

The indifference of the U.S. Treasury and opposition of Wall Street to the codification of a liberal regime for global finance are, when seen from this perspective, more easily understood. Both the Treasury and Wall Street generally favored liberalization and the internationalization of finance. But U.S. policymakers and bankers recognized, as did many Europeans, that the codification of a liberal regime would increase the influence of international organizations and their bureaucracies. The proposed amendment to the IMF's Articles elicited representative responses. Former U.S. Treasury Secretary Lawrence Summers called the proposal "a bureaucratic imperative" for the Fund.[36] Reflecting the sentiment of much of Wall Street, *The Banker* described the amendment as a "Machiavellian device by Camdessus and his lieutenants to wrest back from the market place some of the power it has lost as the principal force in world financial markets."[37] Although the Fund is often construed to have bailed out private financial interests in crises, those same bankers do not, in general, trust the Fund.

Indeed, in retrospect it is surprising that so many observers thought that the U.S. Treasury or Wall Street would push to codify the norm of capital mobility in a way that would empower international organizations.[38] These are straightforward power politics, as rational and self-interested as can be.[39] The U.S. Treasury already effectively governs global finance; it requires little assistance from the European Commission, the CMIT, or IMF management, and with respect to the latter two, has little incentive to delegate to them. The U.S. government was comfortable delegating only to private firms: Moody's and S&P. U.S. banks and financial firms are interested not in worldwide capital mobility, but in access to a handful of emerging markets, access they can, in general, acquire without the liberalizing efforts of policymakers such as Delors, Chavranski, or Camdessus. A recent series of bilateral treaties with countries such as Singapore and Chile is representative of the ability of the U.S. financial community to achieve its goals of access to major emerging markets without the efforts of international organizations.[40]

The Idiosyncrasies of Organization Building

The content of the intergovernmental bargains that promised to strengthen the European Commission, CMIT, and IMF as organizations and bureaucracies also reflected idiosyncratic politics. The single European capital market envisioned by policymakers in Paris and by the Delors Commission in Brussels was not necessarily open to the rest of the world. Even U.K. negotiators, who favored European financial integration, preferred to retain the option of Europe-wide capital controls vis-à-vis third countries as a means to increase Europe's leverage in global financial markets.

The German insistence on the *erga omnes* principle was firm, however. Without financial integration the French could not make progress toward monetary union, one of the ultimate goals. The French government and the Delors Commission acceded to German demands and based Europe's capital liberalization on the principle of freedom of movement to and from all countries. With regard to capital, at least, European integration was equivalent to globalization, and subsequent enlargements of the EU have expanded the scope of nearly absolute freedom of movement for capital.

Liberalism and the Left

For many European policymakers on the Left, their governments' embrace of capital liberalization represented more than expedience or institutional necessity. Important decision makers within the French Left in particular had by the middle of the 1980s come to interpret capital controls primarily as a policy tool that subordinated the middle classes, rather than the traditional means to restrain and tax capital to redistribute wealth and stimulate economic growth.

The French experience with controls to curb capital flight following the election to president of Socialist François Mitterrand profoundly influenced Delors, Chavranski, and Camdessus (all three in the Mitterrand government at the time), as well as many others on the Left. The capital controls seemed to produce perverse distributional consequences: the rich and well-connected removed their money from France, and the middle class remained constrained by controls. "The Left's embrace of liberalization was similar to its fight against inflation," argues Lamy. "Eventually we recognized that it was the middle classes that bore the burden of regulation most, as they did with inflation."[41] Unable to control the rich, the French Left was "obliged to liberate the rest."[42] Many scholars would take issue with Lamy's characterization of the effects of both inflation and capital controls, but this is how policymakers of the French Left interpreted their recent past, and their interpretations guided later decisions.

Although it is often casually asserted that capital controls "do not work," few scholars have explored precisely how they did not work and why their ineffectiveness might matter politically.[43] The diminishing effectiveness of capital controls became politically salient, but not because bankers and managers demanded liberation from unwieldy regulations. Their liberation was already substantial, if still incomplete and full of nuisance. Rather, some policymakers on the Left in Europe liberalized on behalf of their middle classes. Such were the lessons learned by the Left during the era of ad hoc globalization.

Finally, policymakers, politicians, and scholars sometimes have attributed financial globalization to the ascendance of neoliberal economic ideas that propose to empower markets and constrain government discretion. Such neoliberal ideas are most commonly associated with policymakers and politicians of the Right.[44] These ideas were important because they became part of the context of choice faced by governments during the 1980s and 1990s, and therefore they facilitated the deliberate liberalization of capital. This effect was indirect, however. The story of the rise of neoliberalism is, on its own, incomplete, but it complements the account presented in this book. These ideas were put into practice most often and comprehensively by the Left, whose political logic continues to diverge from that of the neoliberal politicians of the Right. To the extent that neoliberalism affected the emergence of a liberal regime to govern global finance, that process was not based on the decisions of identifiably neoliberal policymakers or Rightist politicians. A subtle and complex transformation was at work.

Constitutive Norms and Market Expectations

The sociological analysis I present in this book also complements the conclusion, reached by economists and political scientists, that capital regulations and liberalizations are signals interpreted by financial markets. Market participants, in this way of thinking, infer meanings from policies. Capital liberalizations are interpreted as positive signals, while capital controls are negative signals.[45] If these market expectations and inferences could be treated exclusively as fixed parameters, we might not need to delve further into the social environment of the financial markets.[46]

These expectations and inferences are not parametric, however. In, say, 1958 capital controls signaled neither heresy nor even unfriendliness to financial markets. By 1998, however, capital controls apparently signaled poor international financial citizenship. The capital account regulations themselves were objectively identical during the 1950s and 1990s, and yet international organizations, ministries of finance, credit-rating agencies, financial journalists, bankers, and managers drew different inferences from their implementation.[47]

International organizations affected the international financial system through mechanisms that are at once regulative (rationalist) and constitutive (constructivist or sociological). Once the norm of capital mobility was codified in Europe and the OECD, the European Commission and the CMIT monitored the compliance of members, thereby helping to regulate and constrain their behavior.[48] International organizations also influenced the social context of the international financial system by fixing the meanings of capital controls as policy tools, defining for their members the range of legitimate policies, and disseminating the new orthodoxy of freedom of movement for capital.[49]

The liberal rules of the EU and OECD defined the economic policy "scripts" members were supposed to follow.[50] The EU delineated the boundaries of legitimate policies enacted by "European" states; OECD rules constituted the policy practices of "developed" states. These scripts articulated the obligation of European and developed states to permit capital to move freely. Because these rules define the policy practices that lead members to recognize what constitutes appropriate behavior on the part of other governments, the EU and OECD also informed the expectations of the financial markets. The EU and OECD codified the norm of capital mobility and thereby hardened it into a new orthodoxy.

The EU and OECD then became teachers of their norms and rules, and during the 1990s the organizations found eager pupils among the countries seeking to join their organizations. The real and symbolic benefits of membership encouraged aspiring members to embrace the respective rules, including capital liberalization, often without questioning the content of the constitutive rules that would ensure their recognition as "European" and "developed." A Czech central bank official recalls that central and east European governments competed during the early 1990s to be "the best pupil of the developed market economies."[51] This competition was also apparent from Brussels, where one Commission negotiator remarked on prospective members' "eagerness to be perceived as right up to European standards for openness to capital movements."[52] The countries that joined the OECD and EU readily embraced the script of capital liberalization. Although the Commission and CMIT were enthusiastic proponents of the script, neither could force acceptance of their rules; they merely enforced and interpreted the rules to which members had already agreed.[53]

Outline of the Book

In Chapter 2 I develop further arguments about the causes and consequences of liberal rules for the international financial regime. An important conclusion emerging from my evaluation of the alternate arguments and the conventional wisdom is that an analytical framework informed by social constructivism proves essential to a coherent narrative of the emergence of the current era of global finance. In this chapter I also challenge a variety of alternate arguments for the emergence of liberal rules in the international financial system, including those that emphasize: the U.S. Treasury and Wall Street; the rise of neoliberalism and the Right in the United States and Europe; the accumulation of scientific knowledge of the benefits of capital liberalization; the end of systemwide fixed exchange rates; and technological and other changes that altered the balance of power between governments and financial markets.

Many of these complementary arguments emphasize how the balance of power shifted away from governments and toward financial markets. Financial markets seem to have been enabled by successive trends in the international economy. But trends that enable capital mobility are not the same as, nor do they inexorably lead to, rules that oblige governments further to liberalize capital. Although we now know a great deal about the process and politics of financial internationalization, critical parts of the story remain to be told.

In Chapter 3 I describe the place of capital controls in the compromise of embedded liberalism during the 1940s and 1950s. Drawing on archival and secondary sources, I show how the policymakers who negotiated the IMF's Articles of Agreement, Europe's Treaty of Rome, and the OECD's Code of Liberalization of Capital Movements sought to distinguish between "productive" long-term capital and "speculative" short-term capital movements. For each organization the problem of controlling hot money was paramount. The necessity of regulating short-term capital movements was doctrinal and practical.

Next I trace the evolution of the informal practices and formal rules of Europe (Chapter 4), the OECD (Chapter 5), and the IMF (Chapter 6). Each organization faced a critical moment during which the bureaucracies of the organizations and representatives of some member countries sought to transform fundamentally the nonliberal rules regarding capital controls. These three chapters are based on evidence drawn from recently released archival documents, as well as from interviews conducted between 2002 and 2005 with policymakers situated in the three organizations and eight member countries, as well as representatives of private financial firms (see Appendix).

A book about the evolution of worldviews necessarily engages with the producers and consumers of those ideas, and I have sought to do so directly. Whenever possible I have corroborated the accounts of interviewees with primary documents, contemporary media reports, and the accounts of other interviewees. Only in a few cases have I been forced to rely completely on the admittedly imperfect (and potentially self-serving) recall of one or two individuals for the narratives presented in these chapters. Although I recognize the drawbacks of relying on the testimony of the principals involved in these politics, no superior means of discussing these important moments in recent economic and political history has yet become available. In any event, these additions to the existing evidence will contribute to our understanding of developments as witnessed and influenced by these individuals.

After the case studies of the three organizations in Chapters 4 through 6, I attempt in Chapter 7 to describe the evolution of the informal norms of the international financial system by tracing the doctrines and practices of Moody's and S&P. For this chapter I rely on the content of the rating agencies' official primers on sovereign rating and a number of sovereign rating reports published between the early 1980s and the end of the 1990s, as well as on a handful of interviews conducted with Moody's and S&P managers and analysts.

In Chapter 8 I argue that the financial crisis of 1997–1999 exerted, indirectly and directly, an enormous influence on the three international organizations and the credit-rating agencies. Much as the financial crisis of 1931 became a touchstone for debates about the regulation of international capital flows, so, too, has the financial crisis that erupted in Thailand in the middle of 1997, spread to Russia during the summer of 1998, and culminated in Brazil in January 1999.

The organizations and firms that comprise the international financial community appear to have reconsidered the benefits, risks, and institutional preconditions of capital liberalization.[54] The credit-rating agencies, for their part, have emerged as purveyors of caution in the developing world, emphasizing the risks of liberalization and praising the use of controls by countries with weak domestic financial systems, such as China and India. The OECD's CMIT softened its demands that prospective members liberalize capital flows quickly and comprehensively. The proposed amendment to the IMF's Articles was dealt a fatal blow by the crisis, and IMF staff became reluctant to encourage members to liberalize. When the Slovak Republic joined the OECD in 2000, for example, Elena Kohútiková of the central bank was surprised at how profoundly the message from the international financial community had changed:

> After the crises of 1997 and 1998 the OECD, IMF, and U.S. Treasury encouraged us to slow down our liberalization of short-term capital flows. There was a change in the knowledge base. The dangers of short-term capital flows were recognized more clearly. The shift in sentiment was remarkable: at first it was, "You do have to do everything immediately." Then it became, "You have to do everything step by step, and please be careful about short-term capital movements."[55]

The autumn of 1998 was, in a sense, the high point of the norm and the attempt to codify the rule of capital mobility for all countries. The orthodoxy of capital's freedom was undermined everywhere except in the EU, primarily because the codified norm of capital liberalization for European states is literally not open to interpretation or discussion. The EU, unlike the OECD and IMF, is not the home of experts and their fluid wisdom; the EU is the home of rules. The entire process of European integration through evolving rules enforced by the Commission is built around the idea that it is effective to bureaucratize difficult issues. Few issues in the history of European integration were as difficult as the liberalization of capital movements, but it is now settled definitively. Voices of caution emanate from New York, Washington, and Paris. Only in Brussels does the codification of the norm of capital mobility remain complete and secure from the skepticism that followed the financial crisis of 1997–1999. The emergence of a liberal regime for global finance is not best understood as a conspiracy, and much less as one orchestrated by U.S. policymakers and bankers. The most influential plotters were French socialists, German central bankers, and European bureaucrats.

I conclude with a reflection on the process of interpreting financial crises and their influence on policy orthodoxy and the practices of firms, governments, and international organizations. The lessons of financial crises are not self-evident; they are subject to interpretation and debate.[56] These interpretations evolve with the passage of time. Just as Milton Friedman argued during the early 1950s that the policymakers and economists of the

1940s had overreacted to the crises of the 1930s, soon there may be those who argue that the Asian financial crisis did not warrant a renewed skepticism of international capital flows.[57] In the first years since the most recent crisis, however, with the havoc wrought still fresh in the minds of policymakers, a consensus of caution prevails. Each generation forgets the lessons of the last and renews its awareness of the risks on the occasion of an international financial crisis.[58] What appear to be permanent orthodoxies about capital movements are not permanent at all.

CHAPTER **2**

The Rules of Global Finance: Causes and Consequences

> For it is impossible for any one to begin to learn what he thinks he already knows.
>
> —Epictetus

The ad hoc globalization of finance came into being, incrementally and haphazardly, as the result of a series of unilateral decisions by a handful of countries, particularly the United States and the United Kingdom, between the middle of the 1960s and the end of the 1980s. The extraordinary influence of credit-rating agencies on sovereign borrowers was emblematic of ad hoc globalization.

By the late 1980s, global finance had increasingly become a system of liberal rules. The OECD and EU are constituted in part by rules that oblige members to liberalize capital flows across their borders. In practice, the liberal rules of the OECD and EU apply to some 70 to 80 percent of the world's cross-border finance, which flows primarily from rich countries to other rich countries. In 1998 the IMF nearly adopted a similar liberal rule for its 184 members. Had it passed, this rule would have governed the capital account regulations of nearly every sovereign government in the world according to the norm of capital mobility.

In this chapter, I recover the origins of the rules of global finance and explain the consequences. For the case of the IMF, I focus on the politics of the proposal to amend the organization's Articles of Agreement as a source of evidence for some of the larger debates about the causes of global finance and a liberal regime to govern it.

Causes

The scholarly literature on the internationalization of capital has grown large, and rightly so given the importance of the topic. The arguments and findings of this book require, however, several significant revisions to the conventional wisdom about the political economy of the rise of global capital markets.

First, although the United States promoted globalization, it did so unilaterally and bilaterally; the United States neither proposed nor enthusiastically endorsed the attempts to codify the norm of capital mobility within international organizations. The newly liberal rules of the globalization of finance were written in Europe by Europeans who shared a consensus that favored liberalization.

Second, although the rhetoric of the European Left during the past two decades has largely emphasized their capitulation to the forces of global capital, politicians and parties of the Left throughout Europe in fact embraced—for diverse reasons, to be sure—liberal rules for capital flows.

Third, in their explanations for change within the international financial system, scholars and policymakers have tended to focus on a variety of changes that enabled capital to become more mobile: the advance of knowledge that capital liberalization is simply prudent, growth-oriented policy, bolstered by the common refrain that capital controls "do not work"; the end of systemwide fixed exchange rates; and competitive deregulation, a sort of race to the bottom (or top, if one is a banker or executive who prefers financial deregulation). An element of truth abides in each of these stories, and in the aggregate these influences have enabled capital to become more mobile. They are, as Beth Simmons argues, complementary explanations for the internationalization of capital.[1] But each of these accounts is also factually problematic. None does much to explain the fundamental change in the legitimacy and the signaling content of capital controls, nor do they help explain the efforts of European policymakers to codify the norm of capital mobility.

American Hegemony and the French Paradox

The United States lies at the center of the international financial system, and scholars and policymakers regularly attribute the norms and rules of that system to the exercise of American power. The U.S. Treasury is generally characterized as the country's public agent, while powerful Wall Street financial firms and banks are seen as the private expression of American influence. Because the current era of global finance has greatly favored U.S. strategic and economic interests, the Treasury and Wall Street have welcomed its arrival. But the role of American leadership in its formation is another question entirely.

The widely held belief that attributes the system to U.S. hegemony and design comes from two intellectual traditions. The power politics of Realism, some suggest, naturally led the United States to promote capital liberalization. And the narrow material interests identified by neo-Marxism connect the preferences of the private financial community with the country's broader "national interest."[2] The coincidence of public and private preferences need not indicate conspiratorial design.[3] Scholars, without reviewing the historical record, have taken for granted an American leadership role in the evolution of the system simply because the system benefits the United States. Indeed, as my investigation of the primary archival sources demonstrates, the "Wall Street-Treasury Complex" is a largely passive beneficiary of a liberal regime brought into being by forces elsewhere in the world.

The argument linking U.S. hegemony to the emergence of a liberal international financial system is suspect on both empirical and theoretical grounds. The most important liberal rules of the system are those of the EU and OECD. The empirical record simply does not support the claim that the United States exerted much influence on the processes that created those rules. The United States was irrelevant to the creation of European rules and largely indifferent to the codification of the norm of capital mobility within the OECD.

Observers have particularly presumed an aggressively liberalizing U.S. financial hegemony behind the proposal to amend the IMF's Articles of Agreement in the late 1990s. With different mixes of Realist and neo-Marxist logics, scholars such as Jagdish Bhagwati and Robert Wade argued that the U.S. Treasury and Wall Street financial interests promoted the Fund's embrace of capital liberalization in doctrine and law. Nearly all scholars of globalization maintain that the policy consensus that favored capital's freedom profoundly influenced the process of liberalization. Bhagwati, Wade, and many others have pointed to the consensus that emerged in New York and Washington, D.C.

Bhagwati writes that the IMF "has been relentlessly propelled" by the convergence of preferences of Wall Street and the U.S. Treasury "toward embracing the goal of capital account convertibility."[4] Wade and Frank Veneroso specifically add the Fund to Bhagwati's formulation, thus referring to the "Wall Street-Treasury-IMF complex." Wade and Veneroso also argue that the power of the U.S. Congress helps to underpin this network.[5] They argue that the U.S. and U.K. treasuries are "behind this campaign by the Fund," primarily because the United States "has a powerful national interest in establishing the free movement of capital worldwide." The U.S. Treasury, according to Wade and Veneroso, eventually recognized that those "goals could be advanced more effectively through the IMF by revising the Articles of Agreement." And for its part, "Wall Street wants capital account opening world-wide, and hence supports revision of the IMF's Articles of Agreement."[6]

Scant empirical evidence exists, however, to support these arguments.[7] The archival and recent historical records suggest that the politics of the IMF amendment differed from these conventional accounts of American dominance. The U.S. Treasury emerges as neither originator nor promoter of the amendment. Some senior Treasury officials were indifferent, while others were outright opposed. The private financial community strongly and publicly opposed the amendment as well. And the U.S. Congress was ultimately responsible for the proposal's demise. It may be useful for some empirical questions to specify a Wall Street-Treasury complex, but understanding the politics of the international financial system and the evolution of its rules is not one of them.

This is not to deny the large influence of the United States within the Fund or the veracity of a handful of accounts describing the relationships between the IMF and member countries in which U.S. interests played a decisive role.[8] But it simply does not follow that the United States also would have sought to empower the Fund, an organization that tended to serve the country's needs just as it was.

Thus, I do not conclude that the power politics of Realism are irrelevant to understanding the U.S. approach to the evolution of the international financial system. Those power politics have not yet been correctly derived and specified. The dominant approach of U.S. policymakers and private financial interests has been primarily bilateral and unilateral, and this makes sense from a Realist, rationalist perspective. Neither the U.S. government nor the private financial community has sought to empower international organizations, and, given their status and position in the world, it is difficult to discern why they would want to do so. The U.S. Treasury is already central to global finance. Private bankers and investors already have access to the most important and profitable emerging markets in the world. They have never expressed an interest in, nor have they promoted, literally worldwide capital mobility. Practical thinkers always, bankers and investors have repeatedly witnessed how countries that are not prepared safely to embrace full capital mobility experienced crises. Those crises evidenced a tendency to spread, sometimes to the very emerging markets that were the object of American bankers' and investors' concerns.

Given the extraordinary success of the U.S. Treasury and the American private financial community in achieving their goals by unilateral action and in bilateral negotiations, the assumption that in the 1980s and 1990s they preferred to empower, and delegate to, international organizations is less than convincing. Those international organizations are, after all, run by bureaucracies and officials, frequently European, who have envisioned the creation of a very different organization of global finance. From the perspective of pure power politics, U.S. policymakers, bankers, and investors had every reason to welcome ad hoc globalization. Although the United States has promoted capital liberalization, it has done so unilaterally and bilaterally, and almost never multilaterally.[9] Rather than seeing the IMF as its agent, U.S. Treasury officials frequently understood the Fund as a rival to their own centrality in the international financial system.[10]

Whereas the U.S. approach to globalization has been ad hoc, European policymakers, particularly those situated in the EU, OECD, and IMF, have sought to organize and institutionalize global finance. The codified rules that European policymakers promoted were still liberal, however. EU and OECD rules may build the influence and capacity of those organizations by giving them jurisdiction over members' capital accounts, but those rules also promote liberalization, as the IMF amendment would have. The Europeans were not dragged along by the Americans toward a future of global capital. To the contrary, the Europeans led the way toward a liberal regime for global finance by creating the most consequential rules of the system. The Europeans' "open regionalism" made the current era of globalization possible.[11]

Among these European policymakers, a handful of French civil servants—Jacques Delors as President of the European Commission, Henri Chavranski as Chair of the OECD Committee on Capital Movements and Invisible Transactions, and Michel Camdessus as Managing Director of the IMF—stand out in two respects. First, they represented the emergent French foreign policy doctrine of "managed globalization." Second, they played—

apparently paradoxically—critical roles in conceiving and promoting newly liberal rules for the EC, OECD, and IMF.[12]

All the more paradoxical is that Delors had been, and still is, one of the most influential members of the French Socialist Party. Delors was the architect of French *rigueur*, the macroeconomic austerity that followed crisis in the early 1980s, and the catalyst of the party's rethinking of its approach to finance. Although neither had been involved in French party politics, Chavranski (a member of the Socialist Party) and Camdessus (a Social Christian) had both made their marks as civil servants in the Treasury under Socialist President François Mitterrand, who appointed Camdessus as Governor of the Banque de France. This was a moment, in other words, when the views of the French Left and Right on capital liberalization were indistinguishable. The broader social phenomenon in France became known as *la pensée unique*, an economic orthodoxy embraced across the political spectrum.

The institutional consequences of this paradoxical Left-Right consensus on capital reverberate across the world, yet its origins remain poorly understood. My resolution of this French paradox is premised on three themes that run through the stories of the EC, OECD, and IMF. First, France has displayed a consistent approach to the liberal imperatives of globalization: "managing" globalization with formal rules, even if such rules are essentially liberal. The French foreign policy establishment has conceived the notion and associated doctrine of *mondialisation maîtrisée*, or "managed globalization."[13] The French vision of ruling globalization contrasts starkly with ad hoc globalization of the sort that the United States, as well as the United Kingdom, has nurtured.

Second, of these episodes of rule creation the most decisive was the liberalization of capital movements in Europe. The rewriting of the EC's rules to favor capital freedom was based as well on an idiosyncratic logic: the French accepted capital liberalization because it was part of the European project. Europe's drive toward capital freedom, in the eyes of some observers, constituted a French quid pro quo with the Germans, who had long sought such a rule: capital freedom for the promise of monetary union. The result was profoundly important, for the EU ended up with the most liberal rules imaginable: members were obliged to liberate all capital flows, no matter the source or direction.

Third, the influence of Delors, Chavranski, and Camdessus was, more broadly, the achievement of a vocal minority within the French policy establishment that saw ostensibly liberal policies as instruments for social purposes. Delors reflects:

> Historically there has always been a minority position in France that views inflation as the most damaging for the long-term health of the economy: undermining the value of the currency, tempting capital to flee, and hurting the poor and middle classes. This minority position can be traced back even to [Charles] de Gaulle and [Jacques] Rueff, and more recently a minority in the Left and in the Christian Democrats. This minority has always sought to modernize France: to stabilize the currency, to fight inflation, and to promote healthy growth and employment. And it happened that this minority won in France during the 1980s. It was a long and difficult struggle.[14]

For this minority, which came to power from the Left in the 1980s, the Mitterrand-era capital controls produced perverse distributional consequences: the rich and well-connected spirited their money out of France, and the middle class remained constrained by controls. Although the distributional goals of the Left had not changed, the world had. And the new world of internationalized financial markets meant that capital controls, long one of the Left's tools for macroeconomic management on behalf of the working and middle classes, no longer empowered labor and the intelligentsia. Indeed, from this perspective, they had the opposite effect. Capital controls that constituted a mere nuisance for the rich had become a veritable prison for everyone else. Unable to control the rich, the French Left decided to free everyone else. "We recognized, at last," Chavranski recalls, "that in an age of interdependence capital would find a way to free itself, and we were obliged to liberate the rest."[15]

This modernizing and liberalizing minority of policymakers in the French Treasury and Banque de France won the day in Paris when the country fell into crisis during the 1980s. The march of capital mobility spread beyond France when they left the government and brought their influence to the international organizations that govern globalization. Once there, they proceeded to generalize for the wider world the policies that they had chosen for France. "There was no plan, however, to liberalize capital in all international organizations," reflects Delors. "It was not a conspiracy. Those of us in that modernizing minority shared a common doctrine, and when we were placed in the organizations we continued to promote our doctrine."[16]

Hubert Védrine, one of France's most influential thinkers on international affairs, suggests: "France will share in the adventure of globalization, which will also be marked by France. Our entire foreign policy is built around this idea."[17] The French mark on globalization is nowhere clearer than in the international financial system, where France has taken the lead in devising and writing its rules. The French formulation of rules for capital liberalization was, critically, focused on exactly that: rules, and the organization that was to follow. Pascal Lamy puts it thus: "In Europe, at that time, the French vision succeeded: it was liberalization combined with organization. The stories of the IMF and OECD are similar: these were attempts to liberalize and organize simultaneously."[18]

The kind of globalization that the French fear—uncontrolled, ad hoc, without rules—is precisely the globalization the United States has nurtured. "If there is no system," observes Lamy, "with rules that constrain all states, then we have a problem."[19] Owing to the overwhelming U.S. dominance in international financial markets, neither the U.S. Treasury nor Wall Street has perceived any need to write rules that might ultimately constrain them as well. Most of what either the largest financial institutions or the Treasury secretary would like to accomplish requires the resources of only the United States, and not the EU, OECD, or IMF. Certainly, neither Wall Street nor the U.S. Treasury has evidenced a compelling need to have Delors, Chavranski, or Camdessus advocate liberalization on their behalf. Absent French rulemaking, U.S. unilateral and bilateral policymaking would not have yielded anything like the global system we have now.

Thus, the U.S. approach to ad hoc globalization, befitting a hyperpower with narrow economic ambitions, stands in marked contrast to the French approach to "managed globalization," a strategy befitting a middle power with global ambitions to influence international politics and economics by putting rules and organizations, rather than American power, at the center of the system.

Still, the French doctrine of managed globalization requires significantly more explication, for most of the rhetoric about managed globalization emphasizes the need for more regulation, not more liberalization.[20] The rules that French policymakers helped to write would indeed empower international organizations by giving them jurisdiction over members' capital account policies. But the proposals for these liberal rules also promised to give those organizations a mission to encourage, sometimes by obligation and at other times by persuasion, more liberalization. With regard to the rules of global finance, then, the specific content of the French doctrine was authored by policymakers of the Left who had embraced capital liberalization as a process of removing the unattractive distributional consequences of leaky capital controls.

Neoliberalism and the European Left

Ideological change was part of the evolution of the international financial system, and explanations based on such change are complementary to my own. The rise of neoliberalism during the 1970s and 1980s in the United States, United Kingdom, and the rest of Europe altered the approach that developed countries took with regard to their capital accounts and the organizations of which they were members.[21]

Although much has been made of the rise of neoliberalism, the role of the French and European Left in creating globalization suggests a need for a more nuanced understanding of the role of ideology in the diffusion of liberal policy practices. To be sure, neoliberalism did change the character of the policy debate. During the 1970s and 1980s, and associated with the rise of Margaret Thatcher in Britain and Ronald Reagan in the United States, a new policy consensus that differed from the embedded liberal compromise of the 1940s emerged. Neoliberalism became ideologically dominant throughout the OECD and the EU. The OECD's Pierre Poret, for example, describes a "new era in policy attitudes" in the 1980s:

> The priority objectives ascribed to monetary policies in OECD countries converged towards achieving long-term price stability, and, to this end, building up credibility-enhancing mechanisms. Capital controls, which had in the past aimed at preserving the ability of monetary policy to exploit a possible trade-off between inflation and unemployment, did not fit into this new policy paradigm and risked to distract the authorities from the essential task of maintaining sound and credible economic policies.[22]

Of the EU, political scientist Kathleen McNamara writes, "A neo-liberal policy consensus that elevated the pursuit of low inflation over growth or employment took hold among political elites" throughout Europe. Capital controls, moreover, "run directly counter to the ideology of neo-liberalism."[23] Neoliberalism altered fundamentally how policymakers understood their options, primarily by offering a ready and coherent alternative paradigm to the perceived failure of the Keynesian model. Neoliberal ideas influenced policymakers throughout the developed and developing worlds.[24]

But neoliberalism is, on its own, insufficient as an explanation for the evolution of the rules governing capital in international organizations. It would deprive the word of all meaning to insist that France's Socialist Party, Delors, Chavranski, Camdessus, and the other authors of the liberal rules of global capital were "neoliberals," and that the label offers sufficient insight into the choices they made. The formulation of these rules was driven neither by professional economists nor by policymakers trained in U.S.-style economics, neoliberal or otherwise. There is more to the story of how the formal rules of globalization were written.

The liberal internationalism of the Left during the 1980s was not historically unique in France, or even unusual in comparative context. It has a historical parallel in the first era of globalization, which lasted roughly from 1880 until 1914. The modern French Left argued that workers abroad would improve their standard of living through trade. Political considerations also informed the Left's internationalism. "For the Left to realize its domestic political objectives," Suzanne Berger writes, "it needed to sustain a broad Republican coalition, and it understood that the platform on which such a coalition could be constructed required anti-protectionism and embrace of an open international economy."[25] Indeed, it is a remarkable fact of our era that programs of market-oriented reforms have been implemented much more frequently by putatively left-wing governments than by those on the right.[26]

Scientific Progress and Social Learning

The trade-offs associated with liberating or regulating capital flows are, arguably, as difficult to manage as any in macroeconomic policymaking. The decision to liberalize international capital flows must take account of potential benefits and risks.[27] Many of the benefits are straightforward. By liberalizing, countries increase their access to foreign private capital. Capital mobility facilitates an efficient global allocation of savings, thereby fostering economic growth and welfare around the world. Residents are offered the opportunity to earn higher risk-adjusted returns on their savings. A country's financial sector may increase its competitiveness, as well as attractiveness, to investors. Many economists and policymakers argue, finally, that financial markets impose a useful discipline on macroeconomic policymaking.

The risks of liberalization have worried policymakers for more than a century. Financial markets are more susceptible than goods markets to crises because of asymmetric or imperfect information that might elicit herd behavior among market participants. Moreover, being subject to wide swings in market sentiment unrelated to market fundamentals leaves financial markets susceptible to crises that take the form of self-fulfilling prophesies on the part of market participants.[28] Liberalization thus increases the risk that a country will experience a financial crisis and makes a country more vulnerable to contagion from other countries' crises. Excessive inflows of capital can distort domestic asset prices and thereby introduce inefficiencies. Domestic financial sectors, if they lack the appropriate institutional framework, may be weakened rather than strengthened. Finally, liberalization's most worrisome result from a government's point of view is the attendant obligation to submit to financial-market discipline. In other words, a government that liberalizes capital flows reduces the policy options available to it, particularly if the exchange rate is fixed.

Economists and political scientists have generated a sophisticated scholarly debate on the balance between the benefits and risks of capital liberalization that continues today and is unlikely ever to reach a definitive resolution. One critical question for this book is: Was the policy consensus that favored liberalization—the consensus that provided the intellectual justification for new rules in the EC, OECD, and IMF—based on the evidence produced by scholars that the benefits exceeded the risks? If so, we could then conclude that policymakers chose to liberate capital because they saw that doing so simply makes good economic sense. We would have a case where scientific knowledge—Reason, in short—determined outcomes in international politics.[29]

The short answer to this question is: No. Scientific knowledge did not create the consensus. The policy consensus of the 1980s and early 1990s did not emerge from the accumulation of evidence that capital liberalization promotes economic growth, or that the benefits of liberalization systematically outweigh its risks. Such evidence did not exist then, nor does it exist now.[30] The evidence generated by scores of econometric studies was mixed, even contradictory. The masterly historical synthesis produced by Maurice Obstfeld and Alan Taylor reports that no definitive conclusion can be reached: "Can the benefits and costs of global capital markets be neatly summarized and quantified? The historical record indicates the very contingent nature of any attempt to do so. Some countries have flourished upon financial opening, others have suffered disaster."[31] The economics profession had not reached an evidence-based, scientific consensus that policymakers adopted for a liberalizing agenda.

To the contrary, one of the arguments in favor of the proposed IMF amendment made by then-First Deputy Managing Director Stanley Fischer was motivated not by knowledge but by the lack of knowledge. Fischer saw *not* knowing as a compelling reason for the Fund itself to create a more informed understanding of capital liberalization. The Fund would achieve this understanding by gaining jurisdiction over capital and acquiring a mandate to promote its liberalization. In the Fund, evidence did not drive the agenda; if anything, the lack of evidence lent a sense of urgency to create and institutionalize knowledge. "The difference between the analytic understanding of capital- versus current-account restrictions is striking," argued Fischer in defense of the amendment. "The economics profession knows a great deal about current-account liberalization, its desirability, and effective ways of liberalizing. It knows far less about capital-account liberalization. It is time to bring order to both thinking and policy on the capital account."[32]

Some years and dozens of studies later, the evidence is still wanting.[33] The last major study composed of cross-country regressions with indices of capital account openness (which are widely perceived to be problematic) has probably now been written by Kenneth Rogoff and his team in the IMF's Department of Research. Beginning with the theoretical models of the mechanisms that link capital account liberalization to economic growth, Rogoff and his team concluded: "A systematic examination of the evidence, however, suggests that it is difficult to establish a strong causal relationship. In other words, if financial integration has a positive effect on growth, there is as yet no clear and robust empirical proof that the effect is quantitatively significant."[34]

Rather than supporting the policy consensus, the econometric results of prominent, policy-oriented economists have begun to undermine an ambitious liberalizing agenda within international organizations. As Barry Eichengreen observes, "Given the breadth of support commanded by this synthesis, the lack of empirical substantiation of its fundamental tenets is worrisome indeed. If the evidence is really not there, then it is high time to rethink the conventional wisdom."[35]

The End of Fixed Exchange Rates

Another explanation for the rise of global capital holds that the end of the Bretton Woods fixed-exchange-rate system in the early 1970s undermined part of the rationale for capital controls: without an explicit obligation to maintain a specific exchange rate, governments could in principle liberalize capital flows without undermining their policy autonomy.[36] The end of systemwide fixed exchange rates encouraged governments to experiment with capital liberalization. In practice, however, exchange-rate policy did not change dramatically. Recent reevaluations of the modern history of exchange-rate management suggest that the early 1970s was not such a watershed. More than half the exchange rate arrangements commonly understood to have been "managed floating" were de facto pegs, crawling pegs, or narrow bands.[37] Perhaps more important, generalized floating as a phenomenon does little to explain the rise of obligations to liberalize capital in international organizations.

Indeed, it was in Europe that the movement toward full capital mobility during the 1980s and early 1990s was most thorough, and it was in Europe that the first truly liberal rules for capital flows were written. Yet many European countries had begun to cooperate in exchange-rate management immediately after the Bretton Woods system collapsed. European countries fixed their currencies' values to one another first in the so-called Snake, then in the European Monetary System (EMS), culminating in a monetary union. Certainly the Europeans did not liberate capital because they had given up on fixed exchange rates.

Thus, it was not the elimination of exchange rate commitments that allowed countries to liberalize capital and conduct an autonomous monetary policy. Even more consequential changes in the practice of macroeconomic policymaking were under way.

Capital Controls "Do Not Work"

Policymakers and economists sometimes observe that capital was liberalized simply because capital controls had become too porous. Capital controls, as is so often said, "do not work" to constrain ever more mobile capital.[38] To be sure, over time three important changes in the world economy undermined the effectiveness of controls. At the end of the war in 1945 most countries maintained trade as well as capital restrictions. The return to convertibility for trade transactions at the end of the 1950s afforded opportunities to evade capital account restrictions by, for example, overinvoicing imports or underinvoicing exports.[39] Scholars have also argued that technological change and financial innovation altered the costs and benefits of capital controls. Capital controls, Eichengreen reports, "may have become less attractive because information and communications technologies have grown more sophisticated, rendering controls more porous and their effective application more distortionary."[40] Financial market innovation, in derivatives in particular, made capital controls easier to circumvent. Additionally, once many countries had liberalized capital flows, it became increasingly difficult for any individual country to regulate capital unilaterally. Closely related to a decreasing ability to restrict outflows of capital was an increasing need to attract investors: governments seeking to attract increasingly mobile capital were obliged, according to this argument, to liberalize so as not to lose out to other, more liberal, and presumably more attractive, locations for portfolio investment.[41]

These complementary arguments emphasize how the balance of power shifted away from governments and toward financial markets. Financial markets seem to have been enabled by successive trends in the international economy, each of which compounded the effects of the preceding. But trends that enable capital mobility are not the same as, nor do they inexorably lead to, rules that oblige governments further to liberalize capital. As the three episodes of French policymakers' writing the liberal rules for international organizations reveal, an important motivation of the French Left was to counteract the distributional consequences of ineffective capital controls. The diminishing effectiveness of capital controls thus became politically salient and did indeed drive the creation of a more liberal international monetary system, though *not* for the reasons that many economists and policymakers have assumed. More important, none of these arguments helps to explain how newly liberal rules reinforced the trend toward capital mobility and obliged governments not to reverse course. The sources and effects of the rules of capital require further explanation.

Consequences

The international institutions, without which finance could not have been internationalized, consist of both formal, written rules and informal, unwritten rules. The formal rules of international institutions are often, though not always, interpreted and applied by the bureaucracies of international organizations. The informal rules of international institutions, in contrast, are social norms that emerge from the interactions among governments, firms, and international organizations.

International institutions, and the organizations associated with them, exert a number of distinct influences on governments and markets.[42] Institutions and organizations regulate and constrain behavior by monitoring the compliance of governments with their formal commitments, by providing information about compliance to other governments, and by proposing or introducing punishments and rewards. This conceptualization of the effects of institutions, with its origins in economics, focuses on how they reduce transaction costs.[43] The OECD's CMIT oversaw the Code of Liberalization; the European Commission ensured compliance first with the capital liberalization directive and then with the Maastricht Treaty; and IMF staff undertook surveillance of members' macroeconomic policies. Meanwhile, the credit rating firms Moody's and Standard & Poor's, with increasing formality and quasi-public authority, monitored governments' policies and articulated their perceived implications for sovereign risk, on behalf of financial markets and regulators alike.

Institutions and organizations also constitute state identities and define the boundaries of legitimate policies.[44] The formal rules of organizations specify members' obligations, and the rules thereby define the policy practices that lead other members to recognize what constitutes appropriate behavior on the part of other governments. The rules of the OECD constitute the policy practices of "developed" states, just as the rules of the EU define the boundaries of legitimate policies enacted by "European" states. "Sociology's core insight," observes Frank Dobbin, "is that individuals behave according to scripts that are tied to social roles. Those scripts are called conventions at the collective level and cognitive schemas at the individual level."[45] The codification of the norm of capital mobility in the OECD and EU changed the scripts for "developed" and "European" states: those two scripts articulate an obligation to permit capital to move freely, as well as an intellectual justification for such a policy.

The sociological approach to institutions emphasizes that they are, in the words of Iain Johnston, "social environments" composed of collective understandings, knowledge and information sharing, and fora for learning among policymakers representing their governments.[46] The bureaucracies of international organizations contribute to the "development of consensual knowledge" among member governments.[47] Moreover, interactions among government representatives in international organizations lead them to encourage, cajole, and convince. Above all, policymakers in international organizations talk to and argue with one another.[48] Based entirely on a process of peer review and peer pressure, the OECD, more than most organizations, is designed to benefit members by providing them a forum in which they can discuss and learn from one another's experiences. The EU and IMF be-ing more bureaucratized, most conversations about policy occur not among members but between organization staff and policymakers within member governments. All three organizations nevertheless define and promote norms and rules.[49]

These international organizations have been eager teachers of their norms and rules, and during the 1990s the OECD and EU had some eager pupils among countries seeking to join their organizations. The real and symbolic benefits of membership in the OECD and EU encouraged prospective mem-bers to embrace each organization's rules, including capital liberalization, often without questioning the content of the constitutive rule that would ensure their recognition as "developed" and "European." A Czech central bank official recalls that central and east European governments competed during the early 1990s to determine "who was the best pupil of the devel-oped market economies."[50] The view from Brussels was similar: one Com-mission negotiator recalls in acceding countries an "eagerness to be perceived as right up to European standards for openness to capital movements."[51] The countries that joined the OECD and EU readily embraced the script of capital liberalization.[52] Although the CMIT and European Commission were enthusiastic proponents of the script, neither forced prospective members to accept these rules. And for all the enthusiasm of IMF management for capi-tal liberalization, the Fund never had the legal tools systematically to coerce members to embrace liberalization when their governments were not keen to follow Fund advice. As John Ikenberry and Charles Kupchan argue, so-cialization is most commonly effected through a combination of purposeful behavior by powerful governments or organizations and domestic condi-tions in less powerful states that make policymakers more receptive to a new script.[53]

The international environment in which central and east European states, comprising the vast majority of new OECD and EU accessions, emerged from state socialism was propitious for their embrace of the capital liberal-ization script. OECD and EU members shared a conceptual and codified con-sensus favoring complete capital mobility. And openness to capital as a script for "developed" and "European" states resonated with societies and govern-ments eager publicly to embrace a model of successful economic and politi-cal development. The material incentives of OECD and EU membership created, to be sure, important motivation for accession. But the process of social construction by which the OECD and EU produced these new scripts, as well as the practice of "lesson drawing" by acceding countries suggest a strong sociological underpinning to the spread of the norm of capital mobility from West to East.[54]

These constitutive effects of institutions and organizations on governments' financial regulations are similar to the arguments scholars use to explain the diffusion of policy practices around the world.[55] The scholarly literature on diffusion has not, however, explored the influence of international organizations on the spread of policy practices. Eichengreen observes that countries are more likely to liberalize capital flows "when members of their peer group have done so."[56] Similarly, Beth Simmons and Zachary Elkins explore the possibility that the intellectual justification for liberalization may be spread through communication within or learning from cultural reference groups.[57] Although these studies do not include OECD or EU membership in their operationalization of peer or reference groups, in the chapters that follow I trace the influence of those two organizations on capital liberalization specifically. The OECD and EU are indeed the most influential reference groups in international financial markets.

Conceiving international organizations as bureaucracies makes possible an analysis of the influence of the bureaucrats themselves on the evolution of the formal and informal rules of globalization. Such an analysis is needed if we are to understand precisely how capital came to be globally mobile. The managers of the OECD, EU, and IMF expressed strong preferences about their respective mandates. The IMF's management appeared to adopt its new mandate—capital liberalization—informally, because its policymakers believed in that goal. This informal mandate issued from the self-identified expertise, not the legal basis, of the Fund's management.[58] Appropriating a mandate on the basis of a bureaucracy's interpretation of the truth value of the arguments, as opposed to the bureaucracy's own legal authority, may be described as either, in Louis Pauly's words, "institutional adaptation," or, more critically, according to Michael Barnett and Martha Finnemore, an organizational pathology.[59]

The written rules cannot sufficiently convey how the international monetary system functions. Because the informal rules exist only as the collective understandings of policymakers and markets, such shared beliefs are often held strongly. In an already classic essay, economist Ronald McKinnon, adopting a phrase Keynes had once used to elaborate the principles that governed the gold standard, described the "rules of the game" for each of the international monetary orders of the last 120 years. McKinnon described both formal rules and informal, "implicit rules."[60] The place of capital controls in the postwar orders provides a fitting example. McKinnon characterizes the "spirit" of the Bretton Woods agreement thus: "Free currency convertibility for current-account payments; use capital controls to dampen currency speculation." The "floating-rate dollar standard," 1973–1984, however, was defined in part by a new rule: "Free currency convertibility for current payments, while eventually eliminating remaining restrictions on capital account."[61] In a similar vein, economist Robert Mundell wrote of the "framework of laws, conventions, regulations, and mores that establish the setting of the system and the understanding of the environment by the participants in it."[62]

Three informal institutions influenced this emerging era of global capital. First, international organizations have sometimes shifted their practices without a formal change in rules. In the OECD, for example, the CMIT interpreted the Code of Liberalization less strictly after the international financial crises of 1997 and 1998. An informal shift in IMF policy was also consequential. In the absence of a formal mandate to promote capital liberalization, the Fund began, during the late 1980s and early 1990s, to encourage members to liberalize. IMF management, especially, sought to define the organization's unofficial doctrine as liberal, even before it sought to amend its Articles.[63] Although the Fund's area departments did not promote or advise liberalization systematically or indiscriminately, it is clear that IMF practice had shifted in favor of liberalization.[64]

Second, the beliefs of market participants are a critical determinant of the consequences of capital controls.[65] An ideological consensus, argue Simmons and Elkins, "alters the reputational payoffs associated with policy choice."[66] Market participants infer meanings from policies. Economists have, following this logic, described capital controls and liberalizations as important signals to the markets: liberalizations signal good policies, restrictions signal bad.[67] "Imposing controls on the capital account," observes Geoffrey Garrett, "also sends signals to mobile capital that the country imposing the restrictions is in important senses unfriendly."[68] What is perhaps most remarkable about the signaling content of capital controls—the inference that the market is supposed to draw from their imposition—is that the content changed so radically between the 1950s and 1990s.

Third, although the beliefs of the financial markets are not always easily measured, the beliefs of managers and analysts in three firms—the credit-rating agencies S&P, Moody's, and Fitch—provide an informative window into how specific policies are interpreted by financial markets.[69] These firms' ratings of sovereign issuers and their debt, and the explanations advanced to justify changes in ratings, are profoundly consequential for contemporary international capital markets.[70] Although the rating agencies played no formal role in the design of the international monetary system, the mediation of the rating agencies—given teeth by worldwide incorporation of ratings into national regulations—has become so important to the issuing of sovereign debt that it is no longer possible to understand the governance of debt markets without elucidating the agencies' influence. The views of S&P and Moody's (the so-called Big Two) effectively bridge the formal and informal institutions of the international monetary system. By 2005 S&P and Moody's each rated more than one hundred sovereigns, between them accounting for 90 percent of the sovereign ratings market.

Because the rating agencies' assessments of monetary policies both condition and reflect the reactions of the markets, their analysts must make judgments about the signals that policies convey and the inferences that markets will draw from them. As David Levey, managing director of Sovereign Risk at Moody's for nearly twenty years, observes, "Ratings necessarily rely on a predominantly qualitative methodology. It is all a matter of interpretation." Although Moody's analysts sought not to impose their ideologies on their judgments, they did recognize that capital liberalization came to be seen, in their own eyes, as "a certain inevitability, and appeared to become international dogma."[71] S&P's sovereign analysts, for their part, seemed to reflect and reinforce the prevailing market views, emphasizing that higher-rated sovereigns embrace "orthodox market-oriented economic programs."[72] S&P's Marie Cavanaugh also emphasized the shared "basic economic orthodoxy" among members of a rating committee.[73]

One critical issue, therefore, is the extent to which rating agencies anticipate or follow the markets on whose behalf they analyze sovereigns. Some scholars have found that upgrades have followed market rallies, while downgrades followed market downturns—and still the markets react to the new ratings. This finding suggests a fascinating problem with the market discipline represented by the agencies: not only are the agencies obliged to reflect the beliefs of the markets in an age of potentially self-fulfilling expectations, but, to the extent that ratings are a lagging indicator of creditworthiness, the agencies also help to create procyclical movements of capital.[74]

Moody's and S&P thus participate in the construction of beliefs within the financial markets, self-consciously attempt to incorporate those beliefs into their analysis of the likely responses of markets to a policy change, and, in a sense, have been informally delegated the responsibility of monitoring such policy changes by market participants. Policymakers have also formally delegated to rating agencies responsibility for monitoring sovereigns by incorporating ratings into the financial regulations of the United States, as well as in many other countries. What has come to be called the "private authority" of the rating agencies has in fact been increasingly and overtly public, less informal, and more codified in national regulations over time.[75]

CHAPTER 3

Capital Ruled:
Embedded Liberalism and the
Regulation of Finance

Why, then 'tis none to you; for there is nothing either good or bad,
but thinking makes it so. To me it is a prison.

—William Shakespeare

With war still raging and the economic chaos of the interwar
years fresh in mind, an extraordinary consensus emerged among policymakers in the early 1940s with regard to a postwar international monetary
system. The new order would be founded on capital regulation, not to undermine capitalism but, rather, to rescue it.

Policymakers shared a common vision and a common goal: the creation
of a new order that could avoid the financial crises, disrupted commerce,
wild exchange-rate movements, and political instability of the previous quarter century. From their shared formative experience enduring decades of
unending crisis, the founders of the new monetary system drew essentially
the same lessons and the same conclusions as to causes and cures.

Their consensus was extraordinary for both its cohesion and its content,
which only a few decades earlier would have been considered radical and
anticapitalist. At the time, however, capital regulation marked capitalism's
way forward.

Bretton Woods, the IMF, and Lessons of the Past

Among the legacies of the interwar years, none was as profound as the two
lessons policymakers believed they had learned from their experiences with
the external values of their currencies and the flow of capital across their
borders. Many of these lessons were encapsulated in a League of Nations

publication, regularly attributed primarily to Ragnar Nurkse, as well as the writings of the U.K. Treasury's John Maynard Keynes and the U.S. Treasury's Harry Dexter White. Keynes and White together, literally and figuratively, authored the rules for the Bretton Woods system. The system they envisioned for the postwar years was to be built for economic stability and political autonomy.

Important questions would be answered by reference to past mistakes. Should exchange rates be fixed or free? Nurkse and his colleagues looked to recent history for the answer:

> The twenty years between the wars have furnished ample evidence concerning the question of fluctuating *versus* stable exchanges. A system of completely free and flexible exchange rates is conceivable and may have certain advantages in theory; and it might seem that in practice nothing would be easier than to leave international payments and receipts to adjust themselves through uncontrolled exchange variations in response to the play of demand and supply. Yet nothing would be more at variance with the lessons of the past.[1]

The failures of the interwar years were understood to be almost self-evident, as the League explored "the proved disadvantages of freely fluctuating exchanges."[2] As Robert Skidelsky, one of Keynes's most important biographers, notes, the institution of floating exchange rates was "beyond the practical or theoretical imagination of the times, including Keynes's."[3]

Capital was to be controlled, and with an important purpose: governments were supposed to be autonomous from market forces, free to pursue expansionary monetary and fiscal policies without endangering their exchange-rate commitments or suffering the outflow of capital in search of a higher rate of interest or a lower rate of inflation.[4] Because almost every country would be committed to fixed exchange rates, the regulation of international finance was the only way to provide some measure of autonomy for domestic policymakers.

This logic was clear in the writings and speeches of Keynes and White. By 1944, Keynes and White had been debating their respective proposals for the monetary and financial architecture of the world economy for several years. The Keynes and White plans differed in many respects, but they shared a skepticism of private international financial flows, and both plans relied on capital controls to maintain governments' autonomy.[5] As Keynes explained to the House of Lords:

In my own judgment, countries which avail themselves of the right may find it necessary to scrutinize all transactions, as to prevent the evasion of capital regulations. Provided that innocent, current transactions are let through, there is nothing in the plan to prevent this. In fact, it is encouraged. It follows that our right to control the domestic capital market is secured on firmer foundations than ever before, and is formally accepted as a proper part of agreed international arrangements.[6]

Richard Gardner observed of the U.S. Treasury policymakers, led by Secretary Henry Morgenthau and White, that "They sought to make finance the servant, not the master of human desires—in the international no less than in the domestic sphere."[7] Arthur Bloomfield, a prominent economist of the era, then of the Federal Reserve Bank of New York, summarized this state of affairs for the *American Economic Review:*

It is now highly respectable doctrine, in academic and banking circles alike, that a substantial measure of *direct* control over private capital movements, especially of the so-called "hot money" varieties, will be desirable for most countries not only in the years immediately ahead but also in the long run as well . . . Unfettered freedom of individuals to transfer funds across national boundaries, while conspicuously violated in actual practice since 1914, has long been a hallowed dogma of traditional economic thought, and in this respect the present-day enthusiasm among economists for exchange control over capital movements represents a sharp break with past orthodoxy. This doctrinal *volte-face* represents a widespread disillusionment resulting from the destructive behavior of these movements in the interwar years.[8]

Postwar economists shared this interpretation. "Not only was freedom of international capital movements thought to be unnecessary to achieve the objectives of high income and employment and efficient growth in world trade," Richard Cooper argued, "but also the experience of the interwar period had indicated that such freedom might actually be harmful and disruptive to the pursuit of those objectives."[9] It was not, therefore, that the IMF's founding fathers had failed to consider whether capital should be free and highly mobile, or that they could not reach agreement on the place of capital in the international financial architecture they designed. The place of capital in the Bretton Woods system was carefully considered and purposeful, and the consensus on the usefulness of its control widely shared.[10]

The motivation for controlling capital also went well beyond the reconciliation of what is now thought of as the "impossible trinity," the trade-off among capital mobility, fixed exchange rates, and monetary policy autonomy. Short-term, "speculative" (as opposed, in White's terminology, to "productive") capital flows in particular were deemed unstable. They constituted "hot money." Their instability was thought to yield two consequences. First, as the League's economists argued, short-term capital flows were often "disequilibrating instead of equilibrating, or instead of simply coming to a stop."[11] That is, rather than reconciling payments imbalances, hot money was understood, in modern parlance, to overshoot. Second, such large flows of short-term capital could create the conditions for a crisis, even in what seemed to be a stable financial system. In an intellectual precursor to the modern notion of self-fulfilling speculative attacks, Nurkse worried over "self-aggravating" flows of capital.[12] These flows of short-term capital were understood to be inherently destabilizing, causing contagious crises even where the fundamentals were sound. To the extent that "speculative" could be distinguished from "productive" capital, policymakers of the time believed that capital ought to be tightly regulated regardless of a government's exchange-rate commitments.

No one thought it would be easy to control short-term capital movements, and Keynes, White, and their contemporaries spent a great deal of intellectual effort considering ways to shore up regulators' ability to control financial flows. In each of the two drafts of his Clearing Union plan, Keynes wrote, "It is widely held that control of capital movements, both inward and outward, should be a permanent feature of the post-war system." But if capital controls are "to be effective," they require "the machinery of exchange control for *all* transactions, even though a general permission is given to all remittances in respect of current trade."[13] That is, states would likely maintain the ability to monitor and control all foreign exchange transactions, even if in practice they regulated only those that affected the capital account.

Keynes and White argued that cooperation was crucial for the effectiveness of capital controls. Keynes wrote that "such control will be more difficult to work by unilateral action on the part of those countries which cannot afford to dispense with it, especially in the absence of postal censorship, if movements of capital cannot be controlled *at both ends*."[14] Both drafts of White's plan actually required every member of his proposed Fund to "cooperate effectively with other member countries when such countries, with

the approval of the Fund, adopt or continue controls for the purpose of regulating international movements of capital." For White such cooperation
included a commitment "not to accept or permit acquisition of deposits,
securities, or investments by nationals of any member country imposing restrictions on the export of capital except with the permission of the government of that country and the Fund," as well as a promise to make available
information on the capital flows and holdings of residents "of the member
country imposing the restrictions."[15] In other words, member countries would
be obliged to assist in the enforcement of one another's capital controls. No
such obligation became part of Fund membership; capital controls remained
only a right, not a mutual obligation. But both Keynes and White were
aware of the difficulties of unilateral enforcement of capital account regulation. Still, they assumed, and hoped, that unilateral capital controls would
be effective.

These compromises among the competing logics of economics and politics
cohered into a worldview about the prospects for growth, stability, and international cooperation. Keynes called it "the middle way." Avoiding the
narrow autarky of the interwar years, the "embedded liberalism compromise," John Gerard Ruggie observed, "would be multilateral in character;
unlike the liberalism of the gold standard and free trade, its multilateralism
would be predicated on domestic interventionism."[16] As Ruggie later noted,
"Governments would be permitted—indeed, were expected—to maintain
capital controls."[17]

With respect to the IMF itself, the Fund's internal historian, Margaret de
Vries, clarified the place of capital in the system similarly. She wrote, "The
Fund's regulatory functions apply only to certain kinds of international
transactions, some kinds being deliberately left out."[18] The IMF's Articles
had been "drafted against the background of the disturbing capital movements that had taken place during the 1930s," and so "it was thought that
controls over capital movements might be necessary and beneficial."[19]

Thus, the IMF's Articles were clearly written to avoid the organization's
involvement in most capital account transactions. Article I endows the Fund
with six purposes, which are supposed to guide all of the Fund's policies and
decisions. Several of those purposes deal with the promotion of trade and
the elimination of members' current account restrictions. None deals with
members' capital account restrictions. The Fund therefore may not, without
violating its own Articles, require a member to remove controls on capital
movements as a condition for the use of its resources.[20] Instead, Article VI,

Section 3 specifies that members "may exercise such controls as are necessary to regulate international capital movements."

European Integration and Capital Regulation

Neither were pan-European capital markets a natural outcome of the Treaty of Rome in 1957. The European economy envisioned by the Treaty's logic of integration was not unconditionally liberal. Goods, services, and people were supposed to flow freely. Capital, however, was not, except, according to the Treaty, "to the extent necessary to ensure the proper functioning of the Common Market," and without jeopardizing the internal and external financial stability of members. Trade was the priority. Capital was a second-class citizen of the new Europe.[21]

The caution and conditionality with which the Treaty of Rome dealt with capital was not an oversight. Capital's second-class status in Europe was a self-conscious choice of European negotiators, as well as the result of lopsided bargaining among them. The conditionality of the obligation to liberalize capital was, in part, a reflection of the widespread consensus among policymakers around the world that capital flows ought to be controlled to avoid financial crises and deflationary pressures. Capital was also supposed to be, in the idiom of the time, "disciplined"—constrained to invest at home to create employment and tax revenues, which would then fund the welfare state.

This consensus, which drew on the lessons that European and U.S. policymakers believed were evident from the financial chaos of the interwar years, was, along with fixed exchange rates, the very basis of the postwar international monetary system. An official of the Dutch central bank who had helped to negotiate the Treaty's capital provisions described the conventional wisdom of the time: "The liberal economic doctrines of the nineteenth century, influenced by natural philosophy, took it that with free capital movements flows would go in a direction which would optimize welfare. Nowadays no economist of reputation shares this notion."[22]

The conditionality of capital liberalization in the Treaty also reflected bargaining among Europe's founding members. Germany, whose position was formulated as an ideological principle by the liberal Minister of Economic Affairs, Ludwig Erhard, nicknamed Mr. Convertibility, had been alone in pushing for capital liberalization, whereas France, Italy, and the Netherlands had argued against codifying such an obligation.[23] As former Bundesbank

President Karl Otto Pöhl reflects, "Germany's liberal approach to capital can be traced to Ludwig Erhard. Erhard envisioned a fully convertible D-mark. It was a revolutionary step, which was based on his liberal ideology. At that time everyone else in Europe was in favor of capital controls."[24]

More than ideology was at stake for Erhard and his colleagues. For German policymakers, complete convertibility implied the impossibility of manipulating the currency for political purposes.[25] "Erhard had seen in Europe and especially Germany during the 1930s and 1940s what could happen when capital controls allowed governments to manipulate their currencies for political ends," reflects Hans Tietmeyer, an Erhard protégé who later succeeded Pöhl as Bundesbank president.[26]

The legal implication of the Treaty's wording would later be that members' obligations to liberalize capital could be redefined only by a new treaty or by directives approved unanimously by the European Council and enforced by the Commission. These would, in essence, define what members agreed constituted "the extent necessary" for the common market.[27] As Tommaso Padoa-Schioppa writes, the European legal framework for capital made it "necessary to follow the long road of issuing directives, building European capital market integration step by step."[28] Europe would thus wait for members to catch up with its permanent obligations to allow the freedom of goods, services, and people. With regard to capital, in contrast, the firmness of members' obligations would change over time.

In the years immediately after the Treaty of Rome was negotiated, Germany remained the sole European Community (EC) member that urged greater capital freedom.[29] France, Italy, and the Netherlands continued to highlight the dangers of losing policy autonomy and offering speculators enough freedom to create self-fulfilling crises of confidence in the financial systems of European states.[30] The Dutch even argued in 1959 that the Treaty of Rome applied only to foreign direct investment, for short-term flows of portfolio capital were not, strictly speaking, capital; they were, instead, "money."[31] This division between Germany and the rest of Europe persisted into the 1960s and 1970s.[32]

The Commission began to define and expand members' obligations to liberalize capital with two directives in 1960 and 1962, but no progress was made subsequently.[33] The 1960 directive established a complex list of transaction categories that ranged from those most closely linked to the other basic freedoms in the Treaty (direct investments and personal capital movements, for example) to those considered least necessary (such as "short-term capital movements"). Members were obliged to liberalize only those transactions deemed essential to the functioning of the common market, and, in practice and increasingly over time, that turned out to be a short and narrow list indeed.[34]

Then, for more than twenty years, Brussels did not issue a single new directive for liberalizing capital. At the Commission's initiative a group of experts chaired by Professor Claudio Segré reported in 1966 on the advantages of the formation of a European capital market, but at that time the Commission appeared to be running way ahead of member states.[35] Officials of member states' ministries of finance and central banks continued to discuss capital freedom at the EC's Monetary Committee, which served as a sort of sounding board for the Commission before submitting directives to the Council.[36] The Monetary Committee could not reach a consensus, however.

The Commission did submit a third directive to the Council in 1967, but a decade of negotiations led nowhere. "Opposition came from all sides," writes Age Bakker. "But first and foremost from France and the Netherlands."[37] The only other movement on capital pushed in the direction of more control, rather than liberalization. In 1972 a directive that obliged members to maintain the apparatus of capital controls "to curtail undesirable capital flows" was adopted.[38] When the Germans' enthusiasm for liberalization finally spread to the Dutch and the British in the early 1980s, those three countries sought to return capital liberalization to the agenda in Brussels. Again, France blocked the initiative.[39] Europe's nonliberal rules for finance would not change until France did. "In Europe," the Commission's Jean-Pierre Baché recalls, "progress toward the liberalization of capital was blocked until policy makers in France reversed course in 1983–1984."[40]

The Reluctant Liberalism of the OECD Code

The OECD's Code of Liberalization of Capital Movements has its origins in the European Payments Union (EPU), which, between 1950 and 1958, helped European policymakers on the path toward currency convertibility and, meanwhile, promoted trade among the members.[41] The EPU Executive Committee requested in 1954 that the Managing Board investigate the possibility of liberalizing "investment capital" among member countries.[42] The request resulted in an expert report and modest recommendations, which were brought before the Organization for European Economic Cooperation (OEEC) Council in 1955. Although the Council adopted the expert group's recommendations, which were limited in scope, the members' delegations noted a wide range of exceptions and concerns.[43]

The OEEC's Committee for Invisible Transactions, whose portfolio included the oversight of trade in services, then accepted the task of considering what the organization's position on the liberalization of capital movements ought to be. The committee's 1955 report argued that the OEEC should promote the liberalization of capital, but selectively. The OEEC should distinguish, by this logic, capital movements by their purpose, rather than their form. "Productive" capital flows were to be encouraged, while "hot money" would be discouraged. The committee defined "hot money" broadly. "Movements of capital for the purpose of undesirable speculation or due to political developments or reasons of taxation are often referred to as 'hot money' movements," the Committee noted. "Such funds are, as a rule, either invested in quoted securities, lent on short term, or deposited in cash with banks or other financial institutions."[44] The Committee also urged the OEEC Council to consider the trade-off between the freedom of international capital movements and three other priorities of member governments: a stable balance of payments, monetary policy autonomy, and the promotion of domestic industries.[45]

In December 1957 the OEEC Council reached agreement for the first time on some firm obligations to liberalize capital, in particular encouraging policymakers to allow payments for making and liquidating direct investments.[46] "By concentrating on direct investment and emphasizing the long-term aspect," the OEEC noted, "members avoided committing themselves to allowing capital movements representing purely financial speculation."[47] Greece, Iceland, Spain, and Turkey were exempted from the recommendation in recognition of their more tenuous balance-of-payments positions.

The following summer, in 1958, the Committee for Invisible Transactions recommended that the OEEC Council adopt a new Code of Liberalization of Capital Movements to accompany that for invisible transactions.[48] Again members worried about the implications of hot money, and the Committee failed to reach a consensus on the desirability of a broad Code for capital liberalization.[49] As with the negotiations over the liberalization obligations of the 1957 Treaty of Rome, Germany was alone among its European neighbors in promoting a liberal Code. In 1959 the Committee clarified its interpretation of the liberalization obligations of the OEEC Council's recommendation by reiterating the exclusion of "financial" capital flows. "The Committee would like it to be clearly understood," the authors reasoned, "that the recommendation to Member countries, in Article 1(a), to eliminate restrictions on movements of capital 'as fully as their economic and financial situation permits' shall not be interpreted as limiting in any way the right of a Member country to control 'hot money' movements."[50]

The OEEC Council's discussion of a Code, meanwhile, continued through 1959, and consensus remained elusive. Differences of opinion were serious even about the proposed preamble: "Considering, in particular, the desirability that Member countries should achieve and maintain as complete a liberalization of intra-European capital movements as possible without, however, fostering undesirable speculation." To contemporary eyes such a formulation appears to be eminently reasonable. But at the time even codifying the desirability in principle of capital liberalization was unacceptable to most members, much as it had been for the Treaty of Rome. While the Swiss delegate objected to any suggestion of a link between liberalization and speculation, the U.K. delegate insisted that the Code should do nothing to facilitate "undesirable speculation or hot money movements." The Austrian, Danish, Norwegian, Portuguese, and Swedish delegates spoke in favor of keeping the paragraph. The Belgian, Dutch, French, Greek, and Italian delegates expressed reluctance. In the end the preamble was deleted as a compromise.[51] With its modest proposal for the liberalization of some capital movements associated with direct investment, as well as its circumspect language about other capital flows, the OEEC members finally in 1959 adopted a Code of Liberalization of Capital Movements. The OEEC's reflections on the Code reveal the concerns about liberalization that dominated thinking, in particular the "problems" posed by liberalization. Of these, the most worrisome were "the difficulties that arise when there are significant and sudden movements of short-term funds which conflict with the aims of internal monetary policy."[52] Still, the OEEC's leaders were proud to be "the first international organization to have adopted a legal instrument of this kind for international capital movements."[53]

The Committee for Invisible Transactions was charged with overseeing the new Code. The Committee—referred to as the High Priests of the Codes, as well as the Invisibles Committee—began discussing extensions of the Code's mandate, in particular to portfolio investment, "duly safeguarded," of course, "against hot money movements."[54] When the negotiations over U.S. and Canadian membership began, the Committee began to prepare a Code for the council of the new organization to adopt.[55] "Among the first acts of the new organization," Alexis Rieffel notes, "was the adoption of the Code of Liberalization of Current Invisible Operations and the Code of Liberalization of Capital Movements—modeled on the OEEC Codes."[56] The two OECD Codes, later OECD staff would suggest, represented the organization's "commitment to the philosophy of free and open markets."[57] The OECD vision of "free and open markets" would not, however, embrace all financial markets. The market for hot money was to be permanently excluded.

The postwar international financial system was based on a new orthodoxy of capital regulation that was opposite the liberalism of the late nineteenth century. This regulation was supposed to insulate governments from exchange-rate instability, financial crises, and the deflationary pressures arising from the mobility of "speculative" capital. Policymakers intended to encourage "productive" capital flows among countries, however. The system was not designed to be completely illiberal. Liberalism would be "embedded" in society so that a middle way might be found. Government discretion was to be safeguarded by the codification of the right to regulate capital movements in the international organizations that composed the international financial architecture. The rules of the IMF, EC, and OECD instantiated the logic of an organized international monetary system ruled by the logic of embedded liberalism. Reflecting on the traumatic years just behind them, policymakers in the United States and Europe believed that they had permanently resolved the inherent contradictions between an open, vibrant world economy and the domestic welfare state. Of greatest consequence was the consensus shared across the Atlantic. U.S. and European policymakers embraced these ideas with equal commitment.

Ultimately, the new postwar orthodoxy—capital ruled in the service of embedded liberalism—did not endure. Although this orthodoxy was codified in the rules of the organizations that make up the international financial architecture, over time the day-to-day practices of those organizations would change. Eventually, and incrementally, the organizations' leaders and members rewrote some of the most important rules of the international monetary system, to codify their subsequent rejection of the orthodoxy of capital controls and, by the 1980s, their embrace of freedom for capital movements. The postwar consensus was not merely to be left behind; that consensus was to be turned entirely on its head. In the process the visions of U.S. and European policymakers for a new era of internationalized finance would diverge, and the rupture still has not closed.

CHAPTER 4

The Paris Consensus: European Unification and the Freedom of Capital

Est maître des lieux celui qui les organise. (He who organizes is master of the arena.)

—Jean de la Fontaine

Any lingering doubts about the place of liberalizing capital among the priorities of the Treaty of Rome were definitively dispelled by the European Court of Justice in 1981 when it ruled on the case of Guerrino Casati. Casati, an Italian national residing in Germany, had been arrested on July 16, 1979, on his way from Italy to Austria carrying 24,000 German marks in cash. Italian law prohibited the unauthorized exportation of foreign currency worth more than 500,000 lire. Casati insisted that he had brought the marks into Italy to purchase pasta and ice-cream making machinery he needed for his restaurant in Cologne. Because Casati assumed that he would leave Italy with goods rather than marks, he did not bother to declare the currency upon his arrival. (It was not illegal to remove from Italy the same amount of foreign currency brought into the country, provided it was declared upon entry.)

When Casati arrived at the factory, however, he found that it was closed for summer holidays. Casati decided to return to Germany, by way of Austria. With no record of Casati's having originally brought the marks into the country, Italian authorities arrested him. Poor Casati faced a prison term of one to six years and a fine two to four times the value of the currency in his possession.

After two days in police custody Casati was released, and his trial was scheduled for October 29, 1979, in Bolzano. Casati's attorney argued that, surely, the behavior of the Italian government was not consistent with the spirit of the Treaty of Rome or the laws of the European Community (EC), nor were the potentially severe punishments in proportion to the offense. The local Italian court proceeded deliberately, hearing testimony from Reinell Reinhold, Casati's accountant, who assured the court of the commercial intentions of his client. Eventually the Bolzano court recognized that the potential incompatibility of Italian with Community law would be critical for a final decision.

The European Court of Justice thus was asked by the Bolzano court on October 6, 1980, to interpret the Treaty Articles and European Council directives dealing with the mobility of capital. The governments of Denmark, France, Ireland, Italy, and the United Kingdom argued against the direct effect of Article 67 of the Treaty, which laid out the obligations of Treaty signatories to liberalize capital. Only the German government argued otherwise. The German interpretation of Article 67 emphasized the clause's reference to a "transitional period," rather than the permanence of the conditionality of "to the extent necessary." Advocate General Francesco Capotorti argued that the German position, the outlier, was legally insupportable, even going so far as to deride its logic.

Disappointing Casati, the European Court of Justice ruled that the Italian regulations were consistent with Community laws. The judgment found that the Treaty contained no "general principle" favoring capital freedom. Only Council directives determined which movements of capital would be considered legally necessary for the common market, and existing directives unambiguously excluded movements of currency among the "necessary" capital movements. The judgment confirmed that capital freedom was not implied by the Treaty, and the *Casati* case offered the court an opportunity to reflect on the EC's prevailing wisdom on the relationship between capital and the common market. Its words were unambiguous: "At present, it cannot be denied that complete freedom of movement of capital may undermine the economic policy of one of the member states or create an imbalance in its balance of payments, thereby impairing the proper functioning of the common market."[1] The court thus found that, at least in 1981, the success of the common market depended in part on restricting capital mobility.[2]

Capital's second-class status persisted until the late 1980s. Europe had, by that time, achieved extraordinary success in commercial integration and grown in size (see Table 4.1). The contrast between finance and trade was sharp enough that Benjamin Cohen, among others, could frame an interesting puzzle: "Why is the European Community unable to achieve formal finan-

Table 4.1   EC/EU Members with Dates of Accession

Member State	Accession
Belgium	January 1, 1958
France	January 1, 1958
(West) Germany	January 1, 1958
Italy	January 1, 1958
Luxembourg	January 1, 1958
Netherlands	January 1, 1958
Denmark	January 1, 1973
Ireland	January 1, 1973
United Kingdom	January 1, 1973
Greece	January 1, 1981
Portugal	January 1, 1986
Spain	January 1, 1986
Austria	January 1, 1995
Finland	January 1, 1995
Sweden	January 1, 1995
Cyprus	May 1, 2004
Czech Republic	May 1, 2004
Estonia	May 1, 2004
Hungary	May 1, 2004
Latvia	May 1, 2004
Lithuania	May 1, 2004
Malta	May 1, 2004
Poland	May 1, 2004
Slovakia	May 1, 2004
Slovenia	May 1, 2004

Source: "Key dates in the history of European integration," available at http://europa.eu.int/abc/12lessons/print_index13_en.htm.

cial integration?"[3] Some of Europe's largest and most influential banks had always been in favor of a single European capital market. Certainly German policymakers and bankers had urged Europe toward financial integration since the 1950s. The United Kingdom joined the Germans in their support of more mobile European capital after its own rapid liberalization in 1979. During the early 1980s, British, Dutch, and German policymakers attempted to put capital liberalization on the agenda in Brussels. Yet many European finance ministers and central bankers continued to object to the codification of a new obligation for capital liberalization in Europe for fear of relinquishing their remaining autonomy from financial markets and letting loose crisis-prone capital flows.[4]

The situation changed radically in June 1988, when the European Council adopted a directive (88/361/EEC) proposed by the Commission to oblige members to liberalize all capital movements.[5] At that moment the EC achieved formal financial integration, which was further solidified by the Treaty on European Union. The Treaty, negotiated in Maastricht in 1991 and entered into force on January 1, 1994, promoted capital to a legal status equivalent to that which had been enjoyed by goods, services, and people for nearly forty years. Article 73b of the Treaty was unambiguous: "All restrictions on the movement of capital between Member States and between Member states and third countries shall be prohibited."[6] For the EC as a whole, the transformation represented "a major shift in the appreciation of the pros and cons of free capital flows."[7]

A central question, then, is what changed in Europe between the early 1980s—when an initiative to rewrite the rules of European finance failed despite having the United Kingdom, Germany, and the Netherlands enthusiastically in favor—and the late 1980s, when the institutional foundations of European finance were fundamentally recast? The question relates not only to the history of European integration, but also to the emergence of global capital markets. The answer is deceptively simple: France changed.

The simplicity of the answer marks one of the most consequential turning points in modern economic history. As Age Bakker observes, "the uncompromising, dogmatic attitude of France" was responsible for the failure of the initiatives to bring capital liberalization under the formal authority of the European Commission on behalf of the EC in the early 1980s.[8] Indeed, French policymakers had dealt fatal blows to every initiative for European capital liberalization between the 1960s and the late 1980s, though their allies changed over time. When the French government embraced the freedom of capital in Europe in 1988, then, and only then, was the EC able to embrace that freedom. "The victory of the community project was not determined solely in France," writes Craig Parsons, "but the key battle of European ideas occurred there."[9] Making sense of France's reversal is necessary to understand how European finance became so liberal.

The answer's simplicity is deceptive, however. The French did not merely acquiesce to what seemed to some in the 1980s to be the new reality of globalization. Despite having single-handedly quashed every attempt in Brussels to alter the legal status of capital, the French were not, after all that, dragged by the British, Dutch, and Germans to the 1988 directive. Several French policymakers led the charge for an entirely different set of reasons. Jacques

Delors, as president of the European Commission, and Pascal Lamy, his *chef de cabinet,* played decisive roles in Brussels. French President François Mitterrand himself took responsibility in Paris. Delors, Lamy, and Mitterrand, moreover, were all leaders of the Socialist Party in France. The story of European financial integration is necessarily also the story of how the French Left embraced capital.

Turning France

In the spring of 1981, when Mitterrand was elected president and the Socialist Party won a majority in the National Assembly, the European Left was full of hope, the European Right consumed by fear. The broader significance of the moment, however, was that choice still seemed possible in a world of accelerating economic interdependence that seemed to privilege the needs of capital. Before globalization seemed to be inescapable and inevitable, French Socialists sought to reestablish the policies of Keynesian reflation and redistribution. The ambitions of Mitterrand and the Socialists knew few bounds, and their efforts to remake the French economy were heroic.

Soon after the Mitterrand experiment began, however, it started to unravel, in part because the financial markets did not trust the new French government. So, capital fled France. The French government tightened its controls on outflows of capital first in May 1981, then again in March 1982, and by March 1983 the regulations were rewritten as restrictively as possible. Importers and exporters were not allowed forward exchange transactions, foreign travel allowances were further reduced, personal credit cards could not be used abroad, and the infamous *carnet de change,* a booklet in which the French were to record their foreign exchange transactions, was introduced. According to John Goodman and Louis Pauly, the new regulations amounted to "draconian capital controls."[10]

Still the French government was unable to halt the flight of capital. Anecdotal evidence suggests that the well-to-do and the well-connected—wealthy individuals and powerful firms—continued to evade even the most cleverly designed and stringently enforced controls. By 1983 it was clear that French capital controls constrained the middle classes most of all, while the rich circumvented them with impunity. As Henri Chavranski recalls, "Our capital controls failed not in the sense that everyone was able to elude their grasp; they failed in the sense that those who were less well connected bore their burden most. We recognized, at last, that in an age of interdependence capital would find a way to free itself, and we were obliged to liberate the rest."[11]

Speculators, meanwhile, repeatedly attacked the franc, which had been devalued three times in eighteen months. Mitterrand and the Socialists reversed course in the spring of 1983. The *tournant*, the Mitterrand U-turn, was an admission of defeat: capital had won the battle of wills and ideologies. The socialist experiment had failed. Mitterrand had succeeded only in destroying Keynesian reflation and redistribution as a legitimate alternative once and for all, or so it has seemed since then.

The Meanings of Mitterrand

The scholarly literature on the Mitterrand experiment is wonderfully rich, and virtually every angle has been explored, every conversation among Mitterrand and his advisers recounted. The era of financial internationalization that followed the *tournant* has lent the episode a patina of inevitability. As Peter Hall suggests, the period between 1981 and 1986 can be understood as "the long learning curve of the French Left."[12]

The contest within the Mitterrand administration about how to respond to the worsening economic crisis in the first months of 1983 turns out, in retrospect, also to have been a struggle for the soul of French socialism. Many accounts describe the contest as both hard fought and close run.[13] On one side were Prime Minister Pierre Mauroy and Finance Minister Jacques Delors, who advocated financial austerity—*rigueur*—and European solidarity. France's partners in the European Monetary System (EMS) would not have accepted another significant devaluation of the franc, and floating the franc would have destroyed European monetary cooperation, perhaps once and for all. The alternative was known, literally, as *l'autre politique,* or "the other policy," and the "Albanian solution"—essentially to close off France's markets, to float the franc, and reject the constraints of the EMS. Generations of French governments, including those of the Right, had certainly, as Jonah Levy argues, been content, even resolved to choose autonomy when a crisis loomed.[14] France's choice for Europe, and its acceptance of the international constraints of the EMS, was a radical departure for the country, even more so for the Left.

Delors, a Socialist and long a member of France's financial-administrative elite based in the Banque de France and Trésor, and self-selected for more orthodox leanings regardless of party affiliation, was the architect of *rigueur*.[15] But Delors could not have won the contest among the Socialists alone. Delors was joined by Budget Minister (and Mitterrand protégé) Laurent Fabius and chief of staff Pierre Bérégovoy. Both Fabius and Bérégovoy had been advocates of the other policy, and their conversion by Delors was critical in the finance minister's efforts to convince Mitterrand to choose Europe and austerity. According to David Howarth, "Fabius' change of position appears to have been the determining factor that led to Mitterrand's final decision."[16]

Considering the role that Michel Camdessus would later play in bringing *la pensée unique* to the IMF, it is a remarkable coincidence that as director of the Trésor he helped to convince Fabius that floating the franc would wreak havoc on the French economy. In a meeting that has since been considered a turning point in the internal debate of the Mitterrand administration, Camdessus told Fabius that French foreign exchange reserves were desperately low. Camdessus also warned Fabius that even if the franc were floating, France would lack sufficient foreign exchange reserves to prevent a free-fall. Soon thereafter Delors and Fabius both made the case to Mitterrand and his other advisers that allowing the franc to float would bring disaster, not resolution.[17] With Fabius and Bérégovoy now on his side, Delors won the day: Mitterrand accepted austerity and the constraints of the EMS. The Socialist Party thus permanently lost the ability to adjust through devaluation.[18]

The presence of the highly analytical Delors was thus necessary, but not sufficient. Jonah Levy's reflections on the meaning of Delors' success in convincing his socialist colleagues are revealing:

> Fabius, Bérégovoy, and others like them had multiple motivations in adopting a liberal agenda. At one level, they underwent a genuine conversion . . . The shift in their positions derived from more than learning, however. For Fabius and Bérégovoy, the embrace of the market offered an appealing political identity, a "modern," "competent," profile, in contrast to the "archaic" and excessively "ideological" image of a Chevènement or a Georges Marchais.[19]

The most influential members of the Socialist Party had begun to reinvent themselves. Soon they would also reinvent the economic doctrine and program of the party.

Liberalization, Modernization, and the French Left

The French government began to loosen its draconian capital controls at the end of 1983, continuing in the summer and autumn of 1984. Being committed socialists, not to mention astute politicians, the liberalization campaign of the French Left began with those transactions that had most constrained the middle classes and had been most unpopular among its constituency: limits on travel allowances and the *carnet de change*.

The exchange controls had come to be seen by many socialists as an instrument of the repression of the middle classes, rather than the control of speculators.[20] According to Bérégovoy's chief of staff Jean-Charles Naouri, Bérégovoy, himself a man born to a modest, middle-class family, eventually interpreted capital controls similarly. "Bérégovoy hated the obscure, the opaque, the special deals, the clever gaming of the system," Naouri recalls. "He came to see capital controls in that way as well."[21]

In 1985 the Socialists began to liberalize virtually all transactions, including authorizing Eurobond issues denominated in French francs. When the right-wing government of Prime Minister Jacques Chirac shared the reins of power with Mitterrand between 1986 and 1988, France continued to liberalize, though the pace slowed and focused on other transactions, such as the purchase of secondary residences abroad and exchange purchases and sales by firms. Indeed, the Chirac government, despite being far further to the right than Mitterrand's Socialists, was much more reluctant to liberalize capital so aggressively and quickly, primarily because its establishment constituency opposed such a recasting of the French financial system.[22] The Socialists finished the task on their return to power. By January 1, 1990, France's capital account was almost completely open.

Domestic capital markets also experienced a complete transformation, and the process of deregulation between 1982 and 1985 was just as profound. Oriented around a new banking law in 1984, the French financial reform involved privatizations and, ultimately, the removal of credit controls. Essentially, the domestic financial reform ended the state-organized *dirigiste* financial system, which had been the very basis of French policy activism for forty years.[23]

The domestic financial deregulation marked a radical break for the French government. Naouri, in many respects the author of the domestic reforms, remarks: "We on Bérégovoy's staff knew what had to be done. It had been evident for at least a decade. The first thing to do was to make sure that Bérégovoy was on board. We had many compelling arguments in favor, but

Bérégovoy focused on one simple question: Will it make credit cheaper for the French people?"[24] As with capital liberalization, the Socialists' domestic financial deregulation was intended as a tool to bring the benefits of capital to the middle classes. If capital could not be constrained, it would, the Socialists argued, at least provide benefits for the French. Bérégovoy played an important role: "Even more important than Bérégovoy's shrewd and courageous dealing with the lobbies was this: it was he who convinced Mitterrand."[25]

Some French policymakers saw in these transformations the promise of not just a fairer France but a more modern one as well. "France in the 1980s," Jean-Claude Trichet recalls, "was a country of vast potential, but it was being held back by its own rules. There was an urgency to make France a 'normal' advanced industrialized economy with market institutions. Capital liberalization was a critical part of this market transformation."[26] Transcending divisions of Left and Right, the vision of a more modern, necessarily liberal France was, according to Naouri, pursued by "French technocrats—a technocratic elite from the Treasury. This elite shared a collective culture in favor of modernization. The question was how to lead France into modernity, into the Anglo-Saxon world, but without conflicting with other civil servants and public opinion."[27]

Modernizing France thus implied integration into international capital markets. That integration, once achieved, would be accompanied by the creeping presumption of naturalness and the elegance of intellectual order. Trichet speaks of this

> critical mass of civil servants who believed that the time was ripe for liberalization in France, and were convinced that this logic had some European and universal value. This group was committed to modernization in France, together with the European modernization, and as part and parcel of a global evolution. It had become clear that the market economy, and its codes of conduct, constitute the basic and absolutely insurmountable rules of the game.[28]

More Royalist than the King

The French Right would not have dared to undertake either the foreign or domestic liberalization of capital. As Pascal Lamy reflected, "When it comes to liberalization in France there is no Right. The Left had to liberalize, because the Right would not."[29] What a "conservative government had feared to do," observes Julius Friend, "a Socialist government accomplished."[30] French conservatives in power were, in fact, far less enthusiastic for the liberalization of capital. Naouri argues, "The conservative governments had not been open to financial modernization and capital liberalization. They should have done it, but they did not. It went against powerful lobbies in France, huge opposition from the banks, even from within the Banque de France."[31]

A fascinating contrast to Delors, Mitterrand, Fabius, and Bérégovoy was Jacques de Larosière. De Larosière's background was in the center-right Gaullist tradition, and an important moment in his career was his appointment as *chef de cabinet* to Minister of Finance Valéry Giscard d'Estaing. As Managing Director of the IMF for nearly a decade between 1978 and 1987 and then Governor of the Banque de France until 1993, de Larosière perhaps best represents the economic thinking of the center-right within the French financial-administrative elite. De Larosière speaks of the "mixed blessing" of free capital movements: "Without the right institutions and the right surveillance procedures in place, capital movements could create havoc. And they have."[32] The new enthusiasm of his compatriots did little to convince de Larosière otherwise: "I was never seduced."[33]

The eagerness of the French Left to outdo the Right extended to all matters of economic policy, not just finance.[34] In monetary policy, French economists have observed in the patterns of policymaking over the past decades "an overall financial orthodoxy much stronger than those observed for right-wing governments." Perhaps, according to these scholars, left-wing governments must "overcompensate" in their pursuit of credibility.[35] Others have noted the perceived necessity of exceeding the demands of economic orthodoxy for the French Left. As Serge Halimi describes it, it is the "ambition to prove oneself on the very terrain of the opposition. For the Left, this belief is translated into a policy firmness even more ruthless than the Right when it comes to implementing orthodox economic policies."[36] Similarly, it was, according to David Howarth, "necessary to establish the image of the Socialists as responsible economic managers, as much for domestic political reasons as to challenge international speculation against the franc."[37] The pursuit of credibility in the eyes of the financial markets, according to this logic, required the French Left to become *plus royaliste que le roi,* more royalist than the king himself.

Scholars of French politics continue to debate whether Ricardo's reunion with Marx reinvigorated or destroyed the Socialist Party. Those with sympathies for Mitterrand's original dream describe a keen sense of betrayal and disillusionment, that the Socialist Party offered "orthodox" proposals that "differ little from those of its rivals on the right."[38] George Ross reflects on the consequences for the Left itself:

> They had to live through massive change without any plausible alternative strategy, live in contradiction, and take their lumps with the only recompense—a large one—of staying in power. A certain amount of new cynicism was the product for some, a slow conversion experience to neo-liberalism with a human face was the result for others. The French Left, however, had to go without firm convictions of its own.[39]

The putative necessity of *rigueur* was made a political virtue.[40]

Socialist Goals for a Neoliberal Europe

So much for the French Socialists' grand project of achieving socialism in one country. Abandoning the traditional Socialist project, Mitterrand and the Left decisively embraced a new project in its place, that of Europe. Europe, according to this view, was not the cause of the Mitterrand *tournant*, but rather its legitimation.[41] The renewal of the French commitment to the EMS was what made the EMS a success, whereas its predecessor, the so-called Snake, had been merely a greater Deutsche mark zone.[42] To the extent that the French Left continued to hope for Socialist transformation, its members could see Europe as the only arena in which Socialist goals could be achieved.[43]

The middle of the 1980s was not an auspicious time to imagine the European economy as an opportunity for the traditional policies of the Left, however. The French commitment to the fixed exchange rates of the EMS necessarily implied that the Banque de France would adjust to the monetary policy of the country with the lowest inflation—Germany—or face a continuing need to realign the parities periodically. Policymakers throughout Europe, and particularly in France, interpreted the Mitterrand experiment as the failure of redistributive Keynesianism. Delors recalls France's efforts to bring down inflation in post-Keynesian terms: "The break of 1983 was fundamental. Our struggle against inflation was reinforced. Without the EMS, it would have been impossible to succeed in our struggle."[44]

With Keynesianism discredited, only the German Bundesbank's monetarism remained as a legitimate monetary policy paradigm. Germany's longstanding ability to reconcile low inflation with relatively low unemployment suggested that an alternate model of success could be adopted. The United Kingdom's own embrace of monetarism, still just a few years old at that point, also suggested that European macroeconomic policymaking had turned decisively toward monetary discipline. This new "consensus of competitive liberalism," Kathleen McNamara argues, emphasized low inflation; it also "redefined state interests in cooperation, underpinned stability in the EMS, and induced political leaders to accept the domestic policy adjustments needed to stay within the system."[45]

Germany, during all of this, simply continued to practice and preach financial liberalism. Although Germany had occasionally employed capital controls on inflows to avoid further appreciation of the mark, the country maintained an open capital account and encouraged its European partners to do the same. Whether Germany's partners in fact opened their capital accounts would not, however, affect the government's approach to capital or the Bundesbank's approach to money. "France may have had capital controls during the time of the EMS," recalls former Bundesbank President Karl Otto Pöhl. "So may have Italy. That did not concern us at the Bundesbank."[46]

The Delors Commission

Everything had changed with the *tournant* of 1983. Although French policymakers had merely capitulated to the reality of their capital flight, they also began to reconsider their approach to the freedom of capital movements in Europe. And then on January 1, 1985, the architect of *rigueur*, Delors, became president of the European Commission, a post he would hold for a decade. (For a list of Commission presidents, see Table 4.2.)

After visiting the national capitals, and sensing, according to Andrew Moravcsik, that the time was ripe for an ambitious new integration initiative based on market principles, Delors moved quickly to produce the June 1985 White Paper that was the first outline of a plan to complete the European internal market by January 1, 1993. "Despite personal doubts" about a bold new initiative to deepen the market integration of Europe, Moravcsik argues, "Delors was not one to waste an opportunity."[47]

In June 1985 full capital liberalization was still not on the Commission's

Table 4.2   European Commission Presidents

President	Member State	Tenure
Walter Hallstein	(West) Germany	1958–1967
Jean Ray	Belgium	1967–1970
Franco Maria Malfatti	Italy	1970–1972
Sicco L. Mansholt	Netherlands	1972
François-Xavier Ortoli	France	1973–1977
Roy Jenkins	United Kingdom	1977–1981
Gaston Edmont Thorn	Luxembourg	1981–1985
Jacques Delors	France	1985–1995
Jacques Santer	Luxembourg	1995–1999
Romano Prodi	Italy	1999–2004
José Manuel Durão Barroso	Portugal	2004–present

agenda, however. The White Paper envisioned "greater liberalization of capital movements," but described only small steps toward them. "Unlike the Treaty provisions relating to free trade in goods and services," the White Paper noted, "the principle of freedom of capital movements does not apply directly." The White Paper did not propose to alter the legal status of capital freedom in Europe, and indeed put forward very modest suggestions for further liberalization.[48] "The capital movements directive was not announced in 1985, and was not a part of the road map for 1992," Lamy recalls, "because it was not yet conceived."[49] It would take Delors and his staff another few months, until late 1985 and early 1986, to articulate a plan to create a single European capital market.

The negotiations surrounding the Single European Act of 1986, the first major intergovernmental revision to the Treaty of Rome, provided Delors and Lamy an opportunity to consider seriously the implications of European capital liberalization.[50] In late 1985 Delors came to believe that the "1992 project," as it came to be known, required capital liberalization: "Although I had concerns, I came to the realization that the free movement of capital was essential to the creation of the internal market."[51] Lamy also recalls the reluctance of Delors: "Delors hesitated quite a lot. But the coherence of the plan as it evolved—the logic of the internal market—was powerful."[52] The logic itself held attractions for the Delors Commission.

Once Delors and his advisers had decided that capital liberalization ought to be part of the single market program, the Commission tried—unsuccessfully—to include the freedom of capital in the Single European

Act. In late 1985 and early 1986, before the Treaty was signed in February, the Delors Commission argued that freedom for capital movements ought to have the same privileged status as freedom for goods, services, and people. The Commission's proposal met with resistance in a number of governments, including France, still in the middle of its own transformation, as well as Italy. Instead, the Single European Act did not go so far, and the passage dealing with capital freedom suggested that members were obliged to liberalize capital "in accordance with the provision of the Treaty." The legal basis of capital freedom thus remained as it had been specified in the Treaty of Rome: "to the extent necessary to ensure the proper functioning of the Common Market." The Council's directives still defined the meaning of "the extent necessary."[53] Although many scholars and policymakers continue to assume that the Single European Act defined the liberalization of capital as an objective of the 1992 program, in fact the nonliberal provisions of the 1957 Treaty continued to determine the legal fate of capital within Europe. The Single European Act by itself did little to liberalize capital movements. Capital would remain a second-class citizen in Europe until the Council decided otherwise.

So Delors assembled a team of Commission policymakers to formulate a coherent plan for capital liberalization directives. The team consisted of three Frenchmen—his chief of staff Pascal Lamy, in addition to Jean-Paul Mingasson and Jean-Pierre Baché, both of DGII (Economic and Financial Affairs)—and Joly Dixon, a British national who had long worked in the Commission. Mingasson and Baché focused on capital liberalization, Dixon's responsibility was monetary union, and Lamy coordinated the team.

The Commission unveiled its two-stage plan for capital liberalization before the Council in May 1986. The first directive, which was adopted in November 1986, transferred a number of capital movements from List C of the 1960 directive (the conditional list) to an unconditional list.[54] The November directive still, however, left many of the more controversial capital transactions—"short-term capital movements," most especially—on the conditional list.[55] The second stage would be a directive that moved all capital movements to the unconditional list. (For an overview of the effects of the various liberalization directives, see Table 4.3.)

Although the Single European Act had introduced qualified majority voting to replace unanimity in the Council, the Delors Commission still lacked even a majority in favor of such an ambitious move. The French and Italians, especially, were insistent that the Germans commit to a more symmet-

Table 4.3   EC Council Capital Liberalization Directives and Significant Effects

Directive	Significant Effects
First Directive for the implementation of Article 67 of the Treaty (May 11, 1960)	Members obligated to liberalize intra-Community short-term and medium-term trade-related credits, direct investment, and listed-shares transactions. No obligation to liberalize short-term financial transactions.
Second Council Directive 63/21/EEC adding to and amending the First Directive for the implementation of Article 67 of the Treaty (December 18, 1962)	Obligation to liberalize short-term and medium-term credits under 1960 directive extended to services-related transactions.
Council Directive 72/156/EEC on regulating international capital flows and neutralizing their undesirable effects on domestic liquidity (March 12, 1972)	Members obligated, *erga omnes,* to maintain instruments for the control of certain capital flows, including regulations governing nonresident money market transactions, credit institutions' net external positions, and minimum reserve ratios for nonresident holdings. Extension of general derogation from 1960 directive relating to nonresident loans and credits to residents.
Council Directive 86/566/EEC amending the First Directive of 11 May 1960 for the implementation of Article 67 of the Treaty (November 17, 1986)	Members obligated to liberalize several additional capital movements, though not short-term capital transactions.
Council Directive 88/361/EEC for the implementation of Article 67 of the Treaty (June 24, 1988)	Members obligated to undertake full liberalization of capital movements.

Sources: See cited directives; Age F. P. Bakker, *The Liberalization of Capital Movements in Europe* (Dordrecht: Kluwer, 1996), pp. 87–88, 93, 118, 168, 177, 180, 211.

rical EMS. In a lively discussion in the Monetary Committee in February 1987, the French and Italians offered further capital liberalization if Germany would agree to change the rules so that the burden of adjustment would no longer fall exclusively on the weaker currencies (those that were losing value relative to the stronger currency, always the German mark).[56] Ultimately the result was the Basel-Nyborg agreement of 1987—Basel being where the central bankers met, and Nyborg the location of the finance ministers' meeting. The French agreed in principle to a directive mandating the removal of capital controls throughout Europe. In exchange, the Germans committed to intervene in foreign exchange markets on behalf of the weaker currencies in the EMS and to coordinate interest rate changes with greater communication among EMS members.[57] Basel-Nyborg paved the way for Delors to take the final step toward the codification of the norm of capital mobility in Europe. In October 1987 the Council discussed the last stage of the Commission's capital liberalization plan. Italy was left alone among the EC's largest, most influential members in its skepticism of the proposal.[58]

In June 1988 the final capital movement directive was adopted.[59] No capital transaction or transfer was exempt from this new obligation to liberalize. The Treaty of Rome's qualifier, "to the extent necessary," from the summer of 1988 onward would be defined so that all capital movements were "necessary" for the proper functioning of the common market.[60] Bakker argues that the Commission's claim that short-term capital movements "were an integral part of the Internal Market implied an outright negation of the escape clause of Article 67, which it had tried in vain to remove from the Treaty in the Single Act."[61] The directive established a deadline for the achievement of the full formal mobility of capital within the EC: July 1, 1990.

The most important consequence of the 1988 liberalization directive was its establishment of the legal principle that capital freedom was a fundamental right of EC law, of the *acquis*. In some respects the directive was much more liberal than Delors, Lamy, Mingasson, and Baché had originally wanted. The Delors Commission had argued in favor of amending, but retaining, the 1972 directive obliging member states to maintain the institutional apparatus of capital controls in case they were necessary to regulate capital movements to and from third countries. The Commission's focus was freedom for capital within Europe only, not necessarily with the rest of the world as well.

The Germans, however, insisted that the directive be based on the *erga omnes* principle of applying liberalization to third countries. Hans Tietmeyer, who was then the German finance ministry's senior official with responsibility for the European Community, formulated and articulated the German position on *erga omnes*. The stakes, Tietmeyer recalls, were immense:

We saw in full capital liberalization the possibility for a test of the stability of the ERM—a test by the markets of policy credibility. We wanted a test by world markets, not just European markets. That was why the *erga omnes* principle was so crucial. Liberalization *erga omnes* would demonstrate that we had in Europe a stable fixed exchange-rate system with market-proved stability, rather than artificial stability provided by controls.[62]

Both the French government and the Commission opposed making the *erga omnes* principle legally binding in the directive, as did the British government, which sought to enable Europe to withhold access to its capital market as leverage in negotiating access to other countries' markets. Although a variety of positions on the *erga omnes* principle circulated within Europe, in the end it was "primarily a French-German debate."[63] Pöhl recalls, "The French had very different ideas about a European capital market, as well as for the currency union."[64] The compromise produced a weaker legal obligation with regard to third countries, to "endeavor to attain the same degree of liberalization as that which applies to operations with residents of other Member States" (Article 7).[65] The 1972 directive was also repealed by the 1988 directive.[66]

In other respects the directive was not fully liberal, for it contained a "monetary safeguard clause." Belgium, France, Greece, Ireland, Italy, Portugal, Spain, and the Commission itself all argued that capital controls should not be completely ruled out because of the potential for capital movements to undermine monetary policy or exchange-rate stability. Germany, the United Kingdom, and Denmark opposed the inclusion of any language that permitted capital controls to be reintroduced. The compromise reached by the two sides became Article 3 of the directive, which focused on situations in which "short-term capital movements of exceptional magnitude impose severe strains on foreign-exchange markets and lead to serious disturbances" in monetary and exchange-rate policy. In such a situation, the Commission and a member country could collaborate to take "protective measures," but for no longer than six months.[67]

The change in the French position had been decisive for permitting the codification of any capital liberalization directive.[68] Indeed, the German position on the preconditions for monetary union had been made clear even during policy discussions begun during the 1970s: "The German position was that a single currency of course would imply the free flow of capital."[69] Delors reflects on the ways in which the directive would "have a psychological effect, creating a powerful signal—even more because the proposal was coming from the French."[70] Economist Jacques Melitz describes the significance of the French *tournant* for Europe:

> When economic historians look back at this important juncture in European financial history, I believe that they will conclude that the French liberalization program was the single most important forerunner of the White Paper. With this liberalization program came the French support for an integrated European market for financial services, without which the proposal of a Single Market would never have gotten off the ground.[71]

French liberalization reflected a fundamental victory for the minority of modernizers and liberalizers who had long sought to reorient the Left toward the market and safeguard the value of the French currency. As Delors recalls, however, it "was difficult to convince those in Paris. Many French politicians on both the Left and the Right were against the liberalization of capital." Delors did not lead France to liberalism alone. President Mitterrand played a critical role:

> The firmness of the position of the President of the Republic was decisive. No one has emphasized sufficiently the firmness of the President's view that the French people prefer to be satisfied with the strength of their currency, indeed to be proud of their currency. This was an end in itself for the French government.[72]

"A Transition Period to Help You Change Your Mind"

The Council had, remarkably, passed the capital liberalization directive unanimously. This occurred despite the fact that the Council still lacked consensus—Greece, Ireland, Italy, Portugal, and Spain still objected in principle—and that the Council could have passed the directive easily with a qualified majority vote. "In Europe a unanimous decision does not mean that everyone agrees," Lamy reminds us. "Majority voting does not introduce a system whereby countries are regularly overruled. It creates a new, subtle kind of bargaining."[73]

In the case of the capital liberalization directive, because it was clear that the directive enjoyed the support of both a weighted and a numerical majority of member states, those in the minority were aware that if a vote were called they would be overruled. Their choice was either to follow the lead of the rare consensus among France, Germany, and the United Kingdom, or to choose to make a statement by voting in the minority. Such statements are unpopular among other member states, for they signal isolation from the EC's consensus. Italy, for its part, has always sought to avoid such isolation as a matter of diplomatic principle.[74] Greece had joined the EC only recently, in 1981, and Portugal and Spain had entered just two years earlier, in 1986; 1988 was thus hardly an attractive moment to take a stand against the Franco-German axis at the heart of the Community.

In exchange for their adherence to the EC's consensus, Greece, Ireland, Portugal, and Spain were allowed extra time to complete their processes of capital liberalization. Their "transition periods" extended until the end of 1992.[75] Mingasson recalls the subtlety of the meaning of a transition period from the perspective of the Delors team: "Greece, Portugal, Spain, Ireland, and Italy had not changed their minds. It is standard operating procedure in Brussels to offer transition periods to those who are not convinced. We say it is a transition period for adjusting. But really it is a transition period to help you change your mind."[76]

Within a few years the EC was entirely a community of mobile capital, despite not being a community that entirely agreed on the virtues of such mobile capital. Germany, the Netherlands, and the United Kingdom were already in compliance, while the nine other EC states still had some remaining capital controls to dismantle. Denmark removed its few remaining regulations in October 1988. France lifted nearly all restrictions in March 1989, finishing completely in January 1990. Belgium and Luxembourg eliminated their dual exchange rate, which had created a floating rate for capital transactions that required authorities to monitor and distinguish capital and current transactions.

The capital liberalization directive was, from the perspective of compliance, extremely successful: despite their misgivings, all of the EC's laggards liberalized.[77] In Italy, according to Kenneth Dyson and Kevin Featherstone, "EC pressures for full capital liberalization gave added strength and speed to the domestic process of reform."[78] Furthermore, as Mingasson argues: "Once the directive was in place, Greece, Portugal, Spain, and Ireland really had no choice. The Commission had made it clear that freedom for capital movements was a priority, and that it was prepared to use all of its influence to enforce the directive."[79] Ireland, Portugal, and Spain dismantled their capital controls ahead of the end of 1992 objective.

Only Greece did not meet the Commission's deadline. Greece requested an extension of its transition period to 1995, but the Commission granted an extension only until the end of 1994. Of Europe's laggards, Greece was furthest from having an open capital account. The Greek government had not even accepted the Article VIII obligations of the IMF for an open current account, a transition that took place only in 1992. The Greek financial system in 1988 was as tightly controlled and heavily regulated as the French system had been at the start of the Mitterrand era. The process of capital liberalization went hand in hand, as it had in France, with a broader effort to liberalize the entire system, including the deregulation of interest rates, the abolition of credit controls, and the development of a market for government securities.[80]

Brussels and Athens both had reasons to worry that capital would not be liberalized quickly enough, if at all. Back in 1981, the EC's interest in consolidating Greece's transition to democracy had led the Commission to make an exception for Greece and relax its requirements of compliance with the EC's rules, embodied in the *acquis communautaire*, upon the country's accession, after twenty years of association. Greece's subsequent difficulty complying with liberalization taught the Commission an important lesson that would prove to have great consequence for future accession to the EC: cajoling and enforcing compliance proved much more difficult once a country was already a member. In subsequent accessions, Commission negotiators would insist that much greater progress toward compliance with the *acquis* should precede membership. During the 1980s Greece was widely considered the member that fit least well the legal norms of the EC, and its slowness in transposing Council directives became legendary.

Greece's reluctance to embrace the *acquis* resulted partly from the traditional opposition of both the Socialists and Communists to membership, a political divide that continued into the 1980s.[81] Greek firms, moreover, were not eager to open all sectors of the economy to foreign competition, and the lobby against rapid "Europeanization" was powerful.[82] Greek noncompliance, Elena Iankova and Peter Katzenstein argue, "resulted also from institutional inertia and inefficiency." When the Greek government created a special department within the Ministry of Foreign Affairs in 1986 to manage more efficiently the country's interaction with European law and institutions, the government was able to move much more quickly to embrace its European obligations.[83] The government's redoubled effort to transform Greece from a European problem to an effective member coincided with both the Single European Act and the capital liberalization directives that followed. The decisiveness of the influence of the 1988 directive on Greek capital liberalization thus was partly dependent on the ability of the government to undertake the effort required.[84]

The Greek government began its domestic financial reforms in 1988, leaving the liberalization of capital movements to be accomplished at a breakneck pace between 1992 and the spring of 1994.[85] Between 1988 and 1994, Greece faced a massive economic crisis that put further pressure on the government to adopt European norms for exchange-rate stability and fiscal rectitude. The profligacy of an ambitious government during 1988 and 1989 resulted, the following year, in an inflation rate of 20 percent, a budget deficit that was 16 percent of GDP, and no economic growth. The pressure for macroeconomic adjustment increased the stakes for liberalizing capital movements, in part, from the Bank of Greece's point of view, to deflate the economy.[86]

The Paris Consensus, the Brussels Strategy, and Monetary Union

French policymakers in Paris and Brussels had one further objective in mind when they authored new liberal rules for capital in Europe. The Commission's strategy for capital liberalization, according to Nicolas Jabko, laid the very foundation for monetary union.[87] Both the French government and Delors saw in the liberalization of capital movements a first step in a sequence of events that would lead to monetary union in Europe. The French interest in monetary union heightened with the adoption of the strong franc policy, the *franc fort,* after the Mitterrand decision not to devalue and to remain within the EMS. This meant shadowing German monetary policy ever more closely, and the Bundesbank's independence of every other actor, including the German government, meant there would be very little outside influence on monetary policymaking for all of Europe. For Delors, Economic and Monetary Union (EMU) became a priority, and laying the foundations for union promised to be as great a feat as any Commission president had ever achieved. "EMU, more than everything else," George Ross writes, "was Delors' baby."[88]

The path between the 1988 directive and monetary union was, as everyone knew, long, and the strategy was in many ways extremely risky, for it threatened to unravel the EMS altogether. Though risky, Nicolas Jabko observes, the strategy "was politically quite shrewd."[89] The risk of the strategy was that inflation rates among European countries continued to diverge, while at the same time exchange rate realignments within the EMS were becoming less frequent. The former reflected the fact that central banks throughout Europe did not follow every interest rate increase the Bundesbank announced. Commission officials, Jabko notes, were "acutely aware of the economic incompatibility between fixed exchange rates, freedom of capital movements, and national policy autonomy."[90] Although observant economists pointed out the danger, even the folly, of Europe's embrace of fixed exchange rates, free capital mobility, and nominally autonomous national central banks, Delors, Lamy, Mingasson, Baché, and Dixon knew what they were doing.[91]

The strategy also produced a logic that would appear irresistible, and a path that was inexorable, to governments in Europe. With a single capital market and fixed exchange rates, there could be no place for autonomous monetary policymaking in Europe. Europe's central banks had already essentially relinquished their monetary autonomy to the Bundesbank through the working of the EMS. The Commission thus "raised the political stakes of EMU, acting decisively to liberalize capital movements while exhorting European governments to embrace EMU as a compensatory instrument for regaining monetary sovereignty."[92]

Thus, as Lamy recalls, the "ultimate goal" was monetary union:

> Two logics were critical. Tommaso Padoa-Schioppa, who played a critical role among the plotters, outlined what we then called the Padoa-Schioppa theorem on the incompatibility of fixed exchange rates, capital mobility, and monetary policy autonomy. The Delors plan thus promised to spill over from capital movements to monetary integration. We also needed to erode German resistance, and capital freedom was the price to pay.[93]

A concrete plan for EMU did follow hard upon, and as a direct result of, the capital liberalization directive. French support for the 1988 directive was critical according to Craig Parsons: "Only when they accepted full capital mobility, in June 1988, did Kohl agree to create a committee on EMU under Commission President Delors."[94] The very same month of the capital liberalization directive—June 1988—Mitterrand met Helmut Kohl, the German chancellor, in Evian to discuss the prospects for monetary union. Mitterrand offered Kohl a deal: in exchange for Mitterrand's personally instructing Bérégovoy, then his finance minister, to accept capital liberalization on behalf of the French, Kohl would agree to the formation of the high-level committee on monetary union. The terms of reference for the Committee for the Study of Economic and Monetary Union were set by the European Council only weeks later, on June 27–28, in Hanover.[95] The crux of the German position was that exchange-rate stability should result not only from the fixing of parities in the EMS, but also from macroeconomic policy convergence, and free capital movements would create powerful pressures for convergence.[96] "In the summer of 1988," recalls Hans Tietmeyer, "we made it clear to the Commission and the other European countries that Germany would not accept a monetary union without full mobility of capital both inside and outside. For us capital liberalization was simply a precondition."[97]

The Germans had, of course, agreed only to the study of monetary union, accepting in principle such an objective for the EC, but without a firm timetable or set of enabling criteria. The politics that would lead to an intergovernmental agreement to move forward with monetary union were still elusive, and well beyond the power of Delors and the Commission to cultivate. Still, Delors and Mitterrand took the next step: creating consensus among Europe's skeptical central bankers, not least the head of the fiercely independent Bundesbank, Karl Otto Pöhl.

So Delors, along with Kohl himself, helped to ensure that the Committee would consist of the twelve European central bank presidents or governors. After eight monthly meetings in Basel, meetings during which Delors was careful not to impose himself on the discussion among the central bank governors, the central bankers reached agreement on how European countries could proceed toward unifying their currencies. The central bankers envisioned three stages on the road to monetary union. The first—the removal of capital controls by July 1990—was already under way as a result of the 1988 capital liberalization directive. The second stage, beginning in 1994, involved further convergence of macroeconomic policies and the creation of a European Monetary Institute. Third, and finally, in 1999 criteria to assess the degree of convergence among the macroeconomic policies of member states would be used to determine which countries would unify their currencies, with the newly created currency governed by a European Central Bank modeled closely on the Bundesbank. The committee's report—colloquially known as the Delors Report—helped to relaunch the EMU project. Indeed, the report's outline became, with few modifications, the very text of the Treaty of Maastricht's provisions for the progression toward EMU.[98]

Although Delors and the Commission did not directly cause monetary union, for indeed much debate was still to come, Jabko argues that they "nonetheless performed a pivotal part as recruiting agents for the cause of EMU."[99] Delors and his team also were able to emphasize to policymakers throughout Europe that by the time the Committee for the Study of Economic and Monetary Union had finished its work, Europe had *already* painted itself into a corner. Having chosen free capital and fixed exchange rates, only one choice remained for them, whether it be de facto or de jure. As Padoa-Schioppa, a longtime ally of Delors in the effort to create monetary union and the Delors Committee's rapporteur, argued, the

> Delors Report clearly indicates that the crux of the matter is that there has to be a single monetary policy. The best way to understand this is to make it very clear that what will still be lacking from monetary union once the 1992 program has been fully implemented, with the complete liberalization of banking and financial services, will be the shift from twelve formally independent monetary policies to one single monetary policy.[100]

The choice for monetary union appeared to be perfectly logical. Within an asymmetric EMS, France had only limited monetary autonomy. Monetary policy for all of Europe was essentially made by the Bundesbank in Frankfurt. With monetary union, however, a French central banker would at least have a seat at the table with his or her German and other European colleagues to make monetary policy for all of Europe. France was thus giving up a currency, control over the value of which it had essentially relinquished in 1983 when Mitterrand chose the EMS over the "other policy." Political scientist Joseph Grieco outlines this logic as the opportunity for France to exercise "voice" on the making of European monetary policy.[101] As de Larosière, then governor of the Banque de France, put it in 1990, "Today I am the governor of a central bank who has decided, along with his nation, to follow fully the German monetary policy without voting on it. At least, as part of a European central bank, I'll have a vote."[102]

This logic of French support is useful for understanding the path to monetary union, but three qualifications are necessary. First, and most subtly, the strategy for EMU was formulated in Brussels by Delors and Dixon as much as in Paris by Mitterrand and his advisers, and the Commission's decision to use capital liberalization as both a tool to undermine German resistance and a mechanism for convergence is a necessary piece of the story. Liberal capital rules, authored by French policymakers in Brussels, played a decisive role in encouraging European policymakers to recognize that with monetary union they were giving up a monetary policy autonomy that already was illusory in favor of a seat at the table.

Second, although the logic of French support seems, in retrospect, to be water-tight, in fact the resistance within Paris to monetary union was both significant and dogged. "The French support for full EMU was decided personally by Mitterrand," Parsons reports, "over objections from some of his closest allies and advisors."[103] The strategic logic continued to put Bérégovoy, then finance minister, in an extremely awkward position vis-à-vis his own party. Not only was Bérégovoy obliged to accept European capital liberalization, amidst the harsh criticisms of those further on the Left, but was then asked by Mitterrand to make sense of France's decision to give up its beloved franc. "When Bérégovoy became Minister of Finance, step by step he changed his position," Delors recalls. "Then his role was to convince members of the Socialist Party."[104]

Third, and most important, it was only the French logic that was crystal clear. A critical question is: Why did Germany agree to give up its mark, the very symbol of German stability and postwar prosperity, when the Bundesbank already had power over monetary policy for all of Europe? Perhaps it can be said that France gave up little by pushing for EMU; Germany seemed to give up everything.[105] One part of the answer to this question is based on the institutional logic negotiated among members of the Delors Committee. The new European Central Bank would be politically independent and legally obliged to maintain price stability. Bundesbank officials who were more committed to the goal of low inflation than to the bank's central role in achieving it were reassured that the new central bank would be even more legally insulated from political influence than the Bundesbank itself.

Another part of the answer was Kohl's own commitment to building Europe. Even Kohl, however, could not have brought all of Germany, and the Bundesbank, along with him without some external event forcing his hand. Kohl, moreover, was committed to monetary union in principle and, critically, in the future. It was clear that an intergovernmental conference on monetary union would happen, but the date had not been set.

The fall of the Berlin Wall forced Kohl's hand. The unification of East with West Germany appeared to be inevitable, and public support on both sides of the fallen wall was immense. No German chancellor would have moved forward with unification without the support of the rest of Europe, and certainly not Kohl, who was committed to Europeanizing Germany. In Strasbourg in December 1989 Kohl asked his European partners for their support for unification, and, led by France, Europe embraced the idea of a new Germany in the center of Europe. Mitterrand, however, asked that Kohl accept the French proposal for an intergovernmental conference on monetary union to be held the following December, rather than in 1991 or even later, as Kohl had come to prefer once Germany's unification began to absorb so much of the German government's attention. Although Kohl had originally agreed to the December 1990 date for the intergovernmental conference, the German government backtracked, later offering a series of related conferences: EMU in 1991, institutional reforms in 1992, and political union in 1993. The new German timetable promised to put off Treaty negotiations for several years at least. In part, Mitterrand's request for a 1990 conference on EMU reflected his sense of an opportunity for leverage in the negotiations with Germany over the timing of monetary union, but it was also to be a show of faith that the new Germany would be as committed to Europe as the old Federal Republic had been. In March 1990, the French asked the Germans to commit to a second intergovernmental conference on political union to be held much earlier than 1993. Kohl, presiding over a unification process that appeared increasingly beyond his control, agreed again. In April 1990 the European Council set out these plans, arranged in advance essentially by France and Germany, for negotiating a new Treaty. The Treaty on European Union was finalized in December 1991 in Maastricht. "United Germany was thus," Peter Katzenstein argues, "to be embedded in an integrating Europe."[106]

The Treaty on European Union negotiated in Maastricht did many things. It renamed the European Community the European Union. It laid out the timetable for EMU and codified a firm commitment for monetary union based on the Delors Report. But it is also notable for what it did not do. The Treaty's liberal provisions were, in a sense, moot, for the 1988 directive had already established the legal status of capital movements within Europe. Still, the symbolism, and the subsequent practical effect through rulings of the court, was powerful. The freedom of capital, for the first time in the process of European integration, was a right equivalent to the freedom of goods, services, and people. Rather than an accumulation of directives specifying the capital movements that were "necessary" for the functioning of the common market, the Treaty on European Union offered a simplified, and simple formulation: capital was to be free. The Treaty, moreover, applied directly, rather than, as with the 1988 directive, relying on transposition into national regulations.

The one major difference from the 1988 capital liberalization directive was Maastricht's strengthening of the *erga omnes* principle. In addition to the language of the 1988 directive's obligation that member states "endeavor" to enable capital freedom from third countries as well as within Europe, the Maastricht Treaty added that member states were "prohibited" from restricting capital movements, and not just transfers with respect to capital movements, to and from third countries equally, save some exceptions.[107] The basic principle was clear, however: No European state could restrict capital coming from or going to any state, European or otherwise. When, in 1994, the Treaty entered into force, the EU would henceforth have the most liberal rules for capital in the international financial architecture.

The Delors Commission's strategy of promoting capital liberalization on the way to monetary union almost backfired when, in September 1992, a series of speculative attacks on several of the currencies in the EMS threatened European monetary cooperation. Two currencies, the British pound and Italian lira, left the EMS, and the Portuguese escudo and Spanish peseta were devalued. The very capital markets that the 1988 directive had helped to internationalize were responsible for exchange-rate crises that became crises of confidence in the prospects for EMU. In Frankfurt and Bonn the crises represented tests of the market. "If you can withstand the test of the market," Tietmeyer argues, "you have proven your stability. Only in this way could we create a strong European monetary union and a strong currency." When the markets tested the commitments of European governments to their fixed exchange rates, it was clear to the German government that "the tests were now working."[108]

Continued speculative pressures on EMS currencies, including the franc, eventually provoked European leaders to widen the bands within which EMS currencies fluctuated from plus or minus 2.25 percent to plus or minus 15 percent. It was widely acknowledged that the rigors of following German monetary policy—high interest rates to reduce the inflationary pressures resulting from fiscal deficits associated with the costs of unification—had undermined the market's confidence in the governments' commitments to fixed exchange rates. A June 1992 referendum in which a narrow majority of Danes rejected the Maastricht Treaty further undermined the expectations of a seamless transition from EMS to EMU. Most observers assumed, therefore, that the widened fluctuation bands meant the end of monetary cooperation in Europe, particularly because several countries, France in particular, could use this new leeway to reduce their interest rates and allow their currencies to deviate from the precrisis EMS parities. With the exception of the United Kingdom's and Italy's exiting the exchange rate mechanism of the EMS, European monetary cooperation continued just as intensely as before: EMS governments maintained their exchange rates within much narrower implicit fluctuation bands.[109]

The response of Europe's leaders to the EMS crises of 1992 and 1993 suggests several further conclusions about the process of European financial integration. Although Ireland, Portugal, and Spain introduced temporary, and, apparently, porous capital controls during the crises, EMS members did not, as a rule, attempt to regulate the capital markets that wreaked havoc on the system. Delors himself suggested that the monetary safeguard clause of the 1988 directive could be invoked if governments found it necessary, and he even spoke publicly about the possibility of EC-wide restrictions on capital flows to and from third countries. The Commission president's suggestions were both reasonable and pragmatic: "Cars are free to drive, but they are subject to traffic rules. I see no reason why at the international level we should not study means of limiting monetary traffic." Delors also suggested that Europe could lead the way in such a study: "Bankers cannot act at will. Why should we not draw up some rules of the game? Why should not the Community take the initiative?"

The reaction to Delors in London and Frankfurt was vehement.[110] The EMS crises certainly seemed to fit the scenario European leaders had in mind when the safeguard clause was inserted into the directive. The fact that, even in the midst of a crisis fueled by foreign exchange speculation, the mood among policymakers was very much against new restrictions on capital mobility demonstrates how liberal Europe had become by the 1990s. Finally, Delors was revealed, again, to be a man of the Left with an abiding skepticism of the absolute freedom of capital. For Delors, French modernity and European unification were the ends; capital's freedom was merely the means.

Although Germany remained the focal point for exchange-rate coordination after the 1992 crisis and 1993 widening of the fluctuation bands, the stability of the EMS through the rest of the 1990s depended much less on German leadership and much more on the followership of the EMS countries. Again France was the key to stability as the largest follower state.

Without France, stability in the EMS could be dismissed simply as a greater Deutsche mark bloc comprised of small, open states that had shadowed German monetary policy for years, and in some cases decades. Charles Kindleberger's reflection on the hierarchies inherent in international monetary cooperation suggests how important such a follower is:

> Great powers, typically one great power, have responsibility for the international monetary system. Small countries with no power separately to affect the system have no such responsibility and are free to pursue the narrow national interest. In between, near-great powers face a difficult problem since they have power to hurt the system, generally insufficient power to steady it in the face of disruption on a wide scale, but are tempted to pursue national goals which diverge from the interest of the system.[111]

Germany was the great power of the EMS, while France was its near-great power. French authorities continued to follow German monetary policy, thus keeping the EMS stable through the rest of the 1990s. Not only was the French government unwilling to gamble with the hard-won policy credibility resulting from a decade of *rigueur*, but Mitterrand and his advisers refused to jeopardize monetary union by easing the policies that created *un franc fort*. The EMS remained stable until 1999 when Europe's exchange rates were irrevocably fixed and the euro became Europe's currency.

The Freedom of Capital in a Wider Europe

The 1988 capital liberalization directive and the Treaty on European Union created liberal capital rules for a European Community of twelve members, most of which liberalized their own capital accounts more than thirty years after the Treaty of Rome entered into force. Once codified, these liberal rules were part of the *acquis communautaire*, literally the accomplishments of the community. The thirty-one chapters of the *acquis* are composed of the articles of every treaty, revision, bureaucratic expansion, and Court of Justice ruling, every principle and obligation that constitute the rules of the EU, some 80,000 pages of text. Chapter 4 covers the free movement of capital, and as of 1988 the *acquis* obliged members to be unconditionally liberal in their treatment of capital flows among members and third countries. At the European Council meeting in Copenhagen in June 1993, the "Copenhagen criteria" for the constitutive norms of European-ness were set out: in addition to democracy, the rule of law, the protection of human rights, and a market economy, adherence to the *acquis* was made fundamental. Because the *acquis* prescribes capital liberalization and proscribes capital controls, it follows that the very definition of a "European" state includes a commitment to capital mobility.

The influence of the *acquis* has perhaps been at its most dramatic on each of the occasions that Europe welcomed new members. The "classical method" of enlargement, in the Commission's lingo, mandates that candidate countries fully accept and transpose the *acquis* before joining. With regard to capital, then, any prospective member of the EU must completely liberalize its capital account.[112] When Austria, Finland, and Sweden joined the EU in 1995, the Chapter 4 negotiations were straightforward: Those three countries had, for the most part, already liberalized capital flows in the context of the European Area Agreement.

The influence of the *acquis* on capital liberalization was both more pronounced and more subtle during the accession negotiations leading up to the 2004 admission of Cyprus, the Czech Republic, Estonia, Hungary, Latvia, Lithuania, Malta, Poland, Slovakia, and Slovenia.[113] The Czech Republic, Hungary, Poland, and Slovakia had already liberalized in order to comply with agreements with the EU and subsequently to join the OECD during the 1990s. In part this was also because their leaders recognized that they would have to be fully liberal by the time EU membership was on the horizon. For the others, the prospect of EU membership was the primary impetus behind capital liberalization. Governments in central and eastern Europe eagerly embraced the economic policy practices that defined European-ness. In the Commission, negotiators talked of the "good pupils" to the east who were eager to adopt the practices that would lead others to recognize them as "European," just as the Commission sought to teach European-ness.

The candidates for EU membership therefore liberalized at a pace that would have been inconceivable for France, and in the context of often weak and under-institutionalized domestic financial systems. Stephane Ouaki, one of the Commission negotiators for Chapter 4, observed, in central and eastern Europe, an "eagerness to be perceived as right up to European standards for openness to capital movements."[114] Not a single negotiation between the Commission and candidate countries dealt with the regulation of capital movements for the purposes of macroeconomic management or protection of a weak balance of payments position. No government of a candidate country even asked for a transition period on the liberalization of short-term capital flows.[115] This surprised the Commission negotiators, who often found themselves pushing against an open door. Lars Erik Forsberg, another negotiator, observed that the Commission could not recommend capital controls or a slower pace of capital liberalization, even if the risks to a specific country were clear: "There were a few cases in which transition periods for short-term capital movements might have been useful from an economic point of view, but the Commission cannot grant concessions that are not sought."[116] The only negotiations revolved around the Commission's concern with regulations to deal with money laundering and the acceding countries' concerns over real estate purchases by foreigners. The few transition periods for the free movement of capital in the EU's ten newest members dealt with real estate.

The codification of the norm of capital mobility in the *acquis*, mundane as it may sound, thus proves to be a monumental event in the history of both Europe and capital itself. Rushed into institutional form by French leadership, it unites modern Europe and free capital in a single identity. This new definition of the European is itself the engine of free capital's spread on the world stage. Ouaki describes the inexorable logic of the *acquis* by which the Commission enforces the relationship: "Once an obligation is on the books, the Commission, well-oiled machine that it is, is responsible for enforcing the obligation. It is not the Commission's responsibility, nor its right, to interpret with any flexibility the *acquis*. And on capital movements the *acquis* is now unambiguous."[117] So, too, is its identification as a necessary property of the definition of membership in Europe.

One of the advantages of the EU's process of integration is that it bureaucratizes difficult issues, thereby removing them from the arena of interstate politics and imbuing them with legal legitimacy. So, as Forsberg described the Commission's role, "In the negotiations to accede to the EU we are not to change what has been accomplished."[118] In other words, Europe's fundamental definition as a terrain of free capital is now, to borrow from the French, a fait accompli.

Global financial markets are *global* primarily because the process of European financial integration became open and uniformly liberal. By the end of the 1980s the integration of European capital markets was synonymous with globalization. Given the history of European integration and the persistent protectionism of Europe in other issue areas, it is not difficult to recognize the myriad ways in which it might have been otherwise.

The bargains struck among European governments—but primarily among French and German policymakers—ensured that the EU was central to the global financial system, rather than on its periphery. French policymakers in Paris and Brussels sought to enhance the influence of European institutions by building the capacity and competence of the organizations that govern European integration. Having given up on French mastery of the arena of financial internationalization, Delors, Mitterrand, and Lamy intended for an organized European voice to manage globalization. Ad hoc globalization might thereby be organized, with authority located in Paris, Brussels, and Frankfurt in addition to New York, Washington, and London.

German policymakers found the European embrace of openness comfortable, for it mirrored their own longstanding commitment to financial liberalism. With the exception of Germany's reluctant regulation of capital inflows as the Bretton Woods exchange-rate system collapsed, the German position since the late 1940s and early 1950s had been unambiguously liberal. Formulated against the putative lessons of the manipulative currency practices of Nazi Germany, the German government and the Bundesbank committed themselves to the depoliticization of money, a process that required capital liberalization as well. German monetary and exchange-rate policies always had to meet the test of the market, and German negotiators insisted that European policies would be tested as well.

The consequence of this French-German bargain was a European financial system that was in principle the most liberal the world had ever known. The independence of the European Central Bank was protected by an intergovernmental treaty, not a mere law that might be overturned by a parliamentary majority. European governments were obliged to liberalize capital movements to and from every other country in the world. With one arena organized, and thereby mastered, many of the same European policymakers—French and German—turned their attention to other parts of the international monetary system.

CHAPTER 5

Privilege and Obligation:
The OECD and Its Code
of Liberalization

C'est l'expérience qui dégagera les lois. La connaissance des lois
ne précède jamais l'expérience. (It is experience that yields rules.
Understanding of rules never precedes experience.)

— Antoine de Saint-Exupéry

Membership in the OECD is only for the privileged.[1] Being
part of the OECD signifies that a state has achieved the status of "developed"
country. The organization's headquarters are in the sixteenth arrondisse-
ment of Paris, among the quiet, posh neighborhoods of old money, in the el-
egant Château de la Muette, a site of privilege and power for centuries.

Once a royal hunting lodge, la Muette, as it is known, became the home
of Marguerite de Valois, the first wife of Henri IV and popularly known as
Queen Margot. From 1606 to 1792, la Muette was a part of the royal estates.
King Louis XV entertained his mistresses in the château; Louis XVI honey-
mooned with Marie-Antoinette on its grounds. Upon the completion of a
new château building in 1922, la Muette was the Paris home of Baron Henri
de Rothschild. When Paris was liberated in 1945, the château became the
headquarters of the U.S. Naval Command. Between 1948 and 1961, la
Muette served as the headquarters of the OEEC. The OEEC, which was created to administer the Marshall Plan, was superseded by the OECD when
the United States and Canada joined the eighteen original European members in 1961.[2]

The atmosphere of la Muette is dignified and serene, befitting the membership of one of the most influential, private, and exclusive international
organizations in the world. (For a list of members, see Table 5.1.) As one
senior member of the OECD's Secretariat, whose permanent staff runs the

Table 5.1   OECD Members with Dates of Accession

Member State	Accession
Canada	April 10, 1961
United States	April 12, 1961
United Kingdom	May 2, 1961
Denmark	May 30, 1961
Iceland	June 5, 1961
Norway	July 4, 1961
Turkey	August 2, 1961
Spain	August 3, 1961
Portugal	August 4, 1961
France	August 7, 1961
Ireland	August 17, 1961
Belgium	September 13, 1961
(West) Germany	September 27, 1961
Greece	September 27, 1961
Sweden	September 28, 1961
Switzerland	September 28, 1961
Austria	September 29, 1961
Netherlands	November 13, 1961
Luxembourg	December 7, 1961
Italy	March 29, 1962
Japan	April 28, 1964
Finland	January 28, 1969
Australia	June 7, 1971
New Zealand	May 29, 1973
Mexico	May 18, 1994
Czech Republic	December 21, 1995
Hungary	May 7, 1996
Poland	November 22, 1996
Korea	December 12, 1996
Slovakia	December 14, 2000

Source: "Ratification of the Convention on the OECD," available at
www.oecd.org/document/58/0,2340,en_2649_201185_1889402_1_1_1_1,00.html

organization, informally described it, the OECD is a "gentleman's club," where "finance ministers drink and share their problems." Despite the inevitable hierarchy among members of any such club, the most commonly used word, by far, in la Muette is "peer." Mutual respect is the rule.

The privileges of membership in the OECD are substantial. Some benefits are subtle: the organization is the repository of an extraordinary amount of expert knowledge and country experience on a wide range of policy issues, particularly those related to macroeconomics. Although the effects are difficult to quantify, members value highly their ability to learn from the experiences of their peers.

The OECD is also composed of norms and rules that provide the institutional infrastructure for the economic relations among members. The vast majority of trade and capital flows in the world economy occur among OECD members. Despite all of the hyperbole about financial globalization, nearly 90 percent of the world's foreign direct investment originates in OECD countries, and nearly 70 percent of all foreign direct investment flows into OECD countries. Although the estimates of shorter-term flows are elusive and unreliable, it is fair to conclude that an even greater proportion of portfolio capital also flows within the institutional framework of la Muette's norms and rules. The financial globalization of the past twenty years has been the result of, more than anything else, a vast expansion of capital flows from rich OECD members to other rich OECD members.

Members expect economic responsibility of one another, as do highly internationalized banks. These expectations were embedded in the 1988 Basel Capital Accord, which codifies standards for banks with regard to capital adequacy. The Basel Accord created a relatively unknown but meaningful material benefit for OECD membership. It specifies that banks must keep a risk-weighted 8 percent of their deposits as reserves. Basel's specification of the risks is the critical component. In 1988 the risk weights were set as follows: OECD governments and central banks receive a 0 percent risk weighting; private banks in OECD countries are accorded a 20 percent risk weighting. Non-OECD countries and their banks all receive a 100 percent risk weighting. For more than fifteen years, and during the dramatic expansion of international capital flows during the 1990s, the Basel Accord has thus conferred upon both public and private borrowers based in OECD member countries the benefit of greater access to private international capital markets.

The OECD is not all privileges; membership has its obligations as well, and they are substantial. The most historically consequential obligation of OECD membership is adherence to its Code of Liberalization of Capital Movements.[3] Although the Code of Liberalization allows member governments flexibility in dealing with emergencies and security threats, adherence is nonnegotiable, and the Code's commitments are taken very seriously within la Muette and the national capitals of members. OECD membership thus necessitates the renunciation of other legal rights in the international monetary system. All OECD countries are also members of the IMF, whose rules constitute the legal foundation for the international monetary system. According to Article VI of the IMF's charter, members reserve the right to control capital movements as they see fit. The legal implication of adhering to the OECD's Code, however, is well understood: OECD members have waived the right to control international capital movements. Considering how much of the world's capital flows are among OECD members, the Code is as close as the world has come to global rules for global finance. Until the European Community adopted the 1988 liberalization directive described in Chapter 4, the Code of Liberalization was the only multilateral agreement promoting the liberalization of capital movements. Even still, it is, according to Pierre Poret of the OECD, "the only multilateral instrument promoting comprehensive capital movements liberalization as its primary purpose."[4] The Code followed the progress of OECD members, progressively and gradually including more of the capital account, focusing on long-term flows of direct investment first, and working toward short-term financial flows toward the end of the process.

The Code of Liberalization, despite its importance, is poorly understood. This is partly because of its ambiguous legal status. The Code is not a treaty; it is a collection of binding rules, but most scholars do not consider it to be international law. The Code, technically, is a Decision of the OECD Council, the supreme organ of the organization in which each country has one vote; decisions must be taken unanimously. The Code specifies no explicit sanctions for violating its commitments, although implicitly there is, in the extreme, the threat of expulsion from the organization. Once a country has adhered to the Code and joined the organization, there are no material benefits of increased compliance. "We don't have a stick," explains Rinaldo Pecchioli of the Secretariat. "We don't even have a real carrot, other than international recognition that something has been done."[5]

The organization certainly has not sought notoriety. When Raymond Bertrand retired from his senior post within the Secretariat, he wrote about the OEEC's and then OECD's "rules to enlarge the freedom of international financial transactions." Reflecting on the impressive liberalizing progress that had been made under the Code, Bertrand observes that the organization's work was accomplished behind the scenes. "All this was done in confidential meetings and through secret memos," writes Bertrand, "away from the press and from the people most directly affected by government action or inaction in this area: international money managers, traders, investors, and even the general public."[6] This description still applies to current OECD activities more than twenty years later.

For a dozen years the OECD committee responsible for overseeing the Code of Liberalization—the Committee on Capital Movements and Invisible Transactions (CMIT)—was chaired by Henri Chavranski, a member of the French delegation to the OECD. Chavranski, like Delors in Brussels, played a decisive role in the CMIT's embrace of liberal rules during the 1980s. The French delegation to the OECD is staffed by the *Trésor*, which is part of the finance ministry. These dozen years, from 1982 until 1994, overlapped with some of the most decisive events in the history of the financial internationalization of OECD countries and the organization's rules. As Chavranski recalls, "Little by little, the Code and the Committee pushed the liberalization of capital along. Little by little, we questioned and encouraged, and little by little, governments changed their minds."[7] The Code helped to "consolidate liberalization gains made possible by policy shifts in member countries," and served to "entrench the capital opening process via irreversible undertakings by members and to push the process forward on a broad multilateral and non-discriminatory basis."[8]

The story of the expansion of the Code's mandate and its subtle, persistent effects on the liberalization of capital movements among OECD members is one of the most important narratives of globalization. Almost any finance ministry official of an OECD country would emphasize the importance of the Code. Citigroup's Jeffrey Shafer, who spent nearly a decade in the OECD Secretariat before joining the U.S. Treasury, insists, "The Code of Liberalization of Capital Movements played a critical role in enabling globalization."[9] When the IMF began discussing the possibility of amending its Articles to bring the capital account within its jurisdiction, Fund staff frequently commented on the significant influence of the Code.[10] OECD staff members have been circumspect about the Code's place in the history of globalization, but the role is still there to be explored. "Although," Pierre Poret writes, "policy initiatives by individual governments, regional agreements, and market pressures have been the main driving forces behind the liberalization of capital movements, the strengthening of the OECD Codes has undoubtedly hastened the process."[11]

The critical question facing scholars is how to theorize and evaluate the effects of the OECD's Code on the practices of member governments. I propose to build on existing statistical studies of financial globalization and theoretical trends in the field of international political economy, to which I then apply the tools of history and sociology in order to understand how new norms spread among members. Economist Barry Eichengreen and political scientists Beth Simmons and Zachary Elkins have shown, statistically, that financial globalization has proceeded unevenly, and apparently in groups of countries that appear to be related in one way or another. As Eichengreen reports, "Countries are more likely to liberalize when members of their peer group have done so, holding constant other factors."[12] Eichengreen suggests that perhaps policy emulation or signaling is at work, and Simmons and Elkins add the competition for capital to the list of possibilities.[13] But there is also the possibility that peer groups have independent effects, which are captured better with a more sociological approach to the consequences of the norms of membership and the influence of policy dialogue and mutual learning on policy practices.

"We proceeded," according to Chavranski, "by a process of mutual investigation."[14] This mutual investigation exerted subtle, but powerful influences on the policy practices of OECD members. Most important was the influence of the peer review process on the evolution of members' expectations of one another. The OECD is the most consequential group of peers in the international monetary system, and yet we do not have a full understanding of these peers' influence on one another.

In this chapter I explain the influence of what the OECD itself labels "peer pressure" on capital account liberalization among member countries. I also chart the dramatic transformation in the organization's norms and codified rules regarding capital controls during the postwar era. Then I outline the effects of peer pressure on the liberalization of capital movements among members through the 1980s, as well as the accessions of the 1990s. Developed countries—that is, OECD members—no longer have capital controls.

A Sociology of the Capital Account: Peers and the Code

Little in the formal rules of the Code of Liberalization of Capital Movements would hint at its influence on the international monetary system. The Code's mandate has expanded significantly over time, culminating in the 1989 amendment that placed virtually all capital account transactions within the Code's jurisdiction (see Table 5.2). At any particular moment, therefore, the Code's effect on member country practices was limited to its mandate.

The Code consists of two lists of capital account items—List A and List B. More politically sensitive capital account items, such as shorter-term capital

Table 5.2   Selected Amendments to the Code of Liberalization
of Capital Movements

Amendment	Significant effects
Decision of the Council Amending the Code of Liberalisation of Capital Movements (July 28, 1964), C(64)85/FINAL	Liberalization obligations extended to certain long-term capital flows related to foreign direct investment. Distinction between permanent and reversible liberalization obligations introduced.
Decision of the Council Amending the Code of Liberalisation of Capital Movements (February 27, 1973), C(72)188/FINAL	Liberalization obligations extended to operations in collective investment services.
Decision of the Council Amending the Code of Liberalisation of Capital Movements (April 4, 1984), C(83)106/FINAL	Code jurisdiction of foreign direct investment extended to nonresident investors' right of establishment.
Decision of the Council Amending the Code of Liberalisation of Capital Movements and the Code of Liberalisation of Current Invisible Operations (May 10, 1989), C(89)57/FINAL	Code jurisdiction extended to cover virtually all capital account transactions, including short-term capital flows.

Sources: See cited amendments; OECD, *OECD Code of Liberalization of Capital Movements* (Paris: OECD, 2003).

movements, are on List B. Together with the OECD Secretariat, members catalog all the ways in which they do not meet the liberalization obligations of the Code, thereby lodging "reservations" to the Code. Once reservations are withdrawn from the capital account items on List A they cannot be lodged again. Liberalization commitments are therefore ratcheted up over time. List B, for its greater sensitivity, is more flexible; the withdrawal of a reservation need not be permanent. The Code also includes a range of exceptions for reasons of public order and security and serious balance-of-payments difficulties. A member may also adopt a general derogation from the Code, the so-called safety valve.[15] Only five countries—Greece, Iceland, Portugal, Spain, and Turkey—have ever done so, however. Their, and the OECD's, justification for these countries' general derogations was based on their level of development relative to other members. When it came to the capital account, these five came only recently to be considered peers. Finally, the procedural elements of the Code entail a system of notification, periodic examination by other member countries, and consultation within the Committee overseeing the Code.[16] "The basic commitment of the Code," according to Bertrand, "is in effect voluntary, subject only to moral persuasion and pressure from partner countries." The softness of the formal mandate of the Code was the "result of a compromise, when the Code was being drafted twenty years ago, between countries which favored full liberalization and those who believed only in *ad hoc,* individual relaxations of exchange controls."[17]

The Code of Liberalization of Capital was, until the spring of 2004, overseen by the CMIT, which had previously been nicknamed the Invisibles Committee.[18] The CMIT was an influential committee. Composed of representatives from each of the member countries, the CMIT performed a variety of critical tasks.[19] It monitored members' compliance with the Code, hence their recognition as the guardians of the Code. As with several other powerful committees within the OECD, no new member could join the organization without a positive recommendation from the CMIT. The CMIT was itself responsible for considering and drafting revisions to the rules it was supposed to oversee, with these efforts resulting in recommendations to the OECD Council. The Council invariably accepted the CMIT's interpretations and adopted its recommendations.

One of the CMIT's most important activities for disseminating organizational norms among members is also its least appreciated by outside observers: its practice of peer review—in French, *l'examen par les pairs.* Along with the Economic and Development Review Committee, the CMIT pioneered the use of peer review as a tool for promoting compliance within the OECD. The practice of regular peer reviews is now central to virtually every OECD activity, and OECD staff has, remarkably for the first time, begun systematically to explore the analytical foundations for what OECD policymakers consider to be a tried-and-true form of international cooperation.[20]

The generic practice of peer review in the OECD was recently explored by Fabrizio Pagani, a member of the legal staff of the OECD Secretariat. He writes:

> Peer review can be described as the systematic examination and assessment of the performance of a state by other states, with the ultimate goal of helping the reviewed state improve its policymaking, adopt best practices, and comply with established standards and principles. The examination is conducted on a non-adversarial basis, and it relies heavily on mutual trust among the states involved in the review, as well as their shared confidence in the process.[21]

Pagani also emphasizes a number of critical influences on the effectiveness of peer review, including "value sharing."[22] Peer review is supposed to lead to greater compliance through "soft enforcement," dialogue, and mutual learning, which the OECD also describes as "capacity building."[23] Mutual learning and compliance are closely related. "The effectiveness of peer review relies on the influence and persuasion exercised by the peers during the process. This effect is known as 'peer pressure.'"[24] The OECD's experience with peer pressure has benefited, according to Pagani, from the "homogenous membership and the high degree of trust shared among the member countries."[25]

Peer review and peer pressure within the CMIT were the most important vehicles for improving members' compliance with the Code.[26] The OECD recently described the CMIT's experience with peer review and the Code of Liberalization of Capital Movements:

> The OECD approach does not rely on dogma or political negotiation, nor on detailed prescriptive recommendations for policy implementation. Instead, it involves a process of shared, mutually beneficial learning, where both individual and collective stumbling blocks on the path to open markets are inspected and discussed. It has been found that peer pressure in a multilateral setting can provide strong incentives for authorities to undertake policy adjustment. By "benchmarking" domestic regulations and measures against those implemented by peer participants in this process, countries receive guidance and support in the complex policy area of financial liberalization.[27]

Mechanisms

The mechanisms underlying the effectiveness of the CMIT's peer review and peer pressure rely on a wide range of analytical underpinnings. Three of the mechanisms draw on psychology and sociology, while another is firmly rationalist and strategic. The first, and simplest, mechanism is what OECD staff calls "naming and shaming." The effect of shame—of having one's policy shortcomings discussed in a peer group—depends on CMIT members' caring what their peers think of them. National delegations were occasionally tempted to dismiss the exercise, and there were no material constraints on the seriousness, or lack thereof, with which CMIT members approached a review. But in practice members took CMIT reviews quite seriously for many years. "We had strong norms," Chavranski reports. "It was clear that while your country was examined you had to be a good pupil."[28]

Examination and judgment require standards, and thus we come to the second mechanism: defining the boundaries of acceptable behavior for OECD members. Although the Code has its own formal definitions of adherence, in practice the CMIT's interpretation of the Code is authoritative. Indeed, according to a number of OECD staff members, CMIT members spent the vast majority of their time together arguing about what constituted compliance—that is, whether a specific policy or law required a reservation to the Code or not. The Secretariat would note that such a policy or law warranted a reservation. The country being reviewed would then have a choice to make: it could accept that a reservation would have to be lodged and then attempt to outline the logic of the restriction to the satisfaction of members; or, alternatively, it could insist that the policy or law was not in fact in violation of the Code. In either situation, however, the CMIT's discussions focused on the meaning of conformity to a liberal standard.

Conformity for the CMIT did not imply uniformity. That is, the CMIT's review of a member was also embedded in shared knowledge about the country's ability to meet the Code's demanding obligations. "Flexibility was important to our success," according to Chavranski.

> We distinguished between liberation and liberalization, and we urged the latter. We did not ask the same from each country. In writing the CMIT's recommendations we always had to be sure to be realistic, to find an equilibrium between what the CMIT wanted and what was politically possible.[29]

The staff of the Secretariat speaks of the "genius" of the Code's design: a "clean, clear" obligation to liberalize, but not all members had to undertake it immediately. Still, the obligation is defined as a goal for all. "Our process encouraged dialogue and learning," elaborates Chavranski. "The Secretariat would send a mission to find out where it could get more liberalization. Then the delegation would present to the CMIT what it could and could not do. We would go back and forth. It was a complex game."[30]

The third mechanism is the combination of experience sharing and learning. Although OECD finance ministry and central bank officials certainly would have been aware of the broad patterns of their colleagues' experiences with capital account restrictions and liberalizations, the peer review process was incredibly detailed, recounting both the logic of the restrictions and the logic of removing them. This process also played, according to Shafer, a critical role in "developing a common understanding among governments about how the world works."[31]

Learning in this context was similar to a process of socialization for new members of the CMIT. The story of Jan Nipstad, a member of the Swedish delegation, is particularly illuminating, in part because of the instrumental role Nipstad would play in rewriting the Code in 1989. Nipstad first took part in CMIT discussions in 1974, when he sought to defend Swedish capital controls to the skeptical committee. Nipstad emphasizes that the influence of peers' accounts of their own similar experiences were both instructive and reassuring. The effect was, according to Nipstad, "quite powerful," forcing him to reconsider his most firmly held assumptions about the necessity of particular capital account regulations and the dangers posed by liberalization. Nipstad and the other members of the Swedish delegation paid particular attention to the experience of Denmark, whose situation, they felt, most closely resembled their own. Nipstad recalls:

> Eventually I was convinced by my colleagues on the committee. I learned from their experiences, and returned to Stockholm to share the lessons of our OECD peers. Some of the deepest fears of the Swedish government about capital account liberalization were, it turned out, unfounded. An ardent proponent of controls, I came to embrace the cause of liberalization. Back in Stockholm, however, they began to worry that I was too liberal.[32]

Shafer recalls how influential it was for national policymakers to attempt to justify their restrictions, only to be rebuffed by other policymakers who had already abandoned one mode of thinking for another. "Exposing people to different ways of thinking can be quite powerful," Shafer observes, "particularly in Europe where the intellectual traditions of the governments' elites can be quite insular."[33]

One CMIT practice was particularly useful for enhancing each of these psychological and sociological mechanisms underlying the effectiveness of peer review. At peer review only, the delegation from the country being reviewed was supposed to represent its home government's position. At all other moments CMIT members were to act as "independent experts." On the few occasions when a member would slip, referring to the preferences of his or her finance ministry or central bank, the CMIT chair would inevitably remind the member of the irrelevance of those views.[34] This mode of interacting had a number of interesting effects. One was that it heightened the scrutiny of each peer review. Without having to worry about being accused of living in a glass house, all CMIT members—even from countries with relatively illiberal capital accounts—were enabled, even emboldened, to question their peers aggressively.

This practice also encouraged CMIT members to emphasize their commitment to the committee, the Code, and one another at the expense of their roles in national policymaking bodies. Another recollection from Nipstad suggests this effect. During his conversion to the cause of liberalization, Nipstad notes how influential, and indeed transformative, it was to adopt the perspective of a "Guardian of the Code" when reviewing other members. For those peer reviews Nipstad was "no longer a member of the Swedish delegation," but instead an independent expert whose role it was to encourage further progress toward the "goals of liberalization enshrined in the Code." In this way, Nipstad insists, "One comes to identify with the committee, and with its purposes." New CMIT members were rapidly "indoctrinated."[35] When Nipstad left the OECD to return to the Riksbank in Stockholm, he wrote Henri Chavranski a letter in which he reflected on his own personal transformation as part of the story of the committee. Nipstad recalls,

> I came to the Committee an ardent believer in the usefulness of exchange controls as an additional support for well-balanced economic policies . . . But I could of course not avoid to be contaminated by the liberal spirit which progressively came to dominate the Committee.[36]

The extraordinary continuity in both the Secretariat staff and the CMIT's members heightened the degree of identification with the purposes of liberalization and maintained it over time. That lack of turnover, according to Nipstad, "created an atmosphere of colleagueship and trust."[37]

Fourth and finally, the rationalist mechanism of peer review is the most amenable to empirical scrutiny. OECD peer pressure enabled the reform agenda of those being reviewed. In the language used by the OECD Secretariat, officials would come to Paris to have their reform agendas "blessed by the CMIT," and then return home to their national capitals to relate the opprobrium of the committee and the necessity of "keeping up with our OECD peers." In this sense, OECD staff frequently noted that peer pressure was most effective when government representatives were looking for international support for further liberalization. As Shafer describes, this influence might play itself out in several ways, often by reinforcing the position of a policymaker who is already proliberalization. The liberalizer could strengthen his or her hand in a debate within the cabinet by returning from la Muette with a few possible stories, such as, "We are under a great deal of pressure in Paris; we look like fools." Another claim involved bargaining. "If we do not go along with this," the argument would usually run, "we will never get international support for our priorities."[38]

Moments

There are also three distinct moments in which OECD peer pressure can be understood to have influenced policy. The first is when OECD members contemplated further liberalization of their capital accounts. The influence of peer pressure was always greatest for countries on the verge of taking some new step, "wondering whether it should take this step into cold water," and hoping to "learn from the experiences of peers."[39]

A second moment occurs when an OECD member considers introducing new capital account restrictions, and, thus, lodging new reservations. An OECD member in this situation must come to Paris to justify the restriction, and the CMIT then has an opportunity to question the policy and voice its opinion. This process encourages policymakers to assess all options, and to look for the least damaging way to introduce a restriction—that is, leading to the fewest number of new reservations. "Without a crisis," explains Pecchioli, "a country would not dare."[40]

The third possible moment occurs in the process of negotiating membership itself, before peer review even begins. Governments may not apply to the OECD for membership. The OECD Council, rather, invites new members, and then asks for reports from each of its committees. A favorable report from the CMIT was always essential for the Council to accept a new member. The CMIT therefore had a veto right during this process, for if it issued a negative report a country could not join. The process of producing a report was iterative. The CMIT questioned prospective members, urging them to liberalize further. Liberalization, it seemed, always was the right answer to the committee's questions. The report was written only when it was clear that the outcome would be favorable. It was at these moments that the CMIT had the greatest leverage over policies.

The Evolution of the Code

The Code's evolution followed the shifts in attitudes among its member governments about the desirability and legitimacy of regulating international capital flows. Both the Code's evolution and the process of liberalization were gradual, progressive, and sequenced.[41] The early years of the OECD's Code, as with that of the OEEC, were accompanied by the CMIT's debates on interpretation and jurisdiction that indicated a commitment to long-term capital flows, particularly foreign direct investment, and a deep skepticism of short-term capital flows. According to Bertrand, the omission of short-term flows from the Code's obligations "stems from the recognition that short-term financial transactions, in particular those initiated by banks, can pose problems for the management of money and of exchange reserves, especially under fixed or managed exchange rates."[42]

The Committee for Invisible Transactions began the process of amending the Code by evaluating the logic of capital account restrictions. In 1963 the Committee emphasized members' concerns about the balance of payments, of their "autonomy of monetary policy" (particularly for the three Scandinavian countries and Austria), and strategic selection of inward direct investment (particularly for Greece, Spain, and Turkey).[43] In 1964 the Committee took stock of the positions of OECD members. It divided members into four groups: countries that did not apply exchange controls (Canada, the United States, Switzerland, Belgium, the Netherlands, and Luxembourg); other members in the EEC and Austria, whose aim was full liberalization but that still maintained restrictions; the Scandinavian countries, the United Kingdom, and Ireland, which aimed at progressive, but not necessarily total, liberalization; and the "developing countries," Greece, Iceland, Portugal, Spain, and Turkey.[44]

At that time the committee reported "widespread agreement among Members on the need for complete and early liberalization of direct investments."[45] Capital flows that might affect the practice of domestic monetary policy, however, or that might otherwise reduce the control of policymakers remained controversial. The committee referred to these as "conjunctural" reasons for controlling capital, based on a "desire to restrain foreign capital from disrupting the gradual and orderly evolution of the domestic economy or distorting the economic development plans through massive and sporadic injection (or withdrawal) of foreign capital at inopportune moments."[46]

Hot money, thus, was still the dominant worry of OECD policymakers. As Pierre Poret reports, in 1964 the Council

> took an explicit decision not to extend the scope of the Code to short-term operations on the grounds that their liberalization would make their balances of payments vulnerable to shifts in market participants' sentiments and compromise the independence of their economic policies, in particular undermine exchange rate objectives set out within the framework of the Bretton Woods system of fixed but adjustable exchange rates.[47]

The OECD later reemphasized this perspective. "Certain kinds of flows are excluded from the Code's coverage," the OECD noted in 1971, "which means that governments have not committed themselves to abstain from regulating them." The logic in 1971 was much the same as it had been a decade earlier. "Short-term financial credits and loans are specifically omitted, as are the buying and selling of short-term treasury bills and other short-term money market securities," the review continued, "because they are the vehicle for hot money and because control of such flows is often considered necessary to buttress domestic monetary policy."[48]

The Code was first amended, modestly, in 1964, after these discussions about the extension of liberalization obligations to other capital flows. Only some additional long-term capital flows related to foreign direct investment were made part of the Code's liberalization obligations. It was also in 1964 that the A and B lists were created as a compromise to distinguish liberalization obligations that were permanent from those that were sensitive enough to be considered reversible.[49] The OECD also publicly elaborated the reasons for holding members to different standards with respect to the Code. "Greece, Iceland, and Turkey are completely exempted from their liberalization obligations," according to the OECD in 1971, "because of overall economic and financial problems related to their degree of development."[50] Following the 1964 amendment, the United States, among the more liberal members of the OECD, urged further liberalization, particularly of long-term investment. As Shafer reports, "The United States pressed liberalization in the OECD in the 1960s."[51] With the exception of Germany, the United States found few other proponents for further liberalization.

In 1973, the Code was amended, again modestly, to include operations in collective investment services.[52] This amendment took place against the backdrop of a collapsing international monetary system, with the end of generalized fixing. The OECD members that embraced further capital account liberalization included "both countries that considered a floating exchange rate as an essential element and countries that saw a commitment to fixed exchange rates as a cornerstone of their strategies."[53] By the early 1980s committee members were discussing means to strengthen the Code's stance on foreign direct investment.[54] Consensus was reached quickly, and in 1984 the Code's jurisdiction of foreign direct investment was amended to include the right of establishment for nonresident investors.

Already, however, a number of OECD members had begun to dismantle their capital control regimes on their own: the United Kingdom in 1979, Japan in 1980, Australia and New Zealand in 1983–1984, and the Netherlands in 1986. Most dramatically, the Mitterrand U-turn in France led to a significant relaxation of capital controls. The 1980s, according to a number of OECD papers and publications, ushered in a "new era in policy attitudes."[55] Partly this was an ideological shift toward a renewed liberalism. According to Stephany Griffith-Jones, Ricardo Gottschalk, and Xavier Cirera, "gradualism soon began to wane as a result of a major ideological shift towards greater liberalization in the late 1970s; OECD member countries no longer followed changes in the Code but rather anticipated them."[56] Also at work was a new policy paradigm among OECD finance ministers and central bankers. "Priority objectives ascribed to monetary policies in OECD countries converged towards achieving long-term price stability, and, to this end, building up credibility-enhancing mechanisms," observed Poret.

> Capital controls, which had in the past aimed at preserving the ability of monetary policy to exploit a possible trade-off between inflation and unemployment, did not fit into this new policy paradigm and risked to distract the authorities from the essential task of maintaining sound and credible economic policies.[57]

These sea changes set the stage for the most dramatic amendment to the Code: the inclusion of short-term capital movements, the so-called hot money that had been left out of the Code for so long.

Hot Money and the Code: 1989

The late 1980s was a period of profound change in the OECD—in la Muette as well as in the members' capitals. The legal foundations of central bank independence were spreading among those OECD members that had not had them in place.[58] A decisive shift away from policy discretion among OECD countries was under way. "What the CMIT experienced during my tenure," Chavranski recalls, "was a pendulum swing in sentiment about markets."[59]

In November 1984, shortly after the Code was amended to include the right of establishment for foreign investors, the Committee on Capital Markets and Invisible Transactions and the Committee on Financial Markets agreed to form a Joint Working Group on Banking and Related Financial Services to reconsider the place of short-term capital movements in the Code of Liberalization. "It was exactly the right timing to form a working group on short-term capital movements," according to Nipstad, who was to become chair of the group in 1986.[60] The year 1984 was a moment of relative calm in international financial markets, and many OECD members enjoyed strong balance of payments positions. Also, Nipstad recalls, the internationalization of firms made it "damn difficult to get foreign exchange regulations watertight. The situation in countries that had not liberalized, such as Sweden, was that multinational firms did what they wanted, and only the smaller firms were restricted. So, by the 1980s, many of us saw no advantages, only drawbacks, to capital controls."[61]

Akira Iida, a member of the Japanese delegation, was originally chosen to be chair of the working group, in part because Japan's capital account regime was more restrictive than its peers. According to Nipstad, this was simply good bureaucratic politics, for every chair would like his or her group to achieve a good result. All CMIT member countries were represented in the working group. When Iida was rotated out of the OECD by the Japanese government in 1986, Nipstad took over.

In the first several years, the working group failed to reach a consensus on the desirability of what would amount to a Code of Liberalization that obliged OECD members to liberalize essentially all capital account transactions. "Views differed over how far short-term operations should be liberalized," according to one of the group's first draft reports, "especially the liberalization of money market instruments."[62] After many discussions, "no consensus emerged on this issue" of short-term capital movements.[63] Later meetings, in the summer of 1986, revealed that the traditional argument for controlling short-term capital movements remained foremost in the minds of defenders of illiberal capital accounts. "The main justification," noted the working group, "for excluding such operations from coverage initially was that the level of development of money markets varied considerably from country to country and that short-term capital controls may be needed to assure national monetary independence."[64]

These discussions were, apparently, not heated. "There was no strong opposition to the expansion of the Code," according to Chavranski. "A few countries were reluctant, but there was no big fight. The idea was accepted."[65] A few members were more active, among them the United States, the United Kingdom, the Netherlands, Belgium, Germany, and Switzerland. Several others sat "quietly, and mostly took notes," including Denmark, Finland, Iceland, Norway, Spain, and Turkey.[66]

By the late 1980s, the United States was no longer among the most liberal of OECD members, nor was it even an enthusiastic proponent of a newly liberal Code. As in EC negotiations, France played a critical role mediating between the groups, and indeed it was a reversal of the French position that made the OECD's and EU's rewriting of the rules of capital possible.[67] Chavranski, as chair, played a critical role in forging consensus among the OECD's enthusiastic liberalizers and those members for which a new obligation to free all capital movements would extend well beyond their policy options in the foreseeable future. Thus it was Chavranski's CMIT, with the support of the French and other European governments, that formulated the new rules. And it was after the 1988 capital liberalization directive in Brussels that the Europeans came fully to embrace an amendment to the Code. As Shafer recalls, "I often advised the Treasury not to push or be especially vocal in OECD debates about liberalization. Just be quiet and let the impetus come from the Secretariat and the Europeans who are supportive."[68] Certainly the United States did not oppose the proposed amendment to the Code, instead welcoming the liberal zeal of European countries that had long stymied U.S. efforts toward more freely flowing international capital markets.

In 1988 the working group offered its conclusions to the CMIT's full membership. The most important of these was its recommendation: "The liberalization obligations of the Capital Movements Code should be extended to encompass almost all short-term operations, on either List A or List B of the Code."[69] Indeed, the group suggested that "as far as possible, maturity distinctions in the Code should be eliminated."[70] The rest of the working group's document offers a fascinating insight into the emergence of the norm of full capital mobility in the OECD.

The critical analytical step indeed revolved around maturity distinctions in capital flows as the basis for regulation:

> Both the defense of existing exchange rates in the face of hot money flows
> and the belief in national monetary independence depended on certain ex-
> plicit or implicit assumptions about the state of the financial markets at the
> time and the capacity of monetary authorities to achieve their policy objec-
> tives. In particular, it seems to have been assumed that a sharp distinction
> was warranted between the long-term markets, which were denominated
> by basic considerations related to investment, and the short-term markets,
> which, though more volatile, were subject to fairly direct control by the
> monetary authorities, at least domestically.[71]

Along with flexible exchange rates, the group suggested that "financial markets have developed to the point that the distinction between short-term and long-term financial markets appears to be far less meaningful than in the past."[72]

The group emphasized that its conclusions applied solely to the privileged OECD club. "It has always been assumed, at least tacitly, that the obligations of the OECD Codes," noted the Group, "which apply to a relatively homogenous group of the world's most advanced economies, would be stronger than those concluded in other international bodies whose membership includes developing and centrally-planned economies."[73]

The working group, furthermore, was careful to circumscribe the new obligations, as was always true when the Code of Liberalization was amended. "The obligation to liberalize under the Code is neither immediate nor unqualified," reassured the authors of the report. This is where the function of the CMIT as a discussion forum becomes so crucial for the advance of liberalization. The CMIT engages the authorities of each country in an ongoing dialogue, but it is a dialogue necessarily premised on the objective of progressive liberalization, in which expectations are adapted to the particular circumstances of each member country, its unique economic and financial conditions, and its balance of payments situation.[74]

The working group offered the CMIT both a description of their material reality and what the members considered to be the appropriate interpretation of their material facts. "The development of dynamic internationalized financial markets was basically to be regarded as a positive phenomenon and, in any case, as an accomplished fact of life."[75] The group was also, however, careful to adopt a historical perspective on the potential arrival of hot money within the CMIT's cherished Code; clearly this was not a step to be taken lightly. "The view that controls on short-term operations should also be subject to the obligation of progressive liberalization was much more recent," with most members even of the EC having only just accepted the idea in principle.[76] Some observers have inferred that the Code simply followed policy changes already under way in member states, hence their dismissal of the Code's importance. In fact, the proposals to include hot money among members' obligations preceded the consensus of the members, whose experience and progress were highly varied. "While the trend throughout the OECD area is unmistakably towards liberalization," observed the group, "the degree of progress already achieved varies considerably from country to country."[77]

After the working group reported to the CMIT, the committee began its deliberations about the first major revisions to the Code since the 1960s. The

CMIT's members considered this opportunity historic as well. It was, indeed, opportune, particularly because many of them had not fully liberalized, but were prepared to commit to it as a new obligation. The CMIT reasoned:

> Bearing in mind that such a wide-ranging review of the Code's provisions on banking and financial services is unlikely to be undertaken again for some considerable time, the Group considered it essential to be forward-looking. It therefore sought agreement to define the liberalization obligations in this area as broadly as possible. The Group recognized that not all Member countries would be able to meet the new obligations immediately.[78]

The fully liberal CMIT had traveled a great distance since the 1960s, when the last (and only) review of the Code had taken place. The traditional distinction between short- and long-term capital had broken down. The line between banking and capital market activity had become much less sharp. Euromarkets had grown spectacularly. Most consequentially, capital controls were no longer the rule. Indeed, capital account regulations were increasingly the exception, at least among OECD members, the developed countries. It was not, of course, that OECD countries had been unaware of the consequences of capital account liberalization for their autonomy. "Policy attitudes have moved decisively towards the goal of liberalization and many OECD countries have already taken major steps in that direction," observed the CMIT. "Policymakers are aware," the CMIT continued, "that they have somewhat less autonomy under a regime of free capital movements, but they are increasingly willing to accept this in a world more reliant than ever on international cooperation."[79] The consensus that the working group helped forge within the CMIT, and ultimately in the OECD Council as well, was remarkable for its intellectual distance from the consensus of the original authors of the Code of Liberalization.

A new standard of appropriate behavior was agreed to in 1989. What was ultimately at stake was the relationship between capital mobility as a regulatory or a constitutive norm. Capital account liberalization was becoming the usual behavior of OECD members. In 1989 OECD members agreed that an open capital account was one of the defining—the constituting, the proper—practices of a "developed" country. "While member countries are clearly at different stages of liberalization," reasoned the CMIT, "they now share the view that the complete liberalization of capital movements is a proper goal."[80] Louis Pauly understood the meaning of the OECD's amendment as an attempt "to replace the formal legal right to control capital movements with a new right. The effort to codify the norm of capital mobility continues."[81] The OECD's Robert Ley offered this interpretation of 1989: "Government attitudes have shifted decisively in favor of developed capital and money markets domestically and increased freedom for international operations."[82]

By the end of the decade, then, the presumption among OECD countries that capital controls would be the norm was turned on its head. As Lex Rieffel, an influential member of the U.S. delegation, observed, one could "speak of exchange controls as an anachronism without being considered a heretic or a visionary."[83] To those who were most intimately involved in the process, the new obligations seemed natural.

It took the Secretariat nearly three years, working with the member delegations, to determine the reservations that would need to be lodged vis-à-vis the new obligations. The process complete in 1992, the OECD Council approved the reservations. Two-thirds of the reservations were lodged by Greece, Ireland, Portugal, and Spain.

The 1990s Accessions

Until the 1990s there had been only four accessions to the OECD since 1961: Japan in 1964, Finland in 1969, Australia in 1971, and New Zealand in 1973. Between 1994 and 2000 six more countries joined the OECD. The policymakers in all six countries approached their candidacy with anticipation and pride. OECD membership symbolized their graduation from developing-country to developed-country status. Mexico, the first new member, was obliged to withdraw from the Group of 77 (G77), the most influential group of developing countries in the international economy. Mexico had been a prominent and founding member of the G77. G77 and OECD members almost always, however, found themselves on opposite sides in negotiating the international infrastructure of the world economy.

The context in which the OECD welcomed its newest members differed fundamentally from that of the last accessions, and even more from the founding moments of the late 1950s and early 1960s. The international economy had been transformed. The IMF no longer oversaw a system of fixed exchange rates. Trade flows had been liberalized. International financial markets had grown enormous. The middle of the 1990s was, by many measures, the very high point of the recent era of globalization. The OECD itself was positioned differently relative to international financial markets. The experience of OECD members with capital account liberalization had been gradual and sequenced, and the Code's obligations had evolved along with the practices of members and norms of the club. The Code of Liberalization that new members encountered during the 1990s was no longer the set of rules that privileged foreign direct investment over short-term capital flows. The CMIT now ruled hot money as well.

The accession negotiations between the CMIT and the six prospective members therefore raised a critical question: Which standards should the CMIT apply to new members? Two possible answers were offered for discussion. A few members suggested that the acceding countries should follow the historical path of the current members on their way to capital account liberalization. New members would, in other words, be encouraged to liberalize slowly, sequencing their liberalizing efforts over several years.

The counterargument, which won the day, was composed of the OECD's prevailing norms. The Secretariat articulated the case in late September 1994. "By the end of December 1994, when Iceland will have removed its remaining capital controls, none of the 25 OECD Member countries will maintain exchange controls," the Secretariat's staff observed. The report continued:

> Therefore, a substantially higher level of liberalization of current and capital operations in the what were called the Partners in Transition (PIT) countries in central Europe and Korea would be required if today's OECD *average* standards were to be achieved. The new applicants themselves would have to be aware that their accession progress would be greatly facilitated if they were to take substantial additional liberalization steps before joining the Organization.[84]

Jeffrey Shafer was the U.S. Treasury official responsible for formulating and conveying U.S. positions toward the OECD accession candidates. "We decided," Shafer recalls, "that new members ought to meet the prevailing OECD standards for adherence to the Code. We felt that if this were not something a country was prepared to do, then the country was also not ready for OECD membership."[85] Rieffel, a member of the U.S. delegation, had some years earlier reasoned that "a good test of whether a non-member country is ready to join the 'club' is to see if it is prepared to accept the obligations of these Codes. (The only other important test is the country's commitment to a democratic political system.)"[86] Because the obligations of the

Codes had changed, so, too, the logic went, had the standards of membership.[87]

Of course, the CMIT's encouragement of the minimization of acceding countries' reservations was more easily implemented than the accompanying prudential regulations that the CMIT recommended. Liberating capital is a more straightforward task than building the institutional infrastructure of efficient financial markets. Three of the acceding countries experienced capital account crises within a year or so of accession. "Domestic political constraints," the OECD's Eva Thiel observed, "as well as inertia in the legislative process, prevented the new entrants from introducing the full range of improvements to corporate and public governance practices and to the predictability and transparency of rules and regulations recommended by the CMIT."[88]

As is often the case in exclusive clubs, the sponsorship and strong recommendation of current members can be decisive. It was widely known, for example, that the United States had insisted on rapid negotiations toward Mexican membership in a speech Treasury Secretary Lloyd Bentsen gave in Paris when the North American Free Trade Agreement (NAFTA) was complete. Similarly, Japan was seen as a champion of South Korea's membership. The Americans and Europeans together enthusiastically embraced the four PIT countries: Poland, Hungary, the Czech Republic, and Slovakia. The U.S. delegation, in collaboration with the U.S. government departments in Washington, compiled "road maps" for these four central European countries. Although these documents are not official standards for OECD membership, they reveal a great deal about how one of the OECD's most influential members viewed the criteria.

The U.S. delegation identified four "screens" to gauge readiness for membership: "General philosophy: Economic growth and efficiency and individual liberty"; the "Practice of the Market: Implementation of the OECD's philosophy, sticking to it, and demonstrating performance"; "OECD-specific: Committee review of policies and issues as applicants participate as observers"; and "Commitment and Adherence to OECD Instruments." The delegation's assessment of the standard to be applied by the CMIT with respect to the Code of Liberalization emphasized that current account restrictions should be eliminated. Capital account restrictions should be reduced "to a minimum" (or, in an alternate wording, "to the maximum extent possible").[89]

Thus, although the United States had typically played a passive role in the codification of a norm of capital mobility in 1989, when it came time for the organization to exert its leverage in central Europe, U.S. policymakers saw the OECD as useful leverage for its policy priorities. Clearly the United States had not systematically sought to empower or employ the OECD, but when such an occasion happened to present itself, U.S. policymakers did not hesitate to promote liberalization.

The accession negotiations breathed new life into the CMIT. Just when it seemed that the CMIT's work was done—that OECD members had resolved to liberalize their capital accounts completely—a new round of illiberal countries presented themselves to the committee in search of the knowledge and expectations of the developed world. Some scholars have attempted to judge the character of the negotiations from the outcomes—namely, that the new members lodged very few reservations and none applied a general derogation. "Since this recourse was still available," Griffith-Jones and her colleagues observe, "it suggests that they indeed faced considerable pressure to accept stringent requirements concerning liberalization of their capital account as a requirement for membership."[90] Archival research and interviews reveal that this view is, with the exception of Slovakia, generally correct. "Pressure," however, is not the most accurate way to describe the influence of the OECD. The OECD certainly set liberal standards, but acceding countries were not forced to meet them. Rather, they were eager to adopt the very norms that the OECD sought to disseminate. The process of diffusion was largely cooperative.

The CMIT's experiences with the Czech Republic (1995), South Korea (1996), and Slovakia (2000) represent well the range of outcomes of OECD accession negotiations. The discussions with Prague were hardly negotiations; they were practically instructions. The Czech authorities were eager to please the other OECD members, and to learn the constitutive norms of membership in the developed country club. The negotiations with South Korea, by contrast, were difficult, even occasionally tense as the authorities in Seoul sought to maintain as much autonomy from Paris as possible and to do the minimum required to enter the club. Years later the Secretariat's officials still expressed frustration at the intransigence of the South Koreans, and speculated that the Japanese delegation had coached their east Asian neighbors in how to make life difficult for the CMIT. The Slovaks, by the time they joined in 2000, found a wholly changed CMIT, one made nervous by the financial crises of the 1990s and the weak banking systems on which these crises wreaked havoc. Whereas the CMIT seems to have pushed for any liberalization it could get in the other five acceding countries, the Slovaks were encouraged to reconsider their rapid liberalization, as well as to ensure the suitability of their prudential regulations and the soundness of their banks.

Mexico

The new accessions began with Mexico, which set an incredibly high standard for compliance with the Code of Liberalization of Capital Movements. Acceptance of the Code's obligations was, of course, an "essential condition of Mexico's accession to membership."[91] The critical negotiation concerned Mexico's extension of NAFTA's more liberal obligations to the other OECD members.[92] Mexican authorities agreed to this logic in principle, and the negotiations were quite brief as a result. "Altogether, Mexico has accepted a level of commitments broadly comparable to those of the existing membership," observed Christian Schricke, "and significantly higher than those required from previous new members, because of the increase in the scope and number of OECD instruments over the past twenty years and the narrow scope of its reservations to those instruments."[93] The Secretariat's interpretation of the Mexican experience, when it began to coordinate the CMIT's assessments of the other prospective members, was that Mexico's adherence to the Code would be the new reference point for future members. According to the Secretariat:

> The conditions on which Mexico has adhered to the OECD instruments set a high overall standard in terms of compliance with the general principles of cooperation, transparency, non-discrimination, and stand-still with respect to international capital movements and trade in services. This standard will provide an essential reference point when the Committees come to consider compliance of new candidates with the principles of the Code.[94]

Although few can claim to have foreseen the financial crisis that engulfed Mexico only six months later, the Secretariat was surprisingly optimistic about Mexico's prospects for sustained capital inflows. "Capital inflows in recent years may be considered much more stable," according to this optimism, "than they were during the period preceding the 1982 debt crisis."[95]

Czech Republic

The pursuit of prestige and recognition drove Czech policymakers to liberalize the country's capital account very quickly during 1994 and 1995. When a currency crisis soon followed in May 1997, accompanied by the bursting of a domestic credit bubble, some Czech leaders, former prime minister Vaclav Klaus among them, searched the political scene for the most blameworthy parties. Fingers were pointed at the Czech National Bank (CNB), and ultimately the OECD, whose approval was an important motivation. "In the clash about excessively fast liberalization on the one hand and effects on financial opening on the other," the CNB's Oldřich Dědek observes, "holding the balance was the issue of what was seen as prestigious membership of the Czech Republic in the club of OECD countries. Such recognition for the success of the transformation acted as a catalyst of liberalization efforts."[96]

Prestige, indeed, seems to have been one of the most important benefits central European policymakers saw in the privileged OECD club. For the transition countries, an eagerness to be seen as having rejoined the "developed," "capitalist," and eventually "European" world pervaded political life. As the CNB's Petr Procházka recalls, recognition came in the form of clubs. "We sought the approval of the IMF, OECD, and EU, and during the middle of the 1990s the OECD was the most important of these," Procházka explains. "There was a kind of race to be first into the OECD. We were prepared to follow all OECD advice."[97] The dominant metaphor, pedantic as it sounds, was that of a teacher-pupil relationship. In the early 1990s there was a competition among transition countries to determine "who was the best pupil of the developed market economies."[98] Thus, there would be "prestige" for the "first member of the OECD club and, related to club membership, the first to external currency convertibility."[99]

The Czechs' drive for prestige and international acceptance made them willing to undertake any initiation rite of liberalization that the club required of them. Capital liberalization was pursued for the club doors it would open, with scant consideration given to its soundness as national policy. What was good for developed countries would be good for the Czechs because, after all, the Czechs were developed, as membership would prove. Dědek recalls the "determination to integrate the Czech economy into the family of developed market economies. This will call for the adoption of norms of behavior that are common in these economies. The unfettered mobility that capital flows may at present enjoy is surely one of them."[100]

Some may disagree with the clarity of the causal logic. Dědek puts it simply: "We pursued capital account liberalization in order to become an OECD member."[101]

The CMIT's requirements were strict, but seeking to join was strictly voluntary: no one forced the Czechs to seek the committee's approval. The Czechs' sense of what was required of them to be recognized as a developed market economy was straightforward. "The widespread view during the early 1990s was that more liberal was better," observes Dědek. "The OECD was quite adamant."[102] The view from the Ministry of Finance was the same. "The OECD encouraged us to liberalize as much as possible," recalls a senior official. "The members of the CMIT were very strict; their requirements were very high. The CMIT was extremely proliberalization."[103] The CMIT did not force the Czechs to liberalize; rather, the Czechs forced themselves to accept the CMIT's rules. "The initiative was on the Czech side," Dědek recalls. "The OECD did not have to push us very hard. We wanted the OECD to teach us how to be a developed market economy."[104] Similarly, Procházka suggests that the Czech "commitment to liberalization, as part of our broader reform package, was clear. The OECD enabled and quickened the process."[105]

The negotiations with CMIT began late in the winter of 1995. The Czech government had just liberalized outward foreign direct investment as part of its Europe Agreement, which came into effect on February 1, 1995. The first step, at least as far as the CMIT was concerned, was that the Czechs extend the measures of the Europe Agreement to the rest of the OECD.[106]

The documents associated with the OECD's initial review reveal that the country's capital account regime left much to be desired. "The Czech Republic's regime appears to be quite restrictive," the Secretariat observed, "by today's OECD standards."[107] The OECD only needed to ask, however. Paris quickly found that a common language and set of shared understandings was all that was necessary, and Prague proved an eager student. "The first talks with the OECD," according to Procházka, "entailed a process of our understanding each other, of our making sure that the words we were using to describe the issues of the capital account meant the same things in Prague as they did in Paris."[108] Once this was accomplished, the CNB could then help parliament to draft a law that would satisfy the CMIT. "When we understood their definitions," the CNB's Jana Křelinová recalled, "we were able to craft a new foreign exchange law based on them."[109] The finance ministry's experience was the same: OECD experts spent a great deal of time "teaching us about the capital account and how to liberalize."[110]

While parliamentary negotiations over the letter of the law were going on, the CNB engaged in de facto liberalization. "The accelerated speed of deregulation resulted from the combined effect of the growing pressures from the enterprise and household sectors, on the one hand, and the deliberately weak resistance to these pressures on the part of the regulatory authorities, on the other hand," describes Dĕdek. "The latter originated in the government policy of attracting foreign capital and integrating the Czech economy into the family of developed market economies."[111] Thus, according to the CNB's Tomáš Holub, "De facto liberalization preceded de jure liberalization. Technically many cross-border financial flows were subject to the approval of the CNB. But in the early 1990s the CNB just approved all applications."[112]

The negotiations between Paris and Prague about the new foreign exchange law were therefore quite friendly for two reasons: the liberalization had outpaced the law, and the Czech authorities were eager to follow the advice of OECD experts. "The OECD was quite demanding," Procházka recalls, "but we did not bargain much." Still, there was "quite intensive dialoging" to make all of this happen—visits to Paris, OECD missions to Prague.[113]

When the April 1995 status report was outlined at a joint meeting of the CMIT and Committee on International Investment and Multinational Enterprises (CIME), the OECD welcomed the progress of Czech authorities, but "identified areas where the Czech position needed to be improved to meet the OECD membership requirements."[114] This finding only led the Czechs to redouble their efforts, particularly because the government had staked a great deal of its legitimacy on a rapid transition that would successfully result in OECD membership. "We took CMIT's recommendations very seriously," recalled one senior finance ministry official. "OECD membership was a priority for the government, and we needed CMIT's approval."[115]

All this work culminated in the Foreign Exchange Act, which came into force on October 1, 1995. In the end, Czech policymakers would identify the pieces of their balance of payments linked to the norms and rules of three international organizations: outward FDI for the European Union; the rest of the capital account for the OECD; and the end of the multiple exchange rate system to meet Article VIII of the IMF, which requires current-account convertibility.[116]

The OECD's experts and Czech policymakers began 1996 with optimism. Many Czechs even began to proclaim the era of transition to be at an end. Although the Mexican experience had led the CMIT to be wary of the increased potential for crisis with an essentially open capital account, the view from Paris was sanguine. "In the particular case of the Czech Republic," the Secretariat noted, "the likelihood of serious macroeconomic shocks seems to be small."[117]

Although the Czech experience seems to have had a happy epilogue—by 2004 the Czech economy was growing apace and the country had joined the European Union—its ending, in May 1997, was problematic. The macroeconomic policy mix—the combination of monetary and fiscal policy, banking regulation, and exchange rate policy—created an environment in which capital account liberalization magnified the negative consequences of the policy inconsistencies. The result was a domestic credit bubble, fueled by foreign borrowing, that burst in the middle of 1997.

During 1994 and 1995 the Czech Republic pegged the currency, the crown, to the dollar (35 percent) and German mark (65 percent). The crown fluctuated within a narrow band of plus or minus 0.5 percent. Because interest rates were lower abroad, Czech banks found themselves with an opportunity to borrow in foreign currency and lend domestically at a higher interest rate. The fixed exchange rate ensured that the nominal differential was a real return for Czech banks. Czech banks also had not yet been privatized, and significant pressure was brought to bear to ensure that they continued to lend to domestic firms—in a sense, to finance the transition and postpone the adjustment costs associated with inefficient firms that produced relatively unmarketable products. This was a critical function, given the importance of the Czech banking sector to the economy. With bank lending at 55 percent of gross domestic product (GDP), compared to about 20 percent for neighboring Hungary and Poland, an active banking sector had a massive influence on the state of the economy.[118] The signs of a credit binge were unmistakable: the foreign borrowing of Czech banks peaked at 6 percent of GDP at the end of 1995. Pressure on the exchange rate forced the CNB to widen the fluctuation bands to plus or minus 7.5 percent in February 1996. In the second half of 1996 the CNB tightened monetary policy to cool down the overheating economy. But this action simply raised the incentives to channel the less expensive foreign capital into the economy.

So far this is the usual story, but the usual ending did not fit. The classic problem of a weak, underregulated banking system with unrestricted access to international markets is that banks take on an unsustainable, dangerous foreign exchange exposure.[119] Because developing country banks typically borrow in hard currency and lend in soft, a devaluation of the local currency can devastate banks, which find their foreign currency obligations double or triple in domestic currency terms. Having learned from the countless financial crises of OECD members and developing countries, Czech policymakers had put in place prudential regulations that limited the foreign currency exposure of Czech banks. That is, banks could not borrow, for example, in dollars and then lend in crowns without some offsetting transactions that brought their exposure to the risk of devaluation almost to zero. If banks borrowed in dollars, they were obliged by law to lend in dollars as well. So that is exactly what Czech banks did. Foreign currency-denominated loans to domestic firms were enormous. And although the banks themselves were not exposed to the risk of devaluation, the Czech economy as a whole—resident economic entities taken collectively—were massively exposed.[120]

As a result, the total open foreign exchange position of Czech banks was always close to zero, and was in fact positive in May 1997 when the bubble burst. When the CNB floated the crown and then watched it depreciate steeply, the banks were not directly exposed. This hedge was an illusion, however. By passing the foreign exchange risk on to domestic firms in the form of foreign currency loans, the banks transformed the foreign exchange risk into a credit risk. It mattered little that the banks were hedged if their borrowers were not. And Czech firms were not hedged. When the banking system was ultimately cleaned up in subsequent years, the cost amounted to 15 to 20 percent of GDP, a massive sum.[121]

Czech policymakers look back on their experience with capital account liberalization with remarkable self-reflection. The CNB's Holub and Zdenek Tuma summarize the episode thus:

> The situation can in short be described as a combination of a fixed-but-adjustable exchange rate not supported by an adequate macroeconomic policy mix, weaknesses in the banking sector, and lagging structural reforms. This is probably not a very suitable environment for avoiding the potential problems stemming from the liberalization of capital flows.[122]

As Procházka describes it, "We focused more on the discipline of international markets than on their dangers."[123] The end result was an approach to liberalization that actively encouraged hot money.[124]

Hungary and Poland

Hungarian and Polish policymakers engaged the CMIT in much the same manner as their Czech counterparts, with two exceptions: they were slower to liberalize and more cautious about proclaiming the sufficiency of their prudential regulations; and they privatized and restructured their banks more quickly. Each avoided a currency crisis and credit bubble. Hungary and Poland were able, in a sense, to implement more completely the full range of CMIT advice and adopt the collected wisdom of OECD members.

Hungary's progress toward the complete liberalization of capital flows picked up speed in 1995 when the CMIT handed down its first judgment of the country's ability to take on the obligations of membership. In late May 1995, the CMIT observed that "Hungary's regime appears to be quite restrictive by today's OECD standards."[125] Discussions with the CMIT in the autumn found Budapest still wanting. "The OECD praises Hungary's move toward convertibility of the forint on the current account," it was reported, "but adds that a clear timetable should be established for capital account convertibility as part of a medium-term program for fiscal consolidation and structural reform."[126] Domestic negotiations over a new foreign exchange law stumbled on the issue of controls on short-term foreign investment in state securities designed to "prevent the influx of 'hot,' dubious capital."[127]

Early in 1996 the CMIT and Secretariat reviewed Hungary's position under the Code. The CMIT remained firm. "Still, the large number of remaining reservations concerning capital movements remains a matter of concern," the CMIT pointed out. The committees fully appreciated the need to maintain macroeconomic and financial stability, but urged the Hungarian authorities to bear in mind that capital controls, which create inefficiencies and are often ineffective, cannot be a substitute for appropriate market-oriented economic solutions and policies.[128]

OECD encouragement empowered the liberalizers in Budapest, though the National Bank of Hungary's restrictions on domestic lending to nonresidents remained in place as a means to limit the ability of foreigners to sell short the currency.[129] With the CMIT's stamp of approval for the central bank's liberalization plans, Hungary completed its march toward an open capital account. One final hurdle was the condition that Hungary successfully negotiate a standby credit from the IMF.[130]

By the end of the 1990s Hungary had enjoyed tremendous success in attracting foreign capital. Partly because of the maintenance of some restrictions on short-term capital inflows, policymakers managed to affect the composition of those investments. The vast majority of them constituted foreign direct investment.[131]

Poland's capital account liberalization also progressed relatively slowly, but ultimately successfully. OECD encouragement, and the positive sanction of membership, played an important role in empowering Polish liberalizers. When the December 1994 Foreign Exchange Law was found, on initial review, to be too restrictive by OECD standards, the Ministry of Finance was given authority to make changes without parliamentary approval.[132] A review in the summer of 1995 found Poland's proposed reservations to be unacceptable, despite important progress: "Nevertheless, the Committees," both the CMIT and CIME, "identified a number of areas where Poland's proposed position under the Codes and with respect to foreign direct investment should be improved in order to be considered satisfactory for a new member."[133]

By the beginning of 1996, the advantages of membership—according to the Poles, increased foreign investment and an improved credit rating, as well as prestige—had led the parliament to pass a variety of new laws quickly to strengthen Polish adherence to OECD legal instruments.[134]

As with Hungary, Poland managed to avoid a financial crisis despite attracting massive inflows of capital. Unlike Hungary, the Polish government managed to limit the inflow of the short-term capital that worried Warsaw bureaucrats without resorting to capital controls. The regulatory framework was sound and well enforced for Poland's privatized and restructured banks. The restructuring, begun in 1993, had rapidly instituted a risk-averse credit culture, contrasting sharply with the situation in the Czech Republic.[135] A rapid increase in portfolio investment, which alarmed Polish authorities, led Warsaw to appreciate the currency and widen its fluctuation bands.[136]

South Korea

The accession negotiations for South Korea were unlike the others in a number of respects. Although the South Korean authorities expressed great enthusiasm for membership, they did not adopt the role of eager pupil as had, for example, the Czechs. Instead, the South Korean negotiators resisted many of the conditions for liberalization set by the CMIT. Also, OECD membership was not nearly as popular within South Korea as it was in the other acceding countries.[137] Indeed, membership was controversial: after the financial crisis at the end of 1997, a year after joining, a parliamentary investigation was conducted to examine the relationship between the accession negotiations and the country's vulnerability to a crisis. Both of these unique characteristics of the South Korean accession combined to create a fascinating political economy of financial reform.

The South Korean negotiations also led to discussions of the meaning of OECD membership. Although the South Korean leadership portrayed membership as a graduation to developed-country status in much the same way as Mexico and the central Europeans had, they also wished to retain any advantages of developing-country status in other contexts, particularly the World Trade Organization (WTO). "The Republic of Korea has indicated," the OECD Secretary-General's office observed, "on a number of occasions that its accession to the OECD did not imply that it would relinquish developing country (hereinafter LDC) 'status' in other international fora."[138] The view from la Muette was generally supportive. "In fact, several founding OECD Member countries have been considered, in some cases until fairly recently, as LDCs for the purpose of development assistance in particular," the Secretary-General's office reasoned. "They are Greece, Portugal, Spain, and Turkey." The only exception to this leeway was disallowing concurrent membership in the G77, a decision the council took when Mexico was acceding. The principle, as it was recounted later, was that "belonging to the G77 was not consistent with accession to the OECD given its political role as a negotiating group which was frequently opposed to the OECD in other fora."[139]

In May 1995 the OECD ministerial meeting produced a consensus that South Korea should accede quickly, and the Secretariat was charged with reviewing South Korean progress toward adhering to the Code of Liberalization and other OECD instruments. The process began when the Secretariat sent an eighteen-member delegation to Seoul in October 1995.[140] The delegation concluded that South Korea's five-year financial reform program was "well thought out but needs to be speedier," and suggested that a lack of improvements in the capital account regime would derail the country's progress toward membership. As the *Financial Times'* John Burton reported:

> South Korea argues that it must pursue a gradual liberalization of capital movements because of concerns that a rapid inflow of overseas funds, at-

tracted by the country's high interest rates, would destabilize the economy by increasing the money supply and inflation and cause the South Korean currency to appreciate . . . But the OECD group suggested such fears were exaggerated.[141]

A spring review by the CMIT and CIME found South Korea's numerous proposed reservations unacceptable. "While the Committees fully appreciate the need to maintain macroeconomic stability," as usual, "their consistent view has been that capital controls, which create inefficiencies and become often ineffective, cannot be a substitute for appropriate market-oriented economic solutions and policies, including adequate exchange rate policy."[142] After the spring meeting of the CMIT and CIME to review South Korea, that country's authorities were "quick to warn of the economic chaos if Korea is forced to accept fully" OECD conditions. Their fear was "a surge of 'hot money'" that would lead to inflation and currency appreciation.[143]

In August the South Koreans offered a new liberalization plan to the CMIT. The basis of the plan was to calibrate future liberalizations to the convergence of South Korea's financial market with the world's. "Korea is determined to remove the remaining capital controls, once the domestic-international interest rates differential reaches a level such that excessively large capital inflows would not be induced," the Seoul government responded. "Given the current interest rate levels, the Korean government believes that the differential should narrow down to within two percentage points."[144]

OECD membership remained at once promising and controversial in South Korean politics. "Opponents of 'hasty' OECD membership," John Burton reported, "including the opposition parties and most of the media, also claim liberalization would make Korea heavily dependent on foreign capital and leave it vulnerable to a financial crisis, such as occurred in Mexico in 1994, if 'hot' speculative money left the country."[145] The controversy would persist, of course, when the Asian financial crisis spread from Indonesia and Thailand to South Korea at the end of 1997. Some observers wondered whether the skeptics had been proven right. Scholarship on the crisis reveals complex causation, and the OECD's role in intensifying external pressure to liberalize is an important theme.[146] Those most critical of both the OECD and the Seoul government suggest that the Secretariat was too focused on South Korean adherence to the Code of Liberalization, failing to identify and emphasize the risks of not having the appropriate institutional infrastructure for an open capital account. The Seoul government, in this critique, went ahead with OECD demands for liberalization despite ample unofficial warnings from members of the Secretariat; they thus rushed to receive the benefits of OECD membership without heeding the fragility of their financial sector.[147]

Soogil Young, the former ambassador of South Korea to the OECD, came to the defense of la Muette. Young argued that the issue revolved around the content of the government's concessions for further financial liberalization during negotiations with the OECD. And the OECD "did not," according to Young,

> request Korea to liberalize foreign investment in money market securities and other short-term instruments, including derivatives, and short-term financial credits from abroad . . . Nor did the OECD request Korea to allow the transfer of foreign funds to Korean banks. This was permitted long before Korea's accession negotiations started. And as a matter of fact, at the time of Korea's accession, the OECD drew the attention of the Korean authorities to the need to modernize the banking system and, in particular, to upgrade the prudential supervisory framework.[148]

All of this raises the question of why the Seoul government embraced such a dangerous sequence of capital liberalization. The critical issue was the balance of power between the enormous—and enormously powerful—business conglomerates known as the *chaebol* and the government. If the government liberalized long-term flows of capital first, then the *chaebol's* relative strength would grow further. The banking system, however, was still very much under the control of the South Korean Ministry of Finance. If the finance ministry could strengthen the banks vis-à-vis the *chaebol,* then the government would regain important levers of power within the South Korean economy. The outcome that many have considered perverse—liberalizing short-term flows of capital into the banking sector before allowing long-term flows into South Korean industry—was thus based on political calculations within Seoul. The stability of the plan rested on the finance ministry's effective monitoring of the banks, as well as its ability to convince the banks that they were not fully backed by government finances if capital flows reversed and financial pressures threatened their solvency. Unfortunately, the finance ministry appears to have been unable to perform either of these duties well, and instead managed to encourage South Korean banks and finance companies to borrow massively at the relatively low rates that prevailed at the time without monitoring effectively the increasing fragility of the financial sector.[149]

Aside from the content of the financial liberalization that the OECD required of new members, others have pointed to more subtle effects of the country's accession to the club. Tae-Kyun Kwon, the Counsellor of the South Korean delegation to the OECD, describes the government's decision to keep the exchange rate overvalued to keep the country's per capita income high in U.S. dollar terms. Although the OECD does not have a minimum requirement for per capita income, the view from Seoul was that the U.S. dollar figure was evidence of South Korea's graduation to developed-country status. Another subtle effect, according to Kwon, was the borrowing frenzy of South Korean banks that was enabled by OECD membership. For about one year after accession, and until the crisis struck, South Korean banks and firms were able to borrow from international banks at the favorable interest rates made possible by the OECD risk weightings of the Basel agreement, thereby building up quite rapidly an enormous short-term debt burden.[150]

The OECD did not start out as an organization that favored open capital accounts. Indeed, it deemed regulation essential where hot money was concerned as recently as the 1970s. By the 1990s, however, it had become an engine driving the mobile capital regime across the globe, from central Europe to Latin America to east Asia. Yet the strange thing about this engine is that it runs on something as innocuous as discussion fora, peer review, and the lure of prestige. Member countries are slowly seduced by the expert talk at la Muette—talk that is always already paradigmatically geared toward producing a consensus in favor of free capital. And aspirants to the club pursue the privileges of membership without properly weighing either the costs or their readiness. Only by taking a sociological view can we begin to make sense of how the norms of membership and peer dialogue operate to produce this surprising state of affairs.

Although the U.S. delegation did not object to the progressive strengthening of the Code of Liberalization, neither did it lead the way. As with the process of European financial integration, ultimately the embrace of liberalization by European governments was the fundamental driver of the creation of a truly liberal Code of Liberalization. The United States did not hesitate to employ the accession process as leverage on countries that it considered, in financial terms, strategic priorities. But organization building, the logic that motivated the French and other European governments to build the capacity and authority of the Code, was as a process irrelevant to U.S. policy. The organization did eventually get built, and the Europeans turned their attention from the clubs that they had come to dominate to the only universal organization in the international financial architecture.

CHAPTER 6

Freedom and Its Risks:
The IMF and the Capital Account

Les paradoxes d'aujourd'hui sont les préjugés de demain. (The paradoxes of today are the prejudices of tomorrow.)

—Marcel Proust

The central role of the IMF in the international financial architecture dates to its origins in Bretton Woods, New Hampshire, in 1944. Delegates from forty-four countries met to create a new system of fixed exchange rates and rules to govern the economic relations among members of the newly created organization. The meeting, lasting several weeks, took place in the Mount Washington Hotel, a resort in the White Mountains where New England's wealthiest members of society spent their summers golfing and their winters skiing. The hotel's Gold Room, where the IMF's Articles of Agreement were signed, still memorializes the historic event.

The Bretton Woods system of fixed exchange rates collapsed in the early 1970s, but the Fund, whose central mission had been to oversee the proper functioning of the system, continues to be one of the most influential international organizations in the world. The legacy of Bretton Woods is still with us and will, hopefully, continue. Six decades later the Fund counts among its members nearly every sovereign state in the world, 184 in all (see Table 6.1).

Table 6.1 IMF Members with Dates of Accession and Voting Weights, 2005

Member state	Accession	Voting weight (percentage)
United States	December 27, 1945	17.14
Japan	August 13, 1952	6.15

Table 6.1   (continued)

Member state	Accession	Voting weight (percentage)
Germany	August 14, 1952	6.01
France	December 27, 1945	4.96
United Kingdom	December 27, 1945	4.96
Italy	March 27, 1947	3.26
Saudi Arabia	August 26, 1957	3.23
Canada	December 27, 1945	2.95
China	December 27, 1945	2.95
Russian Federation	June 1, 1992	2.75
Netherlands	December 27, 1945	2.39
Belgium	December 27, 1945	2.13
India	December 27, 1945	1.93
Switzerland	May 29, 1992	1.61
Australia	August 5, 1947	1.50
Spain	September 15, 1958	1.42
Brazil	January 14, 1946	1.41
Venezuela	December 30, 1946	1.24
Mexico	December 31, 1945	1.20
Sweden	August 31, 1951	1.12
Argentina	September 20, 1956	0.99
Indonesia	February 21, 1967	0.97
Austria	August 27, 1948	0.87
South Africa	December 27, 1945	0.87
Nigeria	March 30, 1961	0.82
Norway	December 27, 1945	0.78
Denmark	March 30, 1946	0.77
Korea	August 26, 1955	0.76
Iran	December 29, 1945	0.70
Malaysia	March 7, 1958	0.70
Kuwait	September 13, 1962	0.65
Poland	June 12, 1986	0.64
Ukraine	September 3, 1992	0.64
Algeria	September 26, 1963	0.59
Finland	January 14, 1948	0.59
Iraq	December 27, 1945	0.56
Libya	September 17, 1958	0.53
Thailand	May 3, 1949	0.51
Hungary	May 6, 1982	0.49
Pakistan	July 11, 1950	0.49
Romania	December 15, 1972	0.49
Turkey	March 11, 1947	0.46
Egypt	December 27, 1945	0.45
Israel	July 12, 1954	0.44

Table 6.1   (continued)

Member state	Accession	Voting weight (percentage)
New Zealand	August 31, 1961	0.42
Philippines	December 27, 1945	0.42
Chile	December 31, 1945	0.41
Portugal	March 29, 1961	0.41
Singapore	August 3, 1966	0.41
Ireland	August 8, 1957	0.40
Czech Republic	January 1, 1993	0.39
Greece	December 27, 1945	0.39
Colombia	December 27, 1945	0.37
Bulgaria	September 25, 1990	0.31
Peru	December 31, 1945	0.31
United Arab Emirates	September 22, 1972	0.29
Morocco	April 25, 1958	0.28
Bangladesh	August 17, 1972	0.26
Democratic Republic of Congo	September 28, 1963	0.26
Zambia	September 23, 1965	0.24
Serbia and Montenegro	December 14, 1992	0.23
Sri Lanka	August 29, 1950	0.20
Belarus	July 10, 1992	0.19
Croatia	December 14, 1992	0.18
Ghana	September 20, 1957	0.18
Kazakhstan	July 15, 1992	0.18
Slovakia	January 1, 1993	0.18
Trinidad and Tobago	September 16, 1963	0.17
Côte d'Ivoire	March 11, 1963	0.16
Vietnam	September 21, 1956	0.16
Ecuador	December 28, 1945	0.15
Syria	April 10, 1947	0.15
Uruguay	March 11, 1946	0.15
Angola	September 19, 1989	0.14
Jamaica	February 21, 1963	0.14
Kenya	February 3, 1964	0.14
Luxembourg	December 27, 1945	0.14
Tunisia	April 14, 1958	0.14
Uzbekistan	September 21, 1992	0.14
Myanmar	January 3, 1952	0.13
Qatar	September 8, 1972	0.13
Slovenia	December 14, 1992	0.12
Yemen	May 22, 1990	0.12
Brunei Darussalam	October 10, 1995	0.11
Dominican Republic	December 28, 1945	0.11
Guatemala	December 28, 1945	0.11

Table 6.1   (continued)

Member state	Accession	Voting weight (percentage)
Lebanon	April 14, 1947	0.11
Panama	March 14, 1946	0.11
Cameroon	July 10, 1963	0.10
Oman	December 23, 1971	0.10
Tanzania	September 10, 1962	0.10
Afghanistan	July 14, 1955	0.09
Azerbaijan	September 18, 1992	0.09
Bolivia	December 27, 1945	0.09
Bosnia and Herzegovina	December 14, 1992	0.09
Costa Rica	January 8, 1946	0.09
El Salvador	March 14, 1946	0.09
Jordan	August 29, 1952	0.09
Senegal	August 31, 1962	0.09
Sudan	September 5, 1957	0.09
Uganda	September 27, 1963	0.09
Cyprus	December 21, 1961	0.08
Gabon	September 10, 1963	0.08
Georgia	May 5, 1992	0.08
Lithuania	April 29, 1992	0.08
Bahamas	August 21, 1973	0.07
Bahrain	September 7, 1972	0.07
Ethiopia	December 27, 1945	0.07
Honduras	December 27, 1945	0.07
Iceland	December 27, 1945	0.07
Latvia	May 19, 1992	0.07
Madagascar	September 25, 1963	0.07
Moldova	August 12, 1992	0.07
Namibia	September 25, 1990	0.07
Nicaragua	March 14, 1946	0.07
Papua New Guinea	October 9, 1975	0.07
Guinea	September 28, 1963	0.06
Malta	September 11, 1968	0.06
Mauritius	September 23, 1968	0.06
Mozambique	September 24, 1984	0.06
Paraguay	December 28, 1945	0.06
Sierra Leone	September 10, 1962	0.06
Armenia	May 28, 1992	0.05
Burundi	September 28, 1963	0.05
Cambodia	December 31, 1969	0.05
Republic of Congo	July 10, 1963	0.05
Guyana	September 26, 1966	0.05
Haiti	September 8, 1953	0.05

Table 6.1   (continued)

Member state	Accession	Voting weight (percentage)
Kyrgyz Republic	May 8, 1992	0.05
Mali	September 27, 1963	0.05
Rwanda	September 30, 1963	0.05
Suriname	April 27, 1978	0.05
Tajikistan	April 27, 1993	0.05
Togo	August 1, 1962	0.05
Turkmenistan	September 22, 1992	0.05
Barbados	December 29, 1970	0.04
Benin	July 10, 1963	0.04
Botswana	July 24, 1968	0.04
Burkina Faso	May 2, 1963	0.04
Central African Republic	July 10, 1963	0.04
Chad	July 10, 1963	0.04
Estonia	May 26, 1992	0.04
Fiji	May 28, 1971	0.04
Lao People's Democratic Republic	July 5, 1961	0.04
Macedonia	December 14, 1992	0.04
Malawi	July 19, 1965	0.04
Mauritania	September 10, 1963	0.04
Mongolia	February 14, 1991	0.04
Nepal	September 6, 1961	0.04
Niger	April 24, 1963	0.04
Albania	October 15, 1991	0.03
Equatorial Guinea	December 22, 1969	0.03
Gambia	September 21, 1967	0.03
Lesotho	July 25, 1968	0.03
Somalia	August 31, 1962	0.03
Swaziland	September 22, 1969	0.03
Antigua and Barbuda	February 25, 1982	0.02
Belize	March 16, 1982	0.02
Cape Verde	November 20, 1978	0.02
Comoros	September 21, 1976	0.02
Djibouti	December 29, 1978	0.02
Dominica	December 12, 1978	0.02
Eritrea	July 6, 1994	0.02
Grenada	August 27, 1975	0.02
Guinea-Bissau	March 24, 1977	0.02
Maldives	January 13, 1978	0.02
St. Kitts and Nevis	August 15, 1984	0.02
St. Lucia	November 15, 1979	0.02
St. Vincent and the Grenadines	December 28, 1979	0.02
Samoa	December 28, 1971	0.02

Table 6.1   (continued)

Member state	Accession	Voting weight (percentage)
San Marino	September 23, 1992	0.02
Seychelles	June 30, 1977	0.02
Solomon Islands	September 22, 1978	0.02
Timor-Leste	July 23, 2002	0.02
Vanuatu	September 28, 1981	0.02
Bhutan	September 28, 1981	0.01
Kiribati	June 3, 1986	0.01
Marshall Islands	May 21, 1992	0.01
Micronesia	June 24, 1993	0.01
Palau	December 16, 1997	0.01
São Tomé and Principé	September 30, 1977	0.01
Tonga	September 13, 1985	0.01
Liberia	March 28, 1962	0.00
Zimbabwe	September 29, 1980	0.00

Sources: "IMF Members' Quotas and Voting Power, and IMF Board of Governors," available at www.imf.org/external/np/sec/memdir/members.htm (last modified April 1, 2005); "IMF Members' Financial Data by Country," available at www.imf.org/external/np/tre/tad/exfin1.cfm (last modified February 28, 2005).

The Fund's nearly universal membership makes its codified rules the legal foundation of the entire international monetary system. Although the IMF's rules have, since 1944, obliged members to move toward current account convertibility, they have also reserved for members the right to control capital movements. The IMF's Articles of Agreement thus list among the organization's purposes the liberalization of trade, but not of capital.

When U.S. policymakers speak about the IMF, they often refer to it by the address of its offices in Washington, D.C. From the perspective of 19th Street, it is said, the world looks a certain way. This chapter is, in a sense, about the intellectual distance between Bretton Woods and 19th Street and how it grew—how the view from 19th Street during the middle of the 1990s came to be the opposite of the consensus reached at the Mount Washington Hotel in 1944.[1]

During the late 1980s and early 1990s the IMF began actively, and informally, to promote capital liberalization in the absence of any legal authority or mandate to do so. As one former IMF executive director observes, "Capital account liberalization had become an accepted part of our orthodoxy. It had for some time been Fund policy to promote capital account liberalization."[2] Then, during the mid-1990s the Fund's management sought to amend the Articles to give the Fund jurisdiction over capital movements and to endow the organization with a new formal purpose: the liberalization of capital flows.

An open capital account, in other words, had emerged as a social norm for Fund members, and the organization's leadership sought to codify the norm, to make the movement toward an open capital account an obligation of membership. Former Managing Director Michel Camdessus recalls:

> The idea first emerged at the end of the 1980s and the beginning of the 1990s with the sea changes of that time. It was a moment of the ascendance of some important ideas: globalization, democracy, and the market economy. It was time for us—without rushing—to accompany countries to full liberalization of capital. We would monitor the health of the bank systems and the stability of financial movements along the way. It was time to define the goal, even if it were to take us fifteen or twenty years. The IMF's role would be to help countries adapt to a new world. The natural consequence of this thinking was to change the Articles.[3]

The effort to amend the Articles almost succeeded, and the change would have fundamentally transformed the international financial architecture. Emboldened by the financial crisis in Asia, however, a number of developing country directors on the Fund's executive board began actively to oppose the amendment, which the Canadian executive director, Thomas Bernes, had long resisted.

The proposal to amend the Fund's Articles had been conceived and pushed forward by the management of the Fund itself, and most emphatically by Camdessus. (For a list of the IMF's managing directors, see Table 6.2.) European executive directors in particular strongly favored the amendment. Although the U.S. executive director, White House appointee (and therefore formally apart from Treasury) Karin Lissakers, personally supported the proposal, the U.S. Treasury was ambivalent, if not downright indifferent. Lissakers eventually came to be seen by some Treasury officials as having "gone native" at the Fund—bypassing U.S. national interests for the sake of the Fund's bureaucratic interest in the amendment.[4]

Many observers automatically assumed that U.S. leadership was responsible for the capital account amendment. This assumption could hardly have been more mistaken. The mistake resulted in part from the advocacy of U.S. executive director Lissakers, the amendment's lone supporter in the U.S.

Table 6.2   IMF Managing Directors

Managing Director	Member State	Tenure
Camille Gutt	Belgium	1946–1951
Ivar Rooth	Sweden	1951–1956
Per Jacobsson	Sweden	1956–1963
Pierre-Paul Schweitzer	France	1963–1973
H. Johannes Witteveen	Netherlands	1973–1978
Jacques de Larosière	France	1978–1987
Michel Camdessus	France	1987–2000
Horst Köhler	Germany	2000–2004
Rodrigo de Rato y Figaredo	Spain	2004–present

Sources: "Rodrigo de Rato y Figaredo," available at www.imf.org/external/np/omd/bios/rrf.htm (last updated March 30, 2005); "Horst Köhler," available at www.imf.org/external/np/omd/bios/hk.htm (last updated March 16, 2005).

government. Yet none of the most influential bankers and investors in the United States were consulted when the amendment was first proposed, and, upon learning of the proposal, they opposed it altogether. The possibility of a capital account amendment was ultimately destroyed by the U.S. Congress, when powerful Democrats in the House of Representatives threatened to withhold support for an increase in U.S. contributions to the Fund if the Treasury allowed further progress toward amending the Articles.

The amendment died slowly and quietly, leaving the Fund to reconsider its mandate and role in the international monetary system. Since the crisis, the Fund's management and staff have become increasingly wary of the risks of capital liberalization and, indeed, have urged caution on countries during the early years of the new century. The intellectual distance between Bretton Woods and 19th Street, widest perhaps in September 1997, has since narrowed considerably. The Fund is now once again cautious about capital liberalization, much as its founders, fresh from their own devastating financial crises, had intended.

The IMF's Articles of Agreement and Governance

The IMF's Articles of Agreement, negotiated in July 1944 and entered into force in December 1945, provide the legal foundation for the international monetary system.[5] The Articles are taken seriously within the Fund, and the criteria for amending them are demanding: three-fifths of the members, having 85 percent of the total voting power (which is weighted by financial contributions to the Fund's resources), must accept the proposed amendment. The Articles have been amended only three times: in 1969, to introduce the Special Drawing Right as the Fund's unit of account; in 1978, to establish the right of members to adopt exchange rate arrangements of their choice and to rewrite Article IV; and in 1992, to provide for the suspension of voting and other membership rights for members that fail to fulfill their financial obligations to the Fund.

The Fund's Articles list six purposes for the organization: to promote international monetary cooperation; to facilitate "the expansion and balanced growth of international trade," and thereby employment; to promote exchange stability; to assist in the establishment of a multilateral system of payments "in respect of current transactions between members" and in the elimination of exchange restrictions that hamper the growth of trade; to give confidence to members in dealing with balance of payments adjustments; and to shorten the duration of balance of payments disequilibria. The IMF is supposed to be "guided in all its policies and decisions by the purposes set forth in this Article."[6] Although Fund members are obliged by the Articles not to restrict payments on the current account, members "may exercise such controls as are necessary to regulate international capital movements."[7]

The Fund is governed primarily by its executive board, composed of executive directors (who now number twenty-four) who meet about three times per week. The chair of the board is also the managing director of the IMF. Final authority, however, rests with the Board of Governors, with each member (currently one hundred eighty-four) holding a governor's seat. In most cases each governor is either a finance minister or central bank head.

In between the two boards is a liaison committee created in October 1974. This was known as the Interim Committee of the Board of Governors until 1999, when it was renamed the International Monetary and Finance Committee. Significant power is lodged in this committee, which meets twice per year and essentially issues directions to the executive board. The Committee is composed of twenty-four governors, each of whom has a country counterpart on the executive board.

Fixed Rates and Controlled Capital, 1945–1971

The practice of the Bretton Woods system differed rather substantially from its theory. Still, as economist Barry Eichengreen observes, "Capital controls were the one element that functioned more or less as planned."[8] The Fund's approach to capital controls appears, nevertheless, to have begun to change very early on. By the early 1950s, many Fund publications began to imply, without any explicit change in the thinking of Fund management and staff, that the organization's ultimate goal should be the removal of both current and capital account restrictions.[9] In 1950, the Fund's *Report on Exchange Restrictions* worried that capital controls could be counterproductive: "Exchange restrictions, which have in many cases been devised to prevent the escape of capital have also on occasions strengthened tendencies toward escape."[10] The 1952 *Report* indicated that already "the world situation is considerably different to what it was at the time the Agreement was drawn up at Bretton Woods."[11]

In the mid-1950s some Fund staff members questioned whether the organization's jurisdiction over members' capital account restrictions really was as circumscribed as it appeared to be by the language of the Articles. The legal department analyzed the issue, which ultimately came before the executive board.[12]

A 1956 decision was crucial, for the board itself is supposed to interpret the meaning of the Articles.[13] Although it was clear that important members of the Fund's management and staff deemed capital account convertibility desirable, the board established the definitive interpretation of the rights of members: "Members are free to adopt a policy of regulating capital movements for any reason . . . without approval of the Fund."[14]

By 1971, the eve of the fixed-exchange rate system's collapse, a number of European countries had already liberalized capital movements on their own. While capital controls were no longer as nearly universal as they had been in 1945, they were also neither unusual nor illegitimate. "Capital movements have been progressively liberalized by most countries," Lawrence Krause noted at the time, "but actions which tend to restrict capital movements do not elicit cries of outrage."[15] These cries would not be heard until the 1990s.

Floating and Financial Flows, 1971–1990

The end of systemwide fixed exchange rates threatened the Fund with irrelevance, and the turmoil in international currency markets during the next few years led to several extraordinary changes in the Fund's rules and policies. Capital flows, linked to the end of fixed exchange rates, took center stage. In 1972, the IMF reflected that "alarming growth, in recent years, in the frequency and magnitude of payments imbalances has largely though not exclusively reflected a growth in the scale of temporary and reversible capital flows, which have more and more played a disequilibrating rather than equilibrating role in the balances of payments."[16]

The Fund also, in 1972, organized the leading members of the Board of Governors into the Committee of Twenty. As Louis Pauly notes of the Committee, "a staff taken from the finance ministries and central banks of the leading monetary powers did the real work; they in turn assigned a group of technical experts to examine the problem of speculative capital flows."[17] The Technical Group on Disequilibrating Capital Flows submitted its report to the Committee of Twenty in May 1973.[18] That report, according to Alexandre Lamfalussy, "may be taken as representing the broad trend of official thinking on capital controls at the end of the Bretton Woods era."[19] The report's authors admitted at the outset, however, that "there is no simple and straightforward definition of 'disequilibrating' capital flows."[20]

The technical group reached two important conclusions. First, it envisioned a continuing role for capital controls even after the end of system-wide fixed exchange rates:

> The Group were confirmed in the view that the possibility of disequilibrat-
> ing capital flows continuing in the future could not be neglected, and that
> countries should be able to use a variety of measures, including controls, to
> influence them. A number of countries have in the past found controls to
> be useful in deterring disequilibrating capital flows. They often serve to gain
> time while necessary action is taken or a situation reverses itself. It was
> agreed, however, that it should not be necessary to maintain on a perma-
> nent basis controls introduced to deal with disequilibrating capital move-
> ments, and certain limitations on the use of controls were recognized.[21]

Second, given that capital controls were expected to remain a common practice, the group encouraged the IMF to create a code of conduct for their use. "The use of controls might be governed by a code of conduct which would lay down general principles and more detailed rules, such as the Code of Liberalization of Capital Movements of the OECD," the group wrote. Flexibility would be required, for "experience shows, however, that even when such a code is applied by a group of countries with similar economies and close economic relationships, it is difficult to establish in advance detailed rules which can be applied in all circumstances."[22]

The Committee of Twenty ultimately produced a final report and proposal for reforms. Two sections of the document are particularly instructive. The section on controls indicated some guidelines for the use of exchange restrictions on the capital account, but fell far short of a code of conduct:

> Countries will not use controls over capital transactions for the purpose of maintaining inappropriate exchange rates or, more generally, of avoiding appropriate adjustment action. Insofar as countries use capital controls, they should avoid an excessive degree of administrative restriction which could damage trade and beneficial capital flows and should not retain controls longer than needed.[23]

Also, the section on "Disequilibrating Capital Flows" indicated that the committee considered cooperation to be critical to the success of managing such flows: "Countries will cooperate in actions designed to limit disequilibrating capital flows and in arrangements to finance and offset them." The cooperative efforts the committee had in mind included: harmonization; adjustment of par values; wider margins; floating rates; "and the use of administrative controls, including dual exchange rates and fiscal incentives."[24]

This "Outline of Reform" evolved over the next few years into the Jamaica Accord, which ultimately became the second amendment of the Articles of Agreement. The resulting reform of the international monetary system's legal rules was modest. "In the end," writes Pauly, "all that proved politically feasible was an amendment to the Articles of Agreement of the IMF which legalized floating exchange rates and gave up on trying to achieve a new consensus on the definition and management of disequilibrating capital flows." Thus, according to Lamfalussy, the IMF simply reaffirmed the approach to capital controls already codified in the Articles.[25]

The Fund's rewritten Article IV did give the IMF a role more reminiscent of the organization's precursor in the League of Nations than of Bretton Woods: "firm surveillance over the exchange rate policies of members."[26] The meaning of "firm surveillance," however, was left open, to be determined by the organization's practice and the case law of executive board decisions.

A 1977 executive board decision on the practice of surveillance opened up the possibility for a much greater role for the Fund's management in the conduct of exchange policy. Although the mandate for surveillance was unclear about the place of capital controls in the Fund's review of member countries' policies, the board outlined a broad range of developments that "might indicate the need for discussion with a member of the Fund." These developments included "the introduction or substantial modification for balance of payments purposes of restrictions on, or incentives for, the inflow or outflow of capital," as well as "the pursuit, for balance of payments purposes, of monetary and other domestic financial policies that provide abnormal encouragement or discouragement to capital flows."[27] The Fund's potential role in encouraging capital account convertibility would still be modest, consisting only of surveillance and discussion. That is, the Fund could monitor capital controls and discuss their implementation with members, but in principle it could neither request nor oblige members to liberalize.

Within the Fund, the 1980s were relatively uneventful with regard to the capital account, although they were times of massive change within the EC and OECD. The Fund's publications contain very few references to either capital controls or flows.

Otherwise, as many developed countries liberalized their capital accounts during the decade, the Fund's staff and management appeared to watch quietly. Under the leadership of Managing Director Jacques de Larosière, Fund management intended for the organization to stand apart from the process of financial internationalization:

> We had our catechism: "Thou must give freedom to current payments, but thou must not necessarily give freedom to capital." I was comfortable with the idea that the Fund would not move toward compulsory freedom of capital. By the time I left the Fund in 1987, I was not aware of any discussions of changing the Articles to bring the capital account within our jurisdiction.[28]

De Larosière's authority within the Fund appears to have been a moderating influence among an increasingly liberal-minded staff. Speaking of capital, de Larosière reflects, "I was never seduced." De Larosière, a former managing director of the Fund, continues:

> I was always a little bit skeptical of the leap towards the full freedom of capital movements. It is a mixed blessing. Without the right institutions and the right surveillance procedures in place, capital movements could create havoc. And they have. There have been a lot of casualties in the history of the liberalization of capital.[29]

As the end of the tumultuous decade grew near, Fund doctrine on the capital account remained cautious.

The Age of Capital, 1990–1997

The internationalization of finance made life more difficult for the Fund's management and staff, but by the 1990s many within the IMF had fully embraced the freer movement of capital. The Fund began, for the first time, informally to promote capital liberalization among its members, although the Articles outlined no legal mandate to do so.

Former U.S. Treasury Secretary Lawrence Summers argues that the original mandate of the Articles of Agreement was increasingly interpreted as irrelevant to the enormous challenges faced by the Fund. "By the 1990s," Summers suggests, "no one thought that the Fund was at all faithful to its charter." Instead of the central role envisioned by the authors and signatories of the Articles, the IMF had "morphed into completely new roles, offering commentary on the developed world; managing crises in the developing world; and offering technical advice of various sorts." The Fund was no longer central to the international financial system, in which capital flowed primarily among developed countries that turned to the IMF for neither financial assistance nor advice. "The idea of thinking about the Fund's role in terms of Keynes and White," Summers argues, "was simply impractical. The goals they had outlined—such as fixed exchange rates—were anachronistic."[30]

The Evolution of Fund Practice

In the face of its declining relevance to financial globalization, the Fund's staff recognized that the liberalization of capital had little to do with IMF doctrine, practice, or rules. Instead, the staff attributed the impetus for the liberalization of the 1980s to "the frameworks of the OECD Code and the EU Directives."[31]

In the early 1990s, the content of Fund advice became more liberal, though neither indiscriminately nor particularly forcefully. With developing countries, the Fund had taken a "case-by-case approach to capital account liberalization in its consultations."[32] But the presumption shifted toward the embrace of both current and capital account convertibility. A retrospective analysis within the Fund during the middle of the 1990s found that Fund advice had evolved from the "traditional" approach of promoting current-account convertibility to "encouraging the adoption of full current and capital account convertibility."[33]

Moreover, the Fund had no direct levers with which to force open capital accounts even if it had wished to do so. Although Fund staff recognized that the "asymmetry" of the Articles of Agreement—that members were generally obliged to liberalize current but not capital account transactions—had been by design, the lack of a legal mandate was little deterrence. "Notwithstanding this asymmetry," reported a 1997 review, "the Fund has in recent years sought to promote capital account liberalization in view of the benefits that can accrue from capital movements and their importance in the international monetary system."[34] In other words, the Fund embraced liberalization because it represented, in the view of a staff increasingly reflective of the "neoliberal" training of American economics departments, better policymaking.[35] But this promotion did not consist of organizational demands and country obligations.

The Fund promoted capital account liberalization through two primary mechanisms: surveillance over members' exchange rate policies and technical advice. The Fund had not made capital account liberalization a condition of the use of Fund resources, though apparently it had been considered. The Fund's legal department had, however, clarified that the Fund could only impose conditionality consistent with the purposes of the Fund's Articles.[36]

Fund staff conducted an internal review of the organization's advisory role in the promotion of capital account liberalization as part of the board's consideration of an amendment. The Legal, Monetary and Exchange Affairs (MAE), and Policy Development and Review (PDR) departments reviewed a sample of thirty-four Article IV consultations between 1995 and 1996. Of those thirty-four, staff recommended macroeconomic policy adjustment in thirty-one cases, while in sixteen cases staff supported capital account liberalization, including two (Hungary and South Africa) for which the staff did not recommend macroeconomic policy adjustment. The executive board had supported capital account liberalization in fourteen of thirty-four. In no instances did the board recommend that countries slow down their movement toward capital account convertibility.[37] According to the IMF's Independent Evaluation Office (IEO), which reviewed the IMF's approach to the capital account during the 1990s and first years of the next century, the Fund's advice tended to emphasize the benefits of access to international capital markets, but not the risks of volatility.[38]

The Fund did not literally force liberalization on developing countries, and the Articles prevented the board from systematically making comprehensive capital account liberalization a condition of the use of Fund resources. Fund staff and management also did not encourage liberalization indiscriminately.[39]

Ultimately, countries that liberalized on the encouragement of the IMF through its technical advice or Article IV consultations bear some responsibility also for having followed the Fund's lead. Yet the Fund's informal definitions of legitimate policy are profoundly influential for the monetary and financial practices of states. Political scientist Jeffrey Chwieroth has identified significant effects of this informal norm on capital account liberalization in the developing world.[40] This was a much more subtle exercise of IMF influence than the image of the Fund as an entity that directly obliges governments to liberalize as a condition for using the organization's financial resources during a crisis.

The Origins of the Proposal to Amend the Articles

Locating the origins of the proposal to amend the Fund's Articles is a critical but difficult task. All evidence—interviews, the archival record, and contemporary publications—suggests that the proposal came from within the management of the Fund itself.

This finding contrasts with the widely held assumption that the proposal to amend the IMF's Articles represented the influence of either Wall Street financial firms, the U.S. Treasury, or some combination of those bankers, investors, and U.S. policymakers. Economist Jagdish Bhagwati argues that the "Wall-Street Treasury complex"—a powerful network of shared interest and ideology—pushed the Fund toward "embracing the goal of capital account convertibility."[41] Robert Wade and Frank Veneroso argue that the goal of the "free movement of capital worldwide" is the most important foreign economic policy issue for the United States. They argue that the U.S. Treasury formulated the proposal to amend the Articles so that it could pursue the goal of worldwide capital freedom more effectively. Wade and Veneroso also argue that "Wall Street wants capital account opening world-wide, and hence supports revision of the IMF's Articles of Agreement." Finally, Wade and Veneroso presumed that the U.S. Congress favored the amendment as well.[42] These arguments represent the conventional wisdom on the origins of the amendment.

I have found no evidence that the U.S. Treasury conceived or even, ultimately, embraced the proposed amendment. The proposal required the initial support of the U.S. executive director to get as far as it did, for the United States has a sort of negative power in the Fund by virtue of its large voting weight. Although the U.S. Treasury did not fully embrace the proposal, neither did Treasury officials initially oppose it. Under Lissakers, support for the proposal was, in principle, the U.S. position in board discussions, yet the record suggests that Lissakers acted independently and that her positions were not generally supported by Treasury officials. Lissakers recalls her own interest in greater responsibility for the Fund, noting that "to some extent, the U.S. chair was the instigator, along with Camdessus. We were troubled by the asymmetry in the Articles of the treatment of current and capital transactions."[43]

Treasury officials are unequivocal about the role of the United States. "The idea," a former senior Treasury official argued, "that the Fund was doing the bidding of the Treasury to push openness is totally wrong." The proposal to amend the Articles "came from the Fund. It didn't come from us." Indeed, the Treasury, according to the former senior official, "supported the amendment without doing enough due diligence on the proposal, and especially on why the change to the Articles was desirable or necessary." One outcome of this reliance on the Fund's approach to the amendment was that no one at the Treasury had a portfolio that included shepherding the amendment through the Fund and beyond. Or, as the Treasury official described, "It didn't get adult supervision."[44]

Summers recalls the proposal similarly: "The ideas behind the proposal were sensible enough, but it was not a priority for the Treasury. I gave very little attention to the issue; [Treasury Secretary Robert] Rubin gave it less."[45] There had been no need to block Fund management's agenda at these early stages. Camdessus and the European executive directors required no encouragement from Summers, Rubin, and their colleagues to promote liberalization in practice and as a matter of Fund law.

Even further removed from the proposal, Wall Street financial firms appear to have been altogether unaware of the initial discussions of the amendment. Charles Dallara, Managing Director of the Institute of International Finance (IIF), which represents the interests of highly internationalized banks around the world, insists, "The proposal was by no means a Treasury or Wall Street initiative."[46] When the world's most influential bankers and investors learned of the proposal several years later, the record shows that they reacted with alarm and quickly came to oppose the amendment, thus corroborating Dallara's retrospective assertion. And the decisive, fatal blow to the amendment was struck by the U.S. Congress.

All the available evidence shows that the proposal originated within the management of the Fund. The IMF's former management continues to assert intellectual and political ownership over the proposed amendment, despite the fact that the episode is now widely regarded as infamous. As Camdessus recalls, the idea to amend the Articles "came from within the Fund."[47] Former Executive Director Thomas Bernes also recalls the proposal having originated with Camdessus, with the amendment "part of Camdessus's vision for the Fund."[48]

Several Fund management and staff members were involved in conceiving the amendment. In late 1993 Camdessus approached Philippe Maystadt, chairman of the Interim Committee, with a proposal that the Fund extend its jurisdiction to the capital account.[49]

The concept of Fund jurisdiction was, however, considered by many to be ambiguous. As Fund management later described their interpretation of Fund jurisdiction, it involved a significant expansion of Fund authority: "The amendment will establish the general rule that members are prohibited from imposing restrictions on international capital movements without Fund approval."[50] This involved an extraordinary transformation. Whereas the legal presumption of the Articles as written in 1944 was that capital controls were allowed unless otherwise specified, the amendment would mean that capital controls were prohibited unless specifically approved by the Fund. The burden of proof was to be shifted; restrictions would have to be justified as deviations from openness.

For Fund management, the proposed amendment represented a marriage of a bureaucratic logic and liberal ideas. The logic of the amendment was articulated by senior officials within the Fund, in addition to Camdessus. Jack Boorman, who was then director of PDR, emphasizes the void that the Fund would fill. "There is an absence of a clear international responsibility in this area," Boorman argues. "Capital flows are all over the place, legally speaking. There is no clear jurisdiction. We did not, of course, want jurisdiction for its own sake, but for the sake of defining clear responsibility and the locus of expertise in the international community."[51] The amendment would have given responsibility for the international financial system back to the Fund after decades of recognizing the declining relevance of an international organization with no influence over its members' regulations and liberalizations of capital flows.

The view from the U.S. Treasury was that the Fund's management was searching for a greater role in the international monetary system. According to Summers, "For the Fund it was a bureaucratic imperative. The proposal was less about sound economic policy and more about Fund turf."[52] Consistent with Treasury's interpretation of the proposal was the fact that European executive directors and finance ministers who expressed enthusiasm for the amendment argued that the lack of IMF jurisdiction would lead to global discussions being held in the WTO, thus removing capital movements from the domain of finance ministries and into that of trade ministries.

The private financial community also saw the proposal in these terms. "Some bankers," Charles Dallara observes, "saw the proposal as the Fund's attempt to expand its influence and enhance its role in the international financial system, to bring it back to the center of the financial universe, where it had not been for some time. The Fund has been increasingly marginalized, and the Fund's management appeared eager to play a more important role."[53]

The U.S. Treasury and Wall Street had good reasons for their hesitancy. For the Treasury, according to Summers, the goal was never capital account liberalization for every country: "We were focused on trade in financial services, for which we sought a level playing field, rather than a liberal system per se. Although some Treasury officials did not always distinguish between these two goals, at the highest levels our priorities were clear." As for private sector bankers, according to Summers, "The amendment was not even on the radar screen of Wall Street. No one on Wall Street cared whether the Fund had jurisdiction over the capital account, or thought that it would make much difference."[54]

The private financial community was of two minds regarding the Fund's leadership in capital liberalization. According to Lex Rieffel, a former Treasury and OECD official who chaired the working group on capital account liberalization at the IIF, distinguishing between the freedom of capital movements and the proposed amendment to the Fund's Articles is critical: "Of course, Wall Street was in favor of liberalization. But the financial community had some serious reservations about giving the Fund jurisdiction over the capital account."[55] These reservations included the fear that the amendment would actually legitimize those capital controls that the Fund did approve. Similarly, Dallara recalls that he and his colleagues "sympathized with bankers from emerging markets who warned against premature liberalization and the vulnerabilities that came with it. Although capital account openness is in the broad interest of financial institutions, bankers are much more interested in particular countries, rather than the system as a whole. And the economies that matter most are already mostly open." Lastly, Dallara reflected on the private sector's "confidence in the Fund's ability to see both the public and the private interest. The culture of the Fund is almost always to see the public interest in any situation. The proposed amendment was an example: although the proposal was exactly at the intersection of public and private, in formulating its approach the Fund consulted with the private sector virtually not at all."[56]

Clearly, then, the proposal to amend the Articles was a Fund initiative, with Camdessus as its most influential proponent. Reflecting on the Fund's fiftieth anniversary, Camdessus argued against the putative lessons of the interwar years and naturally sought to replace them with what he considered to be the "lessons about economic policy that have been learned, or re-learned, in the post-war period." According to Camdessus, "we have learned that restrictions on capital movements—allowed as they may be by the Fund's Articles—are generally not to be recommended as an instrument of policy."[57]

The Rise and Fall of the Capital Account Amendment

In July 1994 MAE, headed by Manuel Guitián, first presented a paper to the board that began to lay the intellectual groundwork for an official change in the Fund's approach to the capital account. MAE wrote: "Under the Bretton Woods system controls were seen to make it more difficult for market participants to test the authorities' resolve to defend an exchange rate parity. However, the advent of floating exchange rates and the rapid integration of capital markets have shifted the balance of costs and benefits away from controls."[58] During the next three years, the urge to use the Fund to advance capital mobility would gather momentum.[59]

Economist Stanley Fischer joined the Fund in 1994 as its First Deputy Managing Director and provided considerable intellectual and political support for management's initiative. The proposal to amend the Articles preceded his arrival, however. Although Fischer's role in promoting the amendment later became important, he was not responsible for the idea.

Then, in October 1994, the Interim Committee issued what came to be known as the Madrid Declaration, which "welcomed the growing trend toward currency convertibility and encouraged member countries to remove impediments to the flow of capital."[60] The declaration did not represent marching orders for the board, but it was suggestive of the evolution of orthodoxy. The managing director and board recognized the opening presented by the Interim Committee.

A November 1994 board meeting was devoted to the Interim Committee's assessments of members' approaches to the capital account. The managing director's Summing Up revealed serious divisions:

> Some directors expressed support for an extension of the Fund's jurisdictional responsibility in the area of capital account transactions, noting that we now live in a world that is very different from that faced by the Fund's founding fathers . . . Some other Directors, however, expressed reluctance, noting that, in some circumstances, the use of capital controls could play a useful role in dealing with exchange rate pressures.[61]

The growing enthusiasm for Fund jurisdiction continued to emanate from the developed world.

In 1995, a pivotal year, the Fund's board began to consider seriously amending the Articles of Agreement.[62] A July 1995 board paper observed:

> The Executive Board has thus far not considered comprehensively the specific issue of capital account liberalization with a view to developing guidelines for the membership as a whole . . . Although it has recognized this freedom, the Fund has tended in the context of its multilateral surveillance discussions and bilateral policy advice to welcome members' actions taken to liberalize capital account transactions, and to urge such liberalization in cases where this was deemed to be a crucial element of broader structural reforms.[63]

And thus we see the IMF's journey toward capital liberalization inching forward. This movement forward gathered still more momentum when the Group of Seven (G7) came aboard later that year. The G7, which is the source of nearly all major policy innovations within the Fund, urged the IMF to "consider extending existing obligations regarding the convertibility of current account transactions to the staged liberalization of capital account transactions."[64] Still, the board appeared divided on the issue: developed countries in general favored the proposal, developing countries in general did not.[65]

Within the Fund, MAE, and in particular Guitián, its outspoken and influential director, played a central role in the board's deliberations.[66] In the summer of 1995, Guitián spoke at a critically important board meeting in favor of the amendment, encouraging executive directors to shift discretion regarding the capital account from member countries to the board itself.[67] Guitián, a proponent of an amendment of the Articles, outlined his reasoning: "economic logic advocates the dismantling of capital controls; developments in the world economy make them undesirable and ineffective; and a strong case can be made in support of rapid and decisive liberalization of capital transactions. All these considerations underwrite strongly a code of conduct that eschews resort to capital controls as an acceptable course of action for economic policy."[68] Here we see, yet again, how strong was the appeal of logic and order among these bureaucrats, in lieu of any substantiated case for the soundness of changing policy. By casting his own advocacy as that of logic itself, Guitián implies, as he no doubt believed, that the need to dismantle capital controls was self-evident.

For Camdessus, the case against controls had less to do with universal logic and more to do with his recollection of the French experience, which many others also recognized as pivotal in the history of financial globalization. Camdessus supported the proposal on the grounds that controls themselves, subject to circumvention by the unscrupulous, were more dangerous than the risks of uncontrolled capital:

> There were two views. The first, held by most of the IMF staff, was that it was a more effective strategy to accept to have as an objective full liberalization and to start taking prudent steps in that direction, while the problem of the banking system was starting to be addressed. Both actions could be mutually reinforcing. A few in the staff were more dogmatic and would have preferred a more radical liberalization approach. The second view was to encourage a country to wait behind a protective wall of exchange controls. I have fought against this second tendency. Exchange controls may help insulate a country's authorities, but only for a very short time. Even the best conceived and effective exchange control system will be circumvented within six months. Speculators and crooks are extremely sophisticated. And then, after a year, exchange controls are effective only against the poor. The French experience of the beginning of the 1980s had been extremely convincing for me. I preached on every possible occasion that you cannot trust exchange controls in the long term.[69]

MAE was enthusiastically in favor of the amendment, and generally put forward the view that the way to get sound domestic financial markets was to put pressure on them through liberalization. PDR was basically supportive of the amendment, but hesitant, more concerned about safeguards and how they were organized.

The directors of MAE and PDR, Guitián and Boorman respectively, authored a "staff operational note" and circulated it in December 1995 to the area departments. The note, "Strengthening Discussions and Information on Capital Account Convertibility—Next Steps," was written to offer more guidance on capital account issues. Boorman and Guitián wrote of the "next steps to be followed by the staff in adapting Fund practices to elicit greater emphasis on capital account issues, and to promote more actively capital account liberalization."[70]

The IMF's area departments, however, were generally opposed to the proposal, primarily because their staffs knew that such a mandate would make their lives more difficult in dealing with members.[71] Because the area departments' representatives frequently met with and offered advice to member governments, even strongly held views within MAE and PDR could not determine what the Fund did on the ground. Advice-giving and bilateral surveillance remained decentralized activities, as they always had been.

Within PDR, Boorman worried that the Fund's authority on capital account issues was too widely dispersed. Boorman recalled:

> The Fund was not doing enough in an organized way on capital account issues. Indeed, the research, capital markets, [PDR], and legal departments all had something to do with capital account issues, but without any one of them being in charge and clearly accountable. An amendment would have helped focus organizational responsibility for the Fund's position on this issue.[72]

Some supporters on the board emphasized the credibility to be gained by developing country members. "The key," according to Belgium's Willy Kiekens, "was to give confidence to investors that once a country has opened, it cannot easily go back. At that point the country would be subject to international rules, to an international jurisdiction."[73] European executive directors representing primarily developed countries continued during these discussions to offer colleagues from developing countries arguments that presented the rule change as being primarily in their benefit.

Still, according to the managing director's Summing Up, the board's position at that critical July 1995 meeting was that the staff should continue its efforts to encourage liberalization without an amendment: "In considering whether to amend the Articles to extend Fund jurisdiction to capital account issues, most Directors took the view that sufficient scope was available to the Fund under the present Articles and under the surveillance decision to accommodate increased emphasis on capital account issues."[74] The skepticism of the non-EU and non-OECD members of the board continued to undermine progress toward the amendment.

The minutes of another important July 1995 board meeting indeed reveal limited support for a capital account amendment. Only six executive directors spoke in favor of the amendment, among them the U.S., U.K., and Japanese directors, whose collective voting weight was approximately 38.4 percent. Seven executive directors, representing 25.2 percent of the board's votes, argued that the Fund could continue to promote capital account liberalization effectively without an amendment. Five executive directors, with 22.3 percent of the votes, urged further work. And six developing-country executive directors, with their 14.1 percent of the votes, spoke against a capital account amendment.[75]

The arguments in favor of the amendment reflected an emerging collection of ideas about financial globalization. Kiekens, the Belgian executive director, focused on the acceptability of restrictions: "The legitimate reasons for reintroducing capital account controls are limited."[76] Lissakers emphasized the attractiveness of freer financial markets in principle, noting that "there is a compelling theoretical argument that free capital movements are likely to be welfare enhancing, identical to the argument for the gains from trade in goods and services."[77] Curiously, the Japanese executive director, Hachiro Mesaki, offered an interpretation of the intent of the founders of the Fund that is at odds with the historical record:

> The Articles of Agreement certainly allow capital account restrictions but should not be interpreted to mean that these restrictions are appropriate. The economic circumstances surrounding the drafters of the Articles may have made them hesitate to delve deeply into the capital account convertibility issue, despite their recognition of the desirability of liberalization. That is why the staff has, in effect, encouraged capital account liberalization and why the Board has generally supported it.[78]

Board papers from 1997 reveal that directors, even before the MAE and PDR guidelines of December 1995, had also in July 1995 "encouraged the staff to enhance the Fund's role in the liberalization of the capital account through surveillance and technical assistance."[79] This was to be accomplished through a number of initiatives, including:

> [G]uidance to Article IV missions on strengthening analysis and discussion of capital account issues and assessing the scope for capital account liberalization; allocation of staff resources toward ongoing monitoring and assessment of financial and capital account developments; undertaking a pilot

data collection project for 31 countries on the regulatory regimes governing cross-border capital movements, especially portfolio transactions; and the development of policy proposals regarding the Fund's role in promoting capital account liberalization.[80]

The sequence of events continued to move the proposal forward. In September 1996, the Interim Committee asked the executive board to continue its analysis of capital flows and examine possible changes to the IMF's Articles. In February 1997 the board met to discuss whether it would support an amendment. The amendment was conceived in two parts—first, giving the Fund the purpose of capital account liberalization and, second, giving the Fund actual jurisdiction over capital movements.[81] As the managing director concluded, there was more support on the board for listing capital account liberalization among the Fund's mandates:

> Directors believed that the Fund, as the principal international monetary institution with near universal membership, was uniquely placed to promote capital account liberalization and the smooth operation of international capital markets. It was, of course, observed that the absence of a formal mandate to foster capital account liberalization had not prevented the Fund from playing an important role in encouraging and supporting members' efforts toward liberalization and in monitoring international capital markets. Nevertheless, it was also pointed out that global integration was no longer limited to goods and services, but now encompassed capital flows, and it was in the common interest of all members for the Fund to promote global integration. Therefore, most, if not all, Directors supported an amendment of the Fund's Articles at least to include the liberalization of capital movements in the mandate of the Fund; a few Directors, while not opposed to an amendment, felt that there was no urgency to rush to an amendment and that more work needed to be done, particularly in defining the operations to be covered and the nature of the transitional and emergency measures to be adopted for the implementation of this mandate.[82]

At the same time, the managing director concluded, "many, if not most, Directors agreed that the Fund should be given also jurisdiction over capital movements."[83] There was less support for actual jurisdiction. Camdessus did not, however, accept this view. As he later described: "This position made no sense. How could the Fund have a mandate to promote capital account liberalization without the appropriate jurisdiction and tools?"[84]

"There was never," Matthew Fisher recalls of the jurisdiction issue, "consensus on the Board."[85] Developing country executive directors did not, however, aggressively oppose the amendment as a group, despite their concerns. Among them, Egypt's Abdel Shakour Shaalan and Iran's Abbas Mirakhor objected to the proposal to extend the Fund's jurisdiction to the capital account. They not only argued that the proposal was in direct conflict with the intent of the Fund's founders to encourage current, but explicitly not capital, account liberalization; they also expressed concern that the Fund's staff would become overly enthusiastic in their promotion of liberalization. Indeed, with the legal department having clarified that the Fund could not use conditionality to promote capital account liberalization without a capital account amendment, it appeared to some developing country executive directors that the primary purpose for the amendment was to bring conditionality to the capital account. This fear was heightened by management and staff acknowledgement that the Fund already encouraged capital account liberalization in its surveillance and advisory capacities, with conditionality being the only potential policy lever left to pull. But because of their financial vulnerability, developing countries "on the board are always in an awkward position with respect to new initiatives from Fund management."[86] The Japanese and Australian executive directors, among developed countries, also expressed reluctance.

Even more potentially consequential for the fate of the amendment was the stance of Bernes, the Canadian executive director. Bernes recalls being "surprised at the time that there was very little developing country opposition to the proposal."[87] Canada, a member of the G7, had traditionally embraced the "principle of G7 solidarity," which meant that the group presented a unified front within the Fund. Major new initiatives in Fund policy had come largely from decisions made by G7 finance ministers.[88] Bernes, with the backing of the Canadian finance ministry, objected to the proposal to amend the Articles. His prepared statement outlined a logic based in part on the purposes embedded in the design of the international financial architecture.[89] As a result of his stance, Bernes recalls that he "took a lot of heat from the OECD and G7 countries."[90]

At a February 1997 board meeting, Bernes insisted:

We must also recognize that, inherent in the architecture of the Bretton Woods System was an explicit acknowledgment of the value of a division of labor. This suggests that the notion of "one-stop shopping" for capital account liberalization may not be the most effective configuration and therefore, while I am convinced that the Fund is the most appropriate institution to promote the removal of foreign exchange restrictions with payments and transfers, I am not yet persuaded that it should have jurisdiction on the underlying transactions and indeed, such a proposition raises a number of questions.[91]

The Canadian position was, thus, not that capital account liberalization was a problematic goal in itself, but rather that the Fund's jurisdiction had excluded the capital account for important reasons. Indeed, Bernes "was not convinced we knew what we wanted to do with jurisdiction over the capital account, and that we did not know enough about the preconditions for and sequencing of capital account liberalization."[92] Although Canadian authorities saw capital account liberalization as an appropriate goal—Bernes insists that "no one was debating the objective"—they felt that Fund jurisdiction over capital movements would be unnecessary, and could perhaps actually impede the objective of orderly capital account liberalization.

But by April 1997, enough votes on the board had apparently shifted toward the managing director's position that Camdessus concluded:

> Most Directors supported an amendment of the Fund's Articles to include the liberalization of capital movements in the mandate of the Fund, and supported an extension of the Fund's jurisdiction to capital movements which would allow flexibility in implementation through transitional provisions and approval policies.[93]

The minutes of the meeting do reveal broad support, though not the 85 percent weighted votes necessary to amend the Articles. Fourteen executive directors spoke in favor of amending the Articles to endow the Fund with the purpose of promoting capital account liberalization and jurisdiction over the capital account; those fourteen, including the U.S., U.K., and nearly all European executive directors, accounted for 64.6 percent of the weighted votes. Three executive directors—Bernes, Shaalan, and the temporary alternate executive director for Italy—argued in favor of an amendment that was limited to a new purpose for the Fund, without a new Fund jurisdiction; this view accounted for approximately 10.7 percent of the votes. Seven developing country executive directors, representing nearly 25 percent of the weighted votes, argued against any amendment of the Articles at that time.[94]

As a matter of law, capital liberalization was clearly outside the Fund's purview, as confirmed by the Fund's own General Counsel. In April 1997 a number of executive directors asked the General Counsel, François Gianviti, to clarify the legal issues at stake. His answer is worth quoting at length because it is not yet generally available to the public. According to the board's minutes, Gianviti explained:

> He would find it difficult to confirm that promotion of capital account liberalization fell within the Fund's mandate, even if it were not explicitly within the purposes of the Fund given in Article I. In its exercise of surveillance in the context of Article IV consultations, the Fund looked at all aspects of a member's policies, which included trade policy and capital investment policy, as well as current payments, but that was done for the purpose of assessing the soundness of the member's policies. If, for instance, it was found that the member had had recourse to a particularly strict restriction on capital inflows or outflows, it might show that there was something wrong with the member's exchange rate policies; it would be in that context. The Fund was not promoting liberalization of capital investments or capital transactions as such; the Fund had been assisting members in achieving that purpose, as their purpose and their objective, not as a purpose of the Fund itself. In fact, it would be contrary to the right of members under Article VI to restrict capital transactions. The Fund could perhaps persuade, convince, or explain the benefits, but that was something else . . . During the negotiations on the Second Amendment, compromise wording had been agreed for Article IV. Despite the shortcomings of the logic, however, the law was clear. The beginning of Article IV, Section 1, defined the purpose of the international monetary system, not the purpose of the Fund. The purpose of the international monetary system was to provide a framework that facilitated the exchange of goods, services, and capital. The obligations of members were laid out in Article IV, Section 1. Article IV, Section 3 stated that the Fund had to oversee the compliance of members with their obligations, but the Fund only oversaw the international monetary system in order to ensure its effective operation, the General Counsel pointed out. That did not mean that the Fund had the power to impose additional obligations and, in particular, the obligation to liberalize capital movements. What the Fund could do at the present stage was to tell a member that there was an undesirable state of affairs, and to change, but that was not an obligation.[95]

If capital liberalization were to advance, it would thus require an amendment to the Articles.

The Interim Committee's next meeting, later in April 1997, produced directions for the board that were more resolved. The committee's members "agreed that the Fund's Articles should be amended to make the promotion of capital account liberalization a specific purpose of the Fund and to give the Fund appropriate jurisdiction over the capital movements."[96]

But without an overwhelming majority of board members in favor of the amendment, those in the Fund's management who thought it should still be a priority faced an uphill battle during the spring and summer of 1997. Developing country directors on the board "feared that the United States would use the fund to force developing countries to liberalize."[97] Or, as Kiekens put it, "Some developing country executive directors saw the proposed amendment as undermining sovereignty."[98]

The proposed amendment was dealt another blow when, in May 1997, the British Conservative government was swept from power, along with Chancellor of the Exchequer Kenneth Clarke, who had been an ardent supporter of the amendment. The U.K.'s executive director, Gus O'Donnell, had been one of the most articulate and persuasive advocates of the proposal. The message from the new Chancellor, Gordon Brown, was that the United Kingdom would do nothing to kill the amendment, but that it would also no longer play a major role in its progress.[99] That is, the United Kingdom would join the United States in its modest, but essentially indifferent, support.

Still, Camdessus felt confident enough in May 1997 to announce publicly, "As far as the IMF is concerned, there is unanimity in the membership to give us the mandate to promote capital account liberalization, thereby adding a chapter to the uncompleted work of Bretton Woods."[100] In board meetings, however, Bernes and Shaalan took exception to the managing director's public characterizations of consensus on the board. In June Bernes noted that "the consensus on this issue is clearly moving in the direction of more comprehensiveness in the scope of the Fund's jurisdiction," but that it was "premature" to assert that the board had reached agreement.[101] Similarly, Shaalan argued that "it would be premature to imply that an agreement has already been reached even on the general parameters of extending the Fund's jurisdiction."[102] Although Camdessus generally described the board as having enjoyed consensus and presented the IMF as having a coherent approach, behind the scenes serious divisions in management and staff persisted.

Throughout the summer of 1997 the board discussed every possible angle of the amendment, including emergency approval, exceptions, mechanisms, and transitional arrangements. Still, consensus eluded the board, and each detail raised new concerns. Indeed, executive directors spent the summer noting with regularity that "the devil is in the details," so much so that the phrase characterized the discussions in June, July, and August.[103] Camdessus continued to urge the board to reach agreement by the autumn meeting of the Interim Committee, as had been the board's mandate.

One way to achieve greater consensus on the board was to exclude inward foreign direct investment from the Fund's proposed jurisdiction over capital, as it was seen as too politically sensitive. "With respect to the treatment of inward direct investment," according to the Summing Up of a July 1997 board meeting, "most directors felt that such transactions should fall outside the Fund's jurisdiction in all respects."[104] The political sensitivity of foreign direct investment led to its exclusion from an emerging policy consensus on liberalization, despite the fact that it was direct investment that was generally seen to be more stable and potentially even more beneficial for host countries. In this way the policy consensus began to depart even more dramatically from the emergent professional consensus among economists; to the extent that beneficial effects of capital account liberalization had been increasingly accepted, those benefits were seen primarily to accrue from direct investment.

Another concern that supporters of the amendment worked to assuage was that the Fund would be rigid in its interpretation of its new mandate to promote capital account liberalization. The narrow legal result of an amendment would be that the Fund would have the authority to approve or disapprove of capital controls that member countries introduced. Although it was clear that not all circumstances could be foreseen, a number of board members were eager to construct a set of procedures for the Fund's approval of capital controls that would assure flexibility. The board therefore urged staff to develop approval policies to deal with capital account "restrictions imposed for: (i) balance of payments and macroeconomic management purposes; (ii) market and institutional evolution reasons; (iii) prudential considerations; and (iv) reasons of national and international security."[105]

Although there were still many dissenting voices on the board in July 1997, Camdessus began drafting a report to the Interim Committee for its autumn meeting. In early September, just before the annual meetings in Hong Kong, the board produced its report to the Interim Committee, while, simultaneously and in consultation with the board, the Interim Committee drafted the statement it would make in Asia.[106]

Meanwhile, private financial services firms began to coordinate their efforts to reach a consensus view on the proposed amendment. In September 1997 the IIF, which represents highly internationalized banks, produced a briefing note on the issue. The private sector was unenthusiastic about the proposed amendment for a number of reasons. First, many of these influential bankers expressed concerns about premature capital account liberalization, following the lead of their colleagues operating in emerging markets. Capital account liberalization, the report noted, "encompassing a much larger range of countries could increase the volatility of capital flows."[107] Critics of the Fund and the private financial community have often portrayed concerns about the volatility of internationalized financial markets as exclusive to policymakers, but in this case the situation was essentially opposite: a cautious private financial community warned enthusiastic bureaucrats.

Another important issue concerned the evolution of IMF policy after 1989. Until 1989, it had been Fund policy to withhold its credit from members with payment arrears to commercial creditors until those arrears had been cleared or arranged to be cleared; after 1989, the Fund began to lend even when arrears to commercial creditors were outstanding. Many influential members of the private sector felt that, until the Fund reverted to its pre-1989 policy on lending into arrears, the IIF should oppose a capital account amendment.[108] Finally, from the private sector's point of view, the most worrisome aspect of the amendment was that it had emerged almost as a surprise, and without any involvement of the financial community. As the memorandum noted, "there has been remarkably little consultation and discussion between officials and IIF members on the subject of CAC [capital account convertibility]."[109]

In September 1997, in anticipation of the annual meeting of the Interim Committee, *The Banker* ran a series of articles outlining the perspective of many of the world's most influential financial institutions. The articles, which quote Dallara among others, offered a remarkable list of reasons why financial firms ought to oppose a new IMF amendment. The most important reason was to preserve the central role of private financial firms in the globalization of finance; such a significant increase of influence and power on 19th Street might come at the private sector's expense. "This is power without limit," Dallara explained, "and that is why no one in private markets, investors, bankers, or hedge funds should get on board this amendment."[110] The financial community was also alarmed at the "apparent anxiety by IMF management to have the issue signed and sealed as soon as possible," particularly because private financial interests had not been consulted before management publicly announced the new initiative. Perhaps most ironically, the voice of private finance, to the extent that it was centralized at that moment, was cautious. The Thai financial crisis that began in July 1997 revealed with greater clarity the "need for caution."[111] Dallara worried in particular about the susceptibility of "banking regimes that are not adequately strong" to crisis in an era of financial globalization.[112]

Indeed, by the time the Interim Committee held its forty-ninth meeting in Hong Kong on September 21, 1997, the financial crisis that eventually would sweep across much of southeast Asia had already begun. The worst of the crisis was still to come, and everyone hoped that Thailand's economic collapse would be an isolated problem. The Interim Committee produced, with near unanimity, a statement that came to be known as the Hong Kong Communiqué, which outlined the Fund's official approach to amending the Articles.[113] The Interim Committee also agreed to a $90 billion increase in the Fund's resources, with $18 billion to come from the United States.

The Committee's *Liberalization of Capital Movements under an Amendment of the IMF's Articles* was ambitious, but neither doctrinaire nor inherently inflexible—it was, in the words of the Interim Committee, "bold in its vision, but cautious in implementation." "It is time," the Interim Committee argued, "to add a new chapter to the Bretton Woods agreement." Emphasizing the coordination of national and international authorities, the committee argued that if the liberalization of capital flows were "introduced in an orderly manner," such flows would be "an essential element of an efficient international monetary system in this age of globalization." Finally, the committee

> invites the Executive Board to complete its work on a proposed amendment of the IMF's Articles that would make the liberalization of capital movements one of the purposes of the IMF, and extend, as needed, the IMF's jurisdiction through the establishment of carefully defined and consistently applied obligations regarding the liberalization of such movements. Safeguards and transitional arrangements are necessary for the success of this major endeavor. Flexible approval policies will have to be adopted.[114]

The Interim Committee's chair, Philippe Maystadt, Deputy Prime Minister and Minister of Finance of Belgium, argued that the member countries would simply be transferring sovereignty that they had already ceded to global capital markets back to policymakers, though they would be in an international organization. Making a case that was reminiscent of arguments in favor of European integration, Maystadt suggested that "by allowing sovereignty over capital account restrictions to be transferred from member countries to the Fund, the amendment of the Fund agreement will strengthen the authority of what is, after all, a global institution within an area in which member countries had for practical purposes given up a good deal of their sovereignty already."[115]

The tenor of the discussion within the committee was surprisingly supportive, given the level of disagreement on the board. But it is important to recall that a significant increase in Fund resources was also on the table in Hong Kong. "What was at stake," former Dutch executive director Onno Wijnholds recalls, "was a package of proposals for the IMF, including a quota increase and the capital account amendment. Developing countries were perhaps obliged to go along with the amendment to ensure that the quota increase would go through."[116]

Only a few concerns were raised by committee members. Italian Minister of the Treasury, Budget, and Economic Programming Azeglio Ciampi, who in 1998 succeeded Maystadt as chair, urged the board to reach the "appropriate balance" between greater obligations for Fund members and "appropriate safeguards." Ciampi insisted that in "matters such as these it is more important to be right than to be fast."[117] The Indian Minister of Finance P. Chidambaram argued that it was "important to allow countries to move at their own pace."[118] Remarkably, even Canadian central bank governor Gordon Thiessen, representing Canada on behalf of Finance Minister Paul Martin, expressed support for the amendment, "a logical extension" of the Fund's mandate.[119] This was despite the fact that the Canadian executive director, Bernes, was leading the charge against the proposed amendment on the Fund's board. The Group of 24 raised concerns, however: "While recognizing the benefits for the world economy of greater freedom of capital movements, Ministers emphasize that the capital account liberalization process could put additional stress on the economies that are already straining to adjust to globalization."[120]

Camdessus' plea for the amendment was impassioned. Although the crisis was unfolding in Asia, he urged countries not to begin tallying the costs of capital account liberalization only at the onset of a crisis. "Countries cannot," Camdessus argued, "compete for the blessings of global capital markets and refuse their disciplines." Furthermore, Camdessus insisted that "far from being discouraged by recent events in southeast Asia, the IMF is all the more motivated to continue work on an amendment to the Articles of Agreement that will allow the Fund to promote freedom of capital movements." His strongest argument in favor of an amendment weighed the risks of capital openness against the costs associated with control:

> Freedom has its risks. But are they greater than those of complex administrative rules and capricious changes in their design? Freedom has its risks. But is there any more fertile field for development and prosperity? Freedom has its risks! Let's go then for an orderly liberalization of capital movements. Certainly, the point is not to make a sacrifice on the altar of fashion. The point is not to encourage countries to remove capital controls prematurely, nor to prevent them from using capital controls on a temporary basis, when justified.

Finally, Camdessus claimed that a capital account amendment would fulfill the vision of the IMF's architects: "Let us now add this promising chapter to the work of our founding fathers. This certainly would have been part and parcel of their response to the challenges of today."[121] It is to Camdessus' credit as a student of history that he used the conditional "would have" here, for the founding fathers of the IMF were resolute in their vigilance against hot money and free capital. They "would have" supported Camdessus and capital mobility only if their position had swung around to the diametric opposite of what it actually was.

Jacques de Larosière, Camdessus' predecessor at the Fund, worried over the implications of the Interim Committee's approach. "When I saw the Fund—in Hong Kong, in 1997—promoting the full liberalization of capital movements, I was worried," de Larosière recalls. "I believed that supporters of the amendment were going too far in their effort to formalize capital liberalization, particularly because the system already allowed for the free movement of capital." Describing capital as a river and the institutional infrastructure as its banks, de Larosière saw the proposed amendment as "the river's erosion of that last bit of the IMF, its neutrality on capital controls."[122]

After returning from Hong Kong, Camdessus and Fischer urged the board to consider the Interim Committee's directions as firm and clear. But events in Asia continued to attract attention. When in December 1997 the financial crisis engulfed South Korea, a country that had hitherto appeared to be extraordinarily stable, the amendment was dealt a serious blow. "After the crisis in Korea," Kiekens recalled, "it was all over."[123] The argument that massive capital outflows and widespread currency speculation merely represented the discipline of the financial markets had been undermined. The Thai and Indonesian economic policy transgressions that might require discipline could be at least retrospectively identified, but South Korea's were harder to find. The language of rational market discipline was giving way to words like "contagion" and "panic."

In March 1998 a seminar was held at the Fund to debate the merits of the proposal.[124] Fischer restated his case for an amendment. After being briefed by Lissakers' staff, Summers spoke in favor of an amendment that gave the IMF the "tools" to deal with capital account issues.[125]

From within the IMF, only Jacques Polak, former director of research and Dutch executive director, argued against the amendment, emphasizing the subtle effects of such a mandate. Recognizing that the Fund had "wholeheartedly embraced capital liberalization" already "without being hindered by a lack of mandate," Polak worried that the IMF's staff would become overeager. "If given jurisdiction over such restrictions," Polak reasoned, "the staff is likely to become the enforcer of the new legal code, making sure at each step that any policy it recommends or endorses can pass the test of the new Article."[126] Polak's unique historical perspective on the amendment expressed precisely what had most worried policymakers in the developing world. IMF management continued to ask for trust in enforcing the new obligation, and that trust was lacking.

Meanwhile, the number of IMF executive directors in favor of moving forward quickly to amend the Articles continued to decline. At a contentious board meeting on April 2, 1998, a number of previously acquiescent directors spoke more forcefully. Bernes and Shaalan continued to press Camdessus. Additionally, the Brazilian executive director, Alexandre Kafka, who also represented a handful of Central and South American countries, and Morocco's Mohammed Daïri, Mirakhor's alternate, urged caution.[127] The Japanese executive director, Yukio Yoshimura, also expressed reluctance to approach his parliament with a proposal to expand the Fund's jurisdiction without a clear sense of what that would imply, particularly in light of the unfolding Asian crisis.[128] According to Ralf Leiteritz, these executive board meetings were critical moments during which the proposal to codify the norm of capital mobility was undermined by the arguments of executive directors who saw in the Asian financial crisis ample evidence to warrant caution in expanding the Fund's mandate.[129]

At its next meeting, in April 1998, the Interim Committee also reassured the board of its commitment to extending the IMF's jurisdiction: "The Committee reaffirmed its view, expressed in the Hong Kong Communiqué last September, that it is now time to add a new chapter to the Bretton Woods Agreement by making the liberalization of capital movements one of the purposes of the Fund and extending, as needed, the Fund's jurisdiction for this purpose."[130]

Wall Street and other private financial firms saw spring as another opportunity to weigh in on the proposed amendment, still, surprisingly, not totally undermined by the financial crisis. On the occasion of the next Interim Committee meeting, Dallara of the IIF communicated directly with its chair, Maystadt, to express the concerns of private financial interests about the Fund's effort to increase its authority over international markets.[131]

In the late spring of 1998, the U.S. funding increase for the IMF was being discussed in Congress, and the Fund came under attack from both left and right for a variety of reasons, including concerns about the environment, labor standards, and human rights.[132] When House Minority Leader Richard Gephardt learned of the proposed amendment, he and several of his colleagues sent a letter to Rubin insisting that the U.S. Treasury withdraw its support for an extension of the Fund's jurisdiction, or else the funding increase would be in jeopardy. "People—the anti-globalization crowd—on the Hill, started going nuts," Lissakers recalls.[133] The letter was unequivocal:

> We are troubled by reports that the Administration, as described in the Communiqué of the Interim Committee of the Board of Governors of the IMF, is working to "add a new chapter to the Bretton Woods Agreement by making the liberalization of capital movements one of the purposes of the Fund and extending, as needed, the Fund's jurisdiction for this purpose" . . . Adding a commitment to the complete free movement of capital exacerbates inequality unless it is accompanied by policies that substantially mitigate its impact . . . Finally, we believe that the rapid mobility of capital, especially short-term capital, greatly exacerbated the recent crisis in Asia. Serious consideration should be given to the adoption of measures that retard this volatility. Obviously adoption of the proposed amendment which makes liberalization of capital movements one of the basic purposes of the Fund works against efforts by countries to experiment with measures that could protect their economies from excessively volatile short term capital movements. This approach is exactly the opposite of what is needed to build broad-based support for the IMF. Our support for additional IMF

funding will be in jeopardy if the U.S. government continues to press for the addition of capital account liberalization to the IMF charter.[134]

This opposition within Congress to the capital account amendment led to the Treasury's withdrawal of its support, or, as one former senior Treasury official put it, "We let it fade away." The issue was straightforward: "We were not prepared to spend political capital on this issue either domestically or internationally."[135] Summers recalls the issue similarly:

> The managers of Treasury's scarce political capital were not enthusiastic about the proposed amendment once it involved any expenditure of political capital. When the proposed amendment became a political issue, we dropped it. Although there was substantive sympathy for the idea, we agreed that it was an idea best abandoned.[136]

With the United Kingdom having already backed away from the amendment, Camdessus found that there was no longer any powerful, persuasive constituency on the board for the proposal. As Onno Wijnholds recalls, "The U.S. administration stepped away from the proposal very quickly. It was breathtaking. The Americans fell silent on the issue at board meetings. The U.K. had practically reversed its position."[137]

The eruption of the Russian crisis in August 1998 was the final nail in the coffin of the capital account amendment. Not only was the middle of a contagious financial crisis an inauspicious moment to be pressing for Fund jurisdiction over the capital account, but the Fund's role in the Russia crisis undermined the credibility—in the eyes of critics—of management's assurances that it would embrace capital account liberalization cautiously. "The Fund," Executive Director Kiekens recalled, "had strongly encouraged Russia to liberalize its capital account, and the Russian crisis blew up in our faces."[138] Aleksei Mozhin, the Russian executive director, put it more strongly:

> The Fund messed up in its advice, which turned out to be questionable, to say the least. Russia was an example of a premature, unprepared liberalization of the capital account, and the Fund had encouraged the Russian government to open the GKO market [for high-yield Russian government securities] up to foreigners. With the benefit of hindsight we can see that this was a mistake.[139]

Supporters of the proposal within the Fund were surprised that their intentions could have been misread. "We were trying," Jack Boorman recalls, "to bring order and responsibility." But Boorman acknowledged that the supporters of the amendment had not made their case sufficiently well. "We mishandled it in a way that allowed the critics to portray the initiative as a power grab and as a means for the Fund to force an even more rapid opening of the capital account in emerging markets and developing member countries."[140] Similarly, Mozhin emphasized that the proposed amendment had not been "an attempt to enforce speedier progress." The principle, rather, was to be "that of the current account: no backsliding." Mozhin worried that one must have a "hostile view of the Fund, as some organization always eager to impose its will, to meddle in countries' domestic affairs," in order to see the amendment as a threat to the autonomy of developing country governments.[141] Many policymakers in developing countries hold precisely that view, of course.

The intellectual distance between Bretton Woods and 19th Street grew enormously during the 1990s, but then was compressed again by the emerging market financial crises that marked the end of the decade. And all this occurred without a change in the mandate of the IMF itself. The bureaucracy of the Fund sought to codify authority that some of its management and staff already had informally, and improperly, appropriated.

It was as though the Fund as an organization had forgotten that it was meant to be the agent of its members, who delegated power to the Fund in the first place only because the organization would be governed by laws that protected members' authority over the capital account. By embracing capital liberalization in practice and proposed new law, but in the absence of either a political or professional consensus regarding its desirability, the Fund's management came to misunderstand its role in the world. The IMF was to be the steward of the system and the overseer of its rules, not the creator of the laws. In the early years of the new century a humbled IMF resumed its cautious guardianship of the international monetary system.

As with the new rules of the OECD and EU, European policymakers situated within the organization were responsible for conceiving and promoting the initiative for new rules that would have empowered the organization, and European governments lent the greatest political support. U.S. policymakers did not play decisive roles until the end of the episode, when they were responsible not for the birth or life of the proposal, but rather its death. The private financial community, suspicious of the organization-building endeavors of Fund management, was the amendment's most vocal and influential opponent. The vision of globalization emanating from the U.S. Treasury and Wall Street is not an empowered, capacious multilateral organization representing its interests through codified rules. To the extent that the U.S. approach to ad hoc globalization relies on delegation, it is to two private American firms.

CHAPTER 7

A Common Language of Risk: Credit-Rating Agencies and Sovereigns

L'argent est un bon serviteur, mais un mauvais maître. (Money is a good servant but a bad master.)[1]

—French proverb

More than one hundred governments live, to varying degrees, by the rules of Moody's and Standard & Poor's (S&P). That is, Moody's and S&P rate the risk of lending to more than one hundred sovereigns and their specific issues of debt, the two firms together accounting for 90 percent of the market for sovereign debt rating. The agencies' sovereign ratings indirectly affect every other bond rating in the world because of the so-called sovereign ceiling: the agencies almost never rate a domestic firm's foreign-currency debt higher than that of its government because of the "risk of a sovereign imposing foreign exchange controls."[1]

Sovereign defaults are catastrophic events, for the affected societies and governments as much as for the bondholders.[2] The art of forecasting the likelihood that a government will default on its debt is both subtle and complex, the challenges magnified by the unique characteristics of sovereign borrowing. No third party, no world government or transnational collection agency, can enforce a sovereign debt contract. And countries never really run out of assets to cover their obligations, though they may, of course, fall short of foreign exchange or choose to repay one debt but not another. The assessment of credit risk is always a combination of discerning both the borrower's ability and willingness to pay. When lending to a sovereign, however, the central issue is always willingness. There are always assets to be offered, sectors of society to squeeze, government programs to cut—though such actions may or may not be politically feasible in a given circumstance.

In their analysis of sovereigns, therefore, Moody's and S&P must try to determine which policies are most likely to improve a country's economic performance, and thereby increase its ability and willingness to repay a loan.

The defining challenge is to determine which inferences the markets should draw from a variety of government policy stances. Which policies suggest a greater willingness to meet the sovereign's obligation, and which imply that the government is more likely to refuse to pay? It is plainly impossible to make such a judgment without an analytical framework that allows the agencies' analysts to infer meanings from a range of macroeconomic policies. The rating agencies are obliged to have their own orthodoxy.

As if such a task were not demanding enough, highly internationalized capital markets magnify the interpretive task enormously. An era of globalization is also necessarily an age of "credibility."[3] Government policies may succeed or fail on their own intellectual merit. A policy's success also depends fundamentally, inescapably, on how financial markets react. A credible policy, all understand, will be reinforced by market approval, as capital flows into a country. When the markets believe, a government must go out of its way to fail. But a policy stance that lacks the trust of financial markets is doomed at the start. Such a statement implies no causal relationship between the policy and its failure. It is as simple a fact as the world economy has: when the markets do not believe that a policy will improve a country's economic performance, then that policy cannot succeed. "All macroeconomic policies require public confidence in order to work," argues Jonathan Kirshner. "The astonishing result of this is that on a hypothetical menu of five economic policies, each of which was plausible from the standpoint of economic theory, if three were *perceived* to be illegitimate, they would not in fact be sustainable, *solely for that reason.*"[4]

Even with a closed capital account, a sovereign government will find that the cost of borrowing abroad increases as the markets' skepticism of its policy initiatives translates into a higher risk premium on its bonds. A more open economy is sure to feel the effect more directly. Capital flees domestic banks and equity markets, putting downward pressure on the exchange rate and raising the cost of capital for domestic firms. The logical implication is straightforward: a policy that the financial markets believe can succeed may succeed, or it may not, but a policy that the financial markets believe cannot succeed almost certainly cannot succeed.

An age of credibility thus demands that Moody's and S&P also account for the likely response of the financial markets to a policy stance. Such a response is conditioned by the shared ideas within markets about the meaning of a countercyclical budget deficit, a negative real interest rate, or a restriction on capital mobility. The rating agencies must also know and heed the orthodoxy of the markets.

To borrow the language of John Maynard Keynes, the rating agencies must always negotiate among their own standards of beauty as well as those of the markets themselves. Keynes' classic analogy for investment is perhaps even more evocative when applied to a firm whose business model consists, in part, of predicting and reporting the market's collective prediction of what average opinion expects the average opinion to be:

> [P]rofessional investment may be likened to those newspaper competitions in which the competitors have to pick out the six prettiest faces from a hundred photographs, the prize being awarded to the competitor whose choice most nearly corresponds to the average preferences of the competitors as a whole; so that each competitor has to pick, not those faces which he himself finds prettiest, but those which he thinks likeliest to catch the fancy of the other competitors, all of whom are looking at the problem from the same point of view. It is not a case of choosing those which, to the best of one's judgment, are really the prettiest, nor even those which average opinion genuinely thinks the prettiest. We have reached the third degree where we devote our intelligences to anticipating what average opinion expects the average opinion to be.[5]

The rating agencies have taken on the unenviable task of what Keynes might have called the fourth degree. Moody's and S&P must interpret the signals sent by governments' policies and guess what the markets will infer as well, taking into account, of course, that their own rating changes will influence market sentiment.

Market participants, by many accounts, believe that the rating agencies perform a valuable service. So, too, do the governments that pay their fees, for the business model has also evolved quite substantially. Whereas Moody's and S&P once charged investors for their analysis, the firms now charge issuers for rating their debt. Despite the barrage of criticisms and complaints aimed at the firms' New York headquarters, the business of credit rating remains immensely profitable.[6]

The age of capital brought with it, perforce, market discipline. Rather than the disaggregated, blunt discipline of the financial markets of the late nineteenth century, the voice of today's market discipline is concentrated in the letter ratings of the agencies. This may be a worrisome fact from the perspective of governments around the world, but it is a discipline to which they have willingly subjected themselves. Critics have focused on the magnification of the discipline of fallible markets as the most problematic outcome of the rise of Moody's and S&P. The valorization, and occasional glorification, of the "private authority" of the markets that rating agencies represent offers a fascinating collection of empirical and philosophical questions.[7]

Scholars who write of the privatization of authority in the global economy thus offer important insights into the role of the rating agencies, as long as two rather serious exceptions are taken. The authority of the rating agencies is not actually private, and Moody's and S&P have not wrested from governments an authority that used to be public. They have instead created something completely new, a simplification and magnification of authority that was always private when capital was internationalized. The financial markets were given authority by the governments that liberalized them, and the markets essentially delegated some of their power to the rating agencies. Governments, too, delegated their regulatory responsibilities to the agencies. The reality connecting both of these ideas is underappreciated, but critical: Moody's and S&P's sovereign ratings carry the force of law in the United States and in many countries around the world.[8]

In this chapter I describe the influence of the rating agencies on international capital markets, and in particular their reinforcement of the trends toward capital liberalization. I focus on Moody's and S&P, by a wide margin the two most important firms in the industry.

The agencies offer a remarkable contrast between the two views of financial globalization—Europe's institutionalized global finance compared to the United States' ad hoc globalization—in what is putatively a market outcome: the global dominance of two American firms.

A dominant European view, not to mention a developing-country perspective, is that Moody's and S&P enforce the norms of U.S.-style financial capitalism around the world. Although that argument is frequently overdrawn, the interpretive frameworks and benchmarks used by Moody's and S&P are indeed much more consistent with the organization of firms and banks in the United States, and perhaps the United Kingdom, than elsewhere in the world. No policymakers planned to put the rating agencies at the center of the international financial architecture, and yet, both formally and informally, that is where they are. The influence of agencies does not represent the achievement of the multilateral codification of rules, but rather the ad hoc influence of the United States and its prevailing practices of borrowing and lending. The breadth and depth of U.S. securities markets enhance the significance of U.S. regulations. This outcome, in turn, empowers the rating agencies both within the country and abroad, though the U.S. government can plausibly disavow responsibility for how Moody's and S&P go about making their judgments, just as the agencies can disavow responsibility for the impacts of codifying their ratings.[9]

This is very much the sort of institutional architecture for financial globalization of which the IIF's Charles Dallara would likely approve, and not the vision of, say, Jacques Delors or Pascal Lamy, two proponents of a globalization managed by international organizations. Other European policymakers and politicians have resented, criticized, and attempted to undermine Moody's and S&P, and their struggle continues today.

Origins of the Rating Agencies

The rating agencies are American, and, historically, it hardly could have been otherwise. In the twenty-first century the incumbents of the business of credit rating are protected by regulatory barriers to entry, as well as scale and network economies, so formidable that the chances even of the third-place firm, Fitch, displacing either Moody's or S&P are slim. In the current environment the probability that a newly created firm could ever overtake Moody's and S&P rounds to zero. The path to Moody's and S&P's dominance extraordinarily depended on the starting point. When European managers and policymakers, among many others, wonder how it has come to be that two rating agencies play such an enormous role in their affairs, they often wish that it were French, or German, or even Italian firms that wielded such authority, for then, perhaps, their decisions might be interpreted through eyes more sympathetic to their institutions, histories, and traditions. Unless European policymakers are prepared to regulate a competitor into existence, it is now too late; that train has left the station.

The first rating agencies (the precursors of Moody's and S&P) created the practice of evaluating the creditworthiness of the bonds issued by American railroads in the early twentieth century, selling their analysis to the railroad's potential investors.[10] Everything about U.S. railroads in the nineteenth and twentieth centuries was unique: their regulation; their massive, continental size; and, most dramatically, their financing.[11] "No other enterprises," writes Alfred Chandler of the American railroads, "required such large sums of outside capital."[12] And, perhaps ironically, much of the outside capital that fueled their growth—and thus (at least indirectly) the growth of the U.S.-based rating agencies—came from Europe.[13]

Henry Varnum Poor first began in 1868 to publish *Poor's Manual of the Railroads of the United States,* his annual report on the creditworthiness of the railroads.[14] *Poor's Manual* merely collected information and offered no opinions about the probability that railroad firms would continue to pay their creditors. In 1900 John Moody first published *Moody's Manual of Industrial and Miscellaneous Securities,* which, like *Poor's Manual,* reported on the property, capitalization, management, and credit of the country's firms.

In 1909 Moody invented the modern practice of rating the securities of American railroads by adapting the letter rating symbols that had for a century been used by firms that collected data on customer creditworthiness. Then in 1914, five years after *Moody's Analyses of Railroad Investments* was first published, Moody's Investors Service was incorporated. In 1916 the Standard Statistics Bureau began to assign ratings to bonds as well. Then in 1941, Poor's Publishing Company merged with Standard Statistics to form Standard & Poor's, which was acquired by McGraw-Hill in 1966. Dun & Bradstreet owned Moody's between 1962 and 2000, when Moody's was spun off.

The rating agencies experienced phenomenal growth from their origin through the Great Depression. The 1930s, an unhappy time for issuers and holders of securities, ironically brought an increase in the agencies' influence. The late 1940s, 1950s, and 1960s were happier for both issuers and holders of securities, but for the rating agencies the times were perhaps too good: no one seemed to default. The capital controls of the Bretton Woods international monetary regime, moreover, meant that international private capital flows were minuscule. The U.S. interest equalization tax, among these capital controls, put a serious brake on the firms' potential business from cross-border capital flows, as American investors found the higher returns available abroad diminished by the government's appropriation of the differential. In 1968 the agencies suspended almost all sovereign ratings because of their essential irrelevance.[15] By the late 1960s the rating agencies were unexceptional firms with only modest revenues derived from selling their reports to subscribers, the same business model that John Moody had conceived in 1909. Few businesses were as uninteresting, uneventful, and unimportant.

By the end of the decade, however, the industry had been transformed.

The collapse of the Bretton Woods system in the early 1970s was accompanied, at least in the United States, by the loosening of American capital controls in 1974. Other governments began to experiment with greater mobility for capital as well. Private corporations in the United States and abroad began to tap international capital markets. Governments around the world also began to incorporate the agencies' ratings into their own financial regulations as benchmarks for the investing public's exposure to various categories of default risk.

Although the United States had first incorporated credit ratings into financial regulation in 1931, in 1975 the Securities and Exchange Commission (SEC) took a step that was to influence the industry decisively, and perhaps permanently. The SEC introduced the designation of "nationally recognized statistical rating organization" (NRSRO) for use in U.S. financial regulation. Among the criteria used by the SEC to determine whether a firm ought to be designated an NRSRO, the most important was whether the firm was "nationally recognized" in the United States "as an issuer of credible and reliable ratings by the predominant users of securities ratings." For a security to be widely held in the United States a rating by an NRSRO was simply required by a variety of regulations. Most such regulations were written to limit the exposure of investment funds to risky securities, a quite understandable public policy concern. In 1975 the SEC designated three firms (S&P, Moody's, and Fitch) as NRSROs. Thirty years later there were five NRSROs: S&P, Moody's, Fitch, Dominion Bond Rating Service Ltd and A.M. Best.[16] (see Table 7.1).

The rating agencies also benefited from financial disintermediation, whereby capital flowed directly from investors to issuers of securities, as opposed to going through banks, which had historically "intermediated" this relationship. Disintermediation dramatically changed the process by which capital was allocated.[17] Whereas banks had always scrutinized the creditworthiness of potential borrowers on behalf of depositors, the decision, increasingly widespread, of holders of capital to bypass the bank and invest directly in securities implied that a new premium would be placed on the accumulation and simplification of information about the risks associated with a wide range of securities. All these precursors of the internationalization of capital, indeed of globalization, set the stage for the reemergence of sovereign debt markets, which had essentially been dormant since 1940.

Finally, in the early 1970s both Moody's and S&P fundamentally transformed the business model of ratings. In their heyday, the 1920s, the firms

Table 7.1 Selected Data of the NRSROs

NRSRO (headquarters)	Employees (analysts)*	Total rated securities, U.S.$*	Rated sovereigns	Ownership
Standard & Poor's (New York)	6,000 (1,100)	$30 trillion	107	Operating segment of The McGraw-Hill Companies
Moody's Investors Service (New York)	1,800 (1,000)	$30 trillion	101	Subsidiary of Moody's Corporation
Fitch, Inc. (New York/London)	1,250 (700)	(Not available)	89	Subsidiary of Fimalac, S.A.
Dominion Bond Rating Service Limited (Toronto)	65 (45)	(Not available)	Not rated	Privately owned
A.M. Best Company, Inc. (Oldwick, N.J.)	521 (111)	(Not available)	Not rated	Privately owned

*Number of employees and U.S.$ amounts approximated.
Source: Rawi Abdelal and Christopher M. Bruner, *Private Capital and Public Policy: Standard & Poor's Sovereign Credit Ratings*, Harvard Business School Case 705–026 (2005), p. 20.

had relied on the demand for subscriptions to their reports for topline growth. As a new era of opportunity dawned, managers recognized an opportunity to charge the issuers rather than the investors for their ratings.

The change, as a matter of strategy, was brilliant. Once ratings were publicized, nonpaying consumers of the information could not be excluded. Issuers of securities would, in principle, pass along the fees to investors in the form of lower returns. Although it was possible that some issuers would refuse to pay the fees if their securities were so important that the agencies would rate them anyway, the market evolved such that having one or two (usually two) ratings was essential for the security to be held widely. Moreover, as Richard Cantor and Frank Packer observe, issuers paid the fees and welcomed "the opportunity provided by the formal ratings process to put their best case before the agencies."[18]

Making the Market for Ratings

Duopolies always offer the possibility of success for both firms, though frequently they are unhappy arrangements. When economists model duopolies, there are, generally speaking, only two stable outcomes, a stylized fact that accords with the empirical study of duopolistic markets. The two firms that compose a duopoly sometimes find a way to live harmoniously together either by essentially splitting the market between them, an outcome that may require either implicit or explicit (but in either case, legally problematic) collusion, or by competing on the basis of output rather than price, which is set by the market. By splitting the market, the two firms can ensure that both earn high profits. Often, unfortunately for the managers in the two halves of a duopoly, the firms desperately compete away the rents to be captured until the prices they charge are equal to marginal cost; the epic struggle between Boeing and Airbus comes to mind.[19]

S&P and Moody's have discovered what may be the perfect solution to the dilemma of the duopolist, a sort of third way: S&P and Moody's *both* have *all* the market. S&P commands 99 percent of the U.S. ratings market and 90 percent of the sovereign market—some $30 trillion worth of securities—and so, amazingly, does Moody's. Seemingly a happy outcome for all, the state of affairs is worrisome to Fitch, which is in an extremely distant third place. Fitch's General Counsel, Charles D. Brown, now refuses to call the market a duopoly. "Moody's and S&P are a dual monopoly," Brown wrote to the SEC, "each possessing separate monopoly power in a market that has grown to demand two ratings."[20] When S&P's and Moody's ratings diverge, Fitch is evidently the tiebreaker.[21] Among a worldwide market of some 130–150 mostly tiny, mostly local credit-rating agencies, only two really matter.[22]

The critical feature of the market is the expectation that every security issued will come with two ratings, one as a sort of reality check for the other. When a sovereign is to issue debt, Moody's and S&P are almost always both called in to rate the issue. Their pricing structures, though private, are known to be very similar, and by "tacit agreement," according to Ashok Bhatia, Moody's and S&P "do not hire staff from Fitch or each other."[23] Moody's and S&P thus do not compete with each other in any meaningful sense, though both firms continue to characterize the market as "very" or "intensely" competitive.[24] Neither Moody's nor S&P discloses revenue, cost, or profitability data on its sovereign ratings practice, but by all accounts, and the private admissions of managers, it is a very good business.[25]

Designation, Delegation, and Regulation

Although credit ratings had been part of financial regulations in the United States since the 1930s, the practice of regulators' using ratings to limit exposure to risk became much more widespread within the United States in the middle of the 1970s when the incorporation of ratings into regulations became, literally and figuratively, the rule. "The reliance on ratings extends," write Richard Cantor and Frank Packer, "to virtually all financial regulators, including public authorities that oversee banks, thrifts, insurance companies, securities firms, capital markets, mutual funds, and private pensions."[26]

The dangers of incorporating ratings into financial regulations to limit exposure to risky securities became clear very quickly, however. Rating changes would, and do, literally move markets, particularly in the case of downgrading a security from just-above-investment-grade to just-below-investment grade, prompting a sell-off by institutional investors. With rating agencies making the sorts of judgments otherwise (and previously) reserved for government regulators, the regulators increasingly ceded their responsibility to limit the public's exposure to risk to the rating agencies' analysts.

Rating agencies also benefited from the regulation-driven creation of an "artificial" increase in the demand for their product after 1975. This demand was driven not by the perception that ratings were a source of useful information, but by regulations that obliged an issuer to be agency-rated or suffer exclusion from the large and growing pools of capital allocated by investors subject to the regulations. Credit ratings, by this logic, would grant to issuers of securities what Frank Partnoy calls "regulatory licenses." The market's discipline of the rating agencies for problems in the performance of their ratings would thus be tempered dramatically because issuers could not, as a practical matter, simply refuse to continue to pay fees for ratings. Moody's and S&P, according to Partnoy, no longer capitalize on their reputations as insightful analysts of risk; they flourish because their product is a requirement of myriad financial regulations in the United States.[27]

The rating agencies themselves have historically expressed ambivalence about ratings-based regulations, their managers worrying about significant increases in public scrutiny.[28] Moody's was also opposed to designation and ratings-based regulation because such government policies "create artificial demand for ratings" and may even "enable competitors." The best way for Moody's to maintain its market share, former managing director David Levey argues, is through competition based on reputation: "the market should decide whether it finds ratings helpful."[29] According to S&P:

> Growing worldwide use of credit ratings as eligibility standards, which impose minimum rating levels as the basis for investment or issuance eligibility, can turn ratings into debt market barriers rather than facilitators. Regulations establishing minimum rating requirements actually constrain investors' full use of ratings across the credit spectrum.[30]

The critical assumption underlying the use of ratings in financial regulations was, naturally, that they contain information that the markets have not already brought to bear on yields and prices. Scholars have not reached a definitive conclusion on the information content of credit ratings. The most thorough review of the studies before the Asian financial crisis and U.S. corporate scandals, which were to highlight the agencies' failures to warn investors of the imminent collapse of firms like Enron, finds that the evidence on this point is "mixed."[31] More recent studies have, however, tended to suggest that international markets already largely know what the ratings are meant to reveal, though the markets still react to rating changes (particularly downgrades).[32] The scholars conducting these analyses have, however, subjected the agencies to a test whose appropriateness the agencies' managers might reasonably challenge. The ratings are supposed to describe relative probabilities of default, endstop. They are not, in the first instance, intended to predict any upswing or downswing in either market sentiment or a firm's performance. Thus, the apparent failure of the agencies' ratings to lead, rather than follow, the spreads in bond yields presupposes a task that Moody's and S&P arguably have never tried to perform. It is, however, a function that regulators need ratings to discharge if their incorporation into financial regulations is to benchmark the actual risks faced by an investor—which of course include the risk of future irrational behavior by the market itself.

Perhaps the most vexing problem arising from the regulatory use of rating agencies was, originally, the possibility that firms of dubious capability would enter a regulation-inflated market for ratings. The regulators had to be sure, in other words, that they were delegating to responsible firms. This was the logic behind the SEC's creation of NRSRO status in 1975. Not just any firm's rating could be used in financial regulation. As Cantor and Packer observe, "ratings matter only if they are issued by an NRSRO."[33] Although the credit-rating industry was already highly concentrated in 1975, the SEC's designation of Moody's and S&P among just three NRSROs decisively reinforced their dominance in the U.S. market. A new entry into the ratings market was, by the early years of the new century, difficult to imagine without a relaxation of SEC standards. Without NRSRO status, a firm is essentially irrelevant to regulators and issuers alike. But designation as an NRSRO requires that firms already be "nationally recognized." Many financial systems around the world are based on a similar combination of regulation and designation, with much the same results: Moody's and S&P come out on top. With the profitable U.S. market protected as much by their sheer dominance and the NRSRO designation as by their reputations, the influence of Moody's and S&P was poised to spread worldwide.

Neither Private nor Public

The widespread interpretation—among scholars, managers, and policymakers—that the rating agencies represent a sort of newly privatized authority in the world economy is implausible, if not downright mistaken.[34] Moody's and S&P are, to be sure, private firms. The influence of bondholders, in theory the principals for which Moody's and S&P are agents, has been profound as long as such credit has existed. This is not to argue that there is not something new about Moody's and S&P; indeed, practically everything about them is new, and not well understood. The bondholders now speak twice: first, with many voices, and then with only two.

The rating agencies are not public, nor, however, is their authority in any meaningful sense private.[35] Although the markets act under the questionable assumption that ratings convey new information, they react for two other reasons as well. Just a few firms have been designated by the government as the only credible evaluators of risk and uncertainty, a fact that has enhanced their status, publicity, and influence. Regulators have delegated to the agencies responsibility for assessing risk on behalf of investors, and so the ratings often move markets to the extent that laws and regulations dictate. The opposite of the conventional wisdom is in fact a better description of the current state of affairs: governments have adopted an authority that always had been private, and then codified it post hoc, giving it the force of law.[36]

As John Gerard Ruggie observes, the scholarly literature has overstated the process of regulatory privatization, "obscuring the fundamental fact that in many instances of 'private governance' there has been no actual shift from public to private sectors." Instead, Ruggie observes, "firms have created a new world of transaction flows that did not exist previously," and that could not have come into being without a new "global public domain" of transnational discourse.[37] Rather than ceding new authority to private spokespersons for the bond market, governments have made the bond market's private authority public. This was possible only because John Moody created a way to condense and simplify credit risk into a shorthand that was adopted all over the world. David Beers, S&P's Global Head of Sovereign and International Public Finance Ratings and Managing Director, proudly describes the influence of "a common language of credit risk that we at S&P helped to invent."[38] This common language of risk, originating in private and co-opted by government, was something entirely new, especially for sovereign issuers.

Rating Sovereigns

Moody's began rating sovereign debt in 1919, while S&P entered the business in 1927. Although Moody's greatly expanded its coverage of foreign governments during the 1920s (rating approximately fifty sovereign bond issues by 1929), the vast majority had defaulted by the beginning of World War II.[39] Without significant international flows of capital, to sovereigns or otherwise, between the 1930s and the 1970s, neither firm was obliged, or faced any financial incentive, to rate sovereigns systematically. So they did not. In 1975 S&P rated two sovereigns, the United States and Canada. (Both were rated AAA, the highest possible rating.) Moody's rated three sovereigns in the 1970s, the United States, Canada, and Australia, and as late as the mid-1980s rated only fourteen sovereigns, all of them members of the OECD.[40]

As financial markets internationalized toward the end of the 1970s, the agencies began to rate sovereigns more systematically. Not only were the sovereigns themselves borrowing abroad, but firms within those countries were as well. The agencies could not rate the firms without rating their sovereigns first because of the sovereign ceiling. Sovereign ratings were literally indispensable to the entire analytical apparatus of rating international flows of capital. "As the sovereign rating is the first rating conducted in any new market," S&P observed, "it opens the door for ratings of other public and private entities."[41] Levey, long in charge of sovereigns at Moody's, put it simply: "You can't not have sovereign ratings."[42]

The numbers continued to grow. In 1980 S&P rated eleven sovereigns, all AAA; in 1990 S&P rated thirty sovereigns, and all, save one, were investment grade. The more capital internationalized, the greater the need for the agencies to rate sovereigns. S&P's Beers observes, "globalization helped our business more than anything else."[43] Even governments that did not intend to borrow clearly found it useful to acquire a rating as a signal to markets and to enable the borrowing of domestic issuers. Nonborrowing sovereigns, Beers notes, were "driving the growth in ratings in the sovereign sector."[44]

The 1990s were heady times. The market for higher-yield government debt was helped by the debt-restructuring plan laid out by U.S. Treasury Secretary Nicholas Brady to resolve the ongoing nonpayment of debts associated with the financial crises of the 1980s in Latin America.[45] Toward the end of the 1990s a third of the eighty or so sovereigns rated by S&P were speculative grade.[46] By the early years of the new century Moody's (in 2002) and S&P (in 2004) rated more than one hundred sovereigns with ratings that covered the entire spectrum.[47]

The transition from rating a handful of AAA-rated sovereigns to more than one hundred sovereigns falling into every ratings category placed extraordinary intellectual demands on the agencies' analysts. The methodology for rating sovereigns had not been especially sophisticated in the 1920s and 1930s, and since then decades of neglect had left the practice of rating sovereigns several generations behind that of other parts of the business. "The methodological shift began" in 1986 and 1987, Levey recalls. At the beginning of the process Moody's sovereign analysts found the transition to be a considerable challenge. Because ratings are only relative, and not absolute, measures of risk, until the scale was filled with a number of sovereigns it was not always obvious how to compare newly rated sovereigns with the AAA-rated developed countries that had long been the core of the business. "What," Levey recalls wondering, "is our benchmark?"[48]

Condensing Complexity

"The rating of sovereigns depends more on the art of political economy," according to Fitch, "than on the science of econometrics."[49] Credit rating is, according Moody's Mara Hilderman, "by nature subjective."[50] Levey emphasizes that sovereigns in particular require a combination of quantitative skills with "sensitivity to historical, political, and cultural factors that do not easily lend themselves to quantification."[51] According to Levey, "Ratings necessarily rely on a predominantly qualitative methodology. It is all a matter of interpretation."[52] Empirical studies of sovereign ratings have found that as much as 90 percent of the variation in the ratings can be explained by a small number of quantitative indicators, such as high per capita income, low inflation, and low external debt.[53] "The other 10 percent is where the action is," responds Levey. For such studies "the standard error is about one and a half rating categories."[54]

Ratings are produced by the work of a lead analyst and a rating committee assigned to a sovereign and its security. The committee, usually made up of senior managers as well as junior staff, discusses the analytical basis of a rating put forward by the lead analyst. Although the rating committee seeks to reach consensus, the decision is made by a simple majority vote.[55] For sovereigns, much of the discussion centers on the inferences that ought to be drawn from a government's policy stances and changes. The economic risk, or the government's ability to pay, often can be captured with quantitative analysis of a range of obvious economic variables. "Willingness to pay," however, as S&P's Beers and Managing Director Marie Cavanaugh write, "is a qualitative issue that distinguishes sovereigns from most other types of issuers."[56]

The output is much like a grade. S&P ratings for long-term (with maturity of more than one year) securities range from AAA to D, with BBB– and above considered investment grade, while BB+ and below are noninvestment, or speculative, grade. Moody's ratings range from Aaa to C, with appended numerical modifiers 1, 2, and 3 to rank within a ratings category; for Moody's, Baa3 and above is investment grade. Another difference between S&P and Moody's is the meaning of the rating itself. While S&P's ratings are supposed to reflect the probability of any default, no matter the magnitude, Moody's ratings are intended to convey the expected loss to an investor as well.[57]

Finally, the ratings, which are commonly used as a shorthand for the riskiness of a specific security, are useful only when considered against the spectrum. That is, ratings are supposed to be measures of relative, not absolute, risk. No probability of default can be derived from a sovereign rating of BBB from S&P, for example; one is supposed to infer only that S&P believes the probability that the sovereign will default is lower than a sovereign rated BB and higher than a sovereign rated A. According to a report by the Bank of International Settlements (BIS), "the simplicity of the ordinal ranking system," while useful as a first approximation of credit risk, "inherently obscures a great deal of information about the individual issuer."[58]

Interpretive Frameworks

"Rating agencies disavow any ideological content to their rating judgments," Timothy Sinclair reports with skepticism.[59] As a matter of simple logic, their disavowal cannot support the presumption that the agencies produce ratings that merely reproduce objective criteria. Some interpretive framework must be applied if, as they admit, subjective judgments are being made.[60] Nowhere formally promulgated, their respective frameworks have to be discerned from the self-reflective observations, where we can find or coax them, of Moody's, S&P, and Fitch managers. After providing such a reconstruction, I will then explore the evolution of the agencies' reactions to several episodes when capital was liberalized or restricted by countries during the past several decades. "Rating agency views of management and policy seem to change over time as the prevailing views of economic and financial orthodoxy change," Sinclair observes.[61] But it is important to recognize that there is not a single interpretive framework. Each agency, rather, appears to have its own view of what makes for policies that send signals of the government's willingness to service its debt.[62]

S&P and Moody's are frequently called on by both governments and market participants to explain their judgment process and to clarify the interpretive lenses through which they view data, policies, and institutions. Yet the process itself might not be sufficiently systematic to lend itself to ready explanation. Levey recalls how difficult it was to try to convey the subtleties of what analysts and rating committees actually did. Levey "resisted calls for us to write it down," primarily because the very process of trying to articulate an interpretive lens came across not only as "formulaic," but, worse, "abstract and platitudinous" as well. You cannot, Levey insists, "just apply a rulebook."[63]

The agencies' analysts and managers often use the word "orthodoxy" to describe those economic policy practices that are widely believed within financial markets and policy circles to lead to growth and to signal a government's greater relative commitment to fulfilling its explicit and implicit contracts with investors. In Cavanaugh's experience, the members of an S&P rating committee do indeed adhere to "basic economic orthodoxy."[64] But how is that orthodoxy determined? Bhatia writes of the "invisible ingredient" in the process of rating sovereigns: "committee deliberation," during which discussion often focuses on "intangible issues such as a government's propensity for 'orthodox' vs. 'heterodox' policy responses when under acute debt-service pressure."[65]

A document that Cavanaugh authored on the characteristics of sovereigns in the various rating categories reveals some of the logical connections in that orthodoxy.[66] The most highly rated sovereigns, with ratings of AAA, are characterized by "openness to trade and integration in the global financial system." For BBB-rated sovereigns, that is, those just above investment grade, "orthodox market-oriented economic programs are generally well established," but their governments are "at an earlier stage in the reform process than their more highly rated peers." Just below investment grade, at BB, are sovereigns with "more restrictions" to trade and financial flows. Further down the scale, "orthodox economic policies are usually not well established." Although such sovereigns may be open to trade, "integration into the global financial system is weak and subject to changing circumstances."

Cavanaugh also collaborated with Beers to attempt to describe some of the other inferences S&P draws from the institutions and policies of sovereigns:

> The stability, predictability, and transparency of a country's political institutions are important considerations in analyzing the parameters of economic policymaking, including how quickly policy errors are identified and corrected. The separation of powers, particularly judicial, is an important factor, as is the development of civil institutions, particularly an independent press.[67]

The notion of "policy error" runs throughout S&P's thinking on these issues, implying pragmatism and flexibility, but also a sense that in many cases there are right—and much less right—policy responses to economic problems. "Due to its decentralized decision making processes," Beers and Cavanaugh continue, "a market economy with legally enforceable property rights is less prone to policy error and more respectful of the interests of creditors than one where the public sector dominates."[68]

Less willing to try to write down such an interpretive framework in the abstract, Levey, Moody's erstwhile director for sovereign risk, nevertheless offers several interesting reflections on their thinking. Moody's analysts observed that a "rolling process of liberalization" was under way around the world. Among some policymakers capital liberalization even came to be viewed with a "certain inevitability, and appeared to become international dogma."[69] Levey also recalls that practically everywhere they went in the world, Moody's analysts would arrive at the finance ministry and find that they were spending time with "economists trained in the United States and Britain," an apparent "network for the spread of liberal views" around the world.[70]

Within Moody's Levey insists that there "was never a dogma that capital controls were bad," and certainly countries were not "penalized for having capital controls." To the contrary, among Moody's sovereign analysts liberalization eventually came to be seen as a "source of instability" that had to be managed deftly. "Countries that liberalized almost always had a crisis," Levey reflects. "The question was: How would the government handle the crisis?"[71] By the end of the 1990s it had become clear that the institutional foundations—prudential regulations well conceived and consistently enforced by a capacious government—were decisive for liberalizations that did not lead to debilitating financial crises: "Over time, at Moody's we all became institutionalists."[72]

When Levey did attempt to represent the modes of thought in Moody's, the firm came across as less dogmatic and more circumspect about the interpretive task sovereign analysts have taken on. He wrote in 1990:

> As anyone familiar with the social sciences knows, there is no agreed-upon conceptual framework for thinking about society, history, and political economy . . . The "facts" of history and human behavior do not speak for themselves without interpretation—and rival interpretations derive from strongly differing presuppositions, values, and interests.[73]

With regard to capital, in print Levey expresses skepticism, highlighting the "less benign implications" of capital liberalization.[74] Capital liberalization creates vulnerabilities, and indeed it "may reduce the sovereign's ability to manage its credit status."[75] For Levey the issue is not just whether a policy outcome is economically beneficial, or even whether a government expresses a deep commitment to protecting the interests of investors in the securities it has issued. The political sustainability of a policy stance within the country is important for understanding the effects of capital liberalization:

> In fact, a regime of free financial flows may increase country risk: governments may find less room to manage the economy, speculative capital flows may be more pronounced, and the economy may lose the potential to generate foreign exchange. Market mechanisms, on the other hand, may not work, because they would entail imposing intolerable political costs.[76]

While it is important to characterize the interpretive frameworks of the agencies, as consequential as those frameworks are, none of this is necessarily to suggest that having an "orthodox" interpretive framework is in itself a problem. Indeed, *some* interpretive framework is necessary. Three issues are problematic, however. First, to the extent that the agencies' analysts claim not to have any framework, or that they are somehow above ideology and the prevailing conventions of the world economy, such a contention suggests a lack of self-reflection about how their judgments are formed. Second, even if the interpretive frameworks proved to be extremely useful in predicting sovereign defaults, it would be a worthwhile exercise to try to understand how such a powerful set of predictive analytical tools emerged and developed, and particularly the influence of various organizations and academic disciplines on them. Third, and finally, the large and growing body of econometric evidence that sovereign ratings follow rather than lead market outcomes suggests that greater attention to the improvement or abandonment of existing interpretive frameworks is warranted. As later sections of this chapter demonstrate, the academic scrutiny of the rating agencies became very intense indeed.

Agencies' track record predicting distress or default before the Asian crisis was already seen as problematic, more so than their record for U.S. securities within the United States. Just before the Asian financial crisis began in July 1997 two critical studies were published assessing the information content and effects of sovereign ratings. "Agency announcements of a change in sovereign risk assessments appear to be preceded by a similar change in the market's assessment of sovereign risk," according to Cantor and Packer.[77] Perhaps the ratings are merely lagging indicators of creditworthiness, telling the markets what they already know. After all, the markets' assessment precedes the rating agencies' interpretation of the risk of a security. Their value depends on the objects of analysis: "Rating announcements have a highly significant impact on speculative-grade sovereigns but a statistically insignificant effect on investment-grade sovereigns."[78] Guillermo Larrain and his colleagues also find that rating agencies lag market events, while rating announcements and changes significantly affect the markets. Unlike Cantor and Packer, they find the announcement effect of the agencies' ratings to be significant across the spectrum.[79] These are remarkable findings, considering that sovereign ratings affect nearly every other rating and are incorporated into financial regulations. It seems that one of the most important judgments in the world of international finance—the sovereign rating—encourages sovereign bond markets upward when the markets are enthusiastic and downward when the markets are concerned.

Interpreting Capital's Constraint and Freedom

Analyzing the rating agencies' reactions to new restrictions and liberalizations of the capital account helps us to understand how their interpretive frameworks work in practice, but it is not an easy task.[80] For one thing, the empirical record is spotty. When asked for a set of sovereign ratings reports from the 1980s and early 1990s, a senior manager at Moody's offered to look for the reports but then acknowledged that such documents are not archived systematically. S&P's managers also suggested that it would be difficult to track down such materials quickly or precisely, though publication of *CreditWeek* and (from 1983 to 1996) *CreditWeek International* renders S&P's historical materials more accessible than those of other agencies. In this section I rely first on S&P's *CreditWeek* from 1981 until the onset of the Asian financial crisis. Then, for the financial crisis and the Malaysian experience, I have collected all the relevant agency reports before and after the imposition of capital controls. The period since the crisis, 1998 to 2005, offers much more information from both the rating reports of selected countries and the agencies' overall assessments of the politics of globalization. Although the record is far from definitive, several turning points in the evolution of the agencies' approach to capital freedom and restrictions can be discerned. In the 1980s, when capital mobility was not even a developed-country norm, S&P did not appear to infer heterodoxy from the imposition of capital controls. By the early 1990s, however, S&P associated capital freedom with developed countries and capital controls with developing countries, coming to see liberalization as a sign of financial maturity and commitment to international markets.

As more developing countries liberalized, and especially the so-called emerging markets, S&P's views on capital controls tracked the emergence of what appeared to be the new orthodoxy in both official policy circles, such as the IMF, and among financial market participants. Seen from this perspective, two conclusions stand out as important revisions to the conventional wisdom about the Malaysian capital controls. First, it is clear that S&P did not derive its orthodoxy from the first principles of economics; they followed the orthodoxy, but did so pragmatically and inductively. Second, Malaysia's experience did not represent a long-held perspective that capital controls used by a developing country during a financial crisis necessarily signaled a heightening of political risk. Instead, the Malaysian experience seems to have been the very height of the expectation on the part of financial markets and the rating agencies that developing countries that had already liberalized would not and should not backtrack, even in a crisis.

Moreover, the Malaysian capital controls, in particular, were seen as a violation of an implicit contract with foreign investors not to close off the capital account once they had brought their money into Malaysia. The contrast with Chile is revealing, for Chile's inflow controls were consistently applauded by the agencies, ostensibly because they were up-front and therefore part of the implicit contract with foreign investors from the beginning. Finally, both Moody's and S&P subsequently reversed the position they seemed to hold in September 1998 when Malaysia imposed its controls. Moody's, in particular, has stated that it erred in downgrading Malaysia for its controls, which it had incorrectly interpreted as a signal of reduced creditworthiness. In the early years of the new century both of the major agencies valorized the capital controls of China and India and regularly warned against liberalization without the appropriate institutional foundations.

The Rise of Global Markets and the Fall of Capital Controls

In the early 1980s U.S. policymakers were just beginning to think in terms of the internationalization of finance, and the rating agencies did not yet see a global market for their product. In 1981, certainly, S&P recognized that it served just a small part of the market, the very top. The task itself was prosaic: the sovereigns that sought ratings knew they would receive the highest possible rating, and so did S&P's analysts. "Only a few sovereign names have come to U.S. markets with ratings," one of S&P's staff observed in 1981. "Countries that fail to get the 'AAA' from S&P generally go to non-U.S. markets or do private placements. Countries which do not expect a top rating seldom approach us."[81]

Capital controls, still widespread among developed and developing countries, elicited no condemnation, made no headlines, and, apparently, sent no signals of heterodoxy. As the debt crisis threatened to engulf all of Latin America, the Venezuelan government held out hope that it would not run out of reserves and be forced into default. Far from worrying S&P's managers, the Venezuelan controls were a sign of good sense. "Assuming the controls are maintained effectively," S&P's Philip Bates observed, "they should decrease speculative outflows of capital, thus helping to stabilize international reserves."[82]

During the early 1980s France was in the midst of its own Mitterrand experiment, including a set of policies that might in 1998 have appeared more blasphemous than heretical: nationalizing all major banks and the vast majority of its industry, along with the tightest capital controls since the end of World War II. By 1985, however, S&P had not so much as hinted that France's AAA rating was in jeopardy. "Despite dramatic policy changes in France over the last five years," a writer in *CreditWeek* noted, "S&P maintains its 'AAA' rating on debt guaranteed by the Republic."[83]

The burgeoning Eurocurrency market also encouraged S&P's managers to reflect on what appeared to be a sea change. The market, which had grown in part beyond the authority of national regulators and in part from the indifference of U.S. regulators, put pressure on governments. "The success of the relatively unregulated Euromarket," it was observed, "has had a profoundly liberalizing influence on other national capital markets." But even more profound was the possibility that this market was globalization in the making. As *CreditWeek* guest commentator Philip Hubbard put it: "The Eurobond market of the 1970s which became the international capital market of the early 1980s is developing towards a global financial market."[84]

As early as 1986, after the French had abandoned controls and begun to liberalize, *International CreditWeek*'s authors began to recognize and valorize the trend toward liberalization. The more a country was involved with the liberal, developed world, the better. Wrote Philip Bates and John Chambers,

"S&P also considers the country's degree of political and economic integration with other 'Western' nations. That is, non-economic factors may pose an additional risk of nonpayment of foreign debt for governments with economic and political ideologies that differ significantly with those of the Western mainstream."[85] With Helena Hessel, who analyzed France for S&P, Bates observed that developing countries "have extensive capital controls," while developed countries "have internationally active banking systems and substantial foreign direct and portfolio investments."[86]

After the 1988 liberalization directive in Europe, S&P recognized that it was witnessing the creation of a single European financial space. The new commitments associated with European integration were greeted with approval and excitement within S&P. Not just France and Germany would liberalize, but the rest of Europe, including Italy, would do so as well.[87] When Sweden jumped on the bandwagon in 1989, the process of liberalization was described as being more than internationalization and more than European integration: "The government's actions are in line with the global trend to lower barriers to capital flows."[88] And as the last capital controls were being eliminated in Europe, France again epitomized for S&P the end of the era of national capital and the dawn of a new era of open regionalism in Europe, with a process of financial integration that would tie Europeans to the rest of the world as much as to one another.[89]

For all the criticism that S&P has endured for "failing" to predict the Asian financial crisis, the firm seems to have been given scant credit for having accurately foreseen and warned against the crisis of the European Monetary System (EMS) in September 1992. The potential for crisis, S&P astutely observed, was increased by the very process of European financial integration that had begun in 1986. As Bates observed:

> The market's faith in future [EMU] membership could create a virtuous cycle that facilitates adjustment for countries now facing large imbalances. However, with the removal of the remaining capital controls within the EEC in 1993 and the potential narrowing of interest rate differentials, member countries will be exposed to large swings in capital flows in the event of an unforeseen economic setback. This vulnerability is heightened by the short debt maturity profile of many of the more highly indebted member governments.[90]

Spain's use of capital controls during the crisis, though noted as a potential "deterrent to foreign inflows of capital," raised few concerns among

S&P's observers. S&P did not consider the controls—clearly a crisis measure, rather than a permanent reversal of the liberalization trend—to signal declining creditworthiness, and S&P's managers also did not expect the markets to react negatively. A downgrade for Spain does not seem even to have been considered.[91]

Although S&P's own coverage from 1992 to 1997 expresses enthusiasm about liberalization in emerging markets punctuated by brief anxiety over Mexico's crisis in 1994, concerns were being raised about liberalization's permanence. What seems to have been most worrisome was not that a country like China, with longstanding capital controls, would continue to regulate flows tightly, but rather that one of the liberalizers would reverse course. Just as the crisis was unfolding in Asia, S&P's William Chambers reflected on governments' histories with committing to capital markets and their disciplines. "Some sovereigns have displayed much more restraint in applying controls to private capital movements than others," Chambers wrote, "and such a positive track record is incorporated into the assessment of both the sovereign itself and entities domiciled in that country."[92]

The Financial Crisis and the Malaysian Controls

S&P seems to have questioned early on Malaysia's commitment to the apparently universal norm of liberalization as the crisis began to spread from Thailand. Just a little less than one year before the Malaysian government imposed controls in September 1998, S&P offered what one might read as a warning. Reflecting on the possibility of a downgrade, S&P's Cem Karacadag and Beers expressed concerns about "the government's ambivalent commitment to orthodox economic policies in the wake of volatility in the foreign exchange and share markets."[93] The warning is remarkable for a number of reasons. Karacadag and Beers, first, articulated a version of "orthodoxy" that differed sharply even from the standard applied to Spain during the European crisis of 1992. At the time, Spain's brief use of capital controls was explained, by Spain as much as by S&P, as a temporary measure reflecting the exigencies of managing a crisis of potentially self-fulfilling market expectations. Five years later, as a devastating financial crisis swept across Asia, deviations from orthodoxy even by developing countries in the midst of a crisis were considered signals of an increased readiness to default on the government's foreign debt.

On September 1, 1998, the Malaysian government imposed controls on capital flows. The central bank, Bank Negara, announced that the controls would be temporary measures to manage the crisis, which had treated the Malaysian economy roughly indeed. The Malaysian exchange rate had fallen from 2.5 ringgit to the dollar in June 1997 to a low of 4.5 ringgit to the dollar in January 1998. Asset prices collapsed, share prices on the stock exchange declined precipitously, interest rates rose five percentage points to 12 percent, all while Malaysia accepted the tough medicine of orthodoxy. Under Finance Minister Anwar Ibrahim, Malaysia had tightened its monetary and fiscal policies and hoped to wait out a crisis that increasingly resembled a full-blown financial panic. The controls were designed to eliminate the off-shore market in ringgit, which had been a source of downward speculative pressure on the currency, and to break the link between domestic and international interest rates so that Bank Negara could stimulate recovery with a looser monetary policy. The government clearly sought to distinguish between short-term and long-term capital flows, the former to be managed while the latter would remain as free as before September 1. Among several new regulations, the most important was that nonresidents were required to wait one year to convert ringgit proceeds from the sale of securities.[94]

The Malaysian government also undertook two other significant policy changes. The first became notorious as much for the accompanying surprise as for the human rights abuses that followed. Prime Minister Mahathir Mohamad fired Anwar, his erstwhile protégé and finance minister, on September 2, the day after the controls were imposed. Anwar, who had also emerged as a political rival to the prime minister, was removed more for the political threat he posed than for the failure of his approach to the crisis. On September 3 Anwar was expelled from the ruling party. Shortly thereafter he was arrested and convicted, highly implausibly, for sodomy and sentenced to six years in jail. Without Anwar, the darling of Wall Street and the international financial community, the Malaysian government certainly appeared much less orthodox. In reality, the Malaysian capital controls were implemented primarily to manage the new wave of capital outflows that were certain to result from Anwar's sacking, rather than the year-old Asian financial crisis.[95] The other major policy choice was the fixing of the exchange rate at 3.8 ringgit to the dollar.

Fitch was the first to respond to the controls about one week later. Malaysia's long-term foreign currency debt, which had been rated BBB– (just within investment grade) on August 13, 1998, just two weeks earlier, fell two grades to BB (well below investment grade). "Malaysia's immediate ability to service its foreign currency obligations is not in doubt," Fitch noted, implying that the new rating reflected deterioration in the firm's estimation of Malaysia's willingness to pay. Fitch's analysts and managers also felt that the comparison with more orthodox neighbors cast Malaysia in a negative light, with the government's "imposing capital controls and rejecting the market discipline that has sped reforms in Korea and Thailand." Fitch believed that the markets would react badly to the controls, and their reaction would necessarily undermine the country's prospects. "Although the government has emphasized that the new controls are temporary and should in no way impede foreign direct investment and long-term debt flows," observed Fitch, "foreign investors will be reluctant to take the government at its word in the future and commit further funds." Finally, the most significant issue at stake was Malaysia's lack of respect for an implicit contract with foreign investors. As far as Fitch was concerned, the capital controls signaled a lack of respect for the rights of investors:

> Fitch IBCA believes the recent imposition of exchange controls has seriously undermined foreign investors' confidence in Malaysia and set the economy on an unsustainable policy path that could adversely affect external creditworthiness over the medium term. Exchange controls do not of themselves automatically imply greater likelihood of sovereign default: China and India have long employed a similar battery of controls to those now being put in place by Malaysia. However, the fact that Malaysia has arbitrarily changed the rules, denying some foreign investors access to their capital, is a dangerous precedent.[96]

Moody's reaction came five days later, on September 14, when the foreign currency debt rating was reduced one grade from Baa2 to Baa3, just within investment grade. Moody's was much less dramatic, its judgment more circumspect. For Moody's the problem was that the Malaysian government appeared not to have fully thought through the effect that the capital controls would have on contracts written in ringgit. The Malaysian government was seen as less than fully committed to the needs of the private financial community:

> An important factor behind the downgrades was the effect on private contracts of the exchange controls imposed on September 1, which could have caused defaults on the part of private institutions dealing in ringgit. While this problem has largely been resolved, the action demonstrated a lack of consideration for the interests of private investors in the formulation of economic policy.

Moody's also worried about the reaction of market participants. Although Moody's analysts and managers did not seem to interpret the controls as a signal of extreme heterodoxy, the markets might not forgive the Malaysian government so easily: "Potentially, Malaysia's access to foreign capital, including foreign direct investment, might be jeopardized by the imposition of capital controls, even if they are lifted at some point in the future."[97] Thus, it seems that Moody's managers felt as though they could not ignore the orthodoxy of the markets, regardless of whether they shared it.

S&P's downgrade came the next day: Malaysia's foreign currency rating was reduced two grades from BBB+ to BBB–. Though not as strongly worded as Fitch's interpretation, S&P clearly went beyond Moody's reading of the meaning, purpose, and effects of the controls. S&P considered it a signal of heterodoxy and believed that the market would as well: "The imposition of controls signals a major shift in policy that, if sustained, will depress Malaysia's future growth prospects." The report continued, "the controls likely will discourage domestic savings and all forms of foreign investment."[98] An elaboration of S&P's position on the crisis a fortnight later acknowledged that the Malaysian controls were less disruptive than a government default or moratorium, but emphasized that Malaysia's "damaging policies include the imposition of capital controls."[99]

To keep all of this in perspective, it is crucial to recall that Malaysia did not default on its debt, nor did the government ever consider doing so. As had been promised by Bank Negara, the controls were indeed temporary. In February 1999 the government replaced the one-year moratorium on the repatriation of ringgit proceeds on equity sales with a sliding scale of exit taxes on capital gains ranging from 10 to 30 percent. In September Bank Negara replaced the sliding scale with a flat 10 percent exit tax, which it abolished in February 2001. The offshore ringgit market was eliminated for good, however.

Malaysia also did not, despite the dire predictions, collapse. To the contrary, the capital controls coincided with Malaysia's economic recovery. The Malaysian economy, having declined by 7.4 percent in 1998, grew 6.1 percent in 1999 and an additional 8.2 percent in 2000. There are good reasons to be skeptical of the claim that the controls induced the recovery, however. The depreciation of the ringgit made exports more competitive. U.S. Federal Reserve Chair Alan Greenspan's October 1998 decision to reduce U.S. interest rates reduced the incentives for investors' flight to quality into the United States. Malaysia's neighbors, moreover, all with IMF programs, had also begun to recover from the crisis. Whether the capital controls coincided with or caused Malaysia's recovery is irrelevant from the perspective of this chapter, and I review the evidence elsewhere in collaborative work with Laura Alfaro.[100] The critical observation is this: the capital controls did not lead to catastrophe. The invocations of orthodoxy by S&P and Fitch increasingly appeared, in retrospect, to be orthodoxy-driven overreactions, at least from the perspective of the information content of the controls and their effect on Malaysia's prospects for growth. Fitch upgraded Malaysia to BBB– (again two grades, returning Malaysia to the precapital controls grade) in April 1999; S&P upgraded Malaysia to BBB in November 1999, and Moody's to Baa2 in October 2000. For Fitch and S&P in particular, the Malaysian controls' patina of heterodoxy seemed to have faded quickly. Subsequently, the rating agencies proceeded to reconsider the content of orthodoxy.

Scrutinizing the Judges

The Asian crisis drew new interest from scholars who wanted to know how the credit-rating agencies had grown so powerful that their mere pronouncements—in the form of downgrades—could exacerbate the crisis for Malaysia and its neighbors. Some scholars explored the ways in which Moody's and S&P propagated a set of arm's-length financial transactions that fit well into U.S. and British economic institutions, but that were unusual in continental Europe and the rest of the world. More aggressive critics saw the agencies as instruments of U.S. economic hegemony imposing orthodox standards on powerless sovereigns. Although it was far-fetched to imagine that the U.S. government had empowered the agencies so that they might spread the American model around the world, the agencies' orthodoxies and methodologies did appear, at least to many of the governments that were rated, to represent a range of practices that constitute the U.S. model. Leaders and managers around the world expressed frustration about having to adjust to the agencies' expectations. Even in Germany, hardly a bastion of financial heterodoxy, the agencies' standards were understood to conflict with the traditional relationships between German banks and the *Mittelstand*.[101] "Local markets," Roy Smith and Ingo Walter write, "are subject to political and business pressures that are sometimes very different from those in the key Anglo-American markets" in which the rating agencies are based.[102]

Scholars also returned to the question of whether the agencies provided new information to sovereign debt markets and how large were the effects of their announcements and rating changes, but now with a new data set of announcements, countries, and crises. The consensus remained as worrisome as it had been before the crisis. Rating agencies' reactions continued to lag behind those of the market, and rating changes still significantly affected market outcomes.[103] "Not only do international capital markets react to changes in the ratings," Carmen Reinhart argues, "but the ratings systematically react (with a lag) to market conditions, as reflected in the sovereign bond yield spreads."[104] The agencies, for their part, reminded scholars that the ratings were not designed to predict any market outcome; ratings were only supposed to assign some relative probability of a government's decision to default on its debt. "No sovereign ever rated in the 'A' category or higher has ever defaulted," S&P observed.[105]

This response was not good enough for many European politicians and policymakers, who have called for greater scrutiny, and potentially direct regulation, of the agencies. For European governments, which had pushed forward efforts to codify the rules of the international financial architecture, two U.S. firms exerting massive influence on the world's financial markets without regulatory oversight or competitive discipline was not the sort of globalization they had in mind.[106] The European Parliament's Committee on Economic and Monetary Affairs examined the firms and found them to be U.S. firms with distinctively American worldviews. The committee's report proposed a "European Ratings Authority," which would potentially have the power to regulate Moody's, S&P, and Fitch.[107] The committee's report hardly reflected a European consensus in favor of checking the power of Moody's and S&P, as European bankers, for example, disagreed with the proposal.[108] But clearly there is significant European discontent with the current balance of power, as well as with the combination of ad hoc influence and codified authority of the two big U.S. firms. The European Parliament declined to regulate just yet, but called on the Commission to consider the costs and benefits of a European Registration Scheme under the auspices of the Committee of European Securities Regulators and to report back by July 31, 2005, and periodically thereafter. The Parliament also asked EU competition authorities to investigate Moody's and S&P for potential anti-competitive business practices.[109]

Meanwhile, France began to move on its own as early as 2003, enacting a new securities law imposing document retention requirements on rating agencies doing business in the country. The law also instructs "the newly formed French regulatory authority, L'Autorité des Marchés Financiers (AMF) . . . to publish an annual report on the role of rating agencies," including "their business ethics, the transparency of their methods, and the impact of their activity on issuers and the financial markets." As Moody's relates, the AMF's first report on the agencies "concluded that while there was no evidence of wrong-doing or inappropriate behavior in the industry, some sort of regulatory framework at the European level may be suitable."[110]

The AMF report, issued in January 2005, describes the growth in the ratings business as a reflection of "[f]inancial globalisation and disintermediation"—dating the relevant market transformation and expansion in France to "the mid-1980s"—and explains that the "need for ratings became obvious as the market for private-sector debt underwent unprecedented growth in the euro area as a result of structural changes," including "the integration of the European market."[111] The AMF observes that Moody's, S&P, and Fitch "dominate the credit-rating business in France," and chronicles the trend toward greater reliance on agency ratings by both the private sector and regulators. French regulations incorporating ratings currently "do not make any provision for recognising rating agencies or the rating business," relying rather on agencies' NRSRO designations, which, at least for the time being, "seems adequate."[112]

The AMF clearly envisions broader regulation of the agencies in the future, though it emphasizes the need for a common European approach. The "agencies' structures and locations," it is observed, "are designed to give them European-wide coverage, rather than coverage for each national market," and the AMF report is intended "to inform the French authorities' position in the debate that the European Commission wishes to hold" regarding the agencies.[113] Ultimately, the AMF concludes:

> The only forum for dealing effectively with these issues is the upcoming international talks between regulators. The agencies' organisational structures are pan-European or even worldwide for some functions and they do not lend themselves easily to analysis from a strictly domestic viewpoint . . . The need for consistent assessments and effective oversight of the credit rating business militates in favour of a European system.[114]

Public pressure to investigate, and potentially to regulate, the agencies also was mounting in the United States. While their downgrades as the Asian financial crisis was unfolding had made Moody's and S&P unpopular elsewhere, domestic corporate governance scandals created controversy for the agencies at home. "Enron was a major crisis for the rating agencies. They had gotten emerging markets 'wrong' with the Asia crisis, where they were accused of not signaling early enough the problems in Asia, and then of making the crisis worse by downgrading excessively," Michael R. King and Sinclair write. "Now they had got it 'wrong' in the U.S.A. itself by failing to warn investors of the Enron collapse. This was serious."[115] The Sarbanes-Oxley Act of 2002 thus directed the SEC to conduct a thorough review of the credit-rating industry, considering especially the wisdom of designation and NRSRO status. The Senate banking committee held the first in a series of hearings that would be part of its review of the industry. The committee proposed to evaluate problems arising from NRSRO designation, the firms' business model built on issuer fees, and their methodologies. The central concern expressed by the legislators was that NRSRO designation created unanticipated consequences, not least the increasingly held view that the government had delegated the difficult task of judging risk to experts whose mistakes seemed insulated from market discipline and government review alike. The U.S. Department of Justice had argued that NRSRO designation was inherently anticompetitive.[116] "Once the SEC grants the designation," remarked Senator Richard Shelby, "it does not maintain any form of ongoing oversight."[117]

S&P's and Moody's reactions were revealing and contradictory. S&P argued that NRSRO designation should remain a part of U.S. policy, but insisted that designation should not come with regulation. S&P claimed that its reports and announcements constituted speech protected by the U.S. Constitution; rating processes, the firm argued, are "highly akin to those regularly performed by professional journalists and numerous courts have recognized S&P Ratings Service's entitlement to.the protections of the First Amendment along these lines."[118] Moody's, however, has argued that NRSRO designation should be eliminated. Long Moody's position, the threat that designation in the post-Asia-crisis, post-Enron world would inevitably come with greater public scrutiny, government oversight, and perhaps regulation, clarified the downside even further. For Moody's, it was clear that designation necessarily leads to demands for oversight, notwithstanding protections available to the agencies under the First Amendment.[119]

Basel II

While legislators in Washington and Brussels were reconsidering the wisdom of delegating so much responsibility to the rating agencies, central bankers meeting in Basel were poised to empower Moody's and S&P even further. BIS in Basel is an exclusive club for central bankers and other monetary authority representatives. One of the tasks they take upon themselves is to ensure that the practice of banking, both across borders and within countries, is sound. Toward the aim of financial stability, the Basel Committee on Banking Supervision produced in 1988 a set of standards titled "International Convergence of Capital Measurement and Capital Standards." As mentioned in Chapter 5, the Basel Accord, as it came to be known, specified the percentage of capital that, as a rule, banks should hold in reserve.

The Basel Accord originally weighted the risk associated with loans to sovereigns based on their membership in the OECD. Of the six countries that joined the OECD between 1994 and 2000, three (Mexico, the Czech Republic, and South Korea) experienced a financial crisis within a year or so after acceding. OECD membership, many bankers began to feel, was not the signal of financial solidity that it once was. Many felt that a new method for weighting the risks of borrowers would have to be devised, and this was part of the motivation to arrive at a new Basel Accord—Basel II, as it has come to be called.

Basel II, released in June 2004, was expected to change the practices of nearly all the world's international banks and many financial regulations around the world, just as the first Basel Accord had done. Though just a set of standards, rather than a multilateral obligation, "observance of Basel standards has become a mark of respectability for many developing countries" and, for non-G10 developed countries, "a virtual necessity since many countries, most notably the U.S., require compliance with Basel as a condition for foreign banks to do business."[120]

In place of OECD membership as the internationally recognized benchmark for risk weighting, Basel II envisioned a much finer-grained approach based, in part, on the use of credit ratings.[121] Basel II, scheduled to be fully implemented by the end of 2007, maintains the minimum capital requirement of 8 percent of a bank's risk-weighted assets, but adopts a new ratings-based "standardised approach" to calculating credit risk (applicable to those banks unable to undertake internal credit risk assessments). Sovereign debt is, using S&P's notation as a guideline, weighted as follows: AAA to AA– will be 0 percent; A+ to A– will be 20 percent; BBB+ to BBB– will be 50 percent; BB+ to B– will be 100 percent; below B– will be 150 percent; and unrated assets will be 100 percent. Using ratings as a basis for Basel II naturally creates the same problem that direct incorporation of ratings into financial regulations in the United States and around the world did: producers of ratings worthy of trust have to be identified. Thus Basel II has a counterpart to the NRSRO concept. The BIS specifies that national regulators should designate External Credit Assessment Institutions (ECAIs) to be the only firms whose ratings can be used by banks and regulators for Basel II compliance. As with NRSRO, a number of criteria would be used to evaluate potential ECAIs: objectivity, independence, transparency, disclosure, resources, and credibility.[122]

Basel II seems, so far, to have satisfied few people. Developing countries feared that Basel II would limit their macroeconomic policy discretion as well as their access to international capital markets.[123] Many Europeans felt that Basel II would hurt domestic financial systems based on institutionalized relations with firms, a system that the U.S.-based rating agencies would fail to appreciate.[124] Scholars worried that the BIS would increase the regulatory demand for ratings while simultaneously limiting the supply, just as designation and incorporation had done with NRSRO in the United States.[125] Also, as with NRSRO, ECAI designation was based more on "inputs" (what the agencies do, how, and how frequently) rather than "output" (whether the agencies perform their tasks well), a fact that again would favor incumbents insulated from market discipline by their prior designation.[126] Most worrisome for some scholars, however, was the apparent lack of recognition on the part of the BIS of substantial evidence that ratings may operate procyclically. "A capital adequacy system built around traditional agency ratings might even follow rather than lead, the business cycle," write Edward Altman and Anthony Saunders.[127] In general S&P welcomed Basel II and looked forward to increased demand for their product.[128] Moody's also supported Basel II, but recognized that it could be a source of further political problems for the firm.[129]

The influence of the credit-rating agencies has grown to be immense, and that power is poised to grow further still with the advent of Basel II. The empowerment of these two private U.S. firms continues to frustrate policymakers in Europe and throughout the developing world because they have not chosen to delegate authority over sovereign and other bond markets to S&P and Moody's. Indeed policymakers increasingly, even in the United States, mistrust the rating agencies and their methods. S&P and Moody's epitomize ad hoc globalization. U.S. regulations primarily were responsible for placing the rating agencies into the international financial architecture in the first place.

As judges of the creditworthiness of sovereign borrowers, S&P and Moody's quite literally affect the distribution of beliefs in the market. The origin of the word "credit" is belief, the giving of faith. Credit ratings inform regulators and investors which borrowers are worthy of their faith. A poor track record in discerning among issuers of securities at home, with Enron, and abroad, in Asia, has sullied the reputations of these two firms as effective managers of the American public's exposure to risk. The rating agencies' claim to interrogate and protect the credibility of sovereign borrowers has been called into question.

The current era of global finance demands policy credibility, and thus the raters of credit—of belief—offered an attractive path through a forest of suspect data and opaque policy pronouncements. That attractiveness appears diminished, however. Our own belief in the abilities of the credit raters may have been permanently undermined.

CHAPTER 8

The Rebirth of Doubt

> The war between heaven and hell ignored the money issue, leaving capitalists and socialists miraculously united. Where Ricardo and Marx were as one, the nineteenth century knew not doubt.
>
> —Karl Polanyi

The new orthodoxy of capital mobility was undermined by a wave of financial crises that struck emerging markets in the 1990s. As one country after another was hit, supporters of capital mobility were slow to draw connections. Neither Mexico's financial crisis in 1994 nor Bulgaria's in 1996 had much effect on policy debates and rule trajectories. The Czech crisis of May 1997 was similarly regarded as an isolated incident born of imprudent government policies. Even the financial crisis that erupted in Thailand in the summer of 1997 was initially cast as an unfortunate but explainable problem of inflated asset values and lax prudential supervision. Later in 1997, however, the crisis spread to the Philippines, Indonesia, Malaysia, and South Korea. The series of financial meltdowns, often labeled the "Asian financial crisis," then moved beyond Asia: Russia experienced crisis and default in the summer of 1998, followed by another crisis in Brazil in January 1999. Many of the countries most excitedly hailed for liberalizing their capital accounts fell one after another in a fairly rapid sequence.

Amid the enthusiasm of capital's growing liberation, very few observers foresaw the eruption of these emerging-market crises. When the crises hit, massive outflows of capital bled from developing countries back to the financial markets in developed countries that were their source. Exuberant emerging-market investors and the IMF alike were taken by surprise.

As scholars tried to make sense of what had happened, they found their first hunches largely unsupported by the facts. The usual culprits of a balance-of-payments crisis—budget and current account deficits, overvalued exchange rates—were absent in some of the countries that nonetheless suffered. Other commonalities were investigated: weak financial sectors that were poorly supervised; implicit government guarantees that spurred excessive credit creation; and IMF lending programs that may have worsened the very crises they were intended to resolve.

The most striking shared trait among the crisis-stricken countries, however, was their very openness to capital inflows and outflows. A government that had liberalized its capital account thereby created the possibility of a "self-fulfilling" crisis in which foreign investors, without a change in the country's fundamentals, collectively lost confidence in high returns and removed their funds. The policy debate on the causes of the financial crises has been heated, and consensus appears unlikely. Regardless of the lack of agreement, policymakers within finance ministries and international organizations have been obliged to react in practice.

The EU, OECD, and IMF have since begun a general rethinking within the international financial community of the risks and benefits of capital liberalization. Skeptics of liberalization have felt empowered, if not simply proven right. More consequentially, many policymakers who had accepted the emerging proliberalization consensus have admitted to reassessing the balance of risks and benefits.[1] Interpreting crises, and gleaning their lessons, is an open-ended process, susceptible to the political exigencies of the interpreters.[2] The interpretive process played out differently in the three organizations and within the committees of the credit-rating agencies, in part according to each one's perception of its own culpability.

The End of the IMF's Capital Account Amendment

The crisis emboldened critics of the Fund and of the proposal to endow the organization with the purpose and power to promote capital liberalization. An April 1999 board meeting revealed a return to concerns from years past. "Several Directors," the Acting Chairman of the meeting noted, "pointed to the possible usefulness of capital controls, including temporary capital controls, in certain circumstances." Furthermore, in reflecting on the months leading up to the 1997 Hong Kong meetings, "several Directors felt that a more balanced treatment of the advantages and disadvantages of capital controls would have been desirable."[3]

By 1999 the private sector had also solidified its opposition to the proposed amendment. An influential working group at the IIF recommended that "the private financial community oppose the proposed amendment until it is clear that the amendment would on balance strengthen the legal foundations for private capital flows to emerging market economies." Thus, after producing a comprehensive survey of the benefits and risks of capital account liberalization, as well as the arguments in favor of and against the proposed amendment, the private sector remained skeptical of the usefulness of a new mandate and jurisdiction for the Fund.[4] Lex Rieffel, chair of the working group, had spent several years on the OECD's CMIT, which oversaw the Paris-based organization's Code of Liberalization of Capital Movements. Developed countries' experience with liberalization led the working group to conclude that developing countries should not move quickly in the direction of freedom of capital movements. On the contrary, according to Rieffel:

> The IIF is an association of bankers for whom capital controls are anathema. My role in the working group was to remind them of the OECD's experience with liberalization. OECD countries liberalized their capital accounts slowly, reluctantly, and indeed long after the economic case for openness was overwhelming. Why would we think that developing countries should liberalize sooner and more quickly?[5]

In late 2003 a former senior U.S. Treasury official announced that the proposal to amend the IMF's Articles was "totally dead," a view confirmed by a variety of other sources at the IMF.[6] The circumstances in which a similar proposal could progress as far as the last are difficult to imagine. Policymakers must weigh the material benefits of capital account liberalization against the risks, and consequences, of financial crises. Perhaps naturally, however, the moments after a crisis are not auspicious for the promotion of openness. These choices are fundamentally political, and just as there are politics of financial openness, so, too, are there politics of closure. It is difficult to know whether there would have been an amendment if the financial crisis in Asia had not erupted. Some knowledgeable observers within the Fund suggest that if the G7 had been united and if the U.S. Treasury had been steadfast, the Articles would have been amended. The G7 was not united, however, and was not close to unanimity. And the U.S. Treasury itself did not consider the amendment a priority.

Fund policy also appears to have changed significantly. "We now," Russian Executive Director Aleksei Mozhin observed, "understand the risks very well. If anything, now the Fund is overly cautious on the issue of capital account liberalization."[7] Indeed, the IEO's review of the Fund's approach since the crises reveals a new consensus: the Fund's practice is to spell out for member governments everything that can possibly go wrong during the process of capital liberalization.[8] IMF officials especially have become much less enthusiastic about rapid capital liberalization in developing countries, and Fund staff members have become, in their own words, "allergic" to capital liberalization and "gun-shy" about promoting it. The Fund is often more cautious than its members' finance ministries.[9] When Fund staff members do engage country authorities on capital account liberalization, they emphasize gradualism and sequencing.[10]

The Softening of la Muette

By the time Slovakia joined the OECD club in 2000, the CMIT had lived up to its reputation as a community of shared learning. In previous accession negotiations, the CMIT and Secretariat had sought to ensure that new members acceded with as few reservations to the Code of Liberalization of Capital Movements as possible. With the Slovaks, however, they adopted a very different stance. The crises of the 1990s among new members—in Mexico, the Czech Republic, and South Korea—raised the possibility that the CMIT should also issue warnings more aggressively.

The Slovaks' accession negotiations came essentially to a halt when the regime of Prime Minister Vladimir Meciar (1993–1994 and 1994–1998) turned decisively toward authoritarianism, thus violating one of the key implicit requirements of the OECD community: democratic rule.[11] The accession process had begun in the middle of the decade, and the CMIT's initial review during the summer of 1996 concluded that the Slovaks were not near the standards of liberalization required under the Codes.[12] The Slovak government did not officially submit a response to the CMIT chair's conclusions, even though this was the next step in the process. The response that did come from the Meciar government was so far off the mark that the Secretariat declined even to circulate it among CMIT members, instead informing policymakers in Bratislava that they needed to do much more. Thus, the accession negotiations came to a standstill on a technicality, though both sides were well aware that membership would be impossible while Meciar was in power.

The first post-Meciar government was formed in November 1998, as the Slovaks celebrated their return to democracy. In December 1999 the government responded to the CMIT's initial review with renewed vigor. Having seen the high standard for liberalization set by its neighbors, and demanded by la Muette, the Slovak authorities promised to liberalize almost every capital account transaction. "The new government, inspired by the appeal to soon join the OECD, dropped the past cautious approach," Slovak authorities noted, "which was not in line with the needs to restructure the Slovak economy."[13]

This new liberal and reformist government was extremely keen to join the OECD. As Ivan Mikloš recalls,

> OECD membership was important both politically and symbolically. Within Slovakia it was evidence of the success of our catch-up strategy, an important symbol to Slovakians. Membership was also a signal to investors that Slovakia was a normal, standard, market economy. The reformers within the Slovak government wanted these reforms. OECD pressure strengthened the hand of the reformers within Bratislava. There was no contradiction between what the OECD wanted us to do and the reform program.[14]

Elena Kohútiková of the National Bank described OECD membership in similar terms, noting that "Slovakia was to become a standard country—a normal market economy."[15]

The new government also reenergized its engagement with the OECD Secretariat, from whose experts the Slovaks were extremely keen to learn. As it had done with the other candidate countries, the Secretariat was generous with its advice and the lessons derived from members' experiences with liberalization. As Kohútiková recalls, "The most difficult learning process was our understanding the meaning and logic of the Code. We had to make sure that we were speaking the same language of the capital account. Everyone was willing to help us. We received enormous support from the Secretariat. It was a very good learning process for us."[16]

In the spring of 2000 the CMIT and CIME held their second joint examination of Slovakia. The Slovak authorities' enthusiasm for financial liberalization was interpreted differently than the Czech authorities' similar approach some five years earlier; this time, it was worrisome. The CMIT and CIME "expressed concern about the state of fragility affecting the financial sector and the time lag required to implement fully comprehensive financial sector supervision according to internationally accepted standards," the OECD council reported.

> If the Slovak Republic becomes a member of the Organization, the Committees recommended that the Slovak authorities present an interim report one year after accession on progress in rehabilitation of the banking sector and strengthening of financial sector supervision, which is indispensable for underpinning the move toward full liberalization.[17]

Additionally, the committees urged the Slovaks to liberalize carefully and more slowly, particularly when it came to hot money, a renewed cause for concern. The committees warned that "the timetable for dismantling remaining restrictions on short-term capital flows should be closely tailored to concrete progress on the above-noted reforms."[18] The CMIT also asked the OECD's Committee on Financial Markets, whose narrower portfolio includes analysis of the health of banking sectors, to review Slovak banks' balance sheets and the state of banking supervision in the country as an additional check on the liberalization path of the government. The CMIT had not asked the Committee on Financial Markets to review any other candidates for membership during the 1990s.

The United States had insisted that the process of Slovak accession slow down, while the European members of the CMIT had been prepared to move forward. Essentially, the United States was "blocking" Slovakia's accession. According to Robert Anderson and Stefan Wagstyl, the United States "was concerned about bringing weak and unprepared economies into the OECD prematurely following financial crises which hit other OECD members soon after their accession—including, Mexico, South Korea, and the Czech Republic." The U.S. member of the CMIT was most concerned about the "fragility of the [Slovak] banks and [Slovakia's] vulnerability to liberalized capital flows."[19]

The Slovak accession thus represented a dramatic reversal in the OECD and the U.S. Treasury. Whereas the CMIT and the Treasury had greeted the accessions of the 1990s with enthusiasm for rapid and complete capital liberalization, by the end of the decade the United States had become more cautious than the European members of the CMIT. Edwin Truman, responsible for U.S. policy toward the OECD accessions, recalls that he and his staff relayed a number of concerns from Washington to Paris. The basic issue was the Treasury's fear that Slovakia was simply not prepared to liberalize short-term capital movements safely. It was, Truman argues, "a financial stability issue. We did not think that we were raising the bar so high that the Slovaks could not clear it. In fact, the conditions for membership would be helpful for Slovakia itself to strengthen its own economic and financial system."[20] The most important Treasury concerns were the Slovak government's commitment to bank restructuring and privatization, future fiscal stability, and the effectiveness of institutions for bank supervision.[21] These Treasury concerns were, moreover, warranted. As one adviser to the Slovak finance minister recalls, "In 1998 we were very close to a full-blown financial crisis, and then in May 1999 we were under heavy financial pressure as well."[22]

The U.S. Treasury voiced another, more political concern as well. "We did not want to have Slovakia join and then have another financial crisis six months later," Truman recalls. "That would have been bad policy and bad PR for the OECD club. It looked bad for the organization, having all of these crises in new members." More than the OECD's reputation was at stake. Following the financial crises of 1997 and 1998, the U.S. Treasury had acquired a reputation for having been too enthusiastic, and too insistent, in its encouragement of capital liberalization around the world. The reputation was not fully deserved, but the criticism stung nonetheless. According to Truman, this criticism also led to a great deal of soul-searching within the Treasury: "The U.S. Treasury had been criticized for not having paid enough attention to the health of financial systems prior to liberalization. There was even more self-criticism within Treasury than there was from outside on this issue."[23] The result of this shift in views in the CMIT and in Washington was a subtle, but profound shift in the standards of OECD membership. The CMIT had required that Mexico, the Czech Republic, Hungary, Poland, and South Korea be liberal; in this case, the CMIT required that Slovakia be liberal *and* financially stable—prudentially regulated, privatized, and capitalized.[24]

In Bratislava these new, stricter standards for membership came as an unpleasant surprise just as the reformist coalition was attempting to demonstrate its progress and maintain its power within the Slovak political system. OECD concerns centered on financial stability, while IMF officials worried about the macroeconomic implications of Slovakian structural reforms.[25]

Katarína Mathernová, who played a critical role in the negotiations, argued that the U.S. government, which at the time was "essentially exercising a veto," was not only concerned about issues that it had let pass during previous accession negotiations, but also that the Treasury was asking for institutional changes that the Slovaks had already promised. Mathernová insisted, "We absolutely agreed that the financial sector needed to be sound and prudentially regulated. The U.S. Treasury did not alert us to this idea. Our bank restructuring plan had been in place since April 1999." Thus, the Treasury's concerns were considered legitimate, but Slovak policymakers "did not see why they applied so critically to us. Not only was our bank restructuring under way, the risks of a crisis in Slovakia were minuscule. Our only capital inflows were foreign direct investment. Even if we blew up, moreover, no one would notice."[26] The U.S. position remained firm for several months, however. "We learned from our experiences during the 1990s," Truman recalls. "So of course the standards for OECD membership were adjusted. The world had changed. We were not going to be railroaded into accepting membership just because the standards for membership were not being taken seriously enough."[27]

The United States reversed its position on Slovakia's accession within a few weeks, after intense lobbying from EU governments and the Slovak government's mobilization of experts and resources to reassure the United States that its financial system was sound and its plan for economic reform carefully sequenced and credible.[28] U.S. State Department officials had also intervened in the process on behalf of the Slovak government. Along with the European members of the OECD, the State Department sought to lock in Slovakia's path toward democratization and reform by bringing the country into the OECD club. State Department officials were concerned that the future of the Slovak reforms depended on international validation of the agenda. Failure in the OECD accession process would have been, according to one Slovak policymaker, "disastrous for the reformist coalition."[29] Thus, Mathernová recalls the resolution of what was for the Slovak government a considerable crisis: "When the issue of our accession became highly politicized, and when other parts of the U.S. government—notably the State Department—intervened on our behalf, the U.S. Treasury sat down with us, listened to our arguments, and finally let go."[30] After last-minute negotiations between France and other members about Slovakia's acceptance of EU rules on broadcasting, Slovakia became the OECD's thirtieth member in December 2000. The Slovak authorities did recognize the silver lining of their difficulties in acceding to the OECD: the liberalization required for accession to the EU was already complete.[31]

Despite a measure of recent prudence, the social norms and legal rules of the club of developed countries endure essentially uncontested. By the beginning of the new century, both had evolved considerably. Stephany

Griffith-Jones, Ricardo Gottschalk, and Xavier Cirera offer a critical interpretation of the evolution of OECD practice in assessing compliance with
the Code's obligations: the Code "initially allowed for a long-term, sequenced process that took due account of the heterogeneity of OECD member countries, but it has changed over the past two decades, with a shift in
emphasis towards rapid liberalization, irrespective of countries' conditions
and circumstances."[32] The OECD itself shares this view that capital controls
are no longer considered to be an option for its members: "OECD members
no longer consider for themselves recourse to capital controls as a workable
tool, as part of broader changes in governance approaches and in a context
of highly integrated financial markets."[33] Controls on capital outflows are,
for OECD countries, an even more negative signal, "counterproductive,
indicating lack of effective policies or even panic on the part of authorities
contending with a crisis situation."[34] The newest six members, moreover,
were socialized quickly. "None of the six new members resorted to derogation procedures during the bouts of serious financial turbulence in the recent past, thereby concurring with the by now accepted wisdom that
reimposition of capital controls is negatively perceived by international market participants," the OECD explains.[35]

Cautious Judges

In the last few months of 1998 the rating agencies regularly observed how
capital controls had insulated China and Chile from the financial contagion
in emerging markets. Chile's controls on capital inflows had never been
interpreted as a signal of heterodoxy, and now they were additionally celebrated for having saved the country from crisis by increasing the average
maturity of capital flowing into the country. Even on the occasion of Chile's
removal of the controls, S&P lauded their usefulness: "The judicious use of
inward capital controls is an element of external flexibility, and has been
used appropriately in Chile, positively affecting the structure of its debt."[36]
China, closer to the heart of the crisis, was thought by S&P to have avoided
the crisis primarily by maintaining tight restrictions on capital flows. "Capital
account controls provide insulation against volatile external capital flows,"
S&P's analysts argued, "which have undermined liquidity in other countries
with weak financial systems."[37]

Malaysia offers another case of unexpected support for capital controls by
S&P. As early as March 1999 S&P changed its official "outlook" on Malaysia's

ratings from negative to stable. The announcement suggested that "the risk that capital controls would be followed by imprudent credit policies has abated." The risks appeared to be recast as something other than signaling or harsh market reaction. "Capital flight," S&P's analysts approvingly wrote, "has been halted by the government's imposition and efficient administration of exchange controls on capital-account and selected current-account transactions."[38] In other documents, however, S&P's John Chambers and David Beers, both senior managers in the firm, defended the original downgrade, noting that if defaults were disastrous, "lesser errors include imposing capital controls."[39]

Toward the end of the summer of 2000, with Malaysia's putatively imminent collapse appearing less and less probable, S&P turned to the task of explaining Malaysia's apparently successful management of the financial crisis. S&P's analysts viewed Malaysia's capital controls as having given the government breathing room to rehabilitate the banking sector rather than letting it collapse, as its neighbors had done. The announcement identified Malaysia's strong fundamentals before the crisis, as well as the government's management, as important:

> Malaysia's external strength and stronger banking system at the onset of the crisis relative to Korea and Thailand, coupled with the government's proactive and centralized policy responses, have moderated the impact of the crisis both on the real economy and on the government's books by giving the financial system time to rehabilitate debtors that otherwise would have failed.[40]

This rethinking of the Malaysian experience within S&P raises some deeply problematic issues, however. The attribution of Malaysia's postcrisis rebound to its superior precrisis fundamentals lent greater support to the government's persistent complaint that Malaysia, because it had managed its economy well before July 1997, did not "deserve" to be punished by outflows of capital and speculative attacks on the currency. From this perspective, the spread of the crisis from Thailand and Indonesia to Malaysia resembled a financial panic more than investors' rational response to Malaysia's own policy mistakes.

Moody's Christopher Mahoney was even more self-reflective when offering the firm's reconsideration of the financial crisis and Malaysia's experience. "The 'blame the borrower' approach was highly seductive," Mahoney wrote, conceding that "I myself indulged in this exercise."[41] For Moody's, the crisis, at least in retrospect, was not the result of the deficiencies of the Asian development model so much as exposure to jittery and massive international financial markets. As Mahoney reflected:

> The gist of the revisionist explanation is: (1) that the orthodox model for the global financial system, by tolerating fixed or quasi-fixed exchange rates while encouraging capital account liberalization, has exposed developing countries to the whipsaw impact of volatile capital flows; (2) that outflows can be triggered by all sorts of events reflecting the inherent volatility of international capital movements in a deregulated world; and (3) that the best explanation for the crisis was the degree of exposure to capital flows and the degree to which appropriate policies were in place to cope with such flows.[42]

Both S&P and Moody's have since applied the lessons learned during the financial crisis to a variety of issues and countries. In the abstract, S&P's managers shifted the firm's position from encouraging and valorizing financial openness to highlighting its risks and the importance of a modest pace and careful sequencing. "Past economic crises, particularly in Asia in the late 1990s, suggest," according to Beers and Cavanaugh, that "capital account liberalization should take place in conjunction with current account liberalization, but at an orderly pace that meshes with transparent progress in other areas."[43] Chambers went so far as to endorse "some form of inward capital controls" for "countries that aren't fully integrated with world financial systems, for countries in which regulation or supervision isn't fully developed, or for countries that have low sovereign credit ratings."[44]

In analyses of specific countries, S&P applied the logic rigorously. China, whose place in the international financial system had been transformed by massive flows of foreign direct investment into the country, was often singled out. S&P's advice was to consider the lessons of history and proceed slowly and cautiously. "From the Chinese standpoint," S&P's analysts wrote, "several international experiences highlight the perils of externally driven appreciation (for example, Japan after the Plaza Accord) and capital account liberalization with a weak banking system (Asian countries in 1997)."[45] S&P later warned China of a "too-rapid relaxation" of capital controls.[46] The firm also attributed "India's improving external position" to its growth potential, its competitive exports, and "capital controls, which help build foreign exchange reserves and foreign direct investments."[47]

The content of what Cavanaugh calls S&P's "basic economic orthodoxy" had altered significantly since the firm downgraded Malaysia for imposing controls in September 1998. What used to be a heresy was, by the early years of the new century, endorsed by the rating agencies as orthodox once again.

Capital mobility is still a developed country norm, and the constitutive rules of the EU and OECD continue to inform the agencies' approach to those capital flows among the world's rich countries. "Pervasive investment restrictions on foreign portfolio investment should not exist in developed stock markets," writes S&P, "and their presence is a sign that the market is not yet 'developed.'"[48] Being a "developed" country still means having an open capital account, but a developing country can in 2006 restrict capital and still be considered orthodox, on the right track, and unlikely to default on its sovereign debt. S&P's and Moody's dramatic revisions to their interpretive frameworks do not seem to have captured much attention, but the change is profound.

From the perspective of the agencies, the capital mobility norm need not be universal and unqualified for their business to thrive. The agencies do, however, require capital mobility, and the greater the freedom for capital, the more their revenues may grow. "So long as governments resist the temptation to curb global capital flows, we will be rating many more governments before we reach this limit," observes Beers. "Compared with the 100 we have now, between 25 and 50 additional sovereign ratings would be a realistic target over the next decade, but I would not be surprised if the number turned out to be higher."[49] The implementation of Basel II (described in Chapters 5 and 7) in 2007 also promises to create even greater regulation-induced demand for the services of the rating agencies. Moody's and S&P may well find their, or their competitors', ratings incorporated into most important financial regulations throughout the world.

With this influence has come a responsibility that Moody's and S&P did not want—namely, to protect the world's institutional investors from risky bonds. The current relationship between governments and the rating agencies has proved at best unpalatable and at worst politically unsustainable. There are mounting pressures in the United States for the SEC to exercise greater oversight and perhaps more regulatory authority over the rating agencies.[50] Europeans are also considering ways in which the firms might be regulated by EU authorities, and thus make the industry, from their perspective, better organized and more responsive to the needs of Europe. The

French, naturally, are leading this charge. Even the epitome of American ad hoc globalization may eventually be organized, regulated, and rationalized in Paris and Brussels.

A Europe of Rules

Despite the renewed tolerance for capital controls emerging at S&P and elsewhere, Europe remains confidently untouched by this new challenge to its free-capital orthodoxy. Postwar Europe has much to be proud of, and it counts forging a new global capital regime among its achievements. The accomplishments of the Community, and now of the Union, are impressive, particularly against the backdrop of twentieth-century political and economic history. Many of these accomplishments are famous: peace, sustained cooperation, a common market, a single trade policy, a nearly borderless geographic territory, and, of course, the euro. Much less widely appreciated is the fact that the EU's leadership has enabled the internationalization of finance. Indeed, with the most liberal—and most liberally applied—rules on capital of any international organization in the world, the EU lies at the very center of global finance.

Europe's approach to capital produced a rule-based liberalization initiated by French policymakers in Paris and Brussels and globalized by Germany's insistence on the *erga omnes* principle in the 1988 directive and the Treaty on European Union. France would have preferred a focus only on the liberalization of capital movements within Europe, but ultimately accepted the principle of liberalization with third countries as well, albeit with a number of legal exceptions that could potentially be invoked. Rather than a Europe buffeted from the vagaries of global finance with its own regional capital market, Europe is instead deeply embedded in, even constitutive of, global capital.

In the first decade of the new century, moreover, the EU was the very vanguard of the globalization of finance in at least two respects. First, the Commission continuously monitored the compliance of member states with their obligation to complete capital mobility. The Commission demonstrated on a number of occasions that it would not hesitate to initiate legal action against the governments of member states in the European Court of Justice, a process that has led to the accumulation of case law on the obligations of member states to liberalize.[51] The Commission has sued member governments for infringing on the freedom of capital nine times in the past several years, winning eight of those nine cases. Compliance with the freedom of capital in contemporary Europe is complete enough that the Commission has focused its efforts on policies and laws less obviously implicating capital mobility. For instance, some member states attempted to maintain control in newly privatized firms by retaining a "golden share" that would potentially give the government disproportionate influence over major managerial decisions. The Commission argued that the golden shares discouraged cross-border capital movements, and the Court of Justice agreed in almost every case.[52] The Commission also brought cases against member states for subtle tax policies designed to discourage domestic residents from investing abroad.[53] It is difficult to imagine the Commission softening its attempts to enforce what is, as of 1988, one of the fundamental freedoms that constitute Europe.

Second, the Commission continued to approach accession negotiations with prospective members from the perspective of the "classical method." As with the 1995 and 2004 accessions, complete freedom for capital is a prerequisite for membership. The EU has been consistent on this issue for more than a decade. Many scholars and policymakers argue, however, that the world has changed since the days when Europe embraced total capital mobility.

When the Teachers of Norms Disagree

The orthodoxy of capital's freedom seems to have been undermined everywhere except for Brussels, in part because the codified norm of capital liberalization for European states is literally not open to interpretation. The entire process of European integration through evolving rules enforced by the Commission is built around the idea that it is effective to bureaucratize difficult issues. Few issues in the history of European integration were as difficult as the liberalization of capital movements, but it is now settled definitively. Unrestricted capital mobility is part of the *acquis,* the full body of legal accomplishments, of the community.

The challenges faced by the newest EU aspirants should come as a surprise to those who think of the IMF as the defender of liberal orthodoxy and of Europe as its alternative. Two east European countries—Croatia and Romania—in negotiations with the Commission for membership in 2004 and 2005 found themselves caught between liberal Brussels and cautious Washington. The Commission insisted, as it is obliged to do by the *acquis,* that full capital liberalization is a condition for accession. As all the Commission's reports on the progress of negotiations read:

Member States must remove all restrictions in national law on the movement of capital between themselves, but also with third countries (with some exceptions), and adopt EU rules to guarantee the proper functioning of cross-border payments and transfer of all forms of capital.[54]

The IMF urged the same finance ministry and central bank officials in Croatia and Romania to liberalize more slowly.[55] Fund officials warned of the risk of a financial crisis when these countries' undercapitalized and poorly governed financial systems were opened to free flows of capital.

The Croatian government expressed its concerns about capital liberalization "based on the view that short-term capital flows are the most volatile and thus pose the greatest danger for the country's monetary, exchange rate, and overall economic stability."[56] The IMF staff responsible for Croatia, sharing the Croatian authorities' concerns, encouraged the National Bank of Croatia to consider, if necessary, market-based controls on capital inflows.[57] Croatian authorities indeed followed this advice and increased the marginal reserve requirement for domestic banks to deposit in the central bank, without remuneration, 30 percent of the net increase in their foreign liabilities.[58] The Commission had already made clear, however, that such controls on capital inflows, market-based or not, would not be permitted according to the *acquis*. And so we arrive at the unexpected scenario of Croatia's accession to the free-capital EU being blocked because it followed the illiberal IMF's advice to rely on capital controls.

Romania found itself caught between the same mutually exclusive instructions. The government planned to undertake its final liberalizing measure—allowing foreigners to open bank accounts in the domestic currency, lei—in January 2004, then postponed it to April 2005. This move had been agreed as part of the government's overall plan for liberalization when Romania's Chapter 4 negotiations with the Commission were provisionally closed in 2003.[59] IMF officials argued that the Romanian government should postpone liberalizing those flows of capital because of the spread between inflation (10 to 11 percent) and interest rates in bank accounts (17 percent); such a spread, they suggested, would create an incentive to speculate. The Commission, in contrast, threatened to reopen the already completed Chapter 4 negotiations on capital freedom if Romania did not proceed with the liberalization timetable to which the government and the Commission had already agreed.[60]

Romanian central bankers found the contradictions between the Fund and the Commission all the more frustrating because the IMF had previously encouraged them to liberalize the capital account more quickly during the mid-1990s. At that time Daniel Daianu, formerly Minister of Finance and a senior official at the National Bank of Romania, "supported the opposite point of view, which was validated by subsequent events. Today, the IMF itself is urging us to defer the next step of capital account liberalization, considering the still high interest rates in our country, the possible slipping away from the disinflation target, and the need to limit the external deficits." The Commission, however, continued to press for further liberalization.[61] "Progress has been made on schedule as regards capital movements and payments," observes the Commission, "but the liberalization of capital-account flows needs to be completed and Romania needs to focus on progressing on schedule." The Commission urges that "particular attention should be paid to the timely removal of outstanding restrictions on capital movements and payments, namely concerning access by non-residents to [Romanian lei]-denominated deposit accounts" by April 2005.[62] The very deposits identified as risky were seen by the Commission as one further step toward membership. The Commission was not forcing Romania to liberalize; if Romania were not ready for the *acquis*, then membership ought to wait as well. The Commission did not insist on an open capital account because it was a universal economic truth. It was just the law.

The reasonableness of Brussels negotiators, informed by decades of European legal accomplishments, places the Commission in a vulnerable position, however. The results of accession negotiations, which represent a relationship that is less than coercive but more than imitative, would be interpreted ungenerously were one of the EU's newest or prospective members to suffer a serious financial crisis. After the crises of 1997 and 1998, many policymakers in Asia and Russia, as well as scholars in Europe and the United States, accused the IMF and U.S. Treasury of having urged capital liberalization too aggressively, thereby exposing countries to greater risk. Although more research, and greater archival access, is necessary to determine their responsibility, one fact is clear: the tools of influence available to the EU are far more efficacious than those of the Fund and even the Treasury. A financial crisis in Romania, for example, would lead policymakers to contrast the urgent warnings of Fund staff with the insistence of Brussels. If the sullied reputations of the Fund and the Treasury are any guide, the fact that Europe's standards for membership were merely set, rather than imposed, is unlikely to blunt the inevitable criticisms that ensue.

This state of affairs is almost certainly not what Jacques Delors and his team sought to achieve when they rewrote Europe's capital rules at the end of the 1980s. The codification and bureaucratization of capital's freedom in an institution as well organized as the European Union has constituted the policy practices of European-ness. And it has, simultaneously, created greater leverage for the negotiators whose role it is to recognize the countries of central and eastern Europe as European—or not. As Europe grows, so, too, does the institutional space for the complete freedom of capital movements. Capital mobility is still a European and developed-country norm; it is not the global norm. And the actors widely, but wrongly, thought to be its chief global apostles—the IMF, the U.S. Treasury, the credit-rating agencies—are now backing away in doubt.

CHAPTER 9

Conclusion

For it's no secret that the past proves a most unstable mirror,
typically too severe and flattering all at once, and never as
truth-reflecting as people would like to believe.

—Chang-rae Lee

And so we find ourselves living, once again, in an era of
financial openness and mobile capital. It is not the first time and, unless this
is the end of history, it will probably not be the last time. We have lived
through the end of history more than once, however, and policymakers
continue to relearn old lessons about the difficulties of regulation and the
risks of liberalization.

The idea that capital ought to flow unrestricted across the globe became
the reigning orthodoxy of international finance over the course of the 1980s
and 1990s. Yet less than a decade after the financial crises that hit emerging
markets in the 1990s, that orthodoxy is already in decline and its reign in
question. As a matter of capital flows, global finance is as strong as ever. But
when it comes to the norms and rules of global finance, the very ideas and
laws that sustain the system, the height of this era of globalization has already been reached.

The globalization of finance, in this sense, reached its peak in the autumn
of 1998. The condemnation by the international financial community, and
particularly the credit-rating agencies, of Malaysia's capital controls in September 1998 represented the norm of capital mobility at its purest and most
liberal. Restrictions of the mobility of capital were deemed inappropriate
under any circumstances, even during a financial crisis that began elsewhere; when implemented by a developing country's government frus-

trated by widespread short-selling in the illiquid market for its currency; amid relatively sound economic fundamentals; when foreign direct investment was exempted from the restrictions; or when accompanied by promises of temporariness. In short, all the exceptions that scholars and policymakers had historically reserved from their embrace of open capital markets were ruled out of bounds. The norm of capital mobility was to be universal and unqualified. Deviation was a powerful signal of heterodoxy, and the markets were ready to interpret such signals accordingly. At that very moment in 1998, the IMF Executive Board and Interim Committee were considering codifying the norm for all 184 members, as had the EU and OECD for their own clubs. That autumn was as close as the world has ever come to a consensus—written and unwritten—that capital's right to freedom applied always and everywhere.

Policymakers understand the international financial system very differently, however, in the first decade of a new century. Caution toward full capital mobility now prevails within the international financial community. The IMF, OECD, and credit-rating agencies have been congratulated, occasionally by one another and themselves, for having "learned" valuable lessons from the emerging market financial crises of the 1990s. The organizations and agencies generally include among these lessons: the serious risks of self-fulfilling financial crises and their apparently contagious spread; the dangers of embracing hot money instead of longer-term capital flows; and the importance of a country's domestic institutional foundations for sound banking systems as a precondition for full liberalization.

Every organized voice of authority within the international financial system has backed away from embracing complete, unqualified capital mobility except one: the European Union. The European Commission, in contrast, still approaches its accession negotiations just as it always has: Brussels negotiators insist, correctly, that the EU's rules unambiguously forbid all capital controls, and so potential members are obliged to liberalize fully and, if they are to accede soon, rapidly as well.

Outside the EU and OECD, the rest of the world is actually running on what can only be called ad hoc globalization, led by the United States, the consequences of which are potentially problematic for the maintenance of the bargains that sustain the mobility of capital across national borders. Throughout this period, the United States has consistently turned to unilateral decisions and bilateral trade and investment treaties to advance its national interests. It has largely fallen to the Europeans to exercise leadership in the international organizations that write the rules of capital mobility and socialize new members into the norms of openness. With so much of the world outside the rule of liberal Europe and the OECD club of rich countries, such ad hoc globalization effectively undermines the legitimacy of global financial openness as a universal norm. The system—if such a patchwork can be called a system—that actually governs most countries is anything but the work of deliberate design.

The recent evolution of the norms and rules of the international monetary system raises several important questions for scholars, policymakers, and the private financial community. The international financial community has formulated lessons for itself of the crises of the 1990s that, in both principle and language, are nearly identical to those that policymakers believed they had learned from the crises of the 1920s and 1930s. Yet policymakers today describe the prevailing consensus of caution as having emerged from "new information" or "change in the knowledge base." Why, then, is the rediscovery of the lessons of the interwar years, apparently long forgotten or rejected, so frequently described as "learning"? And why has the European Commission uniquely failed to learn the lessons now shared by the IMF, OECD, credit-rating agencies, and U.S. Treasury?

Of Learning and Forgetting

Members of the international financial community have tended to narrate the past decade of crises and caution as a story of linear progress, a Whig history of new knowledge informing their evolving consensus. Policymakers within the IMF and OECD acknowledge that perhaps management and staff had become overly enthusiastic about capital liberalization, and insufficiently concerned about its risks, during the 1990s. According to this view, they then learned from the experiences of the east Asian, east European, and Latin American financial crises. Like many self-narrated tales, this story has a happy ending: international organizations and credit-rating agencies now recognize the importance of the appropriate pace, sequencing, and institutional preconditions for capital liberalization.

This narrative of continuous progress is implausible for a number of reasons. One is straightforward: the news is not new. These lessons have been learned before, ironically by the very founders of these international organizations, whose rules were written amidst a consensus of caution similar to our own. The IMF and OECD embodied the memory of the interwar years during the early postwar era.

Change within the members and bureaucracies of the organizations slowly undermined that institutional memory. Member countries with increasingly sophisticated and well-governed financial systems enjoyed the benefits of financial internationalization, while domestic institutions and prudential regulations helped to insulate them from the risks. The practice of regulating international capital flows in developing countries became increasingly problematic, as governments that generally lacked capacious institutions fared no better when attempting to control capital. Then, poorly functioning controls engendered inefficiency and corruption. Debates on the desirability of regulation often ended with the prosaic observation that "capital controls do not work." Some policymakers were even tempted to conclude that the problems of capital controls implied that liberalization ought to be embraced. A new generation, exposed more to the drawbacks of controls than to the consequences of financial crises, asserted the superiority of liberalization with increasing confidence.

With regard to international capital flows, however, no stance has ever enjoyed complete superiority, either intellectual or practical. The choice to regulate capital flows has benefits and risks, as does the decision to liberate them. The balance of those benefits and risks is not merely indeterminate, dependent as they are on domestic political and social institutions; the balance can appropriately be struck only by a society and its government.

Another important reason to be skeptical of the narrative of learning is the caution of the private financial community in the United States and elsewhere about worldwide capital mobility. Many influential members of that community of investors and bankers have long recognized that not every country is fully prepared to embrace all capital flows. It is furthermore impossible to deduce for the private financial community an interest in the liberalization of capital flows by all countries. Their profits will be earned in emerging markets, not, say, in the world's poorest countries, whose weak financial systems might easily collapse into a crisis that would affect neighbors. The private financial community is much more interested in avoiding systemic crises than in gaining access to every market in the world.

Discretion and Rules in Brussels

In the early years of the new century, the EU continued to be a force for capital liberalization while the IMF, OECD, and credit-rating agencies counseled caution and pragmatism. In accession negotiations with prospective east European members, the EU insisted that complete capital liberalization was an obligation of membership, while the IMF simultaneously urged east European governments to proceed more deliberately and postpone the liberation of short-term capital flows into the banking sector—essentially to ignore the recommendations of Brussels. With a reputation as "Fortress Europe," the EU's unique liberalism within the international financial architecture is all the more surprising. The bureaucracies of the IMF and the OECD learned caution from the crises for which they were often blamed. The European Commission continues to insist on liberalization in accession negotiations with countries that, from the perspective of Washington, are simply not prepared.

None of this risky behavior by the Commission results from dogma. Commission negotiators are not themselves "neoliberals." Nor is the view from Brussels even informed by economic analysis. For the most part, the negotiators are lawyers. The Commission approaches the enlargement negotiations as a matter of legal, not economic, principle. Accessionwise, the economics of full capital mobility are basically irrelevant, for capital mobility is a long-settled matter of European law. The very status of that European law differentiates the EU from every other international organization in the world. Political authority in the EU is not statelike, nor is it likely to become some sort of superstate. State-building is not the European project, which is sui generis. But the intergovernmental agreements among European members have created a federal authority without parallel in other international organizations.

The EU's *acquis communautaire*, the entire collection of European rules, treaties, directives, and court decisions, unambiguously prohibits member states from restricting capital mobility within the Union and with third countries. In accession negotiations, Commission negotiators are not legally authorized to reconsider the absolute freedom of capital movements, a freedom that was one of the most difficult and celebrated achievements of the community. The EU does not have a stance on capital mobility; it has only rules, settled and codified.

This is not just a matter of the intransigence of an overly bureaucratic Commission, however. Transitional periods are a common compromise on the *acquis* for both existing and prospective members. The EU's current members, for example, authorized the Commission to request that the full mobility of people be phased in slowly for fear of overwhelming immigration from new members.

The constitutive effects of Europe's codified rules are powerful, however:

with the sole exception of land ownership, prospective members have not requested transitional periods for any aspect of full capital mobility. As a matter of law, the Commission cannot insist on transitional periods that no government seeks. This legalistic stance might be useful for absolving both the Commission and new member governments from blame for a financial crisis that results from rapid liberalization of poorly governed, illiquid financial sectors. Blamelessness will not, however, minimize the costs of such a crisis.

Implications for the Study of the International Monetary System

In this book I have put the prevailing orthodoxy in historical and political context. The religious metaphors that pervade the study and policy practices of the international monetary system—dogma, heresy, orthodoxy—suggest, as is often the case with such extreme rhetoric, the absence of firm ground underneath. The evolution of the social norms and legal rules of the system have been driven by politics, not science. Although every orthodoxy has at one moment seemed natural and inevitable, none has been permanent. Each orthodoxy was a contingent product of its time.

Given the mix of conventional wisdom, and, occasionally, ideological dogma, that pervades discussions of the nature and causes of the current regime, the findings of this book may at first seem counterintuitive. Yet all the findings of this book are drawn directly from the ample, though heretofore untapped, documentary record of the relevant archives and the generally corroborated accounts of the policymakers who wrestled with these issues. The empirical narratives and analytical orientation of this book offer two distinct contributions to the study of the international monetary system.

A Revisionist History of the Emergence of Global Finance

The more controversial, and perhaps more important, contribution is a revisionist history of the origins of a liberal regime to govern the internationalization of finance. The OECD's and EU's liberal rules, and the unsuccessful proposal to amend the IMF Articles, generally have been interpreted as the result of a variety of political and economic developments, which I review in Chapter 2. The two most widely credited are U.S. political and economic hegemony and the rise of neoliberal ideology.

A very different narrative emerges from my analysis of the archival documents and firsthand accounts of many of the policymakers who were involved in these extraordinary transformations. Europe's centrality, and its necessity, to the process of financial globalization is the most important revision to the conventional wisdom. A handful of French policymakers, often along with their British, German, and Dutch counterparts, played the decisive roles in the codification of the norm of capital mobility. Moreover, if the process of European financial integration had been more inwardly focused, rather than embracing the principle of *erga omnes,* the financial markets that flourished during the early years of the new century would not have been "global" at all. Many European policymakers, and the mass publics they represent, portray globalization as an impersonal, powerful force beyond their control that limits their autonomy. The invocation of an all-powerful, homogenizing globalization is itself dubious, but even if it were valid Europeans would nevertheless have to acknowledge that this era of global finance was very much of their own making.

Prominent French Socialists, accompanied by policymakers on the Left throughout Europe, decisively influenced the process of capital liberalization within their own countries and subsequently the codification of the norm of capital mobility in the rules of international organizations. The rise of the Right and resurgence of neoliberalism in the United States and Europe affected the policymaking context in which French and European Socialists found themselves. To be sure, the widespread embrace of markets during the late 1980s and early 1990s was important. But this embrace spanned the political spectrum.

With regard to capital controls, the Left became disillusioned with them in an era of internationalized financial markets: the wealthy and well-connected, including multinational firms, eluded controls that had once been designed to prevent the outflow of their capital, while the middle classes lacked the financial sophistication and resources to do the same. Some policymakers on the Left resolved to liberalize—not out of a commitment to neoliberalism, but because the redistributive purpose of capital controls was continually undermined. In France, as throughout Europe, the Left liberalized capital flows more than the Right would have dared. Following the French embrace of an open capital account, a handful of Leftist French policymakers then led the process of codifying the norm of capital mobility in the EU, the OECD, and, unsuccessfully, the IMF.

Rationalism and Constructivism in the Politics of Global Finance

The other contribution of this book is my application of sociological and constructivist theory to an important empirical question of international political economy. Although scholarly debates about the usefulness of rationalist and constructivist theoretical approaches often treat them as analytically incommensurable, my approach is pragmatic. I have focused on complex patterns of international politics: the sources and consequences of organized and ad hoc financial globalization. Some aspects of this research question are better understood with answers derived from a rationalist theory of power politics, while other components demand a more sociological approach. I have drawn on both theoretical traditions to resolve the empirical puzzles that motivate this book.[1]

Power Politics. The U.S. Treasury already is central to global finance; it requires little assistance from the European Commission, the CMIT, or IMF management, and with respect to the latter two, has little incentive to delegate to them. U.S. banks and financial firms are not interested in worldwide capital mobility; they are interested in access to a handful of emerging markets, access they can, in general, acquire without the liberalizing efforts of policymakers like the EU's Jacques Delors, the OECD's Henri Chavranski, or the IMF's Michel Camdessus. Because of the overwhelming dominance of the United States in international financial markets, neither Wall Street nor the U.S. Treasury has perceived any need to write rules that might ultimately constrain them as well. Ad hoc globalization befits the United States' hyperpower and its narrow economic ambitions.

Managed globalization, on the other hand, befits France, a middle power with ambitions to influence international politics and economics by putting rules and organizations, rather than American power, at the center of the system. In the international financial system, French and European policymakers have marked globalization by formulating and codifying the rules. An organizational imperative led the European leaders of the EU, OECD, and IMF to attempt to empower their bureaucracies and expand their jurisdiction.

Social Purpose and Constitutive Rules. The liberal content of the rules that French and other European policymakers proposed requires further explanation, however, given that most of the rhetoric about "managed globalization" has focused on the need for more regulation, not more liberalization. Although the general principle of rule-making and organization-building informed the doctrine of managed globalization, the liberal ideas behind the EU's and OECD's rules resulted in part from the putative lessons of a new age of interdependence for European Socialists. That the Socialists would liberalize due to the worrisome distributional consequences of ineffective capital controls was certainly not an inevitable outcome of the French financial crisis of 1983. The crisis had to be interpreted, and the "modernizing minority" described by Delors had long been prepared to offer an alternate monetary and financial paradigm to the Left. The doctrine that evolved—of a managed globalization that was still liberal, but mastered and organized—won the day.

Furthermore, the German commitment to capital mobility within and outside of Europe dates at least to the 1950s and is derived from a set of influential ideas about the need to depoliticize all matters of currency and capital. Indeed, Germany appears to have been the only consistently and purely liberal country in the sixty years since the Bretton Woods conference. The bargain struck between the organizing initiatives of French Socialists and the liberal commitments of German central bankers resulted in European rules that are unparalleled in their commitment to freedom for capital movements.

The purpose of this French-German bargain was primarily one of deeper European integration on terms that both countries could accept. Neither Paris, nor Bonn, nor Brussels intended at the time to make Europe the vanguard of financial globalization. Yet these accidental globalizers did exactly that. The French and the broader European approaches to globalization have constitutive consequences, regardless of how straightforwardly the policies appear to fit their respective positions within the international distribution of power. The EU's and OECD's clear rules in favor of capital mobility have delineated the practices that are legitimate for "European" and "developed" countries. The codification of the norm of capital mobility in the EU and OECD thus changed the scripts for members of those organizations: those two scripts articulate an obligation to permit capital to move freely, as well as intellectual justification for doing so.

Although these constitutive rules exerted significant influence on the policy practices of existing EU and OECD members, their most powerful effects were felt by the three new EU members in 1995 and the ten new central and east European members in 2004, as well as the six countries that acceded to the OECD between 1994 and 2000. In order to be recognized as "European" and "developed," these countries liberalized their capital accounts rapidly because the EU's and OECD's standards for membership were so clear. Because many of these countries lacked the institutional foundations of well-functioning capital markets, however, they also thereby risked financial crises, which a number of them experienced during the 1990s and may yet still.

A sociological perspective is also necessary to understand the social and organizational construction of the signals conveyed by government policies to financial markets. Market participants are obliged to infer meanings from governments' capital account restrictions and liberalizations. And the social meaning of a capital control changed dramatically more than once during the twentieth century. In addition to the ideological ascendance of liberated markets for capital during the 1980s and 1990s, the EU, OECD, and, to some extent, the IMF helped to define many capital account restrictions as illegitimate policy practices. These international organizations disseminated the practice of full capital mobility to existing and new members, thereby fixing the meanings of capital controls as policy tools for the international financial community. Neither market participants nor policymakers would deny that they comprise a "community" with norms and rules, and yet those very norms and rules are too often treated as self-evident or unproblematic.

The current era of global finance is based in part on market expectations about policy credibility. Credible policies are reinforced by market approval. But a policy stance that lacks the trust of financial markets cannot succeed, as capital flows out and often in overwhelming amounts.[2] In this book I have attempted to explain a fundamental change in the parameters—how a set of policies that once were credible became, to the markets, incredible. At any moment in time it may be possible to model with a purely rationalist analytical framework why prevailing views about the legitimacy of capital controls can create self-reinforcing market reactions. But to understand the dramatic change over time requires an account that takes seriously the process by which the international financial community has changed—collectively—its mind.

Like the rest of us, policymakers, bankers, and investors take things for granted. Day to day, their attention is focused on institutions only to the extent that those institutions structure the costs and benefits of their decisions.

The tasks at hand rarely lend themselves to reflection on the conceptual un-derpinnings of informal institutions or the sources of codified rules. In this book I have attempted to explain several dramatic transformations of the so-cial norms and legal rules of the international financial system, a system that at any moment may be taken for granted by those who operate within it. This project has explored the roles of the EU, OECD, IMF, and credit-rating agencies and why, in the words of German sociologist Max Weber, they are "historically *so* and not *otherwise*."[3]

The international financial system, with its mix of organized and ad hoc governance, could easily have been otherwise. France, Germany, and the European Commission might not have created a liberal, globalizing Europe. U.S. policymakers need not have incorporated Moody's and S&P's ratings into their own financial regulations, the most influential in the world. Nor was it inevitable that the United States would destroy the effort to empower the IMF to promote liberalization and judge members' capital controls.

As with the nineteenth-century regime of financial openness and capital mobility, contingent as it was, a mix of deliberate decisions and unintended consequences created greater legal freedom for the private financial com-munity of the twenty-first century. "There was nothing natural about *laissez-faire*," wrote Karl Polanyi of the earlier era. Instead, "free markets could never have come into being merely by allowing things to take their course."[4] Sixty-odd years after Polanyi wrote those words, the financial markets of the contemporary world are globalized, but not because they were allowed merely to take their own course.

Understanding the institutional foundations of global capital markets should also lead to greater recognition of the sometimes delicate political and social compromises that built them. The globalization of finance is nei-ther inexorable nor inevitable. When the impression of inexorability dis-places our sense of history, we may not recognize the inherent fragility of the underpinnings of a world that allows such extraordinary mobility of capital. The international financial community cannot take each successive orthodoxy for granted. Some have narrated the renaissance of global fi-nance as a story of progress, while others focus primarily on the risks of re-current and devastating crises. These reflections are alternately too flattering and too severe. The unstable mirror of the past is a flawed, but essential source for understanding our own beliefs.

List of Archives and Interviewees

International Organizations

European Commission

OFFICE OF THE PRESIDENT

Jacques Delors, French Minister of Economics and Finance (1981–1984), President of European Commission (1985–1995)

Pascal Lamy, Adviser to French Economics and Finance Minister Jacques Delors (1981–1983), Deputy Chief of Staff to French Prime Minister Pierre Mauroy (1983–1984), Chief of Staff and Representative of European Commission President Jacques Delors (1985–1994), European Commissioner for Commerce (1999–2004), Member of French Socialist Party's Steering Committee (1985–1994)

DG ENLARGEMENT

Lars Erik Forsberg, Negotiator, Chapter 4: Capital Movements

Stephane Ouaki, Negotiator, Chapter 4: Capital Movements

DG ECONOMICS AND FINANCE

Maria Areizaga, Economist, Financial Integration and Capital Movements

Jean-Pierre Baché, Director, Financial Integration and Capital Movements (1973–1989)

Ute Kallenberger, Economist, Financial Integration and Capital Movements

Kenneth Lennan, Deputy Director, Financial Integration and Capital Movements

Jean-Paul Mingasson, Director for Monetary Matters (1982–1987), Deputy Director-General: Economic and Monetary Matters (1987–1989)

Tommaso Padoa-Schioppa, Director-General for Economic and Financial Affairs (1979–1983), Central Director for Economic Research at the Banca d'Italia (1983–1984), Deputy Director General of the Banca d'Italia (1984–1997), Member of the Executive Board of the European Central Bank (1998–2005)

Organization for Economic Cooperation and Development

Official Archives of the Organization for Economic Cooperation and Development, Château de la Muette, Paris

COMMITTEE ON CAPITAL MOVEMENTS AND INVISIBLE TRANSACTIONS

Henri Chavranski, Chair (1982–1994)

Jan Nipstad, Chair of the Joint Working Group on Banking and Related Financial Services (1985–1989)

Lex Rieffel, U.S. Representative to the Committee (1984–1986)

COUNTRY DELEGATIONS

Andreas Breitenfellner, Economic and Financial Attaché, Permanent Delegation of Austria

Tae-Kyun Kwon, Counsellor, Permanent Delegation of the Republic of Korea

Kamal I. Latham, Finance and Investment Adviser, Permanent Delegation of the United States

John L. Weeks, Minister-Counselor for Economic, Financial, and Fiscal Affairs, Permanent Delegation of the United States

DIRECTORATE FOR FINANCIAL, FISCAL, AND ENTERPRISE AFFAIRS

Hans J. Blommestein, Head of Emerging Market Program

Hans Christiansen, Senior Economist, Investment Division

Kathryn Gordon, Senior Economist

Marie-France Houde, Manager, OECD Foreign Investment Policy Reviews

Robert Ley, Counsellor to the Director

Rinaldo Pecchioli, Deputy Director

Pierre Poret, Head of the Investment Division

Eva Thiel, Senior Economist, Investment Division

DIRECTORATE FOR LEGAL AFFAIRS

Fabrizio Pagani, Legal Adviser

International Monetary Fund

Official Archives of the International Monetary Fund, Washington, D.C.

MANAGEMENT

Michel Camdessus, Managing Director (1987–2000)

Stanley Fischer, First Deputy Managing Director (1994–2001)

Jacques de Larosière, Managing Director (1978–1987)

Jacques J. Polak, Director of Research (1958–1980), Economic Counsellor (1966–1980), Executive Director (1981–1986)

Thomas A. Bernes, Canada (and Antigua and Barbuda, the Bahamas, Barbados, Belize, Dominica, Grenada, Ireland, Jamaica, St. Kitts and Nevis, St. Lucia, St. Vincent and the Grenadines) (1996–2001)

Willy Kiekens, Belgium (and Austria, Belarus, Czech Republic, Hungary, Kazakhstan, Luxembourg, Slovak Republic, Slovenia, and Turkey)

Karin Lissakers, United States (1993–2001)

Abbas Mirakhor, Iran (and Algeria, Ghana, Morocco, Pakistan, and Tunisia)

Aleksei Mozhin, Russia

Abdel Shakour Shaalan, Egypt (and Bahrain, Iraq, Jordan, Kuwait, Lebanon, Libya, Maldives, Oman, Qatar, Syria, United Arab Emirates, Republic of Yemen)

J. Onno de Beaufort Wijnholds, Netherlands (and Armenia, Bosnia and Herzegovina, Bulgaria, Croatia, Cyprus, Georgia, Israel, Macedonia, Moldova, Romania, and Ukraine) (1994–2003)

LEGAL DEPARTMENT

Sean Hagan, Deputy General Counsel

Ross Leckow, Assistant General Counsel

MONETARY AND FINANCIAL SYSTEMS DEPARTMENT

Karl Habermeier, Adviser, Immediate Office

R. Barry Johnston, Assistant Director, Financial Market Integrity Division

POLICY DEVELOPMENT AND REVIEW DEPARTMENT

Jack Boorman, Director (1990–2001)

James M. Boughton, Assistant Director

Matthew Fisher, Senior Adviser and Division Chief, Capital Account Issues Division

Member Countries

France

Hervé Hannoun, Technical Adviser to French Prime Minister Pierre Mauroy (1983–1984), Technical Adviser to French President François Mitterrand (1984–1988), Deputy Director of the French Ministry of Economics, Finance, and Budget (1985–1986), Chief of Staff to French Economics and Finance Minister Pierre Bérégovoy (1989–1992), Chief of Staff to French Prime Minister Pierre Bérégovoy (1992), Second Deputy Governor, Banque de France (1992–1999), First Deputy Governor, Banque de France (2000–present)

Pierre Jacquet, Executive Director, Agence Française de Développement

Jean-Charles Naouri, Chief of Staff to French Social Affairs and National Solidarity Minister Pierre Bérégovoy (1982–1984), Chief of Staff to French Economics and Finance Minister Pierre Bérégovoy (1984–1986)

Jean-Claude Trichet, Head of International Affairs, Treasury Department of the

French Ministry of Finance (1985–1986), Chief of Staff to French Economic, Finance, and Privatization Minister Édouard Balladur (1986–1987), Director of the Treasury Department of the French Ministry of Finance (1987–1993), Governor of the Banque de France (1993–1999, 1999–2003), President of the European Central Bank (2003–present)

Germany

Werner Becker, Senior Economist, Deutsche Bank AG

Karl Otto Pöhl, Deputy President (1977–1979) and President (1980–1991) of the Deutsche Bundesbank

Hans Tietmeyer, Permanent Secretary for Financial Policy, International Monetary Policy, and European Community Matters, German Ministry of Finance (1982–1989), President of the Deutsche Bundesbank (1993–1999)

U.S. Department of the Treasury

Caroline Atkinson, Senior Deputy Assistant Secretary for International Monetary and Financial Policy (1997–2001)

Timothy Geithner, Assistant Secretary for International Affairs (1997–1998), Under Secretary for International Affairs (1998–2001)

Mark Jaskowiak, Director, Office of Specialized Development Institutions

James M. Lister, Director, Office of International Monetary Policy (1992–1999)

Jeffrey R. Shafer, Assistant Secretary for International Affairs (1993–1995), Under Secretary for International Affairs (1995–1997)

Mark Sobel, Deputy Assistant Secretary, International Monetary and Financial Policy

Lawrence Summers, Deputy Secretary of the Treasury (1995–1999), Secretary of the Treasury (1999–2001)

Edwin M. Truman, Assistant Secretary for International Affairs (1998–2001)

Czech Republic

MINISTRY OF FINANCE

Věra Břicháčková, Head of International Organizations Department

Šárka Kopřivová, International Organizations Department

Zdeňka Slavíková, International Organizations Department

CZECH NATIONAL BANK

Oldřich Dědek, Vice Governor

Tomáš Holub, Adviser to the Governor

Jana Křelinová, European Union and International Organizations Division

Petr Procházka, Director, European Union and International Organizations Division

Hungary

MINISTRY OF FINANCE

László Akar, Deputy Finance Minister (1995–1999)
Tibor Erhart, Deputy Director General, Economic Policy Department
Ágota Repa, Economist, Economic Policy Department

CENTRAL BANK OF HUNGARY

Péter Ágos Bod, Governor (1991–1994)
Sándor Dávid, Economist, Payments System and Currency Issue Policy Department
György Surányi, Governor (1990–1991, 1994–2001)
György Szapáry, Deputy Governor

Malaysia (conducted jointly with Laura Alfaro)

Mahathir Mohamad, Prime Minister of Malaysia (1981–2003)
Nor Mohamed Yakcop, Special Adviser to the Prime Minister (1998–2004)
Daim Zainuddin, Minister of Finance (1984–1991; 1999–2001)

Republic of Korea

Jun Il Kim, Senior Economist, International Monetary Fund; Senior Counselor to
    Deputy Prime Minister and Minister of Finance and Economy, Republic of Korea
    (1997–1999)

Slovak Republic

MINISTRY OF FINANCE

Katarína Mathernová, Senior Private Sector Development Specialist, Foreign In-
    vestment Advisory Service, World Bank/IFC; Special Adviser to Deputy Prime
    Minister for Economic Affairs, Ivan Mikloš, Government of Slovakia
    (1999–2002)
Ivan Mikloš, Deputy Prime Minister and Minister of Finance
Juraj Renčko, Advisor to the Minister, Head of Bank Privatization and Restructuring
    Unit (1999–2001)

NATIONAL BANK OF SLOVAKIA

Jarmila Hrbáčková, Integration and Foreign Technical Assistance Section, Foreign
    Exchange Department
Elena Kohútiková, Deputy Governor
Tatiana Mikulenková, Integration and Foreign Technical Assistance Section, Foreign
    Exchange Department
Marián Nemec, Director, Institute of Monetary and Financial Studies
Miroslav Šťavina, Director, Foreign Exchange Department

Jozef Makúch, Chairman of the Council
Jana Pohlová, General Director Adviser

Credit-Rating Agencies and the Private Financial Community

Fitch Ratings

Roger M. Scher, Senior Director, Sovereign

Moody's Investors Service

David Levey, Managing Director, Sovereign Risk (1986–2004)
Christopher T. Mahoney, Senior Managing Director
Vincent J. Truglia, Managing Director, Director, Sovereign Risk

Standard & Poor's

David Beers, Managing Director and Global Head of Sovereign and International
    Public Finance Ratings
Laura Feinland-Katz, Managing Director and Chief Criteria Officer for Central and
    Latin America
Marie Cavanaugh, Managing Director, Sovereign Ratings
Lisa M. Schineller, Associate Director, Sovereign Ratings

Institute of International Finance

Charles H. Dallara, Managing Director, Institute of International Finance
Yusuke Horiguchi, First Deputy Managing Director and Senior Economist, Institute
    of International Finance

Other

Group of 24

Aziz Ali Mohammed, Special Adviser

Notes

Chapter 1: Orthodoxy and Heresy

1. The origins of the expression "hot money" can be traced to a speech President Franklin D. Roosevelt gave in November 1936, the first time the phrase was used to describe financial flows. Previously the phrase had referred to marked bills received by gangsters, not to be spent for fear of getting arrested. See Jacques J. Polak, "Hot Money," unpublished manuscript, League of Nations, January 1943, p. 2, n. 2.

2. Bank for International Settlements, *Triennial Central Bank Survey: Foreign Exchange and Derivatives Market Activity in 2004* (Basel: Bank for International Settlements, 2005).

3. John Maynard Keynes, *The Economic Consequences of the Peace* (London: Macmillan, 1919), p. 11.

4. Capital controls, government regulations on transactions that are recorded on a country's capital account in its balance of payments, include: unremunerated reserve requirements; taxes on international capital flows; limits on equity transactions; regulated interest rates for nonresident accounts; mandatory approvals for capital transactions; selective licensing of foreign direct investment; and prohibitions of financial inflows or outflows. Prudential regulations also influence transactions on the capital account. The distinction between capital controls and prudential regulations most often reflects whether they discriminate against international (as opposed to domestic) transactions: capital controls discriminate, whereas prudential regulations do not. The fifth edition of the IMF's *Balance of Payments Manual* (1993) introduced a change in terminology that was adopted around the world. Most of the transactions previously measured in the "capital account" are now in the "financial account." Most economists, policymakers, and IMF officials continue to use the older terminology (that is, to refer to current and capital, not current and financial, accounts), a practice I follow in this book. Thus, "capital account liberalization" and "capital liberalization" are here synonymous.

5. On "open regionalism," see Peter J. Katzenstein, *A World of Regions* (Ithaca, N.Y.: Cornell University Press, 2005).

6. Keynes, *Economic Consequences of the Peace,* p. 12.

7. Karl Polanyi, *The Great Transformation: The Political and Economic Origins of Our Times* (1944; repr. Boston: Beacon, 1957), p. 25.

8. Paul Einzig, *Exchange Control* (London: Macmillan, 1934), chap. 6. Also see Harold James, *The End of Globalization: Lessons from the Great Depression* (Cambridge, Mass.: Harvard University Press, 2001); and Maurice Obstfeld and Alan M. Taylor, "The Great Depression as a Watershed: International Capital Mobility in the Long Run," in *The Defining Moment: The Great Depression and the American Economy in the Twentieth Century,* ed. Michael D. Bordo, Claudia Goldin, and Eugene N. White (Chicago: University of Chicago Press, 1998). On the rise, fall, and rise again of globalization and the influence on multinational firms, see Geoffrey Jones, *Multinationals and Global Capitalism: From the Nineteenth to the Twenty-First Century* (Oxford: Oxford University Press, 2005), chap. 2.

9. John Gerard Ruggie, "International Regimes, Transactions, and Change: Embedded Liberalism in the Postwar Economic Order," *International Organization,* vol. 36, no. 2 (1982), pp. 379–416; and John Gerard Ruggie, "Embedded Liberalism and the Postwar Economic Regimes," in his *Constructing the World Polity: Essays on International Institutionalization* (New York: Routledge, 1998), especially p. 74. On the decidedly nonliberal policy consensus see G. John Ikenberry, "A World Economy Restored: Expert Consensus and the Anglo-American Post-War Settlement," *International Organization,* vol. 46, no. 1 (1992), pp. 289–321; and G. John Ikenberry, "Creating Yesterday's New World Order: Keynesian 'New Thinking' and the Anglo-American Post-War Settlement," in *Ideas and Foreign Policy,* ed. Judith Goldstein and Robert O. Keohane (Ithaca, N.Y.: Cornell University Press, 1993). On the institutionalization of this compromise in European polities, see Peter J. Katzenstein, *Small States in World Markets* (Ithaca, N.Y.: Cornell University Press, 1985). And on the place of capital controls in the embedded liberal compromise, see Eric Helleiner, *States and the Reemergence of Global Finance* (Ithaca, N.Y.: Cornell University Press, 1994), pp. 4 ff. and chap. 2; Barry Eichengreen, *Globalizing Capital: A History of the International Monetary System* (Princeton, N.J.: Princeton University Press, 1996), pp. 3–4 and 93–94; Harold James, *International Monetary Cooperation since Bretton Woods* (Washington, D.C.: IMF; and Oxford: Oxford University Press, 1996), pp. 37–39; Jonathan Kirshner, "Keynes, Capital Mobility, and the Crisis of Embedded Liberalism," *Review of International Political Economy,* vol. 6, no. 3 (1999), pp. 313–337; Jonathan Kirshner, "The Inescapable Politics of Money," in *Monetary Orders,* ed. Jonathan Kirshner (Ithaca, N.Y.: Cornell University Press, 2003), pp. 4–5; Kathleen R. McNamara, *The Currency of Ideas: Monetary Politics in the European Union* (Ithaca, N.Y.: Cornell University Press, 1998), chap. 4; and Beth A. Simmons, "The Internationalization of Capital," in *Continuity and Change in Contemporary Capitalism,* ed. Herbert Kitschelt, Peter Lange, Gary Marks, and John D. Stephens (Cambridge: Cambridge University Press, 1999), pp. 37–38.

10. Among many possible examples, see, especially, Economic, Financial, and Transit Department, League of Nations, *International Currency Experience: Lessons of the Inter-War Period* (Geneva: League of Nations, 1944); Ragnar Nurkse, *Conditions of Monetary Equilibrium,* Princeton Essays in International Finance, no. 4 (1945), pp. 2–5; Arthur I. Bloomfield, "Postwar Control of International Capital Movements," *American Economic Review,* vol. 36, no. 2 (1946), pp. 687–709, especially p. 687; Richard N. Gardner, *Sterling-Dollar Diplomacy* (Oxford: Clarendon, 1956), p. 76; and Richard N. Cooper, *The Economics of Interdependence: Economic Policy in the Atlantic Community* (New York: McGraw-Hill, 1968), p. 27.

11. John Maynard Keynes, "Speech to the House of Lords, May 23, 1944," in *The Collected Writings of John Maynard Keynes,* ed. Donald Moggridge, vol. 26, *Activities, 1941–1946: Shaping the Post-War World: Bretton Woods and Reparations* (London: Macmillan; Cambridge University Press, 1980), p. 17.

12. See Helleiner, *States and the Reemergence of Global Finance,* chap. 4.

13. Ibid., p. 99.

14. Timothy J. Sinclair, *The New Masters of Capital: American Bond Rating Agencies and the Politics of Creditworthiness* (Ithaca, N.Y.: Cornell University Press, 2005). On sovereign ratings see Rawi Abdelal and Christopher M. Bruner, *Private Capital and Public Policy: Standard & Poor's Sovereign Credit Ratings,* Harvard Business School Case 705–026 (2005).

15. Philip S. Bates and William J. Chambers, "Sovereign Policy Update: Denmark," *Standard & Poor's International CreditWeek,* December 1986, p. 16; and Philip S. Bates and William J. Chambers, "Offshore Domestic Currency Debt," *Standard & Poor's International CreditWeek,* May 25, 1987, p. 6.

16. Helena Hessel and Philip S. Bates, "Comparing Countries' External Positions," *Standard & Poor's International CreditWeek,* May 25, 1987, p. 3.

17. Christopher M. Bruner and Rawi Abdelal, "To Judge Leviathan: Sovereign Credit Ratings, National Law, and the World Economy," *Journal of Public Policy,* vol. 25, no. 2 (2005), pp. 191–217.

18. See Kirshner, "Keynes, Capital Mobility," pp. 326–328. For the best study of the decline and fall of embedded liberalism see Mark Blyth, *Great Transformations: Economic Ideas and Institutional Change in the Twentieth Century* (Cambridge: Cambridge University Press, 2002).

19. Benjamin J. Cohen, "Capital Controls: Why Do Governments Hesitate?" in *Debating the Global Financial Architecture,* ed. Leslie Elliott Armijo (Albany: SUNY Press, 2002), pp. 104 ff.; and Benjamin J. Cohen, "Capital Controls: The Neglected Option," in *International Financial Governance under Stress: Global Structures versus National Imperatives,* ed. Geoffrey R. D. Underhill and Xiaoke Zhang (Cambridge: Cambridge University Press, 2003).

20. The liberalization obligations of the 1988 directive were further institutionalized in the 1991 Treaty on European Union, often referred to as the Maastricht Treaty.

21. Author's interview with Jacques Delors, Paris, December 2, 2004.

22. The phrase *erga omnes* is Latin for "toward all." On the concept in international

jurisprudence, see Maurizio Ragazzi, *The Concept of International Obligations erga omnes* (Oxford: Clarendon, 2000); and Christian J. Tams, *Enforcing Obligations erga omnes in International Law* (Cambridge: Cambridge University Press, 2005).

23. Author's interview with Karl Otto Pöhl, Frankfurt, June 29, 2005.

24. Author's interview with Hans Tietmeyer, Königstein, Germany, October 25, 2005.

25. See Hans Tietmeyer, "The Euro—A Denationalized Currency," in his *The Social Market Economy and Monetary Stability* (London: Economica, 1999), p. 215.

26. Maurice Obstfeld and Alan M. Taylor, *Global Capital Markets: Integration, Crisis, and Growth* (Cambridge: Cambridge University Press, 2004), p. 230 and chap. 7 more generally.

27. Article VI, Section 3 of the Fund's Articles reads: "Members may exercise such controls as are necessary to regulate international capital movements." On the IMF's limited jurisdiction over members' regulation of international capital movements see Joseph Gold, *International Capital Movements under the Law of the International Monetary Fund*, no. 21, International Monetary Fund Pamphlet Series (Washington, D.C.: IMF, 1977), p. 1 ff; and Jacques J. Polak, "The Articles of Agreement of the IMF and the Liberalization of Capital Movements," in *Should the IMF Pursue Capital-Account Convertibility?*, Princeton Essays in International Finance, no. 207 (1998). On the IMF's jurisdiction over the current account and its influence on members' liberalization of trade flows, see Beth A. Simmons, "International Law and State Behavior: Commitment and Compliance in International Monetary Affairs," *American Political Science Review*, vol. 94, no. 4 (2000), pp. 819–835; and Beth A. Simmons, "The Legalization of International Monetary Affairs," *International Organization*, vol. 54, no. 3 (2000), pp. 573–602.

28. Independent Evaluation Office (IEO) of the International Monetary Fund, *The IMF's Approach to Capital Account Liberalization* (Washington, D.C.: IMF, 2005).

29. Author's interview with Michel Camdessus, Paris, April 19, 2004.

30. See Jagdish Bhagwati, "The Capital Myth," *Foreign Affairs* vol. 77, no. 3 (1998), pp. 7–12 at p. 12; Jagdish Bhagwati, *The Wind of the Hundred Days: How Washington Mismanaged Globalization* (Cambridge, Mass.: MIT Press, 2000), chaps. 1–3; Jagdish Bhagwati, *In Defense of Globalization* (Oxford: Oxford University Press, 2004), chap. 13; and Robert Wade and Frank Veneroso, "The Gathering World Slump and the Battle Over Capital Controls," *New Left Review*, no. 231 (1998), pp. 13–42, at pp. 35–39. Also see Peter Gowan, *The Global Gamble: Washington's Faustian Bid for World Dominance* (London: Verso, 1999), p. 84–87.

31. Author's interview with Pascal Lamy, Brussels, November 12, 2004.

32. See Philip H. Gordon and Sophie Meunier, *The French Challenge: Adapting to Globalization* (Washington, D.C.: Brookings, 2001), p. 98 ff.

33. Rawi Abdelal, "Writing the Rules of Global Finance: France, Europe, and Capital Liberalization," *Review of International Political Economy*, vol. 13, no. 1 (2006), pp. 1–27.

34. See Miles Kahler, "Bretton Woods and Its Competitors: The Political Economy of Institutional Choice," in *Governing the World's Money,* ed. David M. Andrews, C. Randall Henning, and Louis W. Pauly (Ithaca, N.Y.: Cornell University Press, 2002); Miles Kahler, "Defining Accountability Up: The Global Economic Multilaterals," *Government and Opposition,* vol. 39, no. 2 (2004), pp. 132–158; Ethan B. Kapstein, *Governing the Global Economy: International Finance and the State* (Cambridge, Mass.: Harvard University Press, 1994); Ethan B. Kapstein, "Resolving the Regulator's Dilemma: International Coordination of Banking Regulations," *International Organization,* vol. 43, no. 2 (1989), pp. 323–347; and Beth A. Simmons, "Why Innovate? Founding the Bank for International Settlements," *World Politics,* vol. 45, no. 3 (1993), pp. 361–405.

35. Author's interview with Lamy.

36. Author's interview with Lawrence Summers, Cambridge, Mass., April 30, 2004.

37. "IMF/World Bank: Can Banking Systems Cope? The Historic Hong Kong Meetings Will Discuss Controversial New Powers for the IMF in Response to Recent Financial Crises," *The Banker,* September 1, 1997.

38. On the lack of U.S. support for multilateral, codified rules in a similar context, see Louis W. Pauly, *Opening Financial Markets: Banking Politics on the Pacific Rim* (Ithaca, N.Y.: Cornell University Press, 1988), pp. 172 ff. David Spiro describes a similar contest between the U.S. Treasury and the IMF for control over the process of petrodollar recycling during the 1970s; see his *The Hidden Hand of American Hegemony: Petrodollar Recycling and International Markets* (Ithaca, N.Y.: Cornell University Press, 1999).

39. Thus it is easy to explain U.S. behavior with theories derived within the Realist tradition of international political economy. See Jonathan Kirshner, "The Political Economy of Realism," in *Unipolar Politics: Realism and State Strategies after the Cold War,* ed. Ethan Kapstein and Michael Mastanduno (New York: Columbia University Press, 1999). For classic works of Realist political economy, see Robert Gilpin, *U.S. Power and the Multinational Corporation* (New York: Basic Books, 1975); and Stephen D. Krasner, *Defending the National Interest: Raw Materials Investments and U.S. Foreign Policy* (Princeton, N.J.: Princeton University Press, 1978).

40. See, for example, Edward Alden, "U.S. Backs Curbs on Capital Controls: Free Trade Administration Wants Future Agreements to Be Based on Chile and Singapore Deals," *Financial Times,* April 2, 2003.

41. Author's interview with Lamy.

42. Author's interview with Henri Chavranski, Paris, April 2, 2004.

43. Scholars have generally not paid sufficient attention to the distributional politics of capital controls. A notable exception is Laura Alfaro, "Capital Controls: A Political Economy Approach," *Review of International Economics,* vol. 12, no. 4 (2004), pp. 571–590. The distributional politics of capital liberalization, in contrast, are well studied by political scientists and economists. See Jeffry A. Frieden, "Invested Interests: The Politics of National Economic Policies in a World of Global Finance," *International Organization,* vol. 45, no. 4 (1991), pp. 425–451;

and Jonathan Kirshner, "Disinflation, Structural Change, and Distribution," *Review of Radical Political Economics*, vol. 30, no. 1 (1998), pp. 53–89.

44. The scholarly literature on the influence of these ideas on policymaking is now quite rich, though the effect of neoliberalism on capital liberalization in particular has only recently been systematically explored. See especially Peter A. Hall, "The Movement from Keynesianism to Monetarism," in *Structuring Politics: Historical Institutionalism in Comparative Analysis*, ed. Sven Steinmo, Kathleen Thelen, and Frank Longstreth (Cambridge: Cambridge University Press, 1992); Helleiner, *States and the Reemergence of Global Finance*, pp. 15–16; McNamara, *The Currency of Ideas*; and Blyth, *Great Transformations*. On the role of "neoliberal" ideas in promoting capital liberalization in the developing world, see Jeffrey M. Chwieroth, "Neoliberalism's Role in Capital Account Liberalization in Emerging Markets," paper presented at the Annual Meeting of the American Political Science Association, Boston, August 29–September 1, 2002.

45. The classic source of this argument is Leonardo Bertolini and Allan Drazen, "Capital Account Liberalization as a Signal," *American Economic Review*, vol. 87, no. 1 (1997), pp. 138–154. Other scholars have since emphasized the information content of a variety of policy stances. On capital controls as a negative signal, see Geoffrey Garrett, "The Causes of Globalization," *Comparative Political Studies*, vol. 33, nos. 6/7 (2000), pp. 941–991, at p. 975; and Barry Eichengreen, "Capital Account Liberalization: What Do the Cross-Country Studies Tell Us?" *World Bank Economic Review*, vol. 15, no. 3 (2002), pp. 341–365, at p. 359. On the reputational payoffs of policy choices in the context of ideological consensus, see Beth A. Simmons and Zachary Elkins, "The Globalization of Liberalization: Policy Diffusion in the International Political Economy," *American Political Science Review*, vol. 98, no. 1 (2004), pp. 171–189, at pp. 172–173.

46. As a matter of intellectual principle, however, social meanings, the inferences that audiences draw, can be a result only of social norms. See Max Weber, *Economy and Society*, ed. Guenther Roth and Claus Wittich (Berkeley: University of California Press, 1978), pp. 4–5. A recent evaluation of social norms and signals can be found in Cass R. Sunstein, "Social Norms and Social Roles," *Columbia Law Review*, vol. 96, no. 4 (1996), pp. 903–968, at p. 925.

47. On the importance of the "implicit rules" of the international financial architecture, see also Ronald I. McKinnon, "The Rules of the Game: International Money in Historical Perspective," *Journal of Economic Literature*, vol. 31, no. 1 (1993), pp. 1–44, especially pp. 2–3, 13, 29.

48. These effects have generally been analyzed by scholars operating within the rationalist tradition of institutional analysis. See Robert O. Keohane, *After Hegemony: Cooperation and Discord in the World Political Economy* (Princeton, N.J.: Princeton University Press, 1984); and Lisa L. Martin and Beth A. Simmons, "Theories and Empirical Studies of International Institutions," *International Organization*, vol. 52, no. 4 (1998), pp. 729–757.

49. On constitutive norms, see Peter J. Katzenstein, "Introduction: Alternative Per-

spectives on National Security," in *The Culture of National Security: Norms and Identity in World Politics,* ed. Peter J. Katzenstein (New York: Columbia University Press, 1996), p. 5 ff; and John Gerard Ruggie, "What Makes the World Hang Together? Neo-Utilitarianism and the Constructivist Challenge," in his *Constructing the World Polity,* p. 22ff. On the regulative and constitutive power of international organizations, see Alastair Iain Johnston, "Treating Institutions as Social Environments," *International Studies Quarterly,* vol. 45, no. 4 (2001), pp. 487–515; and Michael Barnett and Martha Finnemore, *Rules for the World: International Organizations in Global Politics* (Ithaca, N.Y.: Cornell University Press, 2004), p. 7.

50. On the sociological insight that "individuals behave according to scripts that are tied to social roles," see Frank Dobbin, "The Sociological View of the Economy," in *The New Economic Sociology,* ed. Frank Dobbin (Princeton, N.J.: Princeton University Press, 2004), p. 4.

51. Author's interview with Oldřich Dědek, Prague, March 24, 2004.

52. Author's interview with Stephane Ouaki, Brussels, November 3, 2004.

53. This diffusion occurred through a combination of normative and mimetic isomorphism. On normative isomorphism, see G. John Ikenberry and Charles A. Kupchan, "Socialization and Hegemonic Power," *International Organization,* vol. 44, no. 3 (1989), pp. 283–315; and Jeffrey T. Checkel, "Why Comply? Social Learning and European Identity Change," *International Organization,* vol. 55, no. 3 (2001), pp. 553–588. On mimetic isomorphism, see Stephen D. Krasner, *Sovereignty: Organized Hypocrisy* (Princeton, N.J.: Princeton University Press, 1999), p. 64 ff. On the diffusion of economic policy practices, see Beth Simmons, Frank Dobbin, and Geoffrey Garrett, "The International Diffusion of Liberalism," unpublished manuscript, June 2004; Simone Polillo and Mauro F. Guillén, "Globalization Pressures and the State: The Worldwide Spread of Central Bank Independence," *American Journal of Sociology* (forthcoming); and Witold J. Henisz, Bennet A. Zelner, and Mauro F. Guillén, "International Coercion, Emulation, and Policy Diffusion: Market-Oriented Infrastructure Reforms, 1977–1999," unpublished manuscript, January 2005.

54. See, for example, Barry Eichengreen, "The International Monetary Fund in the Wake of the Asian Crisis," and Benjamin J. Cohen, "Taming the Phoenix? Monetary Governance after the Crisis," both in *The Asian Financial Crisis and the Architecture of Global Finance,* ed. Gregory W. Noble and John Ravenhill (Cambridge: Cambridge University Press, 2000).

55. Author's interview with Elena Kohútiková, Bratislava, October 27, 2004.

56. Blyth, *Great Transformations;* and Wesley W. Widmaier, "Constructing Monetary Crises: New Keynesian Understanding and Monetary Cooperation in the 1990s," *Review of International Studies,* vol. 29, no. 1 (2003), pp. 61–77.

57. Milton Friedman, "The Case for Flexible Exchange Rates," in his *Essays in Positive Economics* (Chicago: Chicago University Press, 1953), pp. 176–177.

58. John Kenneth Galbraith suggests a twenty-year cycle "from illusion to disillu-

sion and back to illusion." See his *A Short History of Financial Euphoria* (New York: Penguin, 1994), pp. 12–13, 88–89.

Chapter 2: The Rules of Global Finance

1. Simmons, "The Internationalization of Capital," p. 43.
2. Krasner once wrote of the difficulty of distinguishing neo-Marxism from Realism in American foreign economic policy. See his *Defending the National Interest*, pp. 332–333. On the Realist tradition in international political economy, see Kirshner, "The Political Economy of Realism." For a comparison of Realism and neo-Marxism, see Robert Gilpin, *The Political Economy of International Relations* (Princeton, N.J.: Princeton University Press, 1987), chap. 2.
3. Bhagwati, "The Capital Myth," pp. 7–12. Also see Bhagwati, *The Wind of the Hundred Days*, Part I, and Bhagwati, *In Defense of Globalization*, chap. 13.
4. Bhagwati, "The Capital Myth," p. 12.
5. Robert Wade and Frank Veneroso, "The Asian Crisis: The High Debt Model versus the Wall-Street-Treasury-IMF Complex," *New Left Review*, no. 228 (1998), pp. 3–23; Wade and Veneroso, "The Gathering World Slump," pp. 13–42; and Robert Wade, "The Fight over Capital Flows," *Foreign Policy*, no. 113 (1998–1999), pp. 41–54. A similar case is made by Peter Gowan in *The Global Gamble*, pp. 84–87.
6. Wade and Veneroso, "The Gathering World Slump," pp. 35 ["powerful national interest"], 37 ["goals could be advanced"], 38 ["Wall Street wants capital account opening worldwide"].
7. See Abdelal, "Writing the Rules of Global Finance."
8. See, for example, Robert Hunter Wade, "Capital and Revenge: The IMF and Ethiopia," *Challenge*, vol. 44, no. 5 (2001), pp. 67–75. On the U.S. influence within the IMF in general, see Ngaire Woods, "The United States and the International Financial Institutions: Power and Influence within the World Bank and the IMF," in *U.S. Hegemony and International Organizations*, ed. Rosemary Foot, S. Neil MacFarlane, and Michael Mastanduno (Oxford: Oxford University Press, 2003).
9. Helleiner, *States and the Reemergence of Global Finance*, p. 99. The U.S. influence over the terms of the lending agreement between the IMF and South Korea may be an exception to this rule. However, the capital account provisions were in the South Korean government's Letter of Intent, rather than the Fund's conditions.
10. On this struggle in a previous episode, see Spiro, *The Hidden Hand of American Hegemony*.
11. Katzenstein, *A World of Regions*.
12. Author's interview with Pascal Lamy, Brussels, November 12, 2004.
13. Gordon and Meunier, *The French Challenge*, p. 98 and chap. 5 more generally.
14. Author's interview with Jacques Delors, Paris, December 2, 2004.
15. Author's interview with Henri Chavranski, Paris, April 2, 2004.
16. Author's interview with Delors.

17. Quoted in Hubert Védrine, with Dominique Moïsi, *France in an Age of Globalization,* trans. Philip H. Gordon (Washington, D.C.: Brookings, 2001), p. 45.

18. Author's interview with Lamy.

19. Ibid.

20. Gordon and Meunier, *The French Challenge,* pp. 108–111.

21. See Hall, "The Movement from Keynesianism to Monetarism"; Helleiner, *States and the Reemergence of Global Finance,* pp. 15–16; McNamara, *The Currency of Ideas;* and Blyth, *Great Transformations.*

22. Pierre Poret, "The Experience of the OECD with the Code of Liberalization of Capital Movements," paper presented at an IMF seminar on Current Legal Issues Affecting Central Banks, May 1998, pp. 3–4.

23. McNamara, *The Currency of Ideas,* pp. 3, 52.

24. On their role in emerging markets, see Chwieroth, "Neo-liberalism's Role in Capital Account Liberalization in Emerging Markets."

25. Suzanne Berger, *The First Globalization: Lessons from the French,* manuscript, p. 118, published as *Notre Première Mondialisation: Leçons d'un Echec Oublié* (Paris: Seuil, 2003).

26. John Williamson and Stephan Haggard, "The Political Conditions for Economic Reform," in *The Political Economy of Policy Reform,* ed. John Williamson (Washington, D.C.: Institute for International Economics, 1994). Also see Alex Cukierman and Mariano Tommasi, "When Does It Take a Nixon to Go to China?" *American Economic Review,* vol. 88, no. 1 (1998), pp. 180–197; Alex Cukierman and Mariano Tommasi, "Credibility of Policymakers and of Economic Reforms," in *The Political Economy of Reform,* ed. Federico Sturzenegger and Mariano Tommasi (Cambridge, Mass.: MIT Press, 1998); and Dani Rodrik, "Promises, Promises: Credible Policy Reform via Signalling," *The Economic Journal,* vol. 99, no. 397 (1989), pp. 756–772.

27. These potential benefits and risks are reviewed in Rawi Abdelal and Laura Alfaro, *Capital Controls,* Harvard Business School Note 702–082 (2002), pp. 3–6. For a recent comprehensive review, see Richard N. Cooper, "Should Capital Controls Be Banished?" *Brookings Papers on Economic Activity,* no. 1 (1999), pp. 89–141.

28. Charles P. Kindleberger, *Manias, Panics, and Crashes: A History of Financial Crises,* rev. ed. (New York: Basic Books, 1989). John Maynard Keynes offered the classic "beauty contest" metaphor; see John Maynard Keynes, *The General Theory of Employment, Interest, and Money* (1936; repr. New York: Harcourt Brace Jovanovich, 1953), pp. 155–156. An extremely insightful account of these effects in the contemporary international financial system can be found in Mark Blyth, "The Political Power of Financial Ideas: Transparency, Risk, and Distribution in Global Finance," in *Monetary Orders,* ed. Kirshner.

29. If scientific knowledge were the basis for this rethinking of the rules of the international monetary system, then the group of policymakers who proposed, authored, and advocated new liberal rules might be likened to an "epistemic

community." See Peter M. Haas, ed., *Knowledge, Power, and International Policy Coordination* (Columbia: University of South Carolina Press, 1997).

30. This case was made forcefully in Bhagwati, "The Capital Myth." Also see Dani Rodrik, "Who Needs Capital Account Convertibility?" in *Should the IMF Pursue Capital-Account Convertibility?*. Dani Rodrik, "How Far Will International Economic Integration Go?" *Journal of Economic Perspectives* vol. 14, no. 1 (2000), pp. 177–186; and Joseph E. Stiglitz, "Capital Market Liberalization, Economic Growth, and Instability," *World Development* vol. 28, no. 6 (2000), pp. 1075–1086. Compare, however, the positive results associated with the research program of Dennis P. Quinn in "Correlates of Change in International Financial Regulation," *American Political Science Review,* vol. 91, no. 3 (1997), pp. 531–551; Dennis P. Quinn and Carla Inclán, "The Origins of Financial Openness: A Study of Current and Capital Account Liberalization," *American Journal of Political Science,* vol. 41, no. 3 (1997), pp. 771–813; and Dennis P. Quinn, "Capital Account Liberalization and Financial Globalization, 1890–1999: A Synoptic View," *International Journal of Finance and Economics,* vol. 8, no. 3 (2003), pp. 189–204.

31. Obstfeld and Taylor, *Global Capital Markets,* p. 297.

32. Stanley Fischer, "Capital Account Liberalization and the Role of the IMF," in *Should the IMF Pursue Capital-Account Convertibility?,* p. 8.

33. In fact, the research agenda has shifted away from cross-country growth regressions to more microeconomic studies of issues such as equity market liberalization and the cost of capital. See Peter Blair Henry, "Capital Account Liberalization, the Cost of Capital, and Economic Growth," *American Economic Review,* vol. 93, no. 2 (2003), pp. 91–96; and Kristen J. Forbes, "One Cost of the Chilean Capital Controls: Increased Financial Constraints on Smaller Trade Firms," National Bureau of Economic Research working paper 9777, June 2003.

34. Eswar S. Prasad, Kenneth Rogoff, Shang-Jin Wei, and M. Ayhan Kose, *Effects of Financial Globalization on Developing Countries: Some Empirical Evidence,* IMF Occasional Paper No. 220 (Washington, D.C.: IMF, 2003), p. ix. Also see the coverage in "IMF Financial Globalization Study: Opening Up to Capital Flows? Be Prepared before Plunging In," *IMF Survey,* vol. 32, no. 9 (May 19, 2003), pp. 137–141. See the coverage of the seminar discussion in "IMF Economic Forum: Is Financial Globalization Harmful for Developing Countries?" *IMF Survey,* vol. 32, no. 10 (June 2, 2003), pp. 153–155.

35. Eichengreen, "Capital Account Liberalization," p. 360. On the end of the consensus, since "shattered," also see Jean Tirole, *Financial Crises, Liquidity, and the International Monetary System* (Princeton, N.J.: Princeton University Press, 2002).

36. For a version of this argument, see Maurice Obstfeld, "The Global Capital Market: Benefactor or Menace?" *Journal of Economic Perspectives,* vol. 12, no. 4 (1998), pp. 9–30, at pp. 17–18.

37. See Guillermo A. Calvo and Carmen M. Reinhart, "Fear of Floating," *Quarterly*

Journal of Economics, vol. 117, no. 2 (2002), pp. 379–408; and Carmen M. Reinhart and Kenneth S. Rogoff; "The Modern History of Exchange Rate Arrangements: A Reinterpretation," *Quarterly Journal of Economics,* vol. 119, no. 1 (2004), pp. 1–48.

38. For a recent outline of the low and declining effectiveness of capital controls, see Sebastian Edwards, "How Effective Are Capital Controls?" *Journal of Economic Perspectives,* vol. 13, no. 4 (1999), pp. 65–84.

39. Eichengreen, *Globalizing Capital,* p. 94.

40. Eichengreen, "Capital Account Liberalization," p. 350. The strongest form of this argument can be found in Ralph Bryant, *International Financial Intermediation* (Washington, D.C.: Brookings Institution, 1987); Richard B. McKenzie and Dwight R. Lee, *Quicksilver Capital: How the Rapid Movement of Wealth Has Changed the World* (New York: Free Press, 1991); and Richard O'Brien, *Global Financial Integration: The End of Geography* (London: Pinter, 1992). Obstfeld and Taylor consider technological change to have been only a "secondary" influence. See their *Global Capital Markets,* p. 32 ff.

41. See Philip G. Cerny, "The 'Little Big Bang' in Paris: Financial Deregulation in a Dirigiste System," *European Journal of Political Research,* vol. 17, no. 2 (1989), pp. 169–192; Philip G. Cerny, ed., *Finance and World Politics* (Brookfield, Vt.: Edward Elgar, 1993); John B. Goodman and Louis W. Pauly, "The Obsolescence of Capital Controls? Economic Management in an Age of Global Markets," *World Politics,* vol. 46, no. 1 (1993), pp. 50–82; and Helleiner, *States and the Reemergence of Global Finance,* pp. 12–13.

42. On the regulative (rationalist) and constitutive (constructivist or sociological) effects of rules and norms, see Peter J. Katzenstein, "Introduction: Alternative Perspectives on National Security," in *The Culture of National Security,* p. 5, and Ruggie, "What Makes the World Hang Together?," p. 22 ff. On the regulatory and constitutive power of international organizations, see Barnett and Finnemore, *Rules for the World,* p. 7. On the content of identities, see Rawi Abdelal, Yoshiko M. Herrera, Alastair Iain Johnston, and Rose McDermott, "Identity as a Variable," *Perspectives on Politics,* vol. 4 no. 4 (2006).

43. Keohane, *After Hegemony.* For more on the rationalist research agenda in the study of international institutions, see Martin and Simmons, "Theories and Empirical Studies of International Institutions," pp. 729–757. On institutionalist theory in economics, see Douglass C. North, "Institutions," *Journal of Economic Perspectives,* vol. 5, no. 1 (1991), pp. 97–112; Douglass C. North, *Institutions, Institutional Change, and Economic Performance* (Cambridge: Cambridge University Press, 1990); and Avner Greif, "Historical and Comparative Institutional Analysis," *American Economic Review,* vol. 88, no. 2 (1998), pp. 80–84. North has, with colleague Arthur T. Denzau, moved in the direction of a more sociological approach to institutions by focusing on mental models that are "shared intersubjectively." See Douglass C. North and Arthur T. Denzau, "Shared Mental Models: Ideologies and Institutions," *Kyklos,* vol. 47, no. 1 (1994), pp. 3–31.

44. This means that they may also delegitimate policy practices. See Rodney Bruce Hall, "The Discursive Demolition of the Asian Development Model," *International Studies Quarterly,* vol. 47, no. 1 (2003), pp. 71–99.
45. Dobbin, "The Sociological View of the Economy," p. 4.
46. Johnston, "Treating Institutions as Social Environments," pp. 487–515. On sociological institutionalism, see, for example, James G. March and Johan P. Olsen, *Rediscovering Institutions: The Organizational Basis of Politics* (New York: Free Press, 1989); Walter W. Powell and Paul J. DiMaggio, eds. *The New Institutionalism in Organizational Analysis* (Chicago: University of Chicago Press, 1991); Martha Finnemore, "Norms, Culture, and World Politics: Insights from Sociology's Institutionalism," *International Organization,* vol. 50, no. 2 (1996), pp. 325–347; and Martha Finnemore, *National Interests in International Society* (Ithaca, N.Y.: Cornell University Press, 1996). An extraordinarily insightful review can be found in James Johnson, "How Conceptual Problems Migrate: Rational Choice, Interpretation, and the Hazards of Pluralism," *Annual Review of Political Science,* vol. 5 (2002), pp. 223–248, especially p. 232.
47. Kapstein, *Governing the Global Economy,* pp. 12–13.
48. See Thomas Risse, "'Let's Argue!': Communicative Action in World Politics," *International Organization,* vol. 54, no. 1 (2000), pp. 1–39.
49. Barnett and Finnemore, *Rules for the World,* p. 31. Also see Martha Finnemore, "International Organizations as Teachers of Norms," *International Organization,* vol. 47, no. 4 (1993), pp. 565–597; and Wade Jacoby, "Tutors and Pupils: International Organizations, Central European Elites, and Western Models," *Governance,* vol. 14, no. 2 (2001), pp. 169–200.
50. Author's interview with Oldřich Dědek, Prague, March 24, 2004.
51. Author's interview with Stephane Ouaki, Brussels, November 3, 2004.
52. On imitation as a mechanism for the influence of a script, see Krasner, *Sovereignty,* p. 64. For an argument about the influence of persuasion when the source of authority is part of the group that the object of persuasion is eager to join, see Checkel, "Why Comply? Social Learning and European Identity Change," pp. 553–588.
53. Ikenberry and Kupchan, "Socialization and Hegemonic Power," pp. 283–315.
54. On "lesson drawing" and social learning as the two sociological processes—the former driven by acceding states, the latter by international organizations— underpinning the Europeanization of the East, see Frank Schimmelfennig and Ulrich Sedelmeier, "Introduction: Conceptualizing the Europeanization of Central and Eastern Europe," in *The Europeanization of Central and Eastern Europe,* ed. Frank Schimmelfennig and Ulrich Sedelmeier (Ithaca, N.Y.: Cornell University Press, 2005). On the EU members as role models and the constitutive norms thereby created, see also Frank Schimmelfennig, *The EU, NATO, and the Integration of Europe: Rules and Rhetoric* (Cambridge: Cambridge University Press, 2003), pp. 90–91. In the typology produced by Wade Jacoby, the capital liberalization script is a "patch," because it is a firm obligation of membership that acceding countries can only follow faithfully. See Wade Jacoby, *The Enlargement of the Eu-*

ropean Union and NATO: Ordering from the Menu in Central Europe (Cambridge: Cambridge University Press, 2004), pp. 5 ff. On the domestic resonance of international norms as critical to their faithful adoption, see Rachel A. Epstein, "International Institutions, Domestic Resonance, and the Politics of Denationalization," unpublished manuscript, European University Institute, April 2005. For more on the "active" and "passive" leverage exerted by the EU on acceding countries' informal and formal institutions, see Mlada Anna Vachudova, *Europe Undivided: Democracy, Leverage, and Integration After Communism* (Oxford: Oxford University Press, 2005), chaps. 4–7.

55. Simmons, Dobbin, and Garrett, "The International Diffusion of Liberalism." See also Polillo and Guillén, "Globalization Pressures and the State"; and Henisz, Zelner, and Guillén, "International Coercion, Emulation, and Policy Diffusion." An early and insightful analysis of the diffusion of an economic policy practice can be found in Stephen J. Kobrin, "Diffusion as an Explanation of Oil Nationalization," *Journal of Conflict Resolution*, vol. 29, no. 1 (1985), pp. 3–32. On coercive, normative, and mimetic isomorphism, see Dobbin, "The Sociological View of the Economy," pp. 13–14.

56. Eichengreen, "Capital Account Liberalization," p. 350; and Simmons and Elkins, "The Globalization of Liberalization," pp. 171–189.

57. Simmons and Elkins, "The Globalization of Liberalization," pp. 175–176.

58. A similar story is told in Barnett and Finnemore, *Rules for the World*, chap. 3.

59. See Louis W. Pauly, "Good Governance and Bad Policy: The Perils of International Organizational Overextension," *Review of International Political Economy*, vol. 6, no. 4 (1999), pp. 401–424; and Michael N. Barnett and Martha Finnemore, "The Politics, Power, and Pathologies of International Organizations," *International Organization*, vol. 53, no. 4 (1999), pp. 699–732.

60. McKinnon, "The Rules of the Game," esp. pp. 2–3.

61. Ibid., p. 13, Rule Box 2, and p. 29, Rule Box 4.

62. Robert A. Mundell, "The Future of the International Financial System," in *Bretton Woods Revisited*, ed. A. L. K. Acheson, J. F. Chant, and M. F. J. Prachowny (Toronto: University of Toronto Press, 1972), p. 92.

63. See Jonathan Kirshner, "Explaining Choices about Money," in *Monetary Orders*, ed. Kirshner, pp. 270–279; and Joseph E. Stiglitz, "Capital-Market Liberalization, Globalization, and the IMF," *Oxford Review of Economic Policy*, vol. 20, no. 1 (2004), pp. 57–71.

64. See (IEO) *The IMF's Approach to Capital Account Liberalization*.

65. On the content and influence of the prevailing orthodoxy, see Ilene Grabel, "Ideology, Power, and the Rise of Independent Monetary Institutions in Emerging Economies," in *Monetary Orders*, ed. Kirshner. Also see Ilene Grabel, "Creating 'Credible' Economic Policy in Developing and Transitional Economies," *Review of Radical Political Economics*, vol. 29, no. 3 (1997), pp. 70–78; and Ilene Grabel, "The Political Economy of 'Policy Credibility': The New-Classical Economics and the Remaking of Emerging Economies," *Cambridge Journal of Economics*, vol. 24, no. 1 (2000), pp. 1–19.

66. Simmons and Elkins, "The Globalization of Liberalization," pp. 172–173.
67. The classic source of this argument is Bertolini and Drazen, "Capital Account Liberalization as a Signal." Also see Eichengreen, "Capital Account Liberalization," p. 359.
68. Garrett, "The Causes of Globalization," p. 975.
69. An excellent qualitative and quantitative analysis of the beliefs of financial market participants and their interaction with developed and emerging-market economies is Layna Mosley, *Global Capital and National Governments* (Cambridge: Cambridge University Press, 2003).
70. See Abdelal and Bruner, *Private Capital and Public Policy;* Richard Sylla, "An Historical Primer on the Business of Credit Rating," in *Ratings, Rating Agencies, and the Global Financial System,* ed. Richard M. Levich, Giovanni Majnoni, and Carmen Reinhardt (Boston: Kluwer, 2002); and Sinclair, *The New Masters of Capital.*
71. Author's interview with David Levey, New York, February 4, 2005.
72. Marie Cavanaugh, *Sovereign Credit Characteristics by Rating Category* (New York: Standard & Poor's, November 19, 2003).
73. Quoted in Abdelal and Bruner, *Private Capital and Public Policy,* p. 7. Marie Cavanaugh is Managing Director, Sovereign Ratings, Standard & Poor's.
74. See Graciela Kaminsky and Sergio Schmukler, "Rating Agencies and Financial Markets," in *Ratings, Rating Agencies, and the Global Financial System,* ed. Levich, Majnoni, and Reinhardt, p. 229; Helmut Reisen and Julia von Maltzan, "Boom and Bust in Sovereign Ratings," *International Finance,* vol. 2, no. 2 (1999), pp. 273–294; and G. Ferri, L.-G. Liu, and J. E. Stiglitz, "The Procyclical Role of Rating Agencies: Evidence from the East Asian Crisis," *Economic Notes,* vol. 28, no. 3 (1999), pp. 335–356.
75. Bruner and Abdelal, "To Judge Leviathan." I discuss further the legal foundations and increasing national codification of the "private authority" of the rating agencies in Chapter 7.

Chapter 3: Capital Ruled

1. League of Nations, *International Currency Experience,* p. 210.
2. Ibid., p. 211.
3. Robert Skidelsky, *John Maynard Keynes,* vol. 3, *Fighting for Freedom, 1937–1946* (New York: Viking, 2001), p. 193.
4. For the best overviews, see Helleiner, *States and the Reemergence of Global Finance,* esp. pp. 33–38; and Eichengreen, *Globalizing Capital,* esp. pp. 3–4, 93–94. Also see Ragnar Nurkse, *Conditions of Monetary Equilibrium,* Princeton Essays in International Finance, no. 4, 1945, pp. 2–5; Gardner, *Sterling-Dollar Diplomacy,* p. 76; Alfred E. Eckes Jr., *A Search for Solvency: Bretton Woods and the International Monetary System, 1941–1971* (Austin: University of Texas Press, 1975), p. 68; Richard Kahn, "Historical Origins of the International Monetary Fund," in *Keynes and International Monetary Relations,* ed. A. P. Thirlwall (London: Macmillan, 1976), p. 18; Fred L. Block, *The Origins of International Economic Disorder: A Study of United States International Monetary Policy from World War II to the Present* (Berkeley: Uni-

versity of California Press, 1977), pp. 45–46, 51; Armand van Dormael, *Bretton Woods: Birth of a Monetary System* (London: Macmillan, 1978), pp. 69–70; Marcello de Cecco, "Origins of the Post-War Payments System," *Cambridge Journal of Economics*, vol. 3, no. 1 (1979), pp. 49–61, at pp. 49–50; Kenneth W. Dam, *The Rules of the Game: Reform and Evolution in the International Monetary System* (Chicago: University of Chicago Press, 1982), pp. 98–100; James R. Crotty, "On Keynes and Capital Flight," *Journal of Economic Literature*, vol. 21, no. 1 (1983), pp. 59–65; James, *International Monetary Cooperation Since Bretton Woods*, pp. 37–39; Kirshner, "Keynes, Capital Mobility" pp. 313–337; Obstfeld and Taylor, "The Great Depression as a Watershed," pp. 382–383; James, *The End of Globalization;* and James M. Boughton, "Why White, Not Keynes? Inventing the Postwar International Monetary System," IMF Working Paper, WP/02/52, March 2002, pp. 9–10.

5. See Harry Dexter White, "Preliminary Draft Proposal for a United Nations Stabilization Fund and a Bank for Reconstruction and Development for the United and Associated Nations (April 1942)" in *The International Monetary Fund, 1945–1965: Twenty Years of International Monetary Cooperation*, vol. 3, *Documents*, ed. J. Keith Horsefield (Washington, D.C.: IMF, 1969), pp. 63, 64, 66, and 67; Harry Dexter White "Preliminary Draft Outline of a Proposal for an International Stabilization Fund of the United and Associated Nations (July 1943)," in *Documents*, ed. Horsefield, especially p. 96; John Maynard Keynes, "Proposals for an International Currency (or Clearing) Union (February 1941)," in *Documents*, ed. Horsefield, pp. 7 (paragraph 4b), and 13 (paragraphs 45–46); and John Maynard Keynes, "Proposals for an International Clearing Union (April 1943)," in *Documents*, ed. Horsefield, pp. 23 (paragraph 8b), 31–32 (paragraphs 32–33, 35).

6. Keynes, "Speech to the House of Lords, May 23, 1944," p. 17.

7. Gardner, *Sterling-Dollar Diplomacy*, p. 76.

8. Bloomfield, "Postwar Control of International Capital Movements," p. 687.

9. Richard N. Cooper, *The Economics of Interdependence: Economic Policy in the Atlantic Community* (New York: McGraw-Hill, 1968), p. 27.

10. See Richard N. Cooper, "Should Capital Controls Be Banished?" p. 96; and Richard N. Cooper, "A Monetary System Based on Fixed Exchange Rates," in *Alternative Monetary Regimes*, ed. Colin D. Campbell and William R. Dougan (Baltimore: Johns Hopkins University Press, 1986), pp. 85–109, especially p. 104. See also Fred Hirsch, *Money International* (New York: Doubleday, 1969), p. 169.

11. League of Nations, *International Currency Experience*, p. 16.

12. Nurkse, *Conditions of Monetary Equilibrium*, pp. 2–3.

13. Keynes, "Proposals for an International Currency (or Clearing) Union," p. 13 (paragraph 45); and "Proposals for an International Clearing Union," pp. 31–32 (paragraph 33).

14. Keynes, "Proposals for an International Clearing Union," pp. 31–32 (paragraph 33). Similar wording can be found in "Proposals for an International Currency (or Clearing) Union," p. 13 (paragraph 45).

15. White, "Preliminary Draft Outline of a Proposal for an International Stabiliza-

tion Fund of the United and Associated Nations," p. 96. Similar wording can be found in his "Preliminary Draft Proposal for a United Nations Stabilization Fund and a Bank for Reconstruction and Development of the United and Associated Nations," p. 44.

16. Ruggie, "International Regimes, Transactions, and Change," p. 393. On the institutionalization of this compromise in Europe, see Katzenstein, *Small States in World Markets.* For more on the Anglo-American policy consensus, see Ikenberry, "A World Economy Restored," pp. 289–321; and Ikenberry, "Creating Yesterday's New World Order," pp. 57–86. Ruggie briefly describes the place of capital controls in the embedded liberalism compromise, at p. 395, while Ikenberry does not. For the best analysis of the political influence of Keynes and Keynesian economics, see Peter A. Hall, ed., *The Political Power of Economic Ideas: Keynesianism Across Nations* (Princeton, N.J.: Princeton University Press, 1989).

17. Ruggie, "Embedded Liberalism and the Postwar Economic Regimes," p. 74.

18. Margaret G. de Vries, "Exchange Restrictions: The Setting," in *The International Monetary Fund, 1945–1965: Twenty Years of International Monetary Cooperation,* vol. 2, *Analysis,* ed. J. Keith Horsefield (Washington, D.C.: IMF, 1969), p. 224.

19. Ibid., p. 224.

20. The IMF can only impose conditionality consistent with the purposes of the Fund's Articles. See Gold, *International Capital Movements Under the Law of the International Monetary Fund;* and Ross B. Leckow, "The Role of the International Monetary Fund in the Liberalization of Capital Movements," *Wisconsin International Law Journal,* vol. 17, no. 3 (1999), pp. 515–527.

21. The phrase "to the extent necessary to ensure the proper functioning of the Common Market" occurs in Article 67 of the Treaty of Rome. See the discussion in Age F. P. Bakker, *The Liberalization of Capital Movements in Europe* (Dordrecht: Kluwer, 1996), pp. 42–43; Hans O. Schmitt, "Capital Markets and the Unification of Europe," *World Politics,* vol. 20, no. 2 (1968), pp. 228–244; and Peter Oliver and Jean-Pierre Baché, "Free Movement of Capital between the Member States: Recent Developments," *Common Market Law Review,* vol. 26, no. 1 (1989), pp. 61–81. On the "escape clause" for balance of payments difficulties, elaborated in Articles 108 and 109, see Martin Seidel, "Escape Clauses in European Community Law, with Special Reference to Capital Movements," *Common Market Law Review,* vol. 15, no. 1 (1978), pp. 283–308.

22. Quoted in Bakker, *Liberalization of Capital Movements,* p. 37.

23. Germany eliminated all restrictions on capital outflows in 1957, leaving only a few inflow controls in place to dampen upward pressure on the exchange rate, particularly during the early 1960s. Bakker notes that "Germany did not push very hard for its preference of freedom of capital movements." See Bakker, *Liberalization of Capital Movements,* p. 34. On Germany's role in the Treaty of Rome negotiations, see Walter Hallstein, *Europe in the Making,* trans. Charles Roetter (New York: W. W. Norton, 1973); Clement Wurm, ed., *Western Europe and Germany: The Beginnings of European Integration, 1945–1960* (Oxford: Berg, 1995); and Sabine Lee, "German

Decision-Making Elites and European Integration: German 'Europolitik' during the Years of the EEC and Free Trade Area Negotiations," in *Building Postwar Europe: National Decision-Makers and European Institutions, 1948–1963,* ed. Anne Deighton (New York: St. Martin's, 1995).

24. Author's interview with Karl Otto Pöhl, Frankfurt, June 29, 2005. On Ludwig Erhard's liberalism with regard to capital flows, see also Hans Tietmeyer, "The Concept of the Social Market Economy," in his *The Social Market Economy and Monetary Stability* (London: Economica, 1999), pp. 11–12.

25. The Nazi regime had created a wide variety of means to manipulate its monetary relations with neighboring states during the 1930s. See Jonathan Kirshner, *Currency and Coercion: The Political Economy of International Monetary Power* (Princeton, N.J.: Princeton University Press, 1995).

26. Author's interview with Hans Tietmeyer, Königstein, Germany, October 25, 2005.

27. Article 69 of the Treaty specified this role for the Commission. See Tommaso Padoa-Schioppa, "Capital Mobility: Why Is the Treaty Not Implemented?" in his *The Road to Monetary Union in Europe: The Emperor, the Kings, and the Genies* (New York: Oxford University Press, 1994), p. 27.

28. Ibid., pp. 31–32.

29. On Germany's macroeconomic exceptionalism in Europe, see, for example, Christopher S. Allen, "The Underdevelopment of Keynesianism in the Federal Republic of Germany," in *The Political Power of Economic Ideas* ed. Hall. On the influence of Ludwig Erhard, West Germany's economic affairs minister between 1949 and 1963, and his approach to macroeconomic discipline, see A. J. Nicholls, *Freedom with Responsibility: The Social Market Economy in Germany, 1918–1963* (Oxford: Clarendon, 1994), chap. 15.

30. Bakker, *Liberalization of Capital Movements,* pp. 80–85.

31. Ibid., p. 85.

32. Ibid., pp. 34–35.

33. European Economic Community Council, *First Directive for the Implementation of Article 67 of the Treaty* (December 7, 1960); and *Second Directive 63/21/EEC Adding to and Amending the First Directive for the Implementation of Article 67 of the EEC Treaty (Liberalization of Capital Movements)* (December 18, 1962).

34. Oliver and Baché, "Free Movement of Capital," pp. 63–65.

35. Padoa-Schioppa, "Capital Mobility," p. 27.

36. Bakker, *Liberalization of Capital Movements,* p. 7.

37. Ibid., p. 96.

38. Council of the European Communities, *Council Directive 72/156/EEC on Regulating International Capital Flows and Neutralizing Their Undesirable Effects on Domestic Liquidity* (March 12, 1972). See Bakker, *Liberalization of Capital Movements,* pp. 116–118.

39. Bakker, *Liberalization of Capital Movements,* pp. 147–152, 153.

40. Author's interview with Jean-Pierre Baché, Brussels, November 12, 2004.

41. See Jacob J. Kaplan and Günther Schleiminger, *The European Payments Union:*

Financial Diplomacy in the 1950s (Oxford: Clarendon, 1989); and Barry Eichengreen, *Reconstructing Europe's Trade and Payments: The European Payments Union* (Ann Arbor: University of Michigan Press, 1993).

42. "Liberalization of Capital Movements—Report by the Managing Board of the European Payments Union," OEEC Council, December 13, 1954, C(54)327 (OEEC Archives).

43. "Recommendation of the Council Concerning the Liberalization of Capital Movements," OEEC Council, June 22, 1955, C(55)59 (OEEC Archives).

44. "Liberalization of Capital Movements—Report by the Committee for Invisible Transactions," OEEC Council, July 3, 1957, C(57)52 (OEEC Archives), p. 16.

45. Ibid., pp. 17–19.

46. "Decision of the Council Concerning International Capital Movements— Adopted by the Council at Its 387th Meeting on December 6, 1957," OEEC Council, December 16, 1957, C(57)226 (OEEC Archives).

47. OEEC, *Liberalization of Current Invisibles and Capital Movements by the OEEC* (Paris: OEEC, 1961), p. 32.

48. "Codification of the Organization's Provisions for the Liberalization of Capital Movements—Report by the Committee for Invisible Transactions," OEEC Council, July 3, 1958, C(58)172 (OEEC Archives).

49. "Liberalization of International Security Dealing—Report by the Committee for Invisible Transactions," OEEC Council, August 28, 1958, C(58)208 (OEEC Archives).

50. "Codification of the Organization's Provisions for the Liberalization of Capital Movements—Revised Report by the Committee for Invisible Transactions," OEEC Council, May 28, 1959, C(59)119 (OEEC Archives), p. 5.

51. "Comments on the Report by the Committee for Invisible Transactions on Codification of the Organization's Provisions for the Liberalization of Capital Movements—Note by the Joint Trade and Intra-European Payments Committee," OEEC Council, November 2, 1959, C(59)244 (OEEC Archives), pp. 4–5.

52. OEEC, *Liberalization of Current Invisibles and Capital Movements by the OEEC,* p. 19.

53. Ibid., p. 20.

54. "Additional Liberalization Measures in the Field of Capital Movements," Committee for Invisible Transactions, May 5, 1960, TFD/INV/75 (OEEC Archives), p. 8.

55. "Preparation of a Code of Liberalization of Current Invisible Operations and a Code of Liberalization of Capital Movements for Adoption in the OECD," Committee for Invisible Transactions, March 7, 1961, TIR(61)2 (OEEC Archives).

56. Alexis Rieffel, "Exchange Controls: A Dead-End for Advanced Developing Countries?" *The AMEX Bank Review,* no. 12 (July 1987), pp. 1–23, at p. 5.

57. Eva Thiel, "Recent Codes-Based Liberalization in the OECD," in *Capital Liberalization in Transition Countries: Lessons from the Past and for the Future,* ed. Age F. P. Bakker and Bryan Chapple (Cheltenham, U.K., and Northampton, Mass.: Edward Elgar, 2003), p. 85.

Chapter 4: The Paris Consensus

1. European Court of Justice, *Criminal Proceedings against Guerrino Casati (reference for a preliminary ruling from the Tribunale, Bolzano)*, Case 203/80, November 11, 1981. See Oliver and Baché, "Free Movement of Capital" pp. 61–81. On the legal implications of *Casati*, see also Jean-Victor Louis, "Free Movement of Capital in the Community: The *Casati* Judgment," *Common Market Law Review*, vol. 19, no. 2 (1982), pp. 443–452.

2. The Bolzano court finally ruled in 1982 that Casati was not guilty, the general principle being that it is not a crime to export currency from Italy if the exporting will not hurt the Italian economy. Casati thus proved to the court's satisfaction that he had been reexporting currency that he had previously imported. The details can be found in *Giurisprudenza Italiana*, no. 2 (1982), pp. 356–362. For analysis, see also Italo Telchi, "Un occasione perduta: la mancata soppressione delle restrizioni ai movimenti di capitali nella Communità europea," *Giurisprudenza Italiana* 2 (1982), pp. 520–524. I am grateful to Elena Corsi for researching the details of the Casati case in the Italian courts.

3. Benjamin J. Cohen, "European Financial Integration and National Banking Interests," in *The Political Economy of European Integration*, ed. Paolo Guerrieri and Pier Carlo Padoan (Savage, Md.: Barnes & Noble, 1989), p. 145. On the relationship between capital liberalization and the efforts of the Commission to create a single market for financial services, see Jonathan Story and Ingo Walter, *Political Economy of Financial Integration in Europe: The Battle of the Systems* (Cambridge, Mass.: MIT Press, 1997), chap. 1, and pp. 254–257.

4. Cohen, "European Financial Integration and National Banking Interests," p. 164.

5. Council of the European Communities, *Council Directive 88/361/EEC for the Implementation of Article 67 of the Treaty* (June 24, 1988).

6. As of December 24, 2002, the consolidated Treaty renumbered Article 73b; it is now Article 56.

7. Bakker, *Liberalization of Capital Movements*, p. 1.

8. Ibid., pp. 147–152, 153.

9. Craig Parsons, *A Certain Idea of Europe* (Ithaca, N.Y.: Cornell University Press, 2003), p. 2.

10. Goodman and Pauly, "The Obsolescence of Capital Controls?," p. 73.

11. Author's interview with Henri Chavranski, Paris, April 2, 2004.

12. Peter A. Hall, "The Evolution of Economic Policy under Mitterrand," in *The Mitterrand Experiment*, ed. George Ross, Stanley Hoffmann, and Sylvia Malzacher (New York: Oxford University Press, 1987), p. 54. Also see Peter A. Hall, *Governing the Economy: The Politics of State Intervention in Britain and France* (New York: Oxford University Press, 1986), chap. 8.

13. David R. Cameron, "Exchange Rate Politics in France, 1981–1983: The Regime-Defining Choices of the Mitterrand Presidency," in *The Mitterrand Era: Policy Alternatives and Political Mobilization in France*, ed. Anthony Daley (New York: New York University Press, 1996), p. 58.

14. Jonah D. Levy, *Tocqueville's Revenge: State, Society, and Economy in Contemporary France* (Cambridge, Mass.: Harvard University Press, 1999), p. 29.

15. Helleiner, *States and the Reemergence of Global Finance*, pp. 140–143.

16. David J. Howarth, *The French Road to European Monetary Union* (New York: Palgrave, 2001), p. 61.

17. See especially David M. Andrews, "Financial Deregulation and the Origins of EMU: The French Policy Reversal of 1983," in *Structure and Agency in International Capital Mobility*, ed. Timothy J. Sinclair and Kenneth P. Thomas (New York: Palgrave, 2001), p. 20.

18. Michael Loriaux, *France After Hegemony: International Change and Financial Reform* (Ithaca, N.Y.: Cornell University Press, 1991), pp. 239–240.

19. Levy, *Tocqueville's Revenge*, p. 51.

20. Author's interview with Pascal Lamy, Brussels, November 12, 2004.

21. Author's interview with Jean-Charles Naouri, Paris, December 2, 2004.

22. Howarth, *The French Road to European Monetary Union*, p. 93.

23. Two classic treatments are John Zysman, *Governments, Markets, and Growth: Financial Systems and the Politics of Industrial Change* (Ithaca, N.Y.: Cornell University Press, 1983), chap. 3; and Loriaux, *France After Hegemony*, especially chaps. 2 and 4–6. On the domestic financial deregulation, see Cerny, "The 'Little Big Bang' in Paris," pp. 169–192. See also Vivien A. Schmidt, *From State to Market? The Transformation of French Business and Government* (Cambridge: Cambridge University Press, 1996), chaps. 4–6. On the Socialists' reforms and approach to the supply side, see Jeffrey Sachs and Charles Wyplosz, "The Economic Consequences of President Mitterrand," *Economic Policy*, no. 2 (1986), pp. 261–322.

24. Author's interview with Naouri.

25. Ibid.

26. Author's interview with Jean-Claude Trichet, Frankfurt, December 1, 2004.

27. Author's interview with Naouri.

28. Author's interview with Trichet.

29. Author's interview with Lamy.

30. Julius W. Friend, *Seven Years in France: François Mitterrand and the Unintended Revolution, 1981–1988* (Boulder, Colo.: Westview, 1989), pp. 106–107.

31. Author's interview with Naouri.

32. Author's interview with Jacques de Larosière, Paris, April 21, 2004.

33. Ibid.

34. Levy, *Tocqueville's Revenge*, p. 52.

35. Quoted in Ben Clift, *French Socialism in a Global Era: The Political Economy of the New Social Democracy in France* (New York and London: Continuum, 2003), p. 141. The article to which Clift refers is C. Aubin and J.-D. Lafay, "Objectifs politiques et contraintes institutionnelles dans les décisions de politique monétaire. Analyse économétrique du cas français," *Revue Economique*, vol. 46, no. 3 (1995), pp. 869–878.

36. Serge Halimi, "Less Exceptionalism Than Meets the Eye," in *The Mitterrand Era*, ed. Daley, p. 89.

37. Howarth, *The French Road to European Monetary Union*, p. 79.

38. Anthony Daley, "François Mitterrand, the Left, and Political Mobilization in France," in *The Mitterrand Era*, ed. Daley, p. 1.

39. George Ross, "The Limits of Political Economy: Mitterrand and the Crisis of the French Left," in *The Mitterrand Era*, ed. Daley, p. 38.

40. Patrick McCarthy, "France Faces Reality: *Rigueur* and the Germans," in *Recasting Europe's Economies*, ed. David P. Calleo and Claudia Morgenstern (Lanham, Md.: Washington Foundation for European Studies and University Press of America, 1990), p. 37.

41. See, for example, David M. Andrews and Thomas D. Willett, "Financial Interdependence and the State: International Monetary Relations at Century's End," *International Organization*, vol. 51, no. 3 (1997), pp. 479–511, at p. 496; and Andrew Moravcsik, *The Choice for Europe* (Ithaca, N.Y.: Cornell University Press, 1998), pp. 341–343.

42. Rawi Abdelal, "The Politics of Monetary Leadership and Followership," *Political Studies*, vol. 46, no. 2 (1998), pp. 236–259; and Jeffry Frieden, "Making Commitments: France and Italy in the European Monetary System, 1979–1985," in *The Political Economy of European Monetary Unification*, ed. Barry Eichengreen and Jeffry Frieden (Boulder, Colo.: Westview, 1994).

43. David Hanley, "French Political Parties, Globalization, and Europe," *Modern and Contemporary France*, vol. 9, no. 3 (2001), pp. 301–312, at pp. 304–306.

44. Author's interview with Jacques Delors, Paris, December 2, 2004.

45. McNamara, *The Currency of Ideas*, pp. 3, 5–6, 62–65. For more on neoliberalism in Europe, see Helleiner, *States and the Reemergence of Global Finance*, pp. 161–163; John Grahl and Paul Teague, "The Cost of Neo-Liberal Europe," *New Left Review*, no. 174 (1989), pp. 33–50; and Wayne Sandholtz and John Zysman, "1992: Recasting the European Bargain," *World Politics*, vol. 42, no. 1 (1989), pp. 95–128.

46. Author's interview with Karl Otto Pöhl, Frankfurt, June 29, 2005.

47. Moravcsik, *The Choice for Europe*, pp. 361–362.

48. Commission of the European Communities, *Completing the Internal Market*, White Paper from the Commission to the European Council (Milan, June 28–29, 1985), COM(85) 310 (Brussels: Commission of the European Communities, June 14, 1985), pp. 32–34.

49. Author's interview with Lamy.

50. The Single European Act was the first major revision of the Treaty of Rome. On the politics of the Single European Act, see especially Andrew Moravcsik, "Negotiating the Single European Act," *International Organization*, vol. 45, no. 1 (1991), pp. 19–56; and Sandholtz and Zysman, "1992: Recasting the European Bargain."

51. Author's interview with Delors.

52. Author's interview with Lamy.

53. See Bakker, *Liberalization of Capital Movements*, p. 163.

54. Council of the European Communities, *Council Directive 86/566/EEC Amending the First Directive of 11 May 1960 for the Implementation of Article 67 of the Treaty* (November 17, 1986).

55. Oliver and Baché, "Free Movement of Capital," pp. 66–67.

56. Bakker, *Liberalization of Capital Movements*, pp. 191–194.

57. Howarth, *The French Road to European Monetary Union*, p. 92; and Bakker, *Liberalization of Capital Movements*, pp. 202–203.

58. Bakker, *Liberalization of Capital Movements*, p. 205.

59. Council of the European Communities, *Council Directive 88/361/EEC*.

60. See Bakker, *Liberalization of Capital Movements*, p. 211; and Oliver and Baché, "Free Movement of Capital," pp. 66–67.

61. Bakker, *Liberalization of Capital Movements*, p. 168.

62. Author's interview with Hans Tietmeyer, Königstein, Germany, October 25, 2005.

63. Ibid.

64. Author's interview with Pöhl.

65. Technically and legally, the directive applied to all capital movements within the EC, but only transfers in relation to capital movements between EC and third countries.

66. Story and Walter, *Political Economy of Financial Integration in Europe*, p. 256. Also see Bakker, *Liberalization of Capital Movements*, pp. 198–199, 212.

67. Bakker, *Liberalization of Capital Movements*, pp. 196–198.

68. Ibid., p. 212. See also Julius W. Friend, *The Long Presidency: France in the Mitterrand Years, 1981–1995* (Boulder, Colo.: Westview, 1998), pp. 191–192.

69. Author's interview with Tietmeyer.

70. Author's interview with Delors.

71. Jacques Melitz, "Financial Deregulation in France," *European Economic Review*, vol. 34, nos. 2–3 (1990), pp. 394–402, at pp. 394–395.

72. Author's interview with Delors.

73. Author's interview with Lamy.

74. See Tommaso Padoa-Schioppa, "European Italy, Italian Europe," in his *Europe, A Civil Power: Lessons from EU Experience* (London: Federal Trust for Education and Research, 2004).

75. Oliver and Baché, "Free Movement of Capital," pp. 66–67.

76. Author's interview with Jean-Paul Mingasson, Brussels, November 4, 2004.

77. On compliance within the EU, see Peter M. Haas, "Compliance with EU Directives: Insights from International Relations and Comparative Politics," *Journal of European Public Policy*, vol. 5, no. 1 (1998), pp. 17–37. On the capital liberalization directive specifically, see Bakker, *Liberalization of Capital Movements*, pp. 219–223.

78. Kenneth Dyson and Kevin Featherstone, *The Road to Maastricht: Negotiating Economic and Monetary Union* (Oxford: Oxford University Press, 1999), p. 481.

79. Author's interview with Mingasson.

80. George Pagoulatos, *Greece's New Political Economy: State, Finance, and Growth from Post-War to EMU* (New York: Palgrave Macmillan, 2003), p. 176 ff.

81. Susannah Verney, "Greece and the European Community," in *Political Change in Greece: Before and After the Colonels*, ed. Kevin Featherstone and D. K. Katsoudas (London: Croom Helm, 1987).

82. See Pagoulatos, *Greece's New Political Economy*, pp. 178–183; P. C. Ioakimidis,

"The EC and the Greek Political System," in *Greece and EC Membership Evaluated*, ed. Panos Kazakos and P. C. Ioakimidis (London: Pinter, 1994); and P. C. Ioakimidis, "Contradictions in the Europeanization Process," in *Greece in a Changing Europe*, ed. Kevin Featherstone and Kostas Ifantis (Manchester: Manchester University Press, 1996).

83. Elena A. Iankova and Peter J. Katzenstein, "European Enlargement and Institutional Hypocrisy," in *The State of the European Union*, vol. 6, *Law, Politics, and Society*, ed. Tanja A. Börzel and Rachel A. Cichowski (Oxford: Oxford University Press, 2003), p. 280. Also see Dionyssis G. Dimitrakopoulos and Argyris G. Passas, "Greece: An Introduction to Patterns of EU Membership," in *Greece in the European Union*, ed. Dimitrakopoulos and Passas (New York: Routledge, 2004).

84. The Treaty on European Union, signed in Maastricht in 1991, came into force at the end of 1993. Greece's process of capital liberalization thus extended into the period when the Maastricht Treaty was "directly applicable," as opposed to being based on the transposition of a directive.

85. See Iannis A. Mourmouras and Michael G. Arghyrou, *Monetary Policy at the European Periphery: Greek Experience and Lessons for EU Candidates* (Berlin and Heidelberg: Springer, 2000), p. 46 ff.

86. George Pagoulatos, "Financial Interventionism and Liberalization in Southern Europe: State, Bankers, and the Politics of Disinflation," *Journal of Public Policy*, vol. 23, no. 2 (2003), pp. 171–199; and Pagoulatos, *Greece's New Political Economy*. Also see the arguments of Lucas Papademos, who became governor of the central bank in 1994: Lucas Papademos, "Monetary Policy and Financial Markets in the 1990s," in *The Greek Economy*, ed. T. S. Skouras (London: Macmillan, 1992); and Lucas Papademos, "European Monetary Union and Greek Economic Policy," in *Greece, the New Europe, and the Changing International Order*, ed. Harry J. Psomiades and Stavros B. Thomadakis (New York: Pella, 1993).

87. Nicolas Jabko, "In the Name of the Market: How the European Commission Paved the Way for Monetary Union," *Journal of European Public Policy*, vol. 6, no. 3 (1999), pp. 475–495.

88. George Ross, *Jacques Delors and European Integration* (New York: Oxford University Press, 1995), p. 80. Also see Dyson and Featherstone, *The Road to Maastricht*, p. 710.

89. Jabko, "In the Name of the Market," p. 481.

90. Ibid., p. 479.

91. Barry Eichengreen, "European Monetary Unification," *Journal of Economic Literature*, vol. 31, no. 3 (1993), pp. 1321–1357; and Barry Eichengreen and Charles Wyplosz, "The Unstable EMS," *Brookings Papers on Economic Activity*, no. 1 (1993), pp. 51–124.

92. Jabko, "In the Name of the Market," p. 475.

93. Author's interview with Lamy.

94. Craig Parsons, *A Certain Idea of Europe* (Ithaca, N.Y.: Cornell University Press, 2003), p. 205. Also see Moravcsik, *The Choice for Europe*, p. 434.

95. See Dyson and Featherstone, *The Road to Maastricht*, pp. 178–180, 188; and Parsons, *A Certain Idea of Europe*, p. 212.

96. Author's interview with Mingasson.

97. Author's interview with Tietmeyer.

98. Amy Verdun, *European Responses to Globalization and Financial Market Integration: Perceptions of Economic and Monetary Union in Britain, France, and Germany* (New York: Palgrave, 2000), pp. 80–86. Also see Amy Verdun, "The Role of the Delors Committee in Creating EMU," *Journal of European Public Policy,* vol. 6, no. 2 (1999), pp. 308–328.

99. Jabko, "In the Name of the Market," p. 476.

100. Tommaso Padoa-Schioppa, "The Delors Report: From Intentions to Action," in his *Road to Monetary Union in Europe,* p. 114.

101. Wayne Sandholtz, "Choosing Union: Monetary Politics and Maastricht," *International Organization,* vol. 47, no. 1 (1993), pp. 1–39, at pp. 28–30; Joseph M. Grieco, "The Maastricht Treaty, Economic and Monetary Union, and the Neo-Realist Research Program," *Review of International Studies,* vol. 21, no. 1 (1995), pp. 21–40; and Joseph M. Grieco, "State Interests and International Rule Trajectories: A Neorealist Interpretation of the Maastricht Treaty and European Economic and Monetary Union," *Security Studies,* vol. 5, no. 3 (1996), pp. 176–222.

102. Quoted in Hobart Rowen, ". . . Of European Unity," *Washington Post,* October 25, 1990.

103. Parsons, *A Certain Idea of Europe,* p. 203.

104. Author's interview with Delors.

105. Sandholtz, "Choosing Union," p. 30.

106. Peter J. Katzenstein, "United Germany in an Integrating Europe," in *Tamed Power: Germany in Europe,* ed. Peter J. Katzenstein (Ithaca, N.Y.: Cornell University Press, 1997), pp. 1–2. The day-by-day details of Mitterrand's and Kohl's bargaining over the date of the intergovernmental conference can be found in Dyson and Featherstone, *The Road to Maastricht,* pp. 197–198. For more on the politics of Maastricht, see Sandholtz, "Choosing Union," pp. 18–36; Geoffrey Garrett, "The Politics of Maastricht," in *The Political Economy of European Monetary Unification,* ed. Barry Eichengreen and Jeffry Frieden (Boulder, Colo.: Westview, 2001); Verdun, *European Responses to Globalization and Financial Market Integration,* pp. 48–102; and Michael Baun, "The Maastricht Treaty as High Politics," *Political Science Quarterly,* vol. 110, no. 4 (1996), pp. 605–624.

107. Those exceptions to liberal third-country treatment were outlined in Articles 73c-g and included: EU-wide "EMU safeguard measures" with regard to third countries; EU-wide financial sanctions on third countries; and existing individual member restrictions on capital flows to and from third countries. Qualified majority voting within the Council would govern new regimes.

108. Author's interview with Tietmeyer.

109. See Abdelal, "Politics of Monetary Leadership and Followership," pp. 236–241. Also see European Commission, DGII, "ERM Tensions and Monetary Policies in 1993," *European Economy,* no. 56 (1994), pp. 91–104; Heinrich Matthes, "'Damocles Shadowing': An Innovation in the Second Phase of EMU," *Intereconomics,*

vol. 29, no. 2 (1994), pp. 75–77; and Vincent Labhard and Charles Wyplosz, "The New EMS: Narrow Bands Inside Deep Bands," *American Economic Review*, vol. 86, no. 2 (1996), pp. 143–146.

110. See "Delors Calls for Probe of Capital Controls," Press Association, September 15, 1993; Lionel Barber, "Commission Cools Debate on Controls," *Financial Times*, September 17, 1993; and Lionel Barber, "Delors Pushes for Monetary 'Fortress Europe,'" *Financial Times*, September 18, 1993.

111. Charles P. Kindleberger, "The International Monetary Politics of a Near-Great Power: Two French Episodes, 1926–1936 and 1960–1970," in his *Keynesianism vs. Monetarism, and Other Essays in Financial History* (London: Allen & Unwin, 1985), p. 119.

112. Rawi Abdelal and Kimberly A. Haddad, *A Wider Europe: The Challenge of EU Enlargement*, Harvard Business School Case 703–021 (2003).

113. See Claudia M. Buch, "Capital Mobility and EU Enlargement," *Weltwirtschaftliches Archiv*, vol. 135, no. 4 (1999), pp. 629–656; and David Begg, Barry Eichengreen, László Halpern, Jürgen von Hagen, and Charles Wyplosz, *Sustainable Regimes of Capital Movements in Accession Countries*, Center for Economic Policy Research Policy Paper No. 10 (2002). On Poland's compliance with the *acquis* in defense planning and banking, see Epstein, "International Institutions, Domestic Resonance, and the Politics of Denationalization." On the "Europeanization" of central and eastern Europe in general, see Iankova and Katzenstein, "European Enlargement and Institutional Hypocrisy"; Vachudova, *Europe Undivided*; and Schimmelfennig and Sedelmeier, eds., *The Europeanization of Central and Eastern Europe*. On the importance of the eagerness of the objects of persuasion to impress the persuading institution, see Checkel, "Why Comply?," pp. 553–588.

114. Author's interview with Stephane Ouaki, Brussels, November 3, 2004.

115. Author's interview with Lars Erik Forsberg and Ouaki, Brussels, November 3, 2004.

116. Author's interview with Forsberg, Brussels, November 3, 2004.

117. Author's interview with Ouaki.

118. Author's interview with Forsberg.

Chapter 5: Privilege and Obligation

1. On the meaning of OECD membership, see especially Henri Chavranski, *L'OCDE: Au cœur des grands débats économiques* (Paris: La documentation française, 1997), p. 7.

2. See Richard T. Griffiths, "'An Act of Creative Leadership': The End of the OEEC and the Birth of the OECD," in *Explorations in OEEC History*, ed. Richard T. Griffiths (Paris: OECD, 1997).

3. See OECD, *Experience with Controls on International Portfolio Operations in Shares and Bonds* (Paris: OECD, 1980); OECD, *Controls on International Capital Movements: The Experience with Controls on International Financial Credits, Loans, and Deposits* (Paris:

OECD, 1982); OECD, *Controls and Impediments Affecting Inward Direct Investment in OECD Member Countries* (Paris: OECD, 1982); and OECD, *Liberalization of Capital Movements and Financial Services in the OECD Area* (Paris: OECD, 1990).

4. Poret, "The Experience of the OECD with the Code of Liberalization of Capital Movements," p. 1. Also see OECD, "Liberalization of the Capital Movements and Financial Services in the OECD Area," *Financial Market Trends,* June 1991, pp. 19–27, at p. 19.

5. Author's interview with Rinaldo Pecchioli, Paris, September 11, 2003.

6. Raymond Bertrand, "The Liberalization of Capital Movements—An Insight," *Three Banks Review,* no. 132 (1981), pp. 3–22, at p. 3.

7. Author's interview with Henri Chavranski, Paris, April 2, 2004.

8. Thiel, "Recent Codes-Based Liberalization in the OECD," p. 86.

9. Author's interview with Jeffrey R. Shafer, New York, August 12, 2004.

10. See, for one example, Peter J. Quirk, Owen Evans, and IMF Staff Teams, *Capital Account Convertibility: Review of Experience and Implications for IMF Policies,* Occasional Paper No. 131 (Washington, D.C.: IMF, 1995), p. 2.

11. Pierre Poret, "Liberalizing Capital Movements," *OECD Observer,* no. 176 (June/July 1992), pp. 4–8.

12. Eichengreen, "Capital Account Liberalization," p. 350.

13. Simmons and Elkins, "The Globalization of Liberalization," pp. 171–189.

14. Author's interview with Chavranski.

15. Bertrand, "The Liberalization of Capital Movements," p. 8.

16. See OECD, *OECD Code of Liberalization of Capital Movements* (Paris: OECD, 2003); and OECD, *OECD Codes of Liberalization of Capital Movements and of Current Invisible Transactions: User's Guide* (Paris: OECD, 2003).

17. Bertrand, "The Liberalization of Capital Movements," p. 6.

18. In April 2004, the day after I left Paris, the CMIT held its final meeting. The CMIT and Committee on International Investment and Multinational Enterprises (CIME) were merged to form the Investment Committee.

19. Originally, the Invisibles Committee had a limited membership of government representatives who were designated independent experts, a committee structure that was unique even within the OECD. Bertrand, "The Liberalization of Capital Movements," p. 9.

20. See, especially, Fabrizio Pagani, "Peer Review: A Tool for Cooperation and Change—An Analysis of an OECD Working Method," Directorate for Legal Affairs, September 11, 2002, SG/LEG(2002)1 (OECD Archives); and "Investment Policy Peer Reviews: Remarks by the OECD Secretariat at UNCTAD Meeting, 25–27 June 2003," Directorate for Financial, Fiscal, and Enterprise Affairs, CIME, July 3, 2003, DAFFE/IME/RD(2003)15 (OECD Archives).

21. Pagani, "Peer Review," p. 4. Peer review has analogues in regulation ("yardstick competition") and management ("benchmarking").

22. Ibid., pp. 12–13. One measure of commitment is the caliber of people sent by member countries. The more senior the official, the more seriously the country is taking the review.

23. Ibid., pp. 11–12.

24. Ibid., p. 5.

25. Ibid., p. 7.

26. On the role of "multilateral peer pressure" in the OECD's experience with capital account liberalization, see also Jeffrey R. Shafer, "Experience with Controls on International Capital Movements in OECD Countries: Solution or Problem for Monetary Policy?" in *Capital Controls, Exchange Rates, and Monetary Policy in the World Economy,* ed. Sebastian Edwards (Cambridge: Cambridge University Press, 1995), p. 136.

27. OECD, *Forty Years' Experience with the OECD Code of Liberalization of Capital Movements* (Paris: OECD, 2002), p. 8.

28. Author's interview with Chavranski.

29. Ibid.

30. Ibid.

31. Author's interview with Shafer.

32. Author's interview with Jan Nipstad, Stockholm, April 22, 2004.

33. Author's interview with Shafer.

34. Author's interview with Nipstad.

35. Ibid.

36. "Letter by Mr. Nipstad to the Chairman of the Committee," Directorate for Financial, Fiscal, and Enterprise Affairs, CMIT, July 1, 1994, DAFFE/INV(94)24 (OECD Archives), p. 2.

37. Author's interview with Nipstad.

38. Author's interview with Shafer.

39. Author's interview with Nipstad.

40. Author's interview with Pecchioli.

41. See Alexandre Lamfalussy, "Changing Attitudes Towards Capital Movements," in *Changing Perceptions of Economic Policy,* ed. Frances Cairncross (London and New York: Methuen, 1981).

42. Bertrand, "The Liberalization of Capital Movements," p. 6.

43. "Further Liberalization of Capital Movements," Committee for Invisible Transactions, TFD/INV/249 (OECD Archives).

44. "Further Liberalization of Capital Movements—Report by the Committee for Invisible Transactions," OECD Council, March 3, 1964, C(64)13 (OECD Archives).

45. "Supplement to the Report on Further Liberalization of Capital Movements," Directorate for Financial and Fiscal Affairs, Committee for Invisible Transactions, March 31, 1964, TIR(64)1 (OECD Archives), p. 11.

46. Ibid., p. 8.

47. Poret, "The Experience of the OECD with the Code of Liberalization of Capital Movements," p. 5.

48. OECD, "OECD's Code of Liberalization of Capital Movements," *OECD Observer* 55 (December 1971), pp. 38–43, at p. 38.

49. "Decision of the Council Amending the Code of Liberalization of Capital Movements—Adopted by the Council at its 76th Meeting on July 28, 1964," OECD Council, August 14, 1964, C(64)85 (OECD Archives).

50. OECD, "OECD's Code of Liberalization of Capital Movements," p. 40.

51. Shafer, "Experience with Controls on International Capital Movements in OECD Countries," p. 123.

52. "Decision of the Council Amending the Code of Liberalization of Capital Movements—Adopted by the Council at its 317th Meeting on February 27, 1973," OECD Council, March 2, 1973, C(72)118 (OECD Archives).

53. Shafer, "Experience with Controls on International Capital Movements in OECD Countries," p. 134.

54. "The Application of the Code of Liberalization of Capital Movements to Inward Direct Investment—Report by the Committee on Capital Movements and Invisible Transactions," OECD Council, November 23, 1981, C(81)100 (OECD Archives); "Inward Direct Investment under the Code of Liberalization of Capital Movements—Report by the Committee on Capital Movements and Invisible Transactions," OECD Council, September 6, 1983, C(83)106 (OECD Archives).

55. OECD, "Liberalization of Capital Movements and Financial Services in the OECD Area," pp. 22–23; and Poret, "The Experience of the OECD with the Code of Liberalization of Capital Movements," p. 5.

56. Stephany Griffith-Jones, Ricardo Gottschalk, and Xavier Cirera, "The OECD Experience with Capital Account Liberalization," in *Management of Capital Flows: Comparative Experiences and Implications for Africa* (New York and Geneva: UNCTAD, 2003), p. 79.

57. Poret, "The Experience of the OECD with the Code of Liberalization of Capital Movements," p. 5.

58. OECD, *Forty Years' Experience with the OECD Code of Liberalization of Capital Movements*, p. 27.

59. Author's interview with Chavranski.

60. Author's interview with Nipstad.

61. Ibid.

62. "Draft Report by the Joint Group of the CMIT and CMF on Banking and Related Financial Services," CMIT and Committee on Financial Markets, January 15, 1986, DAFFE/INV/86.3 and DAFFE/MC/SC86.1 (OECD Archives), p. 4.

63. Ibid., p. 9.

64. "Work Program and Procedures for the Second Phase—Joint Working Group on Banking and Related Financial Services," CMIT and Committee on Financial Markets, August 25, 1986, DAFFE/INV/86.28 and DAFFE/MC/SF/86.5 (OECD Archives), p. 6.

65. Author's interview with Chavranski.

66. Author's interview with Nipstad.

67. OECD, *Forty Years' Experience with the OECD Code of Liberalization of Capital Movements*, p. 28. See Chapter 2 of this book.

68. Author's interview with Shafer.

69. "The Liberalization of Short-Term Operations under the Code of Liberalization of Capital Movements," Joint Working Group on Banking and Related Financial Services, CMIT, and Committee on Financial Markets, May 19, 1988, DAFFE/INV/87.55 and DAFFE/MC/SF/87.7 (OECD Archives), p. 2.

70. Ibid., p. 3.
71. Ibid., p. 7.
72. Ibid., p. 8.
73. Ibid., p. 4.
74. Ibid., p. 5.
75. Ibid., p. 12.
76. Ibid., p. 16.
77. Ibid., pp. 14–15.
78. "Banking and Financial Services: Review and Proposed Amendment of the Codes of Liberalization of Capital Movements and Current Invisible Operations," CMIT, and Committee on Financial Markets, February 14, 1989, DAFFE/INV/89.4 and DAFFE/MC/SF/89.1 (OECD Archives), p. 4. Also see "Banking and Financial Services: Review and Proposed Amendment of the Codes of Liberalization of Capital Movements and Current Invisible Operations—Report by the Committee on Capital Movements and Invisible Transactions and the Committee on Financial Markets," OECD Council, April 3, 1989, C(89)57 (OECD Archives).
79. "Banking and Financial Services: Review and Proposed Amendment of the Codes of Liberalization of Capital Movements and Current Invisible Operations," CMIT and Committee on Financial Markets, February 14, 1989, DAFFE/INV/89.4 and DAFFE/MC/SF/89.1 (OECD Archives), p. 6.
80. Ibid., p. 8.
81. Louis W. Pauly, *Who Elected the Bankers? Surveillance and Control in the World Economy* (Ithaca, N.Y.: Cornell University Press, 1997), p. 37.
82. Robert Ley, "Liberating Capital Movements: A New OECD Commitment," *OECD Observer,* no. 159 (August–September 1989), pp. 22–26, at p. 22.
83. Rieffel, "Exchange Controls," p. 7.
84. "Assessing Candidates for OECD Membership," Directorate for Financial, Fiscal, and Enterprise Affairs, CMIT, and CIME, September 2, 1994, DAFFE/INV/IME(94)11 (OECD Archives), p. 5.
85. Author's interview with Shafer.
86. Rieffel, "Exchange Controls," p. 6.
87. Robert Ley and Pierre Poret, "The New OECD Members and Liberalization," *OECD Observer,* no. 205 (July 1997), pp. 38–42, at p. 38.
88. Thiel, "Recent Codes-Based Liberalization in the OECD," p. 92.
89. See "Republic of Poland: A USG 'Roadmap' for OECD Accession"; "Republic of Hungary: A USG 'Roadmap' for OECD Accession"; "Czech Republic: A USG 'Roadmap' for OECD Accession"; and "Slovakia: A USG 'Roadmap' for OECD Accession," unpublished memoranda, 1994.
90. Griffith-Jones, Gottschalk, and Cirera, "The OECD Experience with Capital Account Liberalization," p. 90.
91. Pierre Poret, "Mexico and the OECD Codes of Liberalization," *OECD Observer,* no. 189 (August-September 1994), pp. 39–42, at p. 39.
92. "Mexico's Adherence to the Liberalization Codes and the Declaration and Deci-

sions on International Investment and Multinational Enterprises," Directorate for Financial, Fiscal, and Enterprise Affairs, CMIT, and CIME, February 4, 1994, DAFFE/INV/IME(94)1 (OECD Archives), pp. 4–5. Also see "Mexico's Adherence to the Codes of Liberalization and the Declaration and Decisions on International Investment and Multinational Enterprises—Report by the Committee on Capital Movements and Invisible Transactions and the Committee for International Investment and Multinational Enterprises," OECD Council, March 11, 1994, C(94)49 (OECD Archives).

93. Christian Schricke, "Mexico, 25th Member of the OECD," *OECD Observer,* June 1, 1994, p. 4.

94. "Assessing Candidates for OECD Membership," Directorate for Financial, Fiscal, and Enterprise Affairs, CMIT, and CIME, September 2, 1994, DAFFE/INV/IME(94)11 (OECD Archives), p. 5.

95. "Mexico: Proposed Reservations under the Codes of Liberalization of Capital Movements and of Current Invisible Transactions," Directorate for Financial, Fiscal, and Enterprise Affairs, CMIT, and CIME, November 22, 1993, DAFFE/INV/IME(93)6 (OECD Archives), p. 3.

96. Oldřich Dědek, "The Currency Shake-up in 1997: A Case Study of the Czech Economy," in *International Capital Flows in Calm and Turbulent Times,* ed. Stephany Griffith-Jones, Ricardo Gottschalk, and Jacques Cailoux (Ann Arbor: University of Michigan Press, 2003).

97. Author's interview with Petr Procházka, Prague, March 25, 2004.

98. Author's interview with Oldřich Dědek, Prague, March 24, 2004.

99. Ibid. The importance of the prestige of OECD membership was also a theme of the author's interview with Věra Břicháčková, Prague, March 24, 2004.

100. Oldřich Dědek, "Capital Account Liberalization in the Czech Republic," in *Managing Capital Flows in Turbulent Times: The Experience of Europe's Emerging Eco-nomies in Global Perspective,* ed. Zdeněk Drábek and Stephany Griffith-Jones (Armonk, N.Y., and London: M. E. Sharpe, 1999), pp. 109–110.

101. Author's interview with Dědek.

102. Ibid.

103. Author's interview with Břicháčková.

104. Author's interview with Dědek.

105. Author's interview with Procházka.

106. "Adherence of the Czech Republic to the Codes of Liberalization and to the Declaration and Decisions on International Investment and Multinational Enterprises: Principles and Procedures," Directorate for Financial, Fiscal, and Enterprise Affairs, CMIT, and CIME, March 17, 1995, DAFFE/INV/IME(95)2 (OECD Archives). Also see "Czech Republic: Adherence to the Codes of Liberalization and the Declaration and Decisions on International Investment and Multinational Enterprises—Report by the Committee on Capital Movements and Invisible Transactions and the Committee on International Investment and Multinational Enterprises," OECD Council, November 3, 1995, C(95)188 (OECD Archives).

107. "Czech Republic: Proposed Reservations under the Codes of Liberalization of

Capital Movements and Current Invisible Operations," Directorate for Financial, Fiscal, and Enterprise Affairs, CMIT, and CIME, March 17, 1995, DAFFE/INV/IME(95)3 (OECD Archives), p. 3.

108. Author's interview with Procházka.

109. Author's interview with Jana Křelinová, Prague, March 25, 2004.

110. Author's interview with Břicháčková.

111. Dědek, "Capital Account Liberalization in the Czech Republic," p. 106.

112. Author's interview with Tomáš Holub, Prague, March 25, 2005.

113. Author's interview with Procházka.

114. "Response to the Conclusions of the Joint Meeting of CMIT/CIME on the Czech Republic on 21 April 1995—Note by the Czech Authorities," Directorate for Financial, Fiscal, and Enterprise Affairs, CMIT, and CIME, October 2, 1995, DAFFE/INV/IME(95)44 (OECD Archives), p. 2.

115. Author's interview with Břicháčková.

116. Author's interview with Procházka.

117. "Czech Republic: Proposed Reservations under the Codes of Liberalization of Capital Movements and Current Invisible Operations," p. 4.

118. The best account of the complex political economy of the Czech transition is Gerald A. McDermott, *Embedded Politics: Industrial Networks and Institutional Change in Postcommunism* (Ann Arbor: University of Michigan Press, 2002). On reforms in the Czech banking sector in comparative perspective, see Gerald A. McDermott, "The Politics of Institutional Learning and Creation: Bank Crises and Supervision in East Central Europe," unpublished manuscript, The Wharton School, University of Pennsylvania, September 2004.

119. See Ronald I. McKinnon and Huw Pill, "Credible Economic Liberalizations and Over-Borrowing," *American Economic Review,* vol. 87, no. 2 (1997), pp. 189–193; and Ronald I. McKinnon and Huw Pill, "International Overborrowing: A Decomposition of Credit and Currency Risks," *World Development,* vol. 26, no. 7 (1998), pp. 1267–1282.

120. One Czech bank did not, however, indulge in the credit binge, a fact that suggests an important behavioral component to the classic story of "overborrowing." See Rawi Abdelal, Vincent Dessain, and Monika Stachowiak, *Bohemian Crowns: Československá Obchodní Banka (A) and (B),* Harvard Business School Case 705–007 and 705–008 (2004).

121. See especially Tomáš Holub and Zdenek Tuma, "Managing Capital Inflows in the Czech Republic: Experiences, Problems, and Questions," unpublished paper, Czech National Bank, 2001, pp. 16–17.

122. Holub and Tuma, "Managing Capital Inflows in the Czech Republic," p. 32.

123. Author's interview with Procházka.

124. Dědek, "Capital Account Liberalization in the Czech Republic," pp. 102–104.

125. "Hungary: Proposed Reservations under the Codes of Liberalization of Capital Movements and Invisible Transactions," Directorate for Financial, Fiscal, and Enterprise Affairs, CMIT, and CIME, May 23, 1995, DAFFE/INV/IME(95)20 (OECD Archives), p. 3.

126. "OECD/Hungary—4: Constraints on Monetary Policy," *Dow Jones International,* September 13, 1995.

127. Eszter Szamado, "Eyeing OECD Membership, Hungary Wants to Pass New Forex Code," *Agence France-Presse,* November 6, 1995.

128. "Hungary: Position under the Codes of Liberalization and the Declaration and Decisions on International Investment and International Enterprises—Draft Report to the Council," Directorate for Financial, Fiscal, and Enterprise Affairs, CMIT, and CIME, January 11, 1996, DAFFE/INV/IME(96)1 (OECD Archives), p. 5. Also see "Hungary: Position under the Codes of Liberalization and the Declaration and Decisions on International Investment and Multinational Enterprises—Report by the Committee on Capital Movements and Invisible Transactions and the Committee on International Investment and Multinational Enterprises," OECD Council, February 28, 1996, C(96)19 (OECD Archives).

129. Roger Nord, "The Liberalization of the Capital Account in Hungary: Experiences and Lessons," in *Capital Liberalization in Transition Countries: Lessons from the Past and for the Future,* ed. Age F. P. Bakker and Bryan Chapple (Cheltenham, U.K., and Northampton, Mass.: Edward Elgar, 2003), pp. 196–197.

130. "Hungary OECD Membership Depends on IMF Pact—Bokros," *Reuters,* February 8, 1996.

131. Gábor Oblath, "Capital Inflows to Hungary and Accompanying Policy Responses, 1995–96," in *The Mixed Blessing of Financial Inflows: Transition Countries in Comparative Perspective,* ed. János Gács, Robert Holzmann, and Michael L. Wyzan (Cheltenham, U.K., and Northampton, Mass.: Edward Elgar, 2003).

132. Ewa Sadowska-Cieslak, "Capital Account Liberalization in Poland," in *Capital Liberalization in Transition Countries,* ed. Bakker and Chapple.

133. "Joint Meeting of the CMIT/CIME on Poland, 30 June 1995—Conclusions," Directorate for Financial, Fiscal, and Enterprise Affairs, CMIT, and CIME, January 16, 1996, DAFFE/INV/IME(96)5 (OECD Archives), p. 2. Also see "Poland: Position under the Codes of Liberalization and the Declaration and Decisions on International Investment and Multinational Enterprises—Report by the CMIT/CIME," OECD Council, June 6, 1996, C(96)117 (OECD Archives).

134. Wojciech Moskwa, "Poland to Ease Capital Flow Limits for OECD Entry," *Reuters,* February 21, 1996; Martin Grajewski, "Poland Finishes Preparations for OECD Membership," *Reuters,* March 4, 1996; and "Polish President Signs Laws Linked to OECD Entry," *Reuters,* April 5, 1996.

135. John Driffill and Tomasz Mickiewicz, "The Order of Financial Liberalization: Lessons from the Polish Experience," in *The Role of Financial Markets in the Transition Process,* ed. Emilio Colombo and John Driffill (Heidelberg and New York: Physica-Verlag, 2003); and Paweł Durjasz and Ryszard Kokoszczyński, "Financial Flows to Poland, 1990–96," in *The Mixed Blessing of Financial Inflows: Transition Countries in Comparative Perspective,* ed. Gács, Holzmann, and Wyzan.

136. Stanis aw Gomulka, "Managing Capital Flows to Poland," in *Managing Capital Flows in Turbulent Times,* ed. Drábek and Griffith-Jones.

137. See Stephen L. Harris, "South Korea and the Asian Crisis: The Impact of the Democratic Deficit and OECD Accession," in *International Financial Governance under Stress: Global Structures versus National Imperatives* ed. Geoffrey R. D. Underhill and Xiaoke Zhang (Cambridge: Cambridge University Press, 2003).

138. "Accession of Korea and Developing Country 'Status'—Note by the Secretary-General," OECD Council, July 19, 1996, C(96)146 (OECD Archives), p. 2.

139. Ibid., p. 4.

140. In 1994 the OECD Secretariat and the Seoul government had exchanged visits to Paris and Seoul to explore observer status for South Korea.

141. John Burton, "Seoul Urged by OECD to Speed Reforms," *Financial Times,* October 20, 1995.

142. "Korea: Proposed Reservations under the Codes of Liberalization of Capital Movements and Current Invisible Operations," Directorate for Financial, Fiscal, and Enterprise Affairs, CMIT, and CIME, March 14, 1996, DAFFE/INV/IME(96)12 (OECD Archives), p. 5. Also see "Korea: Position under the Codes of Liberalization and the Declaration and Decisions on International Investment and Multinational Enterprises—Report by the Committee on Capital Movements and Invisible Transactions and the Committee on International Investment and Multinational Enterprises," OECD Council, September 11, 1996, C(96)180 (OECD Archives).

143. John Burton, "Seoul Loosens Limits on Foreign Investment: Controls Relaxed as Part of South Korea's Efforts to Meet OECD Membership Terms," *Financial Times,* June 9, 1996.

144. "Korea's Response to the Chairman's Conclusions on the Joint CMIT/CIME Meeting with Korea," Directorate for Financial, Fiscal, and Enterprise Affairs, CMIT, and CIME, August 1, 1996, DAFFE/INV/IME(96)35 (OECD Archives), p. 2. Also see John Burton, "South Korea to Ease Rules on Financial Market: Liberalization Driven by Effort to Meet OECD Membership Demands," *Financial Times,* August 3, 1996.

145. John Burton, "Seoul Hits Impasse Over OECD Entry," *Financial Times,* September 6, 1996.

146. See Ha-Joon Chang, "Korea: The Misunderstood Crisis," *World Development,* vol. 26, no. 8 (1998), pp. 1555–1561, esp. p. 1559.

147. See especially Harris, "South Korea and the Asian Crisis," pp. 144–152.

148. Soogil Young, "Answers to the Four Most Frequently Asked Questions about the OECD in Korea," paper prepared for delivery at the second Korea-OECD Conference on Korea's Five Years in the OECD, Seoul, South Korea, December 13–14, 2001.

149. I have based this account on an enlightening conversation with Jun-Il Kim of the IMF, who at the time was in Seoul in the finance ministry. Author's interview with Jun-Il Kim, Washington, D.C., October 5, 2004.

150. Author's interview with Tae-Kyun Kwon, Paris, April 14, 2004.

Chapter 6: Freedom and Its Risks

1. In writing this chapter I have relied on documents from the IMF archives and interviews with IMF management and staff as well as current and former officials of the U.S. Department of the Treasury. Among the most useful of the documents from the archives is the "Chairman's Summing Up" of each board meeting. Interpreting the language of these documents is an art in itself, and I have followed the key of the Fund's historian, James Boughton. When referring to the positions of the directors, the chair generally means the following: two to four directors are a "few"; five to six are "some"; six to nine are "a number"; ten to fifteen are "many"; fifteen or more are "most"; and twenty or more are "nearly all." The executive board of the IMF recently undertook a significant liberalization of its archival access policies. Currently, executive board documents that are more than five years old are available to the public. Executive board minutes are classified for ten years, however. In June 2004 the executive board granted my special request to read the minutes of a handful of key meetings between 1995 and 1998 at which the proposed amendment to the Articles was discussed. I have tried to cite those minutes judiciously. For archival materials, I have used the IMF's internal classification system. Each series of documents has its own acronym: BUFF refers to statements made by the managing director and staff representatives to the executive board; EBD refers to executive board documents, papers requiring action by, or for the information of, the executive board; EBM refers to executive board minutes, the confidential summary minutes of board meetings; and SM refers to staff memoranda, studies and reports prepared by the staff for consideration by, or the information of, the executive board. See James M. Boughton, *Silent Revolution: The International Monetary Fund, 1979–1989* (Washington, D.C.: IMF, 2001), p. xxi. Boughton's key comes from Minutes of the Executive Board Meeting, January 12, 1983, EBM/83/11 (IMF Archives). I am grateful to Boughton for drawing my attention to this key and for his advice in interpreting these documents.

2. Author's interview with Thomas A. Bernes, Washington, D.C., October 16, 2003.

3. Author's interview with Michel Camdessus, Paris, April 19, 2004.

4. On the role of the U.S. chair, separate form Treasury's own influence in the Fund, see Nicholas D. Kristof and David E. Sanger, "How the U.S. Wooed Asia to Let Cash Flow In," *New York Times*, February 16, 1999.

5. See especially Simmons, "The Legalization of International Monetary Affairs," pp. 573–602; Simmons, "International Law and State Behavior," pp. 819–835; and Beth A. Simmons, "Money and the Law: Why Comply with the Public International Law of Money?" *Yale Journal of International Law*, vol. 25, no. 2 (2000), pp. 323–362.

6. Articles of Agreement of the International Monetary Fund, Article I, "Purposes."

7. Articles of Agreement of the International Monetary Fund, Article VI, Section 3, "Controls of Capital Transfers."

8. Eichengreen, *Globalizing Capital*, p. 94.

9. Robert Alloway, *Capital Controls and the IMF*, Harvard Business School independent student research paper, May 2002, p. 3. Alloway conducted a thorough examination of every official Fund publication between 1945 and 2002 for references to capital account restrictions.

10. IMF, *Report on Exchange Restrictions, 1950* (Washington, D.C.: IMF, 1950), p. 28, cited in Alloway.

11. IMF, *Report on Exchange Restrictions, 1952* (Washington, D.C.: IMF, 1952), p. 14, cited in Alloway.

12. "Legal Aspects of Regulations of International Capital Movements," prepared by the Legal Department, November 16, 1955, SM/55/74 (IMF Archives).

13. Article XXIX specifies that questions of interpretation will be settled by the Executive Board. If a member disputes the board's interpretation, the Board of Governors refers the question to its own Committee on Interpretation, which can be overruled by 85 percent of the voting members.

14. Executive Board of the IMF, Decision No. 541-(56/39), July 25, 1956, in *Documents*, ed. Horsefield, p. 246. See the discussion in the Minutes of Executive Board Meeting, April 6, 1956, EBM/56/24 (IMF Archives).

15. Lawrence Krause, "Private International Finance," *International Organization*, vol. 25, no. 3 (1971), pp. 523–540, at p. 536.

16. IMF, *Reform of the International Monetary System* (Washington, D.C.: IMF, 1972), p. 56, cited in Alloway. It is interesting to note how late into the postwar years the Fund's language continued to rely on concepts—disequilibrating and equilibrating—that were central to the assessment of capital flows during the interwar years.

17. Pauly, *Who Elected the Bankers?*, p. 97.

18. "Report of the Technical Group on Disequilibrating Capital Flows," May 17, 1973, in IMF, *International Monetary Reform: Documents of the Committee of Twenty* (Washington, D.C.: IMF, 1974), pp. 78–92.

19. Lamfalussy, "Changing Attitudes Towards Capital Movements," p. 200. See also Margaret Garritsen de Vries, *The International Monetary Fund, 1972–1978: Cooperation on Trial*, vol. 1, *Narrative and Analysis* (Washington, D.C.: IMF, 1985), pp. 214–215.

20. "Report of the Technical Group on Disequilibrating Capital Flows," p. 78.

21. Ibid., pp. 84–85.

22. Ibid., p. 85.

23. "Final Report and Outline of Reform of the Committee of Twenty," June 14, 1974, in *The International Monetary Fund, 1972–1978: Cooperation on Trial*, vol. 3, *Documents*, ed. Margaret Garritsen de Vries (Washington, D.C.: IMF, 1985), p. 170.

24. Ibid., p. 170.

25. Pauly, *Who Elected the Bankers?*, p. 97; and see Lamfalussy, "Changing Attitudes Towards Capital Movements," p. 201.

26. For more on surveillance, see especially Pauly, *Who Elected the Bankers?*, chap. 6;

James, *International Monetary Cooperation Since Bretton Woods*, pp. 612–613; and Boughton, *Silent Revolution*, chaps. 2–3.

27. Executive Board of the IMF, Decision No. 5392-(77/63), April 29, 1977 (IMF Archives).

28. Author's interview with Jacques de Larosière, Paris, April 21, 2004.

29. Ibid.

30. Author's interview with Lawrence Summers, Cambridge, Mass., April 30, 2004.

31. "Capital Account Convertibility—Review of Experience and Implications for Fund Policies," prepared by the Monetary and Exchange Affairs and Policy Development and Review Departments, July 7, 1995, SM/95/164 (IMF Archives), p. 9.

32. Ibid., p. 10.

33. Ibid., p. 11.

34. "Capital Account Convertibility and the Role of the Fund—Review of Experience and Consideration of a Possible Amendment of the Articles," prepared by the Legal, Monetary and Exchange Affairs, and Policy Development and Review Departments, February 5, 1997, SM/97/32 (IMF Archives), p. 1.

35. See Jeffrey M. Chwieroth, "'How Much,' 'How To?' Testing and Measuring the Role of Norms and Ideas, the Case of Neoliberalism in International Financial Institutions," unpublished paper, European University Institute, 2003.

36. "Capital Account Convertibility and the Role of the Fund," February 5, 1997, pp. 12–13. See also the analysis by a staff member of the Fund's legal department in Leckow, "The Role of the International Monetary Fund in the Liberalization of Capital Movements," pp. 517–518, 521–522.

37. "Review of Experience with Capital Account Liberalization and Strengthened Procedures Adopted by the Fund," prepared by the Monetary and Exchange Affairs, Policy Development and Review, and Research Departments, February 6, 1997, SM/97/32 Supplement 1 (IMF Archives), p. 32.

38. IEO, *The IMF's Approach to Capital Account Liberalization*.

39. IEO, *The IMF's Approach to Capital Account Liberalization*.

40. Chwieroth, "Neo-liberalism's Role in Capital Account Liberalization in Emerging Markets."

41. Bhagwati, "The Capital Myth," p. 12. Also see Bhagwati, *The Wind of the Hundred Days*, Part I, and Bhagwati, *In Defense of Globalization*, chap. 13.

42. Wade and Veneroso, "The Gathering World Slump," pp. 35–39.

43. Author's interview with Karin Lissakers, New York, October 20, 2003.

44. Author's confidential interview with a former senior U.S. Treasury official, Washington D.C., October 6, 2003.

45. Author's interview with Summers.

46. Author's interview with Charles H. Dallara, Washington, D.C., May 26, 2004.

47. Author's interview with Camdessus.

48. Author's interview with Bernes.

49. Author's interview with Willy Kiekens, Washington, D.C., February 17, 2004.

50. Minutes of the Executive Board Meeting, p. 4, April 2, 1998, EBM/98/38 (IMF Archives).

51. Author's interview with Jack Boorman, Washington, D.C., September 23, 2003.

52. Author's interview with Summers.

53. Author's interview with Dallara.

54. Author's interview with Summers.

55. Author's interview with Lex Rieffel, Brookings Institution, Washington, D.C., May 25, 2004.

56. Author's interview with Dallara.

57. Michel Camdessus, "The IMF at Fifty—An Evolving Role but a Constant Mission," address at the Institute for International Economics, Washington, D.C., June 7, 1994, MD/Sp/94/6 (IMF Archives).

58. "Issues and Developments in the International Exchange and Payments System," prepared by the Monetary and Exchange Affairs Department, July 29, 1994, SM/94/202 (IMF Archives), p. 25.

59. For an overview, see Rawi Abdelal, "The IMF and the Capital Account," in *Reforming the IMF*, ed. Edwin M. Truman (Washington, D.C.: Institute for International Economics, 2006).

60. Quirk, Evans, and IMF Staff Teams, *Capital Account Convertibility*, p. 1. Also see IMF, *Annual Report, 1994* (Washington, D.C.: IMF, 1994), p. 26, cited in Alloway.

61. "Concluding Remarks by the Acting Chairman for the Seminar on Issues and Developments in the International Exchange and Payments System," Executive Board Seminar, November 16, 1994, BUFF/94/106 (IMF Archives), p. 2.

62. IMF, *Annual Report, 1995* (Washington, D.C.: IMF, 1995), p. 49, cited in Alloway.

63. "Capital Account Convertibility," July 7, 1995, p. 8. Many of these same sentences later appeared in Quirk et al., *Capital Account Convertibility*, p. 5.

64. G7, "The Halifax Summit Review of the International Financial Institutions," June 16, 1995.

65. "Capital Account Convertibility," July 7, 1995, p. 1. The IMF defines twenty-three countries as industrial: Australia, Austria, Belgium, Canada, Denmark, France, Finland, Germany, Greece, Iceland, Ireland, Italy, Japan, Luxembourg, the Netherlands, New Zealand, Norway, Portugal, Spain, Sweden, Switzerland, the United Kingdom, and the United States.

66. Nearly every member of the Fund's staff and management with whom I spoke emphasized the advocacy of Manuel Guitián.

67. Minutes of the Executive Board Meeting, July 28, 1995, EBM/95/73 (IMF Archives), p. 63.

68. Manuel Guitián, "The Issue of Capital Account Convertibility: A Gap between Norms and Reality," in *Currency Convertibility in the Middle East and North Africa*, ed. Manuel Guitián and Saleh M. Nsouli (Washington, D.C.: IMF, 1996), p. 186. Also see Manuel Guitián, "Capital Account Liberalization: Bringing Policy in Line with Reality," in *Capital Controls, Exchange Rates, and Monetary Policy in the World Economy*, ed. Sebastian Edwards (Cambridge: Cambridge University Press, 1995), pp. 71–90; and Manuel Guitián, "Reality and the Logic of Capital Flow Liberalization," in *Capital Controls in Emerging Economies*, ed. Christine P. Ries and Richard J. Sweeney (Boulder, Colo.: Westview, 1997), pp. 17–31.

69. Author's interview with Camdessus.

70. Quoted in IEO, *The IMF's Approach to Capital Account Liberalization*, pp. 34–35.
71. Author's interview with Matthew Fisher, Washington, D.C., September 26, 2003.
72. Author's interview with Boorman.
73. Author's interview the Kiekens.
74. "The Acting Chairman's Summing Up of Capital Account Convertibility— Review of Experience and Implications for Fund Policies," Executive Board Meeting, July 28, 1995, BUFF/95/83 (IMF Archives), p. 2.
75. Minutes of the Executive Board Meeting, July 28, 1995, EBM/95/73 (IMF Archives).
76. Ibid., p. 20.
77. Ibid., p. 22.
78. Ibid., p. 21.
79. See "Review of Experience with Capital Account Liberalization and Strengthened Procedures Adopted by the Fund," pp. 29–40.
80. "Capital Account Convertibility and the Role of the Fund," February 5, 1997, p. 7.
81. See the board discussion:

> We have reached broad agreement on the text of the amendment to the Articles that would express that purpose in general terms, by amending Article I (ii) and (iv) as follows (modifications are indicated): "(ii) To facilitate the expansion and balanced growth of international trade in goods and services and an efficient international allocation of capital, and to contribute thereby to the promotion and maintenance of high levels of employment and real income and the development of the productive resources of all members as primary objectives of economic policy." "(iv) To assist in the establishment of a multilateral system of payments in respect of current and capital transactions between members, in the orderly liberalization of international capital movements, and in the elimination of foreign exchange restrictions which would hamper world trade and investment."

> "Concluding Remarks by the Acting Chairman of Liberalization of Capital Movements Under an Amendment of the Articles," Executive Board Meeting, April 2, 1998, BUFF/98/41 (IMF Archives), p. 2. Proposed amendments are italicized. The amendment would also involve rewriting Article VI, "Capital Transfers." See "Capital Account Convertibility and the Role of the Fund," February 5, 1997, pp. 30–31.

82. "Concluding Remarks by the Chairman of Capital Account Convertibility and the Role of the Fund: Review of Experience and Consideration of a Possible Amendment of the Articles," Executive Board Seminar, February 26, 1997, BUFF/97/21 (IMF Archives), p. 1.
83. Ibid., p. 2.
84. Author's interview with Camdessus.
85. Author's interview with Fisher.
86. Author's interview with Bernes.
87. Ibid.

88. On the role of the G7 in international financial governance, see Andrew Baker, "The G7 and Architecture Debates: Norms, Authority, and Global Financial Governance," in *International Financial Governance under Stress*, ed. Underhill and Zhang; and Daniel W. Drezner, "Clubs, Neighborhoods, and Universes: The Governance of Global Finance," paper presented at the annual meeting of the American Political Science Association, Philadelphia, August 28–31, 2003.

89. On the skepticism of Paul Martin and Jean Chrétien with regard to the liberalization of capital, as well as their encouragement of the Bernes position on the executive board, see John J. Kirton, "Canada as a Principal Financial Power: G-7 and IMF Diplomacy in the Crises of 1997–99," *International Journal*, vol. 54, no. 4 (1999), pp. 603–624, especially pp. 607–608.

90. Author's interview with Bernes.

91. "Statement by Mr. Bernes on Capital Account Convertibility and the Role of the Fund," Executive Board Meeting, February 26, 1997 (Bernes' copy).

92. Author's interview with Bernes.

93. "Summing Up by the Chairman of Capital Account Convertibility and a Possible Amendment of the Articles," Executive Board Meeting, April 15, 1997, BUFF/97/39 (IMF Archives), p. 1.

94. Minutes of the Executive Board Meeting, April 15, 1997, EBM/97/38 (IMF Archives).

95. Ibid., pp. 37–39.

96. Communiqué of the Interim Committee of the Board of Governors of the IMF, IMF Press Release #97–22, April 28, 1997. For the organization's coverage of the spring meetings, see David M. Cheney, "IMF Wins Mandate to Cover Capital Accounts, Debt Initiative Put in Motion," *IMF Survey*, vol. 26, no. 9 (May 12, 1997), pp. 129–130.

97. Author's interview with Boorman.

98. Author's interview with Kiekens.

99. Author's interview with Matthew Fisher, Washington, D.C., April 26, 2002.

100. Quoted from the opening press conference of the IMF's spring meeting, "Camdessus on Globalization, Capital Account, IMF Support for Social Spending," *IMF Survey*, vol. 26, no. 9, (May 12, 1997), p. 134.

101. Minutes of the Executive Board Meeting, June 30, 1997, EBM/97/66 (IMF Archives), p. 59.

102. Ibid., p. 71.

103. See Ibid.; Minutes of the Executive Board Meeting, July 15, 1997, EBM/97/72 (IMF Archives); and Minutes of the Executive Board Meeting, August 26, 1997, EBM/97/87 (IMF Archives).

104. "Concluding Remarks by the Acting Chairman of Capital Movements Under an Amendment of the Articles—Concepts of 'International Capital Movements' and 'Restrictions,'" Executive Board Meeting, July 2, 1997, BUFF/97/69 (IMF Archives), p. 1. For more on the board's deliberations of inward direct investment, see Minutes of the Executive Board Meeting, June 30, 1997, EBM/97/66 (IMF Archives); Minutes of the Executive Board Meeting, July 15, 1997, EBM/97/72 (IMF Archives); Minutes of the Executive Board Meeting, August 26,

1997, EBM/97/87 (IMF Archives); "Capital Movements under an Amendment of the Articles—Treatment of Inward Direct Investment," prepared by the Legal Department, June 27, 1997, SM/97/168; and "Capital Movements Under an Amendment of the Articles—The Treatment of Inward Direct Investment—Selected Issues for Discussion," prepared by the Legal Department, July 11, 1997, SM/97/168 Supplement 1 (IMF Archives). The background paper is "Capital Movements Under an Amendment of the Articles—Concepts of 'International Capital Movements' and 'Restrictions,'" prepared by the Legal Department, June 10, 1997, SM/97/146 (IMF Archives).

105. "Concluding Remarks by the Acting Chairman of Capital Account Convertibility—Transitional Arrangements, Approval Policies, and Implications for Financing; and Capital Movements Under an Amendment of the Articles—the Treatment of Inward Direct Investment," Executive Board Meeting, July 18, 1997, BUFF/97/74 (IMF Archives), p. 2. See also Minutes of the Executive Board Meeting, July 15, 1997, EBM/97/72 (IMF Archives); "Capital Account Convertibility—Transitional Arrangements, Approval Policies, and Financing Under an Amendment," prepared by the Policy Development and Review, Monetary and Exchange Affairs, and Legal Departments," July 1, 1997, SM/97/173 (IMF Archives); "Capital Movements Under an Amendment of the Articles—Transitional Arrangements, Approval Policies, and Implications for Financing: Status of Deliberations and Further Considerations," prepared by the Legal, Monetary and Exchange Affairs, and Policy Development and Review Departments, August 12, 1997, SM/97/210 (IMF Archives).

106. For the board's report, see "Report to the Interim Committee on the Liberalization of Capital Movements Under an Amendment of the Articles," September 10, 1997, ICMS/Doc/49/97/12 (IMF Archives). For the evolution of the language of the executive board's report, see "Draft Report to the Interim Committee on the Liberalization of Capital Movements Under an Amendment of the Articles," September 4, 1997, SM/97/230; September 9, 1997, SM/97/230 Revision 1; September 10, 1997, SM/97/230 Revision 2 (IMF Archives). For the evolution of the language of the Interim Committee's statement, see "Draft Statement of the Interim Committee on the Liberalization of Capital Movements Under an Amendment of the Articles," September 8, 1997, EBS/97/171; September 11, 1997, EBS/97/171 Revision 1 (IMF Archives).

107. *Capital Account Convertibility as an IMF Obligation: A Briefing Note for the IIF Board of Directors*, unpublished memorandum, Institute of International Finance, Washington, D.C., September 9, 1997, p. 3.

108. Ibid., p. 5.

109. Ibid., p. 2.

110. Quoted in "Fuse Lit Under IMF Powers: Proposed New Powers for the IMF, Intended to Help Avert or Lessen the Impact of a Financial Crisis, Have Caused Alarm in Sections of the Financial Community," *The Banker*, September 1, 1997.

111. Ibid.

112. Quoted in "IMF/World Bank: Can Banking Systems Cope? The Historic Hong

Kong Meetings Will Discuss Controversial New Powers for the IMF in Response to Recent Financial Crises," *The Banker,* September 1, 1997.

113. Communiqué of the Interim Committee of the Board of Governors of the IMF, IMF Press Release #97–44, September 21, 1997. For a record of the discussion in Hong Kong, see "Forty-Ninth Meeting of the Interim Committee—Formal Plenary Meeting—Record of Discussion," September 21, 1997, ICMS/Mtg/ 49/97/1 (IMF Archives).

114. Interim Committee of the IMF, *The Liberalization of Capital Movements Under an Amendment of the IMF's Articles,* Hong Kong, September 21, 1997. Also see "Capital Liberalization Essential to an Efficient Monetary System," *IMF Survey,* vol. 26, no. 18 (October 6, 1997), pp. 302–303.

115. "1997 Annual Meetings—Excerpts from Speeches by Governors," October 6, 1997, EBD/97/111 (IMF Archives), p. 26.

116. Author's interview with J. Onno de Beaufort Wijnholds, Washington, D.C., February 17, 2004.

117. "Forty-Ninth Meeting of the Interim Committee," p. 22.

118. Ibid., p. 30.

119. Ibid., p. 71.

120. Communiqué of the Intergovernmental Group of Twenty-Four on International Monetary Affairs, September 20, 1997. Also see Aziz Ali Mohammed, "Issues Relating to the Treatment of Capital Movements in the IMF," in *Capital Account Regimes and the Developing Countries,* ed. G. K. Helleiner (New York: St. Martin's and UNCTAD, 1998). The Group of 24 (G24), a chapter of the G77, was established in 1971 to coordinate the positions of developing countries on international financial issues.

121. "Address by Michel Camdessus, Chairman of the Executive Board and Managing Director of the International Monetary Fund, to the Board of Governors of the Fund, Hong Kong, China," September 23, 1997, MD/Sp/97/111 (IMF Archives). Also see the coverage in David M. Cheney, "Annual Meetings: IMF Given Role in Fostering Freer Capital Flows; Quota Increase, SDR Allocation Agreed," *IMF Survey,* vol. 26, no. 18 (October 6, 1997), pp. 289–292.

122. Author's interview with de Larosière.

123. Author's interview with Kiekens.

124. Sara Kane, "Seminar Discusses the Orderly Path to Capital Account Liberalization," *IMF Survey,* vol. 27, no. 6 (March 23, 1998), pp. 81–84.

125. "Deputy Secretary Summers' Remarks before the International Monetary Fund," March 9, 1998, U.S. Treasury Press Release RR-2286. This statement is much more supportive of the amendment than later reflections of Treasury officials. Apparently the statement was drafted primarily by the U.S. executive director's staff.

126. Polak, "The Articles of Agreement of the IMF and the Liberalization of Capital Movements," pp. 50, 52.

127. Minutes of the Executive Board Meeting, April 2, 1998, EBM/98/38 (IMF Archives), pp. 8–9.

128. Ibid., pp. 18–19.
129. Ralf Leiteritz, "Explaining Organizational Outcomes: The International Monetary Fund and Capital Account Liberalization," *Journal of International Relations and Development*, vol. 8, no. 1 (2005), pp. 1–26.
130. Communiqué of the Interim Committee of the Board of Governors of the IMF, IMF Press Release #98–14, April 1998.
131. Letter from Charles H. Dallara, Managing Director of the Institute of International Finance, to His Excellency, Minister Philippe Maystadt, Chairman of the Interim Committee, April 8, 1998.
132. See Robert Rubin and Jacob Weisberg, *In an Uncertain World: Tough Choices from Wall Street to Washington* (New York: Random House, 2003), pp. 266–271.
133. Author's interview with Lissakers.
134. Letter to the Honorable Robert E. Rubin, Secretary, Department of the Treasury, from Reps. Richard Gephardt, David Bonior, Nancy Pelosi, Barney Frank, Maxine Waters, and Esteban Edward Torres, May 1, 1998. Also see Eric Schmitt, "Democrats Threaten to Oppose I.M.F. Bill," *New York Times*, May 2, 1998; and Nancy Dunne, "Democrat Obstacle to IMF Funding," *Financial Times*, May 4, 1998.
135. Author's confidential interview with a former senior U.S. Treasury official.
136. Author's interview with Summers.
137. Author's interview with Wijnholds.
138. Author's interview with Kiekens.
139. Author's interview with Aleksei Mozhin, Washington, D.C., February 18, 2004.
140. Author's interview with Boorman.
141. Author's interview with Mozhin.

Chapter 7: A Common Language of Risk

1. Marie Cavanaugh, *Credit FAQ: Foreign/Local Currency and Sovereign/Nonsovereign Ratings Differentials* (New York: Standard & Poor's, September 22, 2003). Factors that can allow an issuer to receive a rating higher than the government of the country in which it is based include an offshore parent company and having a significant percentage of its business or assets abroad.
2. On the origins of sovereign debt markets, see Niall Ferguson, *The Cash Nexus: Money and Power in the Modern World, 1700–2000* (New York: Basic, 2001), chaps. 4–6.
3. See Grabel, "The Political Economy of 'Policy Credibility,'" pp. 1–19.
4. Jonathan Kirshner, "The Study of Money," *World Politics*, vol. 52, no. 3 (2000), pp. 407–436, at p. 423.
5. Keynes, *The General Theory of Employment, Interest, and Money*, pp. 155–156. On the "herding" of investors with short horizons on information that may be irrelevant to fundamentals, see Kenneth A. Froot, David S. Scharfstein, and Jeremy C. Stein, "Herd on the Street: Informational Inefficiencies in a Market with Short-Term Speculation," *Journal of Finance*, vol. 47, no. 4 (1992), pp. 1461–1484.

6. See Abdelal and Bruner, *Private Capital and Public Policy.*

7. See, for example, Claire A. Cutler, Virginia Haufler, and Tony Porter, eds., *Private Authority in International Affairs* (Albany, N.Y.: State University of New York Press, 1999); and Rodney Bruce Hall and Thomas J. Biersteker, eds., *The Emergence of Private Authority in Global Governance* (Cambridge: Cambridge University Press, 2002). On the rating agencies see especially, Timothy J. Sinclair, "Global Monitor: Bond Rating Agencies," *New Political Economy*, vol. 8, no. 1 (2003), pp. 147–161, and Sinclair, *The New Masters of Capital.* In *The New Masters of Capital,* Sinclair focuses on the agencies in general, rather than on sovereign ratings, which he covers on pp. 137–147.

8. Bruner and Abdelal, "To Judge Leviathan," pp. 191–217. On the use of ratings in U.S. and other countries' financial regulations, see Securities and Exchange Commission, *Report on the Role and Function of Credit Rating Agencies in the Operation of the Securities Markets,* January 2003, pp. 3–5; and Bank for International Settlements, *Credit Ratings and Complementary Sources of Credit Quality Information,* Basel Committee on Banking Supervision Working Paper No. 3, August 2000, p. 40. The Bank for International Settlements reported that of the twelve member countries of the Basel Committee on Banking Supervision, eleven used ratings in national financial regulations (Germany was the exception). Of six "interesting nonmembers"—Australia, Argentina, Chile, Hong Kong, Mexico, and New Zealand—only one (Mexico) did not use ratings in national financial regulations. The same three firms—Moody's, S&P, and Fitch—were those whose ratings were used by regulators in all sixteen of these countries.

9. See, for example, Dieter Kerwer, "Rating Agencies: Setting a Standard for Global Financial Markets," *Economic Sociology European Electronic Newsletter,* vol. 3, no. 3 (2002), pp. 40–46, at p. 45 (describing the "accountability gap" resulting from the codification of agency ratings).

10. See especially Sylla, "An Historical Primer on the Business of Credit Rating," pp. 22–24.

11. On the evolution of the U.S. approach to the regulation of railroads, see Thomas K. McCraw, *Prophets of Regulation* (Cambridge, Mass.: The Belknap Press of Harvard University Press, 1984), chaps. 1 and 2. On the divergence of regulatory approaches to the railroads in the United States and Europe, see Frank Dobbin, *Forging Industrial Policy: The United States, Britain, and France in the Railway Age* (Cambridge: Cambridge University Press, 1994).

12. Alfred D. Chandler, Jr., *The Visible Hand: The Managerial Revolution in American Business* (Cambridge, Mass.: The Belknap Press of Harvard University Press, 1977), p. 187.

13. John C. Coffee, Jr., "The Rise of Dispersed Ownership: The Roles of Law and the State in the Separation of Ownership and Control," *Yale Law Journal,* no. 111 (2001), pp. 1–82, at pp. 25–26.

14. See Alfred D. Chandler, Jr., *Henry Varnum Poor: Business Editor, Analyst, and Reformer* (Cambridge, Mass.: Harvard University Press, 1956). Chandler, Henry Poor's great-grandson, had completed his doctoral dissertation at Harvard on Poor as well in 1952: *The Pen in Business: A Biography of Henry Varnum Poor.*

15. Only Canada, exempt from the interest equalization tax, was still rated. See Abdelal and Bruner, *Private Capital and Public Policy*, p. 4. Also see *Sovereign Ratings before the Interest Equalization Tax* (New York: Standard & Poor's, April 5, 1999).

16. See Abdelal and Bruner, *Private Capital and Public Policy*, p. 9; BIS, *Credit Ratings and Complementary Sources of Credit Quality Information*, pp. 14–15; SEC, *Report on the Role and Function of Credit Rating Agencies*, pp. 5–13. NRSRO status was also extended to four other firms, all of which were acquired by or merged with the original three. Other NRSRO criteria are: organizational structure; financial resources; size and quality of staff; independence from issuers; rating procedures; and internal mechanisms to prevent abuse of nonpublic information.

17. Timothy J. Sinclair, "Between State and Market: Hegemony and Institutions of Collective Action under Conditions of International Capital Mobility," *Policy Sciences*, vol. 27, no. 4 (1994), pp. 447–466; and Michael R. King and Timothy J. Sinclair, "Private Actors and Public Policy: A Requiem for the Basel Capital Accord," *International Political Science Review*, vol. 24, no. 3 (2003), pp. 345–362.

18. Richard Cantor and Frank Packer, "The Credit Rating Industry," *Journal of Fixed Income*, vol. 5, no. 3 (1995), pp. 10–34, at p. 15.

19. When firms split the market, economists refer to the outcome as a Cournot duopoly; when firms compete away the rents, it is a Bertrand duopoly. The logics were first outlined by the nineteenth-century French scholars Antoine Augustin Cournot and Joseph Bertrand.

20. Charles D. Brown, Response Letter to SEC Concept Release: Rating Agencies and the Use of Credit Ratings under the Federal Securities Law, July 28, 2003.

21. See Jeff Jewell and Miles Livingston, "A Comparison of Bond Ratings from Moody's, S&P, and Fitch IBCA," *Financial Markets, Institutions, and Instruments*, vol. 8, no. 4 (1999), pp. 1–45, at p. 3.

22. BIS, *Credit Ratings and Complementary Sources of Credit Quality Information*, p. 14.

23. Ashok Vir Bhatia, "Sovereign Credit Ratings Methodology: An Evaluation," IMF Working Paper WP/02/170, October 2002, p. 46.

24. See The McGraw-Hill Companies, Inc., Quarterly Report for the quarter ended June 30, 2004, p. 20, and Moody's Corporation, Annual Report on Form 10-K for the fiscal year ended December 31, 2003, p. 28.

25. See, for example, the discussion in Lawrence J. White, "The Credit Rating Industry: An Industrial Organization Analysis," in *Ratings, Rating Agencies, and the Global Financial System*, ed. Levich, Majnoni, and Reinhart, pp. 41–42.

26. Cantor and Packer, "The Credit Rating Industry," pp. 15–16.

27. Frank Partnoy, "The Siskel and Ebert of Financial Markets? Two Thumbs Down for the Credit Rating Agencies," *Washington University Law Quarterly*, no. 77 (1999), pp. 619–712, at p. 690. Partnoy distinguishes between "reputational capital" and "regulatory licensing." The same distinction, using different terminology, is drawn by Smith and Walter, who write of "signaling" and "certification." See Roy C. Smith and Ingo Walter, "Rating Agencies: Is There an Agency Issue?" in *Ratings, Rating Agencies, and the Global Financial System*, ed. Levich, Majnoni, and Reinhart, p. 292. Similar concerns are raised by White, who writes of the

"growing regulatory demand" for ratings, a demand that implies that "the current presence of the major incumbents is no automatic assurance that they continue to meet a market test." See his "The Credit Rating Industry," p. 44. Thus, although Partnoy has put his case forward provocatively, the ideas have received widespread support. "Partnoy's complaint needs to be taken seriously," Sylla writes. See Sylla, "An Historical Primer on the Business of Credit Rating," p. 37.

28. Smith and Walter, "Rating Agencies," p. 308.
29. Author's interview with David Levey, New York, February 4, 2005.
30. Hendrik J. Kranenburg, "Ratings as Eligibility Criteria," *Standard & Poor's Credit-Week International,* September 6, 1993, p. 27.
31. Cantor and Packer, "The Credit Rating Industry," p. 20.
32. For example, see generally Reisen and von Maltzan, "Boom and Bust and Sovereign Ratings," pp. 273–293; and Manfred Steiner and Volker G. Heinke, "Event Study Concerning International Bond Price Effects of Credit Rating Actions," *International Journal of Finance and Economics,* vol. 6, no. 2 (2001), pp. 139–157 (examining Eurobond returns following agency announcements).
33. Cantor and Packer, "The Credit Rating Industry," p. 18.
34. Sinclair, "Between State and Market," esp. p. 448; King and Sinclair, "Private Actors and Public Policy," esp. p. 346.
35. Alternatively, one might argue that the agencies are both private and public. That is, they are private entities that play a distinct and specialized global and public "governance function." See Alexander Cooley, *Logics of Hierarchy: The Organization of Empires, States, and Military Occupations* (Ithaca, N.Y.: Cornell University Press, 2005), chap. 7.
36. For a longer discussion of this issue, see Bruner and Abdelal, "To Judge Leviathan."
37. John Gerard Ruggie, "Reconstituting the Global Public Domain: Issues, Actors, and Practices," *European Journal of International Relations,* vol. 10, no. 4 (2004), pp. 499–531, at pp. 503–504.
38. Quoted in Abdelal and Bruner, *Private Capital and Public Policy,* p. 1.
39. David Levey and Elina Kolmanovskaya, "Sovereign Rating History," in *Moody's Rating Methodology Handbook: Sovereign* (New York: Moody's Investors Service, 2002), p. 77; and Richard Cantor and Frank Packer, "Sovereign Credit Ratings," *Federal Reserve Bank of New York Current Issues in Economics and Finance,* vol. 1, no. 3 (1995), pp. 1–6, at p. 2.
40. See Alec Klein, "Smoothing the Way for Debt Markets: Firms' Influence Has Grown Along with World's Reliance on Bonds," *Washington Post,* November 23, 2004, and Levey and Kolmanovskaya, "Sovereign Rating History," p. 77.
41. The McGraw-Hill Companies, Inc., *2004 Investor Fact Book* (New York: McGraw-Hill, 2004) and On the importance of sovereign ratings for the rest of the market, see also Bhatia, "Sovereign Credit Ratings Methodology," p. 47.
42. Author's interview with Levey.
43. Quoted in Abdelal and Bruner, *Private Capital and Public Policy,* p. 4.
44. David T. Beers, *Credit FAQ: The Future of Sovereign Credit Ratings* (New York: Standard & Poor's, March 23, 2004).
45. Levey and Kolmanovskaya, "Sovereign Rating History," p. 78.

46. John Chambers and David T. Beers, *Sovereign Ratings Display Stability over Two Decades* (New York: Standard & Poor's, April 5, 1999).

47. Few other firms rated sovereigns. Fitch is an exception, and by 2005 rated eighty-nine sovereigns. Toronto-based Dominion, rates only one sovereign, Canada, for purposes of rating Canadian issuers.

48. Author's interview with Levey.

49. *Fitch Sovereign Ratings: Rating Methodology* (New York: Fitch, 2002), p. 4.

50. Mara Hilderman, *Opening the Black Box: The Rating Committee Process at Moody's* (New York: Moody's Investors Service, 1999), p. 1.

51. David Levey, "Sources and Uses of Moody's Country Credit Statistics and Ratios," in *Moody's Rating Methodology Handbook: Sovereign*, p. 89.

52. Author's interview with Levey.

53. See, for example, Richard Cantor and Frank Packer, "Determinants and Impact of Sovereign Credit Ratings," *Federal Reserve Bank of New York Economic Policy Review*, vol. 2, no. 2 (1996), pp. 37–54, at pp. 40–41.

54. Author's interview with Levey. Cantor and Packer report "a residual standard error of about 1.2 rating notches." Cantor and Packer, "Determinants and Impact of Sovereign Credit Ratings," p. 41.

55. See International Organization of Securities Commissions, *Report on the Activities of Credit Rating Agencies*, September 2003, p. 4. Also see Rawi Abdelal and Christopher M. Bruner, *Standard & Poor's Sovereign Credit Ratings: Scales and Process*, Harvard Business School Note 705–027 (2005); *Fitch Sovereign Ratings*, pp. 5–8; and Hilderman, *Opening the Black Box*, esp. pp. 3–6.

56. David T. Beers and Marie Cavanaugh, *Sovereign Credit Ratings: A Primer* (New York: Standard & Poor's, March 15, 2004).

57. Bhatia, "Sovereign Credit Ratings Methodology," pp. 4–5.

58. BIS, *Credit Ratings and Complementary Sources of Credit Quality Information*, p. 127.

59. Sinclair, "Between State and Market," p. 454.

60. Sinclair describes this as the "mental framework of rating orthodoxy," in *The New Masters of Capital*, p. 17. I am inclined to be less sweeping in characterizing the interpretive frameworks of the agencies, first because they differ among the firms, and second because they may be related in complex ways to the market's prevailing conceptions of orthodoxy.

61. Sinclair, "Between State and Market," p. 459. Also see Sinclair, *The New Masters of Capital*, chap. 1.

62. I do not delve into Fitch's documentation of its interpretive framework, though it appears from a reading of a few documents about methodology that Fitch's is significantly more ideologically derived, and less inductive, than either S&P's or Moody's. Fitch's official elaboration of its own interpretive framework appeared to celebrate the end of history: "The conspicuous failure of world communism removes any plausible alternative to the capitalist mode of development." See *Fitch Sovereign Ratings*, p. 3.

63. Author's interview with Levey.

64. Quoted in Abdelal and Bruner, *Private Capital and Public Policy*, p. 7.

65. Bhatia, "Sovereign Credit Ratings Methodology," pp. 26–27.

66. The following quotations are from Marie Cavanaugh, *Sovereign Credit Characteristics by Rating Category* (New York: Standard & Poor's, November 19, 2003).

67. Beers and Cavanaugh, *Sovereign Credit Ratings: A Primer.*

68. Ibid.

69. Author's interview with Levey.

70. Ibid.

71. Ibid.

72. Ibid.

73. David H. Levey, "Sovereign Nations," in *Global Credit Analysis* (New York: Moody's Investors Service, 1990), p. 161.

74. Ibid., pp. 182–183. Moody's methodological statements have been interpreted, however, as "favour[ing] what [Stephen] Gill has called the 'new constitutionalism,'" a doctrine that, among things, "'is intended to guarantee the freedom of entry and exit of internationally mobile capital without regard to different socioeconomic spaces.'" Sinclair, "Between State and Market," p. 458.

75. Levey, "Sovereign Nations," pp. 169–170.

76. Ibid., p. 186.

77. Cantor and Packer, "Determinants and Impact of Sovereign Credit Ratings," p. 45.

78. Ibid., p. 47. Interestingly, Cantor and Packer also found that "Announcements by Moody's . . . have a larger impact than announcements by Standard and Poor's," at p. 48, suggesting that despite their joint dominance, the market does not necessarily view their perspectives as entirely interchangeable.

79. Guillermo Larrain, Helmut Reisen, and Julian von Maltzan, "Emerging Market Risk and Sovereign Credit Ratings," OECD Development Centre Technical Paper No. 124, April 1997.

80. Sinclair observes the rating agencies' orthodoxy with respect to the separation of powers and fiscal deficits. See Sinclair, *The New Masters of Capital*, pp. 137,145. My focus is on the agencies' interpretations of capital controls and liberalizations.

81. Mahesh K. Kotecha, "Future of International Ratings," *Standard & Poor's CreditWeek*, November 9, 1981, p. 489.

82. Philip S. Bates, "Venezuela (Republic of)," *Standard & Poor's International CreditWeek*, Second Quarter 1983, p. 34.

83. Barbara Nunemaker, "France's 'AAA' Debt Guarantee Affirmed," *Standard & Poor's International CreditWeek*, June 1985, p. 12.

84. Philip M. Hubbard, "International Market Comes of Age," *Standard & Poor's CreditWeek*, June 23, 1986, p. 39.

85. Philip S. Bates and William J. Chambers, "Sovereign Policy Update: Denmark," *Standard & Poor's International CreditWeek*, December 1986, p. 16. For the same language, nearly verbatim, see Philip S. Bates and William J. Chambers, "Offshore Domestic Currency Debt," *Standard & Poor's International CreditWeek*, May 25, 1987, p. 6.

86. Helena Hessel and Philip S. Bates, "Comparing Countries' External Positions," *Standard & Poor's International CreditWeek*, May 25, 1987, p. 3.

87. See especially Helena Hessel, "Cautiously Optimistic Ratings Outlook," *Standard & Poor's International CreditWeek*, December 5, 1998; Guido Cipriani, "Italy (Republic of)," *Standard & Poor's International CreditWeek*, December 5, 1998; and Pablo Scheffel, "Portugal (Republic of)," *Standard & Poor's International CreditWeek*, December 5, 1998.

88. David Munves and Lars Björkland, "Sweden's Capital Market Enters New Era," *Standard & Poor's International CreditWeek*, April 3, 1989, p. 14.

89. Helena Hessel, "France (Republic of)," *Standard & Poor's International CreditWeek*, June 5, 1989, p. 41.

90. Philip Bates, "European Monetary Union Alters Credit Landscape," *Standard & Poor's CreditWeek International*, May 4, 1992, p. 52.

91. George Dallas, "Waiting for the Spanish Fixed Income Market," *Standard & Poor's CreditWeek International*, November 2, 1992, pp. 101–102.

92. William J. Chambers, *Understanding Sovereign Risk* (New York: Standard & Poor's, August 20, 1997).

93. Cem Karacadag and David T. Beers, *Malaysian Ratings Outlook Revised to Negative by S&P* (New York: Standard & Poor's, September 25, 1997).

94. See Rawi Abdelal and Laura Alfaro, *Malaysia: Capital and Control*, Harvard Business School Case 702–040 (2002).

95. Rawi Abdelal and Laura Alfaro, "Capital and Control: Lessons from Malaysia," *Challenge*, vol. 46, no. 4 (2003), pp. 36–53.

96. Paul Rawkins, *Malaysia Downgraded to 'BB'* (London: Fitch IBCA, September 9, 1998).

97. Vincent Truglia and Steve Hess, *Moody's Downgrades and Leaves on Review for Possible Further Downgrade Malaysia's Foreign Currency Country Ceilings* (New York: Moody's Investors Service, September 14, 1998).

98. Ashok Bhatia, David T. Beers, and John Chambers, *Malaysia's Ratings Cut by S&P; Outlook Still Negative* (New York: Standard & Poor's, September 15, 1998).

99. David T. Beers et al., *Government Policy Responses Key to Ratings in Emerging Markets Says S&P* (New York: Standard & Poor's, September 24, 1998).

100. Abdelal and Alfaro, "Capital and Control."

101. See, for an excellent example, Jeffrey Fear, *Banking on Germany?*, Harvard Business School Case 703–028 (2003).

102. Smith and Walter, "Rating Agencies," p. 313.

103. Reisen and von Maltzan, "Boom and Bust in Sovereign Ratings"; Ferri, Liu, and Stiglitz, "The Procyclical Role of Rating Agencies," pp. 335–355; Kaminsky and Schmukler, "Rating Agencies and Financial Markets," and Carmen Reinhart, "Sovereign Credit Ratings before and after Financial Crises," both in *Ratings, Rating Agencies, and the Global Financial System*, ed. Levich, Majnoni, and Reinhart.

104. Reinhart, "Sovereign Credit Ratings before and after Financial Crises," p. 264.

105. John Chambers and Daria Alexeeva, *2003 Transition Data Update for Rated Sovereigns* (New York: Standard & Poor's, January 30, 2004).

106. On European resentment toward the rating agencies, see Sinclair, *The New Masters of Capital*, pp. 133–134. This resentment has been building for some time. See Klaus Engelen, "A European Nightmare: Unchecked American Rating

Agencies Become Continent's New Boss-Men," *International Economy,* vol. 7, no. 6 (1994), pp. 46–50.

107. European Parliament Committee on Economic and Monetary Affairs (Giorgos Katiforis, rapporteur), *Report on Role and Methods of Rating Agencies,* January 29, 2004, 2003/2081(INI).

108. Nikolaus Bömcke, Letter to Giorgis Katiforis on Draft Report on the Role and Method of Credit Rating Agencies, January 8, 2004.

109. European Parliament Resolution on Role and Methods of Rating Agencies (2003/2081[INI]), February 10, 2004.

110. Moody's Corporation, Annual Report on Form 10-K for the fiscal year ended December 31, 2004, p. 9.

111. Autorité des marchés financiers, *2004 AMF Report on Rating Agencies,* January 2005, p. 35.

112. Ibid., pp. 31–32, 37–39.

113. Ibid., pp. 4, 5.

114. Ibid., p. 55.

115. King and Sinclair, "Private Actors and Public Policy," p. 348. Also see Sinclair, "Global Monitor," pp. 155–156; and Sinclair, *The New Masters of Capital,* chap. 7.

116. *DOJ Urges SEC to Increase Competition for Securities Rating Agencies* (Washington, D.C.: U.S. Department of Justice, March 6, 1998).

117. Statement of Richard Shelby, U.S. Senate Committee on Banking, Housing, and Urban Affairs, "Examining the Role of Credit Rating Agencies in the Capital Markets," February 8, 2005.

118. Leo C. O'Neill, Response Letter to SEC Concept Release: Rating Agencies and the Use of Credit Ratings under the Federal Securities Laws, July 28, 2003.

119. Raymond W. McDaniel, Response Letter to SEC Concept Release: Rating Agencies and the Use of Credit Ratings under the Federal Securities Laws, July 28, 2003.

120. Hal S. Scott, *International Finance: Law and Regulation* (London: Sweet & Maxwell, 2004), p. 193.

121. For a comprehensive review and analysis, see King and Sinclair, "Private Actors and Public Policy."

122. *Basel II International Convergence of Capital Measurement and Capital Standards: A Revised Framework, Part 2: The First Pillar—Minimum Capital Requirements,* Basel Committee Publications No. 107, June 2004; and *Basel II: International Convergence of Capital Measurement and Capital Standards: A Revised Framework,* Basel Committee Publications No. 107, June 2004.

123. See, for example, Brendan Murphy, "Credit Ratings and Emerging Economies," *Freidrich Ebert Stiftung Digitale Bibliothek* (2000), Section III. See also King and Sinclair's observation in "Private Actors and Public Policy," at p. 352: "The new capital adequacy framework will stunt the growth of firms in developing countries by raising their cost of capital relative to firms in the wealthy countries."

124. Fear, *Banking on Germany?*

125. White, "The Credit Rating Industry," pp. 41–42.

126. Ibid., p. 56.
127. Edward I. Altman and Anthony Saunders, "The Role of Credit Ratings in Bank Capital," in *Ratings, Rating Agencies, and the Global Financial System*, ed. Levich, Majnoni, and Reinhart, p. 102. For more on the potentially procyclical effects of Basel II, see King and Sinclair, "Private Actors and Public Policy," pp. 348–351.
128. Standard & Poor's, *Basel Committee on Banking Supervision Third Consultation Paper: Standard & Poor's Response* (New York: Standard & Poor's, August 22, 2003); Abdelal and Bruner, *Private Capital and Public Policy*, p. 10.
129. See Jerome S. Fons, "Policy Issues Facing Rating Agencies," in *Ratings, Rating Agencies, and the Global Financial System*, ed. Levich, Majnoni, and Reinhart, p. 343.

Chapter 8: The Rebirth of Doubt

1. See, for example, Eichengreen, "The International Monetary Fund in the Wake of the Asian Crisis," and Cohen, "Taming the Phoenix?"; Morris Goldstein, *The Asian Financial Crisis: Causes, Cures, and Systemic Implications* (Washington, D.C.: Institute for International Economics, 1998); Wade and Veneroso, "The Gathering World Slump," pp. 13–42; Wade, "The Fight Over Capital Flows," pp. 41–54; Joseph E. Stiglitz, *Globalization and Its Discontents* (New York: W. W. Norton, 2002); Widmaier, "Constructing Monetary Crises," p. 74.; and Jacqueline Best, "From the Top-Down: The New Financial Architecture and the Re-embedding of Global Finance," *New Political Economy*, vol. 8, no. 3 (2003), pp. 363–384. On the crisis in general, see especially Wing Thye Woo, Jeffrey D. Sachs, and Klaus Schwab, *The Asian Financial Crisis* (Cambridge, Mass.: MIT Press, 2000); and T. J. Pempel, ed., *The Politics of the Asian Economic Crisis* (Ithaca, N.Y.: Cornell University Press, 1999).
2. Blyth, *Great Transformations;* Widmaier, "Constructing Monetary Crises"; Wesley D. Widmaier, "Keynesianism as a Constructivist Theory of the International Political Economy," *Millennium*, vol. 32, no. 1 (2003), pp. 87–107; and Wesley D. Widmaier, "The Social Construction of the 'Impossible Trinity': The Intersubjective Bases of Monetary Cooperation," *International Studies Quarterly*, vol. 48, no. 2 (2004), pp. 433–453.
3. "Summing Up by the Acting Chairman of Countries' Experiences with the Use of Controls on Capital Movements and Issues in Their Orderly Liberalization," Executive Board Meeting, April 6, 1999, BUFF/99/45 (IMF Archives), p. 2.
4. "IIF Working Group on the Liberalization of Capital Movements: Executive Summary," unpublished memorandum, Institute of International Finance, Washington, D.C., January 20, 1999, p. v.
5. Author's interview with Lex Rieffel, Washington, D.C., May 25, 2004.
6. Author's confidential interview with a former senior U.S. Treasury official, Washington, D.C., October 6, 2003.
7. Author's interview with Aleksei Mozhin, Washington, D.C., February 18, 2004.
8. IEO, *The IMF's Approach to Capital Account Liberalization*.
9. Ibid., p. 9.
10. Ibid., pp. 8, 36–37, 57–58.

11. See especially Martin Bruncko, "Political and Technical Conditionality in Slovakia's Accession into the OECD," *Slovak Foreign Policy Affairs*, no. 2 (2000).

12. "Adherence of the Slovak Republic to the Codes of Liberalization and to the Declaration and Decisions on International Investment and Multinational Enterprises: Principles and Procedures—Note by the Secretariat," Directorate for Financial, Fiscal, and Enterprise Affairs, CMIT, and CIME, June 12, 1996, DAFFE/INV/IME(96)22 (OECD Archives); and "Slovak Republic: Proposed Reservations Under the Codes of Liberalization of Capital Movements and Invisible Operations," Directorate for Financial, Fiscal, and Enterprise Affairs, CMIT, and CIME, June 12, 1996, DAFFE/INV/IME(96)24 (OECD Archives).

13. "The Official Response of the Slovak Authorities to the Chairman's Conclusions on the Joint CIME/CMIT Meeting of the Organization for Economic Cooperation and Development Held on 2–3 July 1996," Directorate for Financial, Fiscal, and Enterprise Affairs, CMIT, and CIME, December 17, 1999, DAFFE/INV/IME(99)9 (OECD Archives), pp. 2–3.

14. Author's interview with Ivan Mikloš, Bratislava, October 28, 2004.

15. Author's interview with Elena Kohútiková, Bratislava, October 27, 2004.

16. Ibid.

17. "Slovak Republic: Position Under the Codes of Liberalization and the Declaration and Decisions on International Investment and Multinational Enterprises—Report by the Committee on Capital Movements and Invisible Transactions and the Committee on International Investment and Multinational Enterprises," OECD Council, June 13, 2000, C(2000)114 (OECD Archives), p. 9.

18. Ibid., p. 10.

19. Robert Anderson and Stefan Wagstyl, "U.S. Blocks Slovakia's Early Joining of OECD," *Financial Times*, May 16, 2000. The following day the *Financial Times* published an editorial critical of the U.S. position. See "Joining the Club," *Financial Times*, May 17, 2000. Also see Bruncko, "Political and Technical Conditionality."

20. Author's interview with Edwin M. Truman, Washington, D.C., September 23, 2004.

21. Author's interview with Juraj Renčko, Bratislava, October 26, 2004.

22. Ibid.

23. Author's interview with Truman.

24. See Katarína Trajlinková, "Review of Slovakia's Accession to the OECD," *BIATEC*, vol. 9, no. 2 (2001), pp. 33–36, at p. 34; and Bruncko, "Political and Technical Conditionality."

25. Author's interview with Renčko.

26. Author's interview with Katarína Mathernová, Washington, D.C., September 22, 2004.

27. Author's interview with Truman.

28. Robert Anderson, "U.S. to Support Slovakia on OECD," *Financial Times*, May 27, 2000.

29. Author's interview with Renčko.

30. Author's interview with Mathernová.

31. Author's interview with Kohútiková. Other Slovak authorities shared this view

as well. According to an adviser of the finance minister, "By the time we began accession negotiations with the EU, we had already met virtually all of the demands from Brussels with regard to capital flows. The OECD countries that joined the EU were already liberal." Author's interview with Renčko.

32. Griffith-Jones, Gottschalk, and Cirera, "The OECD Experience with Capital Account Liberalization," p. 72.

33. OECD, *Forty Years' Experience with the OECD Code of Liberalization of Capital Movements*, p. 11.

34. Ibid., p. 18.

35. Ibid., p. 102.

36. Alexei Remizov, *Chile Weathering Asian Storm* (New York: Standard & Poor's, October 28, 1998).

37. Joydeep Mukherji and Paul Coughlin, *China's BBB+ for Curr Rating Affirmed by S&P* (New York: Standard & Poor's, November 9, 1998).

38. Chew Ping, Takahira Ogawa, and Ashok Bhatia, *Malaysia's A-/A-2 LC and BBB-/ A-3 FC Ratings Affirmed; Outlook Revised to Stable from Negative* (New York: Standard & Poor's, March 31, 1999). Also see Chew Ping, Ashok Bhatia, and John Chambers, *Malaysia's Global Bond Rated BBB−; Foreign and Local Currency Ratings Affirmed* (New York: Standard & Poor's, May 31, 1999). Contrary to S&P's assertion, Malaysia had not restricted any current account transactions.

39. John Chambers and David T. Beers, *S&P's Sovereign Ratings Focus on Fundamentals* (New York: Standard & Poor's, May 26, 1999).

40. Chew Ping, Ashok Bhatia, and Takahira Ogawa, *Outlook on Malaysia's Foreign Currency Rating Revised to Positive; All Ratings Affirmed* (New York: Standard & Poor's, August 31, 2000). The same paragraph can be found in Chew Ping, *Malaysia (Federation of)* (New York: Standard & Poor's, November 6, 2000).

41. Christopher T. Mahoney, "What Have We Learned? Explaining the World Financial Crisis," in *Moody's Rating Methodology Handbook: Sovereign*, p. 54.

42. Mahoney, "What Have We Learned?" p. 55.

43. Beers and Cavanaugh, *Sovereign Credit Ratings: A Primer.*

44. John Chambers, *The Role of Credit Rating Agencies in Market Development* (New York: Standard & Poor's, August 1, 2004).

45. Ping Chew and Paul Coughlin, *Risky Move to Float China's Exchange Rate* (New York: Standard & Poor's, September 15, 2003).

46. David T. Beers, *Resilient Asian Economies Emerge from Fiscal Shadows of Yesteryear* (New York: Standard & Poor's, December 1, 2003).

47. Ping Chew and Paul Coughlin, *India (Republic of)* (New York: Standard & Poor's, August 31, 2004).

48. *The S&P Emerging Market Indices: Methodology, Definitions, and Practices* (New York: Standard & Poor's, February 2000), p. 2.

49. Beers, *Credit FAQ: The Future of Sovereign Credit Ratings.*

50. See, for example, "Who Rates the Raters?," *Economist,* March 26, 2005.

51. See, for example, Leo Flynn, "Coming of Age: The Free Movement of Capital Case Law, 1993–2002," *Common Market Law Review,* vol. 39, no. 4 (2002), pp. 773–805; A. Landsmeer, "Movement of Capital and Other Freedoms," *Legal*

Issues of Economic Integration, vol. 28, no. 1 (2001), pp. 57–69; and Niamh Maloney, "New Frontiers in EC Capital Markets Law: From Market Construction to Market Regulation," *Common Market Law Review,* vol. 40, no. 4 (2003), pp. 809–843.

52. These cases include *Commission v Italian Republic* (Case C-58/99, May 23, 2000), and three decisions handed down on June 4, 2002: *Commission v Portuguese Republic* (Case C-367/98); *Commission v French Republic* (Case C-483/99); and *Commission v Kingdom of Belgium* (Case C-503/99).

53. See *Commission v Kingdom of Belgium* (Case 478/98, September 26, 2000); *Commission v French Republic* (Case C-334/02, March 4, 2002); and *Commission v Italian Republic* (Case C-279/00, February 7, 2002).

54. See, for example, Commission of the European Communities, *2004 Regular Report on Romania's Progress towards Accession,* October 6, 2004, COM(2004) 657/1200, pp. 62–63; and Commission of the European Communities, *Opinion on Croatia's Application for Membership of the European Union,* April 20, 2004, COM(2004) 257, p. 63.

55. Author's interview with Lars Erik Forsberg and Stephane Ouaki, Brussels, November 3, 2004. Another east European country, Bulgaria, had already satisfied almost all of the Commission's requirements for capital freedom. See Commission of the European Communities, *2004 Regular Report on Bulgaria's Progress Towards Accession,* October 6, 2004, COM(2004) 657/1199, pp. 55–56. Bulgaria was granted transitional periods for secondary residences and agricultural and forestry land.

56. Government of the Republic of Croatia, *Response to the Questionnaire of the European Commission* (2003), chap. 4, p. 3.

57. IEO, *The IMF's Approach to Capital Account Liberalization.*

58. The previous requirement was 24 percent. See Croatian National Bank, *Additional Measures to Reduce External Borrowing,* Press Release, February 9, 2005.

59. Under the agreement with the Commission, Romania had been granted transitional arrangements concerning the acquisition of land for secondary residences by EU citizens and agricultural and forestry land.

60. Author's personal communication with a senior official of the National Bank of Romania, January 31, 2005. On the Fund's encouragement of Romania to postpone the capital liberalization plan already negotiated with the EU, see IEO, *The IMF's Approach to Capital Account Liberalization.*

61. See Daniel Daianu, "Pragmatism, Poise in Public Discourse and Fairness Are Needed," *Nine O'clock,* no. 3,353, January 27, 2005.

62. Commission of the European Communities, *2004 Regular Report on Romania's Progress Towards Accession,* pp. 64, 65.

Chapter 9: Conclusion

1. For a useful discussion of treating theoretical traditions pragmatically, see Peter J. Katzenstein and Rudra Sil, "Rethinking Asian Security: The Case for Analytical Eclecticism," in *Rethinking Security in East Asia: Identity, Power, and Efficiency,*

ed. J. J. Suh, Peter J. Katzenstein, and Allen Carlson (Stanford, Calif.: Stanford University Press, 2004).

2. See Kirshner, "The Study of Money"; and Grabel, "The Political Economy of 'Policy Credibility.'"

3. Max Weber, *The Methodology of the Social Sciences*, trans. Edward A. Shils and Henry A. Finch (1904–1906; repr., Glencoe, Ill.: Free Press, 1949), p. 72, emphasis in original.

4. Polanyi, *The Great Transformation*, p. 139.

Acknowledgments

Almost certainly I would not have tried to write this book if I were a professor somewhere other than Harvard Business School. As a political scientist hired to teach international political economy and macroeconomics in a school of management, I felt extraordinarily well situated to explore these issues while in continuous dialogue with MBA students, managers, and my colleagues. Those colleagues generously offered insights and reactions informed by training in a variety of academic disciplines and the experience of practice. I am especially grateful to Thomas McCraw, Julio Rotemberg, Debora Spar, Richard Tedlow, Richard Vietor, and Louis Wells, all of whom took a special interest in this project and how it related to my professional development. Laura Alfaro, with whom I coauthored a Harvard Business School case on the Malaysian capital controls as I began this project, offered frequent encouragement and, as always, tough criticism that helped me sharpen my arguments. The intellectual and professional environment in which I wrote was wonderfully supportive.

I also cannot imagine having been able to marshal the financial resources necessary to accomplish the research for this book without the abundant and unsparing support of the School's Division of Research and Faculty Development. With this support, as well as a year of developmental leave, I was able to collect and review primary documents and conduct interviews with policymakers and the private financial communities in Bratislava, Brussels, Budapest, Frankfurt, Kuala Lumpur, New York, Paris, Prague, Stockholm, and Washington, D.C. I thank Paul Gompers and Geoffrey Jones, the two Research Directors who supported this project and continually replenished my research budget.

I am grateful to the nearly one hundred policymakers who spoke with me on the record, as well as the many others who shared their reflections in confidence. I learned an extraordinary amount from my interviewees, and I believe that their reflections enliven the prose of this book. Some of these policymakers also took a personal interest in my project—offering to read draft chapters or put me in touch with current and former colleagues. Pascal Lamy and Lawrence Summers were especially gracious in explaining their interpretations of events and encouraging former colleagues to speak with me.

I spent time as a visiting scholar at several international organizations while conducting my research. For graciously hosting and advising me I thank Marie-Odile Forges, Pierre Poret, and Eva Thiel at the OECD, and Ashoka Mody at the IMF. I also spent a significant amount of time in archives and interpreting primary documents. For invaluable assistance navigating the IMF archives in Washington, I thank Premela Isaac, Jean Marcouyeux, and Norma Samson. I am grateful for the guidance and patience of Jan-Anno Schuur of the OECD archives in Paris.

Shinji Takagi of the IMF's Independent Evaluation Office invited me to consult to his team's evaluation of the Fund's approach to capital account liberalization, and from that experience I learned a great deal. Shinji also became extremely supportive of my own project. I am grateful for his guidance, encouragement, and profound insight, as well as for the opportunity to work with his research team to influence the very policy practices that I was evaluating as a scholar.

My research in Europe was enabled by the efforts of Harvard Business School's European Research Center in Paris. I thank Daniela Beyersdorfer, Elena Corsi, Vincent Dessain, and Monika Stachowiak for their advice, logistical support, and research assistance.

The research for this book was supported by a series of very able and efficient individuals. For their research assistance I thank Nicholas Bartlett, Dana Brown, Yordanka Chobanova, Jana Grittersova, Kimberly Haddad, Lane LaMure, and Marie-Anne Verger. Thanks also to Juliana Seminerio, who cheerfully managed all manner of logistics and correspondence and otherwise kept things under control in Boston when I was away.

I am extremely grateful to Christopher Bruner, who worked with me during the year I finished the first full draft of the manuscript. Christopher was more colleague and peer than research assistant. He mastered the scholarly and policy literature on the credit-rating agencies and then helped me to make sense of it for myself. The rating agencies chapter would not yet exist without Christopher's efforts. Christopher also contributed to and commented on countless drafts of all the other chapters.

My students in two courses—Business, Government, and the International Economy and Managing International Trade and Investment—contributed to this book in a variety of ways. I explored some of the ideas for this book in Harvard Business School cases that adopted the point of view of both policymakers and managers, and class discussions often helped me to see the connections among international norms and rules, policy practices, and managers' decisions. Two students became more directly involved in this project. Alexis Chiyo Martinez spent a summer charting the evolution of EU and OECD rules regarding capital controls, and I later built on her initial research project. Robert Alloway spent two terms during his second year tracing the subtle shifts in the treatment of capital account regulations in every IMF publication between the organization's founding and the end of the century. Robert also joined me for initial interviews at the Fund in the spring of 2002. I am grateful for Robert's keen intellect, dry wit, and meticulous research in the early stages of the project.

As I look over the list of people who read and commented on my manuscript as it developed, I am quite astonished at the size of my debt for all of this generosity and advice. But it is a debt that I am incredibly fortunate to have. For their careful readings and insightful reactions to parts of this manuscript, I thank Regina Abrami, Munir Alam, Laura Alfaro, Robert Alloway, Henri Chavranski, Jeffrey Chelsky, Nazli Choucri, Thomas Christensen, Jeffrey Chwieroth, Katherine Cousins, Joly Dixon, Frank Dobbin, Rachel Epstein, Niall Ferguson, Jeffry Frieden, Kenneth Froot, Edna Judith Armendariz Guizar, Peter Hall, Rodney Bruce Hall, Lakshmi Iyer, Nicolas Jabko, Joseph Joyce, Elli Kaplan, Ethan Kapstein, Tarun Khanna, Ulrich Krotz, Kathryn Lavelle, David Levey, Ralf Leiteritz, Richard Locke, George Lodge, Noel Maurer, Gerald McDermott, Sophie Meunier, Ashoka Mody, Andrew Moravcsik, David Moss, Aldo Musacchio, Craig Parsons, Louis Pauly, Thierry Pech, David Peretz, Huw Pill, Jacques Polak, Eswar Prasad, Forest Reinhardt, Martin Rhodes, Dani Rodrik, Pierre Rosanvallon, John Gerard Ruggie, Bruce Scott, John Simon, Edwin Truman, Gunnar Trumbull, Gayle Tzemach, Wesley Widmaier, and David Yoffie.

I am even more deeply indebted to those scholars and practitioners who read and commented on entire drafts of the manuscript. For their efforts to see the whole, I am grateful to Suzanne Berger, Mark Blyth, Christopher Bruner, Benjamin Cohen, Alexander Cooley, Rafael di Tella, Jeffrey Fear, Ilene Grabel, Eric Helleiner, Yoshiko Herrera, Geoffrey Jones, Peter Katzenstein, Jonathan Kirshner, Kenneth Lennan, Kathleen McNamara, Thomas McCraw, Jan Nipstad, Julio Rotemberg, Matthew Rudolph, Herman Schwartz, Adam Segal, Debora Spar, Jeff Strabone, Randall Stone, Shinji Takagi, Richard Tedlow, Richard Vietor, Christopher Way, and Louis Wells.

I thank the participants in seminars at Cornell, Georgia Tech, the European University Institute, Harvard, MIT, Princeton, and the University of Pennsylvania for their reactions to preliminary presentations of my ideas and arguments. I am especially grateful to Eric Helleiner and Jonathan Kirshner for inviting me to present the first full draft of the manuscript over a long weekend in Ithaca in their Money Manuscript Workshop, which is funded by the International Political Economy Program at Cornell. Eric and Jonathan managed to attract a fantastic crowd (including Benjamin Cohen, Ilene Grabel, Kathryn Lavelle, Kathleen McNamara, Herman Schwartz, Randall Stone, and Christopher Way) just to discuss and propose revisions to my manuscript. Although spending a weekend in a seminar room listening humbly to accomplished senior scholars discuss the merits and flaws of one's manuscript is not for the faint of heart, this book was improved immeasurably by such generosity.

I asked Peter Katzenstein and Jonathan Kirshner to cochair my dissertation committee at Cornell more than a decade ago, and I continue to seek their counsel regularly. As with my first book, Peter and Jonathan have advised me every step of the way with this, the second. I offer my heartfelt thanks for their guidance, friendship, and occasional reality checks. Peter is still my hero. Jonathan still, more than anyone else, understands where I am trying to go and talks me through the twists and turns on the way there.

I am fortunate to have piqued the interest of Michael Aronson in the early stages of this project. I am grateful to Michael for his support, insight, and excellent instincts. Working with Michael has made publishing with Harvard University Press truly a pleasure. I also thank the Press's three anonymous reviewers, whose advice for the final draft of the manuscript has proven so useful.

My family was warmly supportive. My mother, Phyllis Kuehn, has remained constant in her support, even editing with great care every initial chapter draft. I still have never run out of apricot jam, an essential ingredient. My father, Ahmed Abdelal, told me in myriad subtle ways that he is proud of me, and I think every day about how to make sure that remains true. My most heartfelt thanks to Laila, David, Max, Jim, Martha, and Jeanine for cheerfully tolerating the presence of my computer in Marin, Sonoma, Almanor, Atlanta, and Seagrove, as well as for patiently waiting for me to finish another few sentences before dinner. Adam Segal, long one of my closest friends, became, in a sense, family as we worked simultaneously on our second books surrounded by several new babies. For unfailing support, my thanks to (now) Uncle Adam.

My wife, Traci Battle, and son, Alexander James Battle Abdelal, understand better than anyone the sacrifices that were necessary to write this book, for they were obliged to make some themselves. Alexander has lived with this book since his birth, and he has experienced its writing through gifts and phone calls from around the world and an extensive tour of the gardens and bakeries of Paris. My eager anticipation of Alexander's tender greetings at each homecoming made the field research bearable, and his encouragement reminded me why I was working so hard. Traci supported my ambitions for this book even when my own resolve occasionally faltered. In addition to managing her own career as a research scientist, Traci ensured that I had all the space, comfort, and baked goods that I needed to write. I could not have written this book without her, and most likely I would not have dared even to try. This book is dedicated to Traci and Alexander, and I hope that they both recognize my intention to dedicate everything else to them as well.

Index